Business Valuation & Bankruptcy: Case Law Compendium

2ND EDITION

BVR
What It's Worth
1000 SW Broadway, Suite 1200, Portland, OR 97205
(503) 291-7963 • www.bvresources.com

BVR
What It's Worth

Printed in the United States of America.

Editor: Jan Davis

Publisher: Sarah Andersen

Managing Editor: Janice Prescott

Chair and CEO: David Foster

President: Lucretia Lyons

Vice President of Sales: Lexie Gross

Customer Service Manager: Retta Dodge

ISBN: 978-1-62150-042-1

Library of Congress Control Number: 2014946524

Table of Contents

INTRODUCTION

As I reflect upon the numerous business cycles I have witnessed since the late 1980s during my career as a bankruptcy practitioner, I am surprised by both the similarities and the uniqueness in each of those cycles. Lax lending standards, an overextension of credit, and departures from basic principles of finance always seem to accompany peaks prior to a downturn in the business cycles. Yet the combination of catalysts and drivers and the severity of each economic downturn has made each one unique.

Financially distressed and bankrupt businesses have always behaved in erratic and unpredictable ways. Such behavior adds to the challenges of developing logical and supportable conclusions of value. The unique elements of each economic downturn add further complexity to valuing such businesses. In response to such complex issues, more robust and sophisticated methods are constantly being developed to address the challenges of assessing the value of business interests and assets in context of financial distress and bankruptcy.

Valuation issues are at the heart of virtually every bankruptcy case and arise at almost every stage as the case proceeds. Whether in connection with adequate protection, plan confirmation, or the assessment of solvency in the context of avoidance actions, bankruptcy matters and valuation issues are always connected.

In an effort to help valuation experts stay abreast of case law and specialized methods and techniques that apply to the valuation of financially distressed businesses and assets, Business Valuation Resources has published this second edition of *BVR's Business Valuation & Bankruptcy: Case Law Compendium*. This new edition offers abstracts of some 130 bankruptcy-related court decisions, as well as several articles that provide insights about the challenges of valuing financially distressed businesses. The articles take up recent issues in bankruptcy valuation, consider methods for developing discount rates for distressed businesses, and highlight the opportunities for valuation engagements in the context of dividend recapitalizations.

Paul N. Shields, Director
Berkeley Research Group, LLC

Editor's Note: **BVR is pleased to offer you access to the courts' full opinions of all cases referenced in this compendium. Please visit www.bvresources.com/bankruptcycases and log in to access this resource.**

Chapter 1. Ten Current—and Controversial—Issues in Bankruptcy Valuations[1]

By Robert F. Reilly, CPA

Editor's note: *This article is based, in part, on a presentation made by Robert F. Reilly, Willamette Management Associates managing director, at the AICPA Forensic & Valuation Services Conference 2013. Also, this article represents a small sampling of the expert information contained in* A Practical Guide to Bankruptcy Valuation *by Reilly and Dr. Israel Shaked (The Michel-Shaked Group), published by the American Bankruptcy Institute and available from BVR at www.bvresources.com/bankruptcy.*

Valuation analysts who become involved in bankruptcy-related assignments should expect their work to be subject to a rigorous contrarian review because most of these valuations are performed within a litigation or other contrarian environment. The valuation analyst needs to be aware of current hot-button issues in order to be able to defend his or her work.

A valuation analyst may be asked to perform a valuation within a bankruptcy context for any number of reasons, including debtor in possession (DIP) asset sales, DIP financing collateral determination, claims of insolvency and fraudulent conveyance, creditor protection considerations related to any DIP transaction, testing of reasonably equivalent value for transfers into or out of the bankruptcy estate, testing the reasonableness of a proposed plan of reorganization, assessing whether a debtor is operating within the zone of insolvency, and implementing post-Chapter 11 bankruptcy fresh-start accounting. The analyst may also be asked to perform related financial advisory services, such as a fairness opinion, solvency opinion, or economic damages analysis.

A number of controversial issues have emerged that analysts will encounter when performing bankruptcy valuation services. Here are 10 of the most common.

1 This article was originally published in the April 2014 issue of the *Business Valuation Update.*

1. Definition of the term 'value.' Unlike the Internal Revenue Code, the U.S. Bankruptcy Code doesn't define "fair value," "fair market value," or any other standard of value. The closest definition of the term "value" is presented in Bankruptcy Code Section 506a:

> Such value shall be determined in light of the purpose of the valuation and of the proposed disposition or use of such property, and in conjunction with any hearing on such disposition or use or on a plan affecting such creditor's interest.

Other than the limited guidance presented in Section 506a, analysts (and legal counsel) have to look to judicial precedent to see what value definitions the courts have accepted. However, even these definitions from judicial precedent provide limited guidance as to which standard of value is appropriate in which bankruptcy circumstances.

Of course, the analyst is not the legal counsel; however, an experienced bankruptcy valuation analyst should be familiar with the relevant sections of the Bankruptcy Code and the Bankruptcy Rules. But even the most experienced bankruptcy analyst should not be making legal decisions. And the analyst should not hesitate to request (and accept) legal instructions from counsel with regard to any bankruptcy-related legal issues.

2. The use of hindsight. In a bankruptcy valuation, the use of hindsight is discouraged. This analyst caveat is usually true with regard to valuations prepared for most purposes—whether the purpose relates to an estate tax issue, a family law issue, a shareholder appraisal rights dispute, etc. Nonetheless, in the bankruptcy environment, the use of hindsight in the valuation is particularly controversial. This is because the use of hindsight (albeit inappropriate) is quite common in many bankruptcy-related considerations because all parties know what actually happened to the debtor company, i.e., it filed for bankruptcy protection.

Most bankruptcy valuations (whether prepared for notation, transaction, or litigation purposes) apply a retrospective valuation date. This is because the bankruptcy valuation typically relates to a specific historical event, such as a dividend payment or a financing transaction. However, in the bankruptcy valuation, the analyst should consider only that information that was known or knowable as of the time of the valuation date.

3. Reliance on management-prepared financial projections. The adequacy of the analyst's due diligence with regard to management-prepared projections is often questioned in bankruptcy controversy cases. Accordingly, the analyst should perform adequate due diligence procedures before accepting the management-prepared projections. For example, the analyst should consider how contemporaneously prepared were the financial projections compared to the selected valuation date. If possible, the analyst should avoid relying on either stale projections (i.e., projections prepared quite a while before the subject valuation date) or those prepared as of a date after the subject valuation date. Also, if possible, the analyst should avoid relying on projections prepared after the bankruptcy litigation is filed. Even if such post-petition filing projections are perfectly reasonable, some party in interest may allege that the projections are biased and litigation-driven.

The debtor company's management may have to prepare projections subsequent to the valuation (or petition) date because, for example, the debtor company did not have financial projections in place as of the valuation date. If the only available projections were prepared after the valuation date, those projections should be based on variables that were known or knowable as of the subject valuation date. But even then the analyst should expect that such subsequently prepared projections will be challenged.

In addition, the analyst will want to know whether debtor management had prepared various versions of financial projections for the same period. In that case, the analyst will inquire as to whether the various projections were prepared for purposes other than (or inconsistent with) the bankruptcy-related valuation purpose. It is not uncommon for debtor company management to prepare various financial projection versions. One version could be prepared for the debtor board, one for the debtor's bank, one for a potential acquirer, and one for a joint venturer. In such an instance, the analyst should perform sufficient due diligence regarding these projections to conclude which version is most appropriate for the purpose and objective of the bankruptcy valuation.

Due diligence procedures are important any time the analyst relies on management projections for a valuation, fairness, solvency, or other financial analysis. The analyst will try to learn who prepared the projections and whether those individuals were qualified to prepare them. Typically, the debtor company's president, CEO, CFO, or controller will prepare the company's financial projections. However, if these same executives were also responsible for the debtor's financial distress, then the analyst may question their expertise to prepare reliable financial projections.

4. Selection of the valuation analysis variables. The analyst has to make many decisions when valuing a distressed company (whether or not that company has filed for bankruptcy protection). In many bankruptcy-related purposes, the judicial precedent provides mixed guidance to the analyst with regard to the methodology for selecting valuation variables. Even prior to selecting the appropriate methodology, the analyst may have to consider conceptual issues with regard to the bankruptcy valuation.

For example, the analyst may need to decide whether the valuation variables should reflect the current state of the debtor or the reorganized state of the debtor. Typically, the debtor company was experiencing financial distress before the bankruptcy filing. Typically, the debtor company is relieved from currently paying certain historical liabilities while it is in bankruptcy protection. And, typically, the reorganized debtor company will operate with lower operating expenses and less long-term debt. Therefore, the selection of which debtor company financial condition to analyze on the subject valuation date can impact the value conclusion.

The analyst may also consider how the assumed financial condition of the debtor company affects its cost of debt, its cost of equity, its debt/equity capital structure ratio, and its WACC. If the analyst assumes a reorganized debtor company, the analysis may incorporate a different discount rate than the one appropriate for a financially troubled debtor company. The analyst may also consider how the assumed financial condition of the debtor company affects its expected long-term growth rate.

If the debtor company is financially troubled, the debtor may have a constraint on its long-term growth rate. For example, it may not be able to fund future capital expenditures, working capital investments, or R&D expenditures. If the analyst assumes that the debtor company is reorganized, both operating expenses and capital-related expenses may be reduced. In that case, the analyst may project a higher expected long-term growth rate.

The analyst may also consider whether the selected discount rate reflects the business risk of the debtor company or the performance risk of the specific financial projections. There is performance risk associated with the debtor company's financial projections. If the analyst does not adjust the discount rate for that performance risk, any projected increase in revenue or cash flow will simply result in a higher value conclusion. But that increased value conclusion may not be reasonable. If there is greater risk inherent in the enhanced cash flow projections, then there should be a correspondingly risk-adjusted discount rate. With more aggressive financial projections, it is often appropriate to apply a larger (risk-adjusted) discount rate. And, with less aggressive financial projections, it is often appropriate to apply a lower discount rate.

When selecting the valuation variables, the analyst has to decide whether the selected variables should reflect the likely actions of the actual debtor company, of a typical willing buyer for the debtor company, or of the average company in the industry in which the debtor participates. This decision may impact the selected valuation variables.

In a bankruptcy valuation, the analyst should be particularly sensitive to documenting the selection process with regard to the valuation variables used in the analysis. In particular, the analyst will want to show that the process for selecting valuation variables was unbiased, transparent, and replicable. And the analyst should be prepared to justify the quantity and quality of data elements considered in the selection of the valuation variables.

5. Current interest rates. The current commercial debt interest rates are still at or near a historically low level. The risk-free rate is still at or near a historically low level (due to the monetary policy actions of the Federal Reserve). U.S. Treasury bond rates are also at or near a historically low level. Therefore, corporate bond interest rates are at or near historically low levels. The analyst has to determine whether the use of such interest rates is appropriate in determining the debtor company's WACC. The analyst may consider whether the DIP (or any financially troubled company) could actually borrow at such low interest rates. The analyst should be concerned that an understated WACC (caused by an unreasonably low cost of debt) may overstate the debtor company's value.

6. Due diligence. The reasonableness of the analyst's due diligence is often questioned, in bankruptcy litigation matters even more than in general commercial litigation matters. The analyst has to perform sufficient due diligence procedures to develop a comfort level regarding the debtor company's historical and prospective financial data.

Access to debtor company management or to other parties in interest may be limited in a bankruptcy dispute. It is also common in a bankruptcy valuation for the analyst to have limited access to the debtor company's financial or operational documents. One reason for this limitation is that the debtor company may no longer be operating. If the debtor company is still operating, it may not be operating with the same management team that existed as of the valuation date. Even if the analyst does have access to debtor company management, the manager's memories and perceptions may have changed over time. This condition is particularly common within a bankruptcy environment. This is because current debtor management often has to reflect back on what was happening with the debtor company as of a historical valuation date. The debtor company's operations (and fortunes) may have changed significantly since the company filed for bankruptcy protection. Therefore, the analyst may receive different answers to due diligence questions now than if the analyst had asked the same due diligence questions, say, two years earlier. And the analyst should realize that in bankruptcy cases hindsight is always 20/20.

7. Income tax effects on the debtor company's value. In a bankruptcy valuation, fairness, or solvency analysis, the analyst should consider the debtor's effective income tax rate, actual cash income tax expense, and deferred income tax assets or liabilities. In particular, the analyst should consider the debtor company's expected use of any net operating loss (NOL) tax attributes. In a bankruptcy, it is common for a creditor to forgive (or restructure) some of the debtor's long-term debt. Such a debt forgiveness (or restructuring) may cause the debtor company to recognize cancellation of debt (COD) income under the Internal Revenue Code. The debtor company may be able to avoid the recognition of COD income in certain circumstances. The debtor company may be able to avoid the COD income recognition if it is in Chapter 11 bankruptcy protection or to the extent that it is insolvent. However, the use of those exemptions to the recognition of COD income will cause the debtor company to lose the benefit of certain tax attributes, such as its NOL.

8. Rules of thumb. The use of industry valuation rules of thumb is often questioned. Two types of pricing metric rules of thumb are considered in valuations: (a) financial metrics, such as price/earnings multiples or price/revenue multiples; and (b) operational metrics, such as price/customer. Analysts are cautioned not to use industry rules of thumb as a primary valuation method in the preparation of a bankruptcy-related valuation. One reason for this caution is that valuation rules of thumb reflect an average company in the subject industry. However, the debtor company is most likely *not* the average company in the subject industry since it is in financial distress and in bankruptcy protection.

9. The cash flow test within a solvency analysis. In a fraudulent conveyance claim analysis, the analyst will typically perform the three fraudulent transfer tests: (a) the balance sheet (or solvency) test; (b) the cash flow (or debt service) test; and (c) the capital adequacy test. In the performance of the cash flow (or debt service) test, the analyst concludes whether the debtor company is able to meet all of its debt service obligations as they become due. In performing the cash flow test related to an alleged fraudulent transfer, the analyst has to decide whether to consider possible cash inflows from future new debt issues or new equity issues. The professional guidance from judicial precedent is mixed with regard to this issue.

Of course, if the analyst assumes that the debtor company can generate cash inflows either by liquidating its assets or by selling new debt or equity instruments, then just about any debtor company can pass the cash flow test. That is, just about any company can meet a principal or interest payment if the analyst just assumes it will borrow new debt to pay off its old debt.

The analyst also has to decide whether to consider the current credit availability of the debtor company when performing the cash flow test. It is not uncommon for analysts to include this source of debtor company cash flow if the debtor actually has unused lines of credit available to it. However, given the actual financial condition of the debtor company, the debtor may not be able to draw down on its unused lines of credit. That is, the unused credit may not actually be available for the financially distressed company if it has already violated several debt covenants.

The analyst also has to decide whether to consider debtor company asset sales in the cash flow test. If the debtor company's projected asset sales include nonoperating property, then this cash inflow consideration may not be unreasonable. However, if the analyst assumes the sale of the debtor company's operating assets, then the analyst may not be performing a going concern analysis in the cash flow test. Rather, if the analyst projects the sale of debtor company operating assets, then the analyst may actually be performing a liquidation analysis in the cash flow test.

10. Using the market approach in an inactive market. In the valuation of a financially distressed company, the analyst may not be able to identify sufficiently comparative guideline public companies. This is not because such financially distressed guideline companies do not exist. Rather, the likely guideline companies are not in the same distressed financial condition as the debtor company. For the same reason, the analyst may not be able to identify sufficiently comparative guideline M&A transactions. To make meaningful comparisons between selected guideline companies/transactions and the financially distressed debtor company, the analyst may have to make numerous normalization adjustments. However, because of the debtor's financial condition, such normalization adjustments may be quite large. As a result of such normalization adjustments, the analyst may have to adjust the market-derived pricing multiples by 30%, 40%, or 50%. If the pricing adjustments become so material, the analyst will have to decide whether it is really appropriate to apply the market approach in the subject bankruptcy valuation.

The analyst also has to decide whether it is appropriate to use the market approach backsolve method in the subject bankruptcy valuation. If there were actual sale transactions of the debtor company's securities over the last (say) year, the analyst may consider these actual sales of the company's securities and extrapolate ("backsolve") the transaction pricing data to conclude a value indication. In valuations performed for many purposes, it is often reasonable to use the backsolve valuation method. The analyst may have to decide whether it is appropriate in the subject bankruptcy valuation.

Before relying on the backsolve method, the analyst will assess two factors. First, the analyst will consider whether the recent debtor company transactions are actually arm's-length transactions. The transactions may not qualify as arm's-length transactions if the debtor company was experiencing severe financial distress. For example, the distressed debtor company may be willing to exchange any amount of equity to be relieved from a maturing debt obligation. Second, the analyst will consider whether the debtor company's financial condition has materially deteriorated between the backsolve transaction date and the current valuation date.

Summary and conclusion. Analysts are often asked to perform bankruptcy-related valuations, fairness opinions, solvency opinions, and other financial analyses for many reasons. And numerous parties in interest in the typical business bankruptcy may need valuation-related services. Nonetheless, these bankruptcy-related valuation analyses are complicated. The analyst should consider the 10 issues listed above and the associated analyst caveats when performing valuations (and related financial analyses) within a bankruptcy environment.

The analyst is not expected to be the legal counsel in the bankruptcy matter. In fact, the analyst should not hesitate to request (and rely on) legal instructions to legal questions—including with regard to the valuation issues listed above.

In particular, the analyst should be prepared to withstand a rigorous contrarian challenge related to the bankruptcy valuation. In addition to the selected valuation variables, methods, and conclusions, the analyst's due diligence procedures are often challenged during a controversy in a bankruptcy environment.

Robert F. Reilly, CPA, *is managing director of Willamette Management Associates. He can be reached at* rfreilly@willamette.com *and 773-399-4318.*

Chapter 2. Traditional Valuation Approaches Are Only the Starting Point When Valuing a Company in Distress

By Bernard Pump, CPA, ABV, CFF

Valuing a company in financial distress can be difficult. The methodologies that analysts use to value financially healthy, profitable companies do not work as well when we apply them to distressed companies.

Financially distressed companies do not behave like the market. Traditional valuation approaches, such as the market and income approaches, use market-based benchmarks such as the S&P 500 and comparable companies to value the subject company. The assumption behind these methods is that the value of a subject company is correlated with the values of other similar companies in the industry and with the stock market in general. In the market approach, the subject company is benchmarked using earnings multiples developed from similar public companies. In the income approach, the subject company's discount rate is benchmarked using the price relationship (CAPM) between similar public companies and a market index, such as the S&P 500. These methods work for financially healthy companies because the assumption that values are correlated is generally true. This assumption does not generally hold for companies in financial distress.

Exhibit 1 provides a graphic example of the issue. In Exhibit 1, I present the stock price history of two companies plotted against the S&P 500 index. One company is Procter & Gamble, which is a large, financially healthy, packaged goods company. I chose Proctor & Gamble (P&G) because it is a good example of a large profitable company that is included in most institutional portfolios, but Exhibit 1 would look similar with any large profitable U.S. company. The other company we will call "Company X," which is a financially distressed company in the energy industry. The period of Exhibit 1 is January 2010 through January 2012. Company X filed for Chapter 11 bankruptcy protection in December 2011.

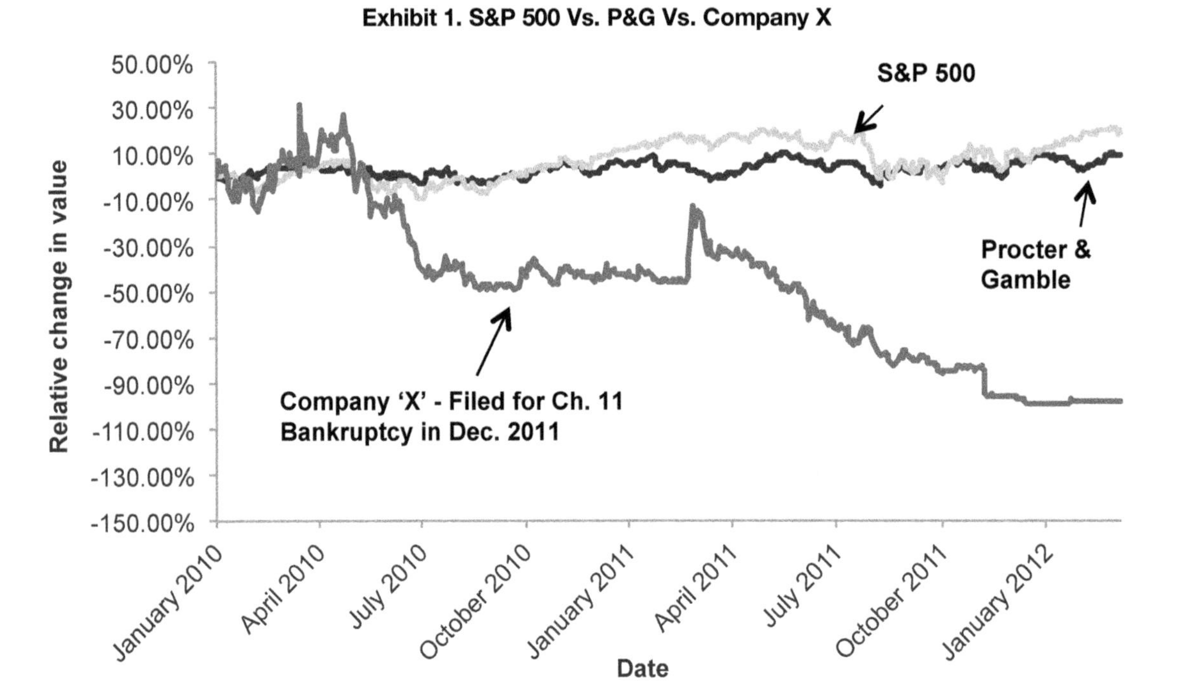

Source of data: Capital IQ

As Exhibit 1 demonstrates, traditional methods would work well to value a company such as P&G because its stock price movements are correlated with the S&P and presumably with other companies in the packaged goods industry. You could use P&G's peer companies, the S&P 500, and other market indicators to develop a discount rate and market multiples for P&G.

On the other hand, valuing Company X is more challenging because normal economic events are not necessarily driving its stock price. Company-specific events, such as news about the company's negotiations with creditors, restructuring events, and bankruptcy proceedings, are driving its stock prices as much as or more than economic and industry events. Therefore, if you look to the market alone for indicators to estimate the earnings multiple or discount rate for Company X, you may be missing a significant component of the valuation equation: company-specific factors.

Moreover, if you use public company data from healthy companies to benchmark the value of a subject company that is in distress, you are likely going to underestimate the level of risk associated with that investment and overestimate the value. Note that January 2010 through January 2012 was a volatile period for the stock market, but, when compared with the highly volatile stock price of a financially distressed business, the S&P index looks as if there was very little volatility during the period. The higher stock price volatility reflects the higher level of risk inherent in financially distressed companies versus healthy companies.

Risk, Return, and Uncertainty Go Hand-In-Hand. Just as it is difficult to value financially distressed companies using traditional methods, so too is it difficult to value a distressed company's debt. It is well established that risk and return are correlated. This is especially true for debt.

Companies with low credit quality have to pay higher yields on their debt than companies with high credit quality. However, estimating the appropriate yield for low-quality debt securities can be much more difficult than estimating the yield on investment-grade debt. In Exhibit 2, I have plotted observed yields on selected publicly traded debt with different credit ratings as of mid-2012. The chart presents the observed yields for debt securities, with a five- to seven-year maturity, across the range of credit quality for corporate debt. Exhibit 2 presents the yields that investors received in the public market for debt with S&P credit ratings of "AAA" down to "CCC" and lower.

For the debt of financially healthy companies with an "A" credit rating or higher, the job of estimating a market-based yield is fairly straightforward. The yields for debt rated "A," and higher, fall within a relatively tight range. In other words, you can use the yields reported in the public market to benchmark the yield for debt with a rating of "A" and above and be fairly confident with the result.

At credit ratings of "BBB" and "BB," the yields begin to rise, and we also see a widening of the range of observed yields. The wider range of yields makes estimating the appropriate yield for a subject company debt more difficult. The wider range of yields is driven by company-specific factors among the companies that issue the debt. The selected yield must then be applied to the subject company debt, which will have its own company-specific factors that must be considered.

At credit ratings below "BB," the yields go much higher and the dispersion of market yields around the mean is even greater. At the low end of the credit quality spectrum, the risk of default becomes

Exhibit 2. U.S. Corporate Debt Yields by Rating

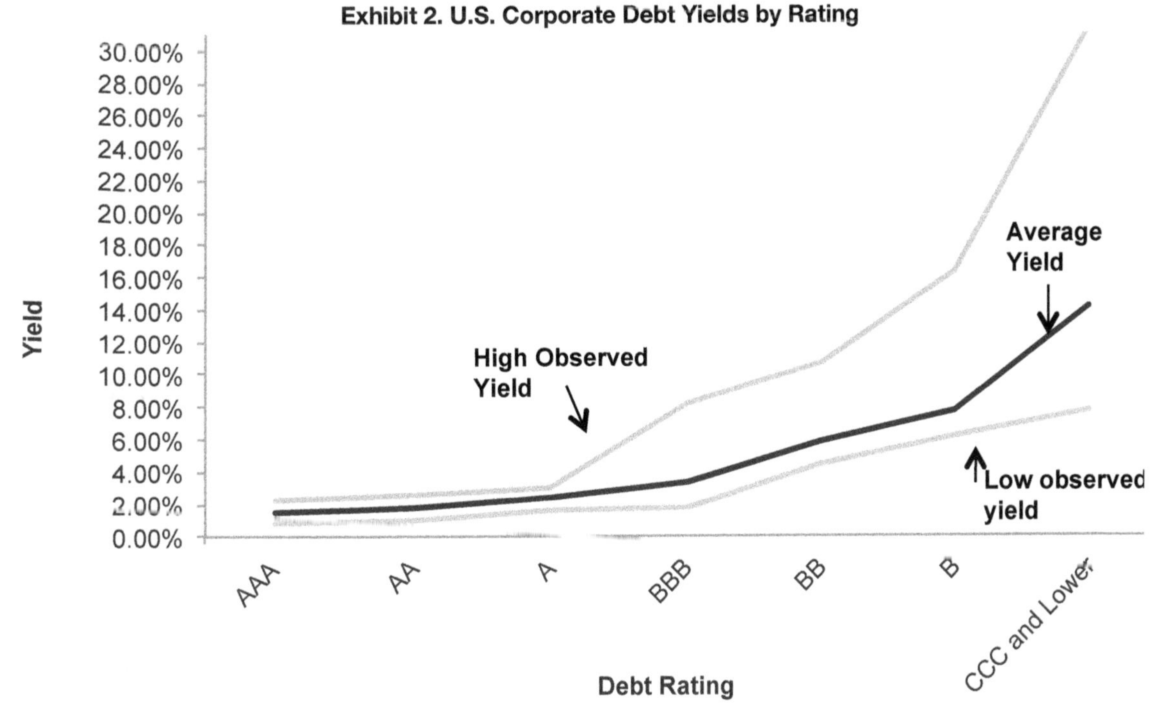

Source of data: Capital IQ

a significant consideration and company-specific factors begin to drive yields as much as or more than market factors do. The influence of company-specific factors on the yields of financially distressed debt can make it difficult to select market yields when valuing distressed debt.

In addition, the availability of market data on yields for low credit quality debt can be very limited. Institutional investors are often prohibited from holding debt below investment grade in many of their portfolios. Trading in these securities can be thin and sporadic. In other words, you may find a comparable debt security to benchmark a subject company's yield against, but it may not have traded for a week, or a month, and the trade prices may be far apart.

The implication for valuing distressed debt is that you have to accept a wider range of confidence in estimated values than for investment grade debt. Moreover, you will need to take into consideration company-specific factors that bridge the difference between yields observed in the market and the selected yield for the subject debt.

Company-Specific Factors Drive the Value of Distressed Securities. To demonstrate the impact of company-specific factors on the value of securities of distressed companies, I have plotted the trading prices of Company X's publicly traded debt in Exhibit 3. The prices are for the senior convertible notes that mature in 2037 and carry a 3.5% coupon. I have plotted Company X's equity trading price in Exhibit 3 as a reference point. The debt trading pattern for Company X's debt is typical of distressed debt. The price volatility increases, and the notes begin to trade sporadically prior to the filing of Chapter 11. At some points the debt is trading at 60 cents on the dollar and

Exhibit 3. Company X Equity and Debt Prices

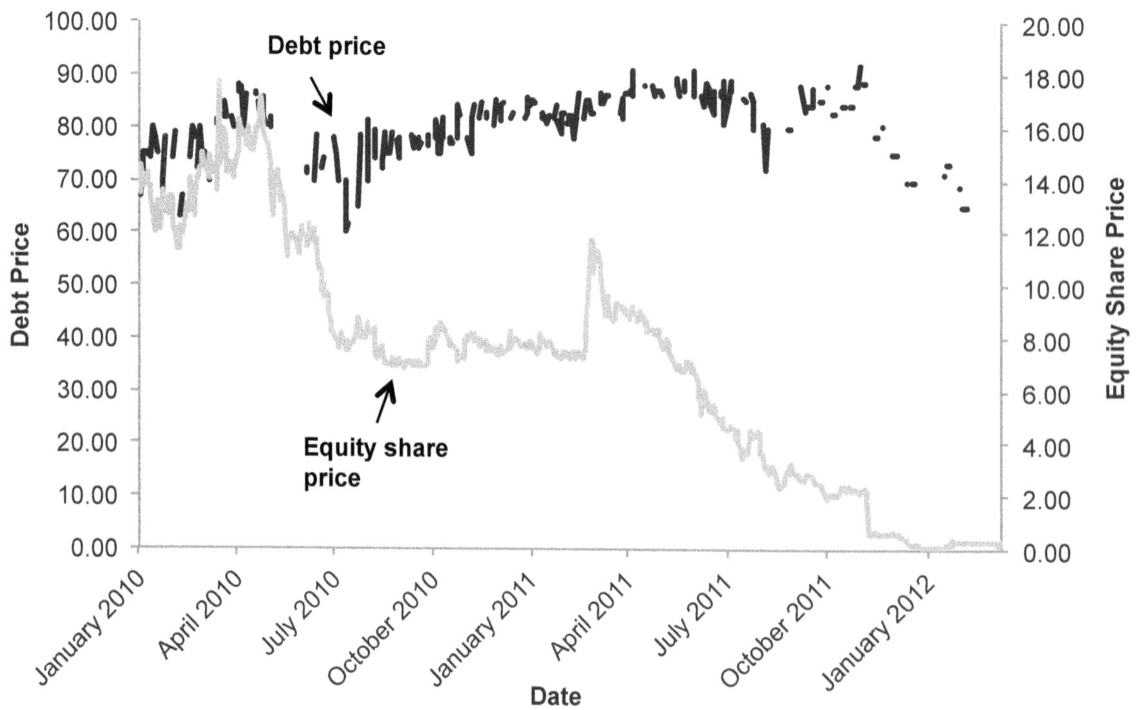

Source of data: Capital IQ

at other points it's trading at 90 cents on the dollar. There are days and even weeks that go by at certain times with no trading activity.

The important observation in Exhibit 3 is that, even after Company X files for Chapter 11 and its stock price is near zero, the notes continue to trade at levels above 60 cents on the dollar. I benchmarked this debt security, based upon the financial metrics of the company and where it stood in the capital structure, and estimated that it would have carried a rating of approximately "CC" at that time. Using an average yield for "CC" debt, a traditional income approach would have produced a value of about 20 cents on the dollar, not 60 or 70 cents on the dollar. The question then becomes: Why is the trading price so high? The answer is in the company-specific details. Company X is in the energy business. It owns land and proven oil and gas reserves, and the debt is senior. The market apparently believed that the holders of the notes were going to receive a significant recovery from their investment based on the value of the underlying company assets and the seniority of the notes in the capital structure. That is presumably why the note continued to trade at relatively high levels even after the company entered bankruptcy.

Company-specific factors are the key to understanding the trading value of Company X's notes. A traditional valuation approach underestimated the value of the notes, and company-specific facts were necessary to bridge the gap to the higher traded value.

Now Comes the Hard Part. When valuing distressed businesses, our first instinct may be to find other distressed businesses similar to the subject company. We may be tempted to think that, if these comparable companies are in a similar industry and going through distress, the stock multiples and the debt yields will be similar, but that is not necessarily true because the value of the comparable company, even if it is in distress, is not going to behave the way the value of the subject company is going to behave. Both companies' values will be driven by their own unique company-specific factors. Think of what a chart with the stock prices of two distressed companies, like Company X, might look like. Each company's stock price would likely follow a different, and largely uncorrelated, path over time. Using one to predict the other might be worse than using a healthy company in the same industry. By using another distressed company as a benchmark, you may find a low equity multiple, or a high market debt yield, that seems to make sense, but it will be based upon a completely different set of company-specific factors.

The problem is that there are not many viable substitutes for the traditional methodologies. We need to use the tools that we have even though they may not be perfectly suited for valuing financially distressed business securities. The results of the traditional methodologies become the starting point in the process when valuing the securities of distressed businesses.

In other words, you may need to start with what the company's equity and debt might be worth if it were financially healthy and then make company-specific adjustments to estimate the value in financial distress. This may require an analysis of the company at a very granular level in order to identify the company-specific factors and to determine which factors are driving value. The really challenging part is then to quantify the impact of these factors in a supportable analysis.

As with any valuation exercise, it is important to validate the results using multiple valuation approaches. Looking at value from multiple points of view is even more important where the valuation methods are prone to high error rates. This is the case when valuing the securities of companies in financial distress.

Bernard Pump, CPA, *is a partner in the Valuation Services practice of Deloitte Financial Advisory Services LLP. He can be reached at bpump@deliotte.com or 312-486-2834.*

Chapter 3. Determining a Distressed Debtor Company's Discount Rate[1]

By Michael D. Pakter

Financial analysis in contested bankruptcy proceedings often involves distressed business valuation issues. Whether a debtor company was solvent at a particular date is often critical in contested bankruptcy proceedings. The fair value of certain assets of the debtor company (or the business as a whole) is often pivotal in proving or disproving that solvency. (Generally, individual asset values will be determined based on the future cash flows expected from that individual asset.[2])

Valuation issues are also important in other areas of the bankruptcy process. Valuations of assets (or the business as a whole) are often critical determinants of the viability of the plan of reorganization of a formerly distressed debtor company intending to emerge from bankruptcy. In bankruptcy proceedings, proper values are key to determine whether holders of secured claims are adequately protected, to determine the changing value of collateral over time, or to establish the "fresh start" financial reporting of a reorganized debtor company's assets and liabilities.

As the adversarial parties and their expert financial analysts defend their respective valuations—or reasonably equivalent values—a key element for the distressed (or formerly distressed) business as a whole (or selected asset classes) is determining a suitable discount rate. The purpose of this article is to provide guidance to the financial analyst regarding the proper discount rate to be applied to a distressed debtor company's cash flows for business valuation purposes.

For the purposes of this article, the author has defined:

- A "distressed debtor company" as one with financing problems (difficulty in meeting obligations) and / or operating problems (apparent lack of operating success) of a magnitude such that it may seek the protection of the Bankruptcy Court;[3]

1 Originally published in two parts in the January 2014 and February 2014 issues of the *Business Valuation Update.*

2 Extracted from *Bankruptcy and Insolvency Accounting—Practice and Procedure,* 7th ed. Vol. 1, by Grant W. Newton, at page 555.

3 Extracted from the Newton textbook at page 745.

- A "reorganizing debtor company" as a distressed debtor company going through a restructuring or reorganizing process; and
- A "reorganized (formerly distressed) debtor company" as a debtor company allowed to resume business in a new form without the burden of loss-making operations and/or debt that existed prior to the bankruptcy proceeding.

This article assumes that the distressed (or formerly distressed) debtor company is being valued as a going concern.[4] This article considers only valuation analyses in bankruptcy proceedings performed using discounted cash flows.[5]

Valuation based on discounted cash flows. A common method to determine the solvency of a debtor company is to calculate the present value of the debtor company's debt-free cash flow.[6] The resulting present value is often referred to as the debtor company's market value of invested capital or its business enterprise value. The business enterprise value reflects the value of the debtor company's operating assets (net of its current operating liabilities—excluding debt).

Typically, to determine solvency, the value of the debtor company's long-term interest-bearing debt is subtracted from the invested capital value. Although other valuation methods in calculating solvency are frequently employed, this discussion summarizes the application of the discounted cash flow method.

To apply the discounted cash flow method, the financial analyst projects expected future cash flows through a discrete projection period, determines a terminal value (with the terminal value capitalized first), determines an appropriate discount rate, and applies that discount rate to both the discrete period cash flow and the terminal value.

Discounted cash flow valuation methods are commonly cited in business valuation literature, considered relevant and appropriate in many valuation settings, and recognized by bankruptcy courts. The financial analyst should assess the applicability of this method in each debtor company valuation situation.

The financial analyst should consider both the quality and quantity of information available before developing and applying a discounted cash flow method model. In applying the discounted cash flow valuation method, the analyst should be able to obtain and/or develop a credible projection of the debtor company's future cash flow.

The fact that the debtor company was or is distressed—or is in bankruptcy—affects the financial

4 The author recognizes that certain valuation analyses in bankruptcy proceedings can or will be based on the liquidation premise of value (or even that part of the business that continues while parts are liquidated). This merely adds to the complexity of the moving parts that the financial analyst should take into account in the performance of his or her work.

5 The author recognizes that other valuation methods exist. This article does not attempt to discuss or differentiate between the fair value versus a fair market value standard of value and, among other issues, ignores discounts for lack of control and/or for lack of marketability.

6 This section, and subsequent paragraphs, extracted from *Solvency Analysis: A Primer on Applying the Discounted Cash Flow Method,* by Robert Reilly, at page 115.

analysis of cash flows. A distressed business may have less data available regarding its cash flows than the average company—and that data may be more difficult to retrieve.

A distressed or bankrupt debtor company may have experienced significant turnover in personnel and/or loss of institutional knowledge. Distress may impact the quality and quantity of a debtor company's available financial information. The debtor company's accounting books and records may be in disorder.

The author experienced a situation where the password to the debtor's accounting books and records maintained using the QuickBooks software was no longer available after the controller quit her job. The author has experienced numerous situations where developing realistic future cash flow projections necessitated first reconstructing the true financial historical performance of the debtor company and its materially misrepresented financial reporting.

Proper identification of cash flows may have additional difficulties for a distressed, reorganizing, and/or reorganized debtor company. Cash flows may be measured at a consolidated parent level or at one or more subsidiary levels—but not all companies may be distressed, reorganizing, and/or reorganized using Chapter 11 of the Bankruptcy Code.

Taxes complicate the analysis. Tax carryforwards, if any, may result in the absence of taxes associated with cash flows for a period of time—at the parent and/or subsidiary levels. The financial analyst should be especially diligent in assembling the financial information needed for the valuation analysis.

The financial analyst should be careful to adjust historical data properly to take into account that the reorganization of the distressed business may have eliminated and/or restructured the entity's debt—and when that occurred. The financial analyst should ensure that the projected cash flows take into account the elements of the plan of reorganization and correlate with the discount rate determination—for example, pretax cash flows used together with pretax cost of capital elements, subsidiary-level cash flows giving rise to subsidiary-level values, debt service costs associated with correct levels of debt service, etc.

Point in time valuation is performed. "Courts will have to determine value on a case-by-case basis, but clearly value is to be determined in light of the purpose of the valuation and proposed disposition or use of the property."[7] (Also important in valuing the asset may be its benefit to the creditor.[8])

Generally, the Bankruptcy Code does not define the time at which the value is to be determined, leaving this matter to case-by-case interpretation and development.[9] In determining the date of valuation or the debtor company's stage of distress, the financial analyst should consider several issues on a case-by-case basis, including the purpose of the valuation in the bankruptcy proceed-

7 Extracted from the Newton textbook at page 558. Also see *Barash v. Public Finance Corp.*
8 Extracted from the Newton textbook at page 559.
9 Extracted from the Newton textbook at page 555.

ing; the prepetition and post-petition chronology of events; and the nature, timing, and extent of reorganization and restructuring efforts. It also may be useful to learn whether the industry as a whole—or the guideline companies within that industry—has been reorganized and restructured, and when.

The financial analyst should consider whether the valuation is being performed for purposes of determining the adequate protection of a secured creditor, the solvency of the enterprise as a whole for avoidance actions, or the enterprise value for purposes of establishing the acceptability or feasibility of the plan of reorganization. Such considerations will guide the date(s) of the valuation(s), the information and/or documentation to be gathered, the cash flows to be measured, and the assets or businesses to be valued.

The financial analyst should be mindful that many sections of the Bankruptcy Code require valuations and/or prescribe the elements and/or conditions of those valuations. In several instances, case law has weighed in further on those specifics.[10]

The financial analyst should have an understanding of the chronology of events that led the debtor company to reorganize and/or seek the protection of the Bankruptcy Court. Dates in which one or more significant transactions took place—such as the date of a leveraged buyout, the dates of transactions that allegedly led to the debtor company being unable to pay its debts in the ordinary course of business, or the dates when specific locations were closed down—frame the date(s) of financial analysis and the corresponding historical or projected cash flows.

Valuations typically are performed on information known and knowable at the date of the valuation. What was known and knowable at a particular date, in itself, may drive the date(s) of valuation(s).

The financial analyst should consider the stage of a debtor company's distress and/or restructuring so that proper comparisons can be made to guideline metrics during the valuation process. Whether the debtor company is distressed or reorganized affects the financial analyst's assessments of risk and return, study of debt structure, and evaluation of sustainability of cash flows.

The date(s) of the valuation(s) depends on the purpose(s) of the valuation(s). For purposes of establishing plan acceptability or feasibility, the valuation is performed currently—at or near the date of the plan of reorganization, for a reorganized entity compared to other nondistressed businesses. The value of collateral for purposes of classifying debt in a plan of reorganization should be determined close to the effective date of the plan and/or plan confirmation.[11]

For an avoidance action, the valuation is performed historically—at or near the date(s) of a transaction that may be alleged to have rendered the debtor insolvent. To determine the adequate protection of a secured creditor, the valuation may be needed at the petition date, the time the secured creditor sought relief from the automatic stay, or close to the time of the hearing.

10 A list of Bankruptcy Code sections with value mentions may be found in the Newton textbook at pages 573-574.
11 Extracted from the Newton textbook at page 560(b).

There is considerable uncertainty as to the date the creditor is entitled to adequate protection and the related date on which the valuation should be made: as of the petition date or as of the date the creditor first asked for adequate protection. Courts have held that the creditor is entitled to protection of the value of its collateral: (a) as of the petition date; (b) as of the date the right to adequate protection commences; or (c) as of the date the creditor first sought relief for adequate protection.[12]

While the financial analyst should perform the valuation as of the date of any challenged transfer, the courts have recognized that businesses do not prepare daily balance sheets. The *Litigation Services Handbook*[13] notes that the courts allow for retrojection spanning the gap between a transaction date and the balance sheet date for the solvency determination.

In a retrojection analysis, the financial analyst should demonstrate that no material changes in the financial condition of the debtor company occurred between a date when solvency (or insolvency) can be established and the date of the challenged transaction, such that the condition of solvency (or insolvency) established at a particular measurement date can be inferred for the date of the challenged transfer.

Appropriate discount rate. Generally, the selected discount rate reflects the debtor company's weighted average cost of debt capital and equity capital.[14] Solely for the purposes of this article, the author has defined "debt capital" as capital that the company raises by taking out a loan to be repaid at a future date regardless of the company's financial position and "equity capital" as invested money that is not repaid to investors during the ordinary course of business—and cannot be repaid while the debtor company is insolvent.

Generally, the debtor company's debt-free cash flow represents its cash flow from operations less its investing cash flow. The greater the risk of realizing the debtor company's projected cash flow, the higher the selected discount rate. The mathematical effect of increasing the discount rate is to reduce the present value of the debtor company's cash flow. Generally, a discount rate that is too low may reflect a bias toward solvency, while a discount rate that is too high may inappropriately indicate that the debtor company is insolvent.

Generally, selecting the discount rate involves the use of the capital asset pricing model or some other cost of equity capital model. If the debtor company is privately owned, the financial analyst may consider guideline public companies during the process of estimating the cost of equity capital.

When using such guideline companies, the financial analyst should be careful to select companies that provide meaningful valuation guidance from an investment risk and expected return perspective—one that properly takes into account the distressed, reorganizing, or reorganized

12 Extracted from the Newton textbook at page 557.

13 Extracted from *Litigation Services Handbook—The Role of the Financial Expert*, authored by Roman L. Weil, Peter B. Frank, Christian W. Hughes, and Michael J. Wagner, at Chapter 22, page 31, Section 22.3(ii).

14 Extracted from the Reilly textbook at page 115.

nature of the debtor company.

Another procedure for considering projection performance risk is to use a probability weighted set of projected scenarios: High probability scenarios will get more weight than those having a low probability, resulting in a probability weighted cash flow analysis. The financial analyst should appropriately apply a discount rate that takes risk into consideration.

Deriving the cost of capital. The cost of capital represents the required return that must be earned if the value of the entity at issue is to remain unchanged.[15] Cash flows are discounted at the cost of capital to determine the value of the emerging entity. A debtor company's capital structure may consist of common equity, preferred equity (if any), and debt (long term and short term).

Each of these capital components has an associated cost. To compute a debtor company's cost of capital, it is necessary to compute the blended cost of its capital structure. Use of the weighted average cost of capital is appropriate when the entire enterprise or invested capital of the business is being valued.

The weighted average cost of capital takes into account both the cost of the debt and the cost of the equity, each weighted by the market value of that individual capital component. The debt and equity weighting used in the calculation of the weighted average cost of capital are based on market values (not book values) as the cost of capital should measure the cost of issuing securities (and these are issued at market value). The weights that are used should be those that are planned or targeted over the projection period.

Deriving the cost of equity. The cost of equity of a distressed (or reorganized) debtor company is the implicit rate of return necessary to attract investors to purchase the debtor company's stock. It is the return that must be earned on new projects to leave the value of the shareholders' equity unchanged.[16] The debtor company's cost of equity can be determined using the capital asset pricing model.

The capital asset pricing model is used to develop the debtor company's cost of equity based on portfolio management theory. The capital asset pricing model determines the debtor company's cost of equity by establishing the following:[17]

- The risk-free rate,[18] generally the rate on long-term Treasury bonds. The financial analyst should correspond the period of the Treasury bonds with the debtor company's projection period.
- Beta,[19] a measure of the stock's volatility relative to an average stock. The financial analyst should consider that the debtor company's historical beta values may have limited use in

15 This section, and subsequent paragraphs, extracted from the Newton textbook, page 579, Section 11.13.
16 This section, and subsequent paragraphs, extracted from the Newton textbook, page 582.
17 Risk-free rates, betas, and equity risk premiums are publicly published, including by Morningstar/Ibbotson, Merrill Lynch, and other financial service firms.
18 Extracted from the Newton textbook, page 583.
19 Extracted from the Newton textbook, page 583.

bankruptcy proceedings and should be carefully evaluated. The financial analyst should look to betas of similarly sized companies within the industry, taking care to understand whether those companies have or have not been reorganized and restructured, vis-a-vis the debtor company. Because published betas reflect actual capital structure, the financial analyst should unlever and relever beta to adjust for the appropriate capital structure. The financial analyst should gain an understanding of any other unique risks present in the debtor company's unique financial structure—especially considering the stage of distress, restructuring, or reorganization.

- The equity risk premium,[20] the expected market rate of return less the risk-free rate. The financial analyst should consider whether the distressed debtor company's circumstances warrant an adjustment of the publicly available equity risk premium.

The traditional capital asset pricing model is often modified[21] to capture the risk associated with smaller distressed debtor companies by making an adjustment for company-specific risk (i.e., for size and unsystematic risk)—alpha risk.[22] The financial analyst should build into alpha risk the risks associated with a small-sized company[23] and the specific risks associated with the company.[24] The latter is discussed in additional detail later in this article.

A popular alternative method to the modified capital asset pricing model, to determine a debtor company's cost of equity capital, is the build-up method.[25] The build-up method uses essentially the same components as the capital asset pricing model but applies them differently. The build-up method implicitly assumes that beta is 1.0.

It is a common practice in the build-up method to make an additional adjustment to the alpha risk as follows:

- To reflect an industry risk premium—to recognize that an industry is more or less risky than the market as a whole. The financial analyst should consider the number of data points available for the industry. If the number of data points is limited, the financial analyst should consider whether the use of the industry risk premium is warranted. (An industry risk premium can be a negative number.)
- To reflect a small-sized risk premium—to recognize that investors in a smaller company require extra returns for investing in that smaller company. Many financial analysts rely, for size-based risk adjustments, on the size premia analysis, based on market capitalization, that is part of the Ibbotson/Morningstar equity risk premium studies.[26] The financial analyst

20 Extracted from the Newton textbook, page 584.

21 Extracted from the Newton textbook, page 585.

22 Assistance in determining a suitable alpha may be found in publications by Morningstar/Ibbotson, Duff & Phelps, and other financial service firms.

23 Professor Newton's analysis on page 586 appears to suggest that the small size portion of alpha risk may vary from 1% to 6%.

24 Company-specific risks include risk factors that are often interrelated including small company (size), key person dependence, key supplier dependence, customer concentration, changing technology, regulatory change, pending litigation, and forecast uncertainty (achievability).

25 Extracted from the Newton textbook, page 587.

26 Extracted from *The Financial Valuation and Litigation Expert,* Issue Number 35, February/March 2012, page 16, "Current Issues in Developing the Cost of Capital," by William Quackenbush.

should consider: (1) that even the smallest companies in the additionally subdivided 10th-decile size of those studies may have market capitalizations far greater than the subject debtor company; and (2) that the 10th-decile size may contain companies that are large but performing poorly—hence having a low market capitalization.

There are several methods to determine discount and capitalization rates. The method used by the financial analyst will depend on the information available. Using the build-up method to determine these rates involves adding rates of return and return premiums based on the qualitative risk analysis of the distressed debtor company.

The typical build-up method for estimating the cost of equity consists of:[27]

1. A risk-free rate

2. A premium for risk, including any or all of these subcomponents:

   a. General equity risk premium;

   b. Small company risk premium; and

   c. Company-specific risk premium (incorporating an industry risk premium, as appropriate).

The author submits that the fact that the debtor company is distressed, reorganizing, or reorganized is a factor to be taken into account primarily in the financial analyst's determination of the company-specific risk premium.

The company-specific risk premium is the component of the build-up method that is most specific to the subject debtor company and based on the financial analyst's professional judgment.[28] The determination of this portion of the overall discount or capitalization rate should be based on a detailed financial analysis of the subject debtor company.

The financial analyst uses ratio analyses and common size financial statements to compare the debtor company's current performance with its past performance as well as benchmarking to compare the subject debtor company with industry and guideline company data. The financial analyst also considers nonfinancial risks such as those associated with the subject's industry, size (as measured by revenues and/or assets), depth of management (or lack thereof), operations, environmental laws and regulations, and so forth.

Dr. Israel Shaked and **Robert F. Reilly**[29] note that "valuation analysts do not have established procedures for measuring company specific risk" and "there is no generally accepted formula, equation or model for quantifying the [company-specific risk premium]." Shaked and Reilly state

27 Extracted from *Cost of Capital in Litigation*, by Shannon Pratt and Roger Grabowski, page 26.

28 Extracted from *Understanding Business Valuation*, 4th edition, by Gary Trugman of Trugman Valuation Associates; Fort Lauderdale, Fla., page 39.

29 Extracted from *A Practical Guide to Bankruptcy Valuation*, by Dr. Israel Shaked and Robert Reilly, page 19.

that the company-specific risk premium is based on the [financial] analyst's informed assessment of company-specific internal and external factors that may be both financial and operational in nature, as well as both historical and prospective in nature.

The author submits that the assessment and/or determination of company-specific risk are additionally complicated by the nature, timing, and extent of the debtor company's distress and/or its involvement in actual, pending, or threatened litigation.

The author further submits that the stage of distress, reorganization, and/or restructuring is an additional consideration in determining the company-specific risk premium. Professor Newton notes[30] that the extent of the restructuring of a specific debtor company's operations typically creates greater risk than a plan of reorganization that simply modifies the financial structure of the business. The risks of major strategic and operational changes to the business may be tantamount to the risks of a startup entity.

Research indicates that "[a]ny such company specific risk premium is applicable during the time the company is in distress, as the premium reflects the added risk that plans to work out of the distressed situation simply will fail."[31]

The publications and training materials of the National Association of Certified Valuation Analysts include the following factors to be considered in determining the company-specific risk premium: competition, financial strength, management ability and depth, profitability and stability of earnings, national economic effects, and local economic effects.[32] Clearly the nature, timing, and extent of a debtor company's stage of distress and/or reorganization have an impact on most if not all of these factors.

Warren Miller[33] suggests using a competitive advantage/strategic analysis structure to determine the company-specific risk premium. Miller groups into four categories the company-specific risk factors to be considered in a strengths, weaknesses, opportunities, and threats (SWOT) analysis based on the groundbreaking strategic planning and analysis work of Michael Porter.

In his textbook, *Understanding Business Valuation* (4th edition), **Gary Trugman**[34] presents a comprehensive discussion of the factors that financial analysts should consider in determining the company-specific risk premium. Trugman presents a compendium of factors that various financial analysts have suggested with respect to determining the company-specific risk premium.

Trugman presents three categories of factors. The first category relates to risk factors such as economic, market, and regulatory risk. The second category relates to nonfinancial factors such as location of the business and barriers to entry into the market. The third category relates to company-specific

30 Extracted from the Newton textbook, page 587.
31 Extracted from the Newton textbook, page 588, where Newton sources to Pratt and Grabowski who, in turn, source to Gilson, Hotchkiss, and Ruback. Also, see footnote 73.
32 Extracted from the Shaked and Reilly textbook, page 30.
33 Extracted from the Shaked and Reilly textbook, page 30.
34 Extracted from the Shaked and Reilly textbook, page 32.

factors such as depth and quality of management.[35]

Financial analysts should consider each of these quantitative and qualitative factors when judgmentally selecting the appropriate company-specific risk premiums.

Deriving the cost of debt.[36] The rate that would generally be used for the cost of debt is the long-term yield currently being demanded by bondholders over the number of years in the projection period.[37] Debt includes the current portion of long-term debt, any interest-bearing short-term debt, and long-term debt.

The cost of debt is the debtor company's interest expense. The interest rate selected should be the current market rate. However, since that rate is not generally available for distressed companies, it must be determined from alternative sources.

Prof. Newton identifies three methods of establishing the cost of debt for a distressed debtor company.[38]

The first method is to determine the cost of debt from the debtor company's bond rating. The financial analyst would determine the debtor company's default risk as measured by its bond rating and then determine the current interest rate of debt with similar default risk, which should be consistent with the financial condition of the debtor company based on a comparative analysis of its average ratios.

Alternatively, the financial analyst can determine the interest rates paid most recently by the debtor company on its borrowings. The financial analyst should consider that smaller companies might have a higher cost of debt than larger companies.[39]

The second method is to determine the cost of debt from the default spread bond rating. The financial analyst would determine the spread between low-quality and high-quality debt. Because of default risk, the true cost of capital is the yield-to-maturity on corporate bonds less the expected default loss. When the economy is poor, the default spread widens. The financial analyst's conclusions still should be consistent with the relative distressed financial condition of the debtor company.

The third method is to determine the cost of debt from comparable companies. The financial analyst would estimate the bond rating of a privately held company through a comparison to guideline comparable public companies. The financial analyst selects the most comparable guideline companies based on appropriate quantitative and qualitative factors. The financial analyst's conclusions still should be consistent with the relative distressed financial condition of the debtor company.

Conclusion. Financial analysts should recognize that the Bankruptcy Court has noticed that

---

35 Extracted from the Shaked and Reilly textbook, pages 32-33.
36 The calculation for the cost of preferred stock is similar to that of debt other than the absence of a maturity date and the non-tax-deductibility of dividends. Extracted from the Newton textbook, page 582, Section (B) Cost of Preferred Stock.
37 Extracted from the Newton textbook, page 580.
38 The three sources discussed below are all extracted from the Newton textbook, Chapter 11 Section (A) Cost of Debt.
39 Extracted from the Newton textbook, page 581 regarding footnotes 66-68 sourcing to Shannon Pratt and Roger Grabowski, *Cost of Capital*, 3rd ed., page 52.

valuation of assets "is not an exact science and has inherent vagaries."[40] Financial analysts have the opportunity to exercise their professional judgment within a structured methodology when they determine the proper discount rate to be applied to a debtor company's cash flows for business valuation purposes.

Unfortunately, despite the widespread use by financial analysts of a company-specific risk premium in a build-up or capital asset pricing model, there is limited academic research on quantification of any company-specific risk premium, which generally remains within the realm of the financial analyst's judgment.[41] If true for average, "run-of-the mill" companies, then how much more so for distressed, reorganizing, or reorganized debtor companies?

The author submits that the determination of the discount rate of a distressed, reorganizing, or reorganized debtor company in general—and the company-specific risk premium in particular—may be the most significant of those inherent vagaries. The financial analyst's response, therefore, should be an in-depth study of the nature, timing, and extent of the debtor company's distress, reorganization, or restructuring and its impact on the company-specific risk premium.

Michael D. Pakter, CA, CPA, CFE, CIRA, CDBV, CFF, CFFA, CVA, CGMA, *has more than 35 years' experience in accounting, financial analysis, financial forensics, and investigations, including more than 15 years' experience in economic damages and business valuation issues.*

40 Extracted from the Newton textbook, page 559, regarding footnote 18 sourcing to *Savloff v. Continental Bank.*

41 Extracted from the Pratt and Grabowski textbook at page 32.

Chapter 4. Case Studies Reveal How BV and Bankruptcy Issues Are Intertwined

This article is adapted from A Practical Guide to Bankruptcy Valuation, *by* ***Robert Reilly*** *(Willamette Management Associates) and* ***Dr. Israel Shaked*** *(The Michel-Shaked Group), published by the American Bankruptcy Institute. The book helps navigate the complex task of valuing a bankrupt or other financially distressed business. For more information, go to www.bvresources.com/bankruptcy.*

Business valuation issues often play a major role in bankruptcy litigation. Valuation analysts are frequently retained to opine on the valuation of a company that either is contemplating, has filed for, or is trying to emerge from bankruptcy. The outcome of the bankruptcy process often hinges on valuation-related issues.

The case studies presented are a representative sample of actual bankruptcy cases chosen to illustrate how bankruptcy issues and valuation issues are intertwined.

Bankruptcy hearings. A common issue in a bankruptcy valuation hearing is determining the distributable value of the debtor company and comparing that value to the value of the company's liabilities. In general, if the court determines that the debtor company's distributable value is less than the value of the company debt, shareholders are unlikely to participate in the debtor company post-emergence. In contrast, if the debtor company's distributable value is greater than the value of the company debt, then, upon emergence, shareholders are likely to retain a stake in the company.

In the proposed reorganization plan, debtor company management typically projects how the restructured entity will perform following various restructuring initiatives. These initiatives may include closing nonprofitable divisions, realigning the workforce, modifying the company's trade-credit policy, improving its inventory management system, revising its warranty policy, and the like. Valuation may play an important role in assessing a financially distressed company's options. One valuation method that is commonly used to assess these alternatives is the discounted cash flow (DCF) valuation method.

Paper company: When restructuring, a debtor company may elect to discontinue operations or sell a nonperforming division. In a recent bankruptcy hearing, a paper company chose to both discontinue certain divisions and sell other underperforming divisions. The valuation analysts in this case used generally accepted income approach and market approach valuation methods, reflecting the post-reorganization changes to the business. As expected, the opposing valuation analysts disagreed on the specific types of measures to be taken, the impact of these measures, and the time it would take to implement those measures. As the debtor company was expected to be restructured, the historical financial performance did not fully reflect the expected financial position of the company after it was restructured.

For this reason, the company's historical financial results—although still important—provided less valuation guidance than did the company's financial projections. Often prepared by the proposed management of the restructured entity, financial projections involve assumptions and estimates. Based on financial projections, financial advisers are able to perform a valuation analysis based on projected income and cash flow. In this case, the projected income was used in market approach valuation methods, including the guideline publicly traded company (GPTC) method and the guideline merged and acquired company (GMAC) valuation method.

When a debtor company's recent financial performance is less relevant to the company's expected post-emergence performance, the market approach may be applied based on prospective (rather than historical) financial fundamentals. Unfortunately, the market-derived data needed to calculate prospective pricing multiples are not always available to use in the GPTC and the GMAC methods.

Fraudulent conveyance. A fraudulent conveyance occurs when a debtor company transfers assets out of its possession while it is insolvent. One aspect of litigating fraudulent conveyance claims is determining whether the debtor company was solvent at the time of the subject transfer transaction. This may involve performing the valuation of the debtor company many years after the subject transaction occurred. In some cases, the debtor company is no longer in existence. While the ultimate outcome of the debtor company may be known, it is a generally accepted procedure for the valuation analyst to use only information that was known or knowable at the time of the transaction.

Insurance company: For example, consider a case related to the bankruptcy of an insurance company. At the time of the transfer transaction, the debtor company expected to have sufficient funds available to pay claims for more than 50 years. However, these funds only lasted 18 months after a transfer transaction. When valuing the debtor company, all of the valuation analysts ignored the fact that the company ultimately filed for bankruptcy. The analysts considered only those actuarial models based on information available at the time of the transaction, without the benefit of hindsight.

Energy company: Access to reliable information may be limited in the case of an energy company. For example, in the bankruptcy of an energy company where the management of the company was fraudulent, historical financial information was not reliable. Financial projections made by the fraudulent management were equally unreliable. It was important for the valuation analyst to consider alternative measures of valuation.

It may be possible for the analyst to prepare financial projections if sufficient contemporaneous data exist about the subject company and the subject industry. When valuing a fraudulent debtor company, it is often insufficient to merely restate the historical financial statements to adjust for the fraud. Empirical evidence and academic research show that, following a restatement caused by fraud, a company loses value in excess of what would be expected based solely on the accounting adjustment. The valuation analyst should consider this factor in the valuation analysis.

Preference claims. If, within 90 days prior to the bankruptcy date (one year for company insiders), a payment is made to a creditor out of the ordinary course of business, it is potentially regarded as a preference payment. This payment is made at the expense of the other unsecured creditors and may, therefore, be avoided. After returning the money, the creditor may then file a claim together with all of the unsecured creditors. One of the procedures required by the trustee of a bankrupt company to prove that a payment is a preference payment is to show that the debtor was insolvent at the time of the payment. When performing a valuation in a preference matter, it is necessary to estimate the value of the debtor company at the time of the preferential payment.

Clothing retailer: In the case of a large clothing retailer, the debtor company was valued for preference claim consideration at a time when financial information was not readily available. For example, for payments that occurred on May 15, the debtor company did not have financial information at that date. Instead, the debtor company issued quarterly financial statements on March 31 and June 30.

It was proven that the debtor company was insolvent on both statement dates and that no significant events could have altered this opinion between the two quarter-end dates. Accordingly, the debtor company was also insolvent on May 15. Similarly, in some instances, the debtor company made multiple payments that could be considered preferential payments. The valuation analyst may be required to prove that the debtor company was insolvent at the time of each payment or throughout the period when the payments were made. As in the example relating to the clothing retailer, the valuation analyst may "bookend" the valuation by proving solvency or insolvency at the beginning and end of the payment period. Then, the analyst may review all material events regarding the debtor company that occurred throughout the period.

Fair consideration. A necessary condition for proving a fraudulent conveyance claim is showing that there was a lack of fair consideration. In some cases, the issue is relatively simple. For example, in a leveraged buyout (LBO), the acquirer borrows money using the target's assets as collateral, and the majority of the proceeds from the issuance of the debt are used to pay exiting shareholders. In these cases, the company is burdened with debt, whereas the cash raised does not stay in the business. Therefore, there may be no fair consideration in such an LBO. However, the determination of lack of fair consideration is not always a simple issue.

Financial services company: In the case of the acquisition of a financial services company that subsequently filed for bankruptcy, each of the components of the transaction had to be valued to assess whether the company received more than it gave up. The transaction was evaluated, and the purchase price consisted of various components including a complex swap agreement, a management agreement, various exchanges of real estate, and the exchange of a business not related to the core operations of the debtor. Each component of the transaction was valued to assess whether the debtor received fair consideration in the transaction.

Public relations company: In the case of a public relations company, the company repurchased its own stock. At issue was whether a debtor company could ever receive fair consideration for the purchase of its own stock. Similar to a dividend, cash leaves the company to fund the repurchase of the shares, but the cash goes straight to the selling shareholders. Alternatively, if the repurchase was funded by debt, then debt would increase on the balance sheet without a corresponding increase in a company asset. Even though the remaining shareholders may have benefitted from the repurchase, the debtor company did not receive any direct benefit from this transaction.

Liquidation. When valuing a financially distressed company, one of the questions that the analyst considers is whether the stakeholders are better off with the company operating as a going concern or the company implementing an asset liquidation. In some situations, the liquidation of the company's assets represents the highest and best use (HABU) of the assets. In other situations, some form of corporate reorganization and restructuring may enable the debtor company to turn around and operate as a going-concern entity. In either case, a valuation analyst may be retained to assess the best alternatives for the stakeholders. For example, consider the following cases.

Cruise ship company: In a bankruptcy relating to a cruise ship company, the debtor company acquired several new cruise ships over a few years. The valuation of the debtor company indicated that the company was not profitable. The debtor valuation company also indicated that the net present value of each newly acquired ship was negative. In other words, the company equity became less valuable with each cruise ship acquisition. Therefore, the analysts made an assessment of whether the company could continue to operate as a going concern. In this case, the debtor company was clearly better off liquidating and not continuing to operate as a going concern. In such a case, the debtor business valuation was based on an orderly liquidation premise of value.

Imaging technology company: In certain cases, the majority of the company value is derived from the nonoperating assets of the debtor company. For example, an analyst was retained to value an imaging technology company that produced very low operating cash flow. However, the company had won a patent-infringement lawsuit. As a result, the debtor company was awarded a large amount of money that was not yet collected as of the valuation date. In addition, the company owned valuable vacant land that could be sold for a significant amount. In such a case, the value of the nonoperating assets was added to the value of the operating assets to conclude the value of the debtor company's invested capital.

Bankruptcy-related asbestos claims. A common practice in asbestos-related bankruptcies is for the debtor to set up a trust to deal with the asbestos claims that may arise in the foreseeable future. The party responsible for setting up the trust contributes assets to the trust to fund the payment of future claims. In these instances, it may be necessary to value the expected proceeds of the contributed assets or to assess the debtor's post-reorganization viability to operate as a going concern.

Flooring company: In the bankruptcy of a flooring company, the focus of the valuation analysis was on a note contributed to the trust. The note's indenture included many provisions and contingencies that depended on the debtor company's value at a future point in time. However, considering the fact that the debtor company was a defendant in asbestos litigation, the debtor company's future value was highly uncertain.

Asbestos claims-processing company: In the case of an asbestos claims-processing company, the focus of the dispute was the question of whether the debtor company could emerge from bankruptcy as a viable going concern. Shares of the post-reorganization debtor company were contributed to a trust. The assessment of the company's future viability included two analyses: a valuation analysis, which was performed to assess the value of the debtor company shares that had been contributed to the trust, and a cash-flow analysis, which was performed to assess whether the projected future cash flow would be sufficient to fund the expected company obligations.

Damages. In certain cases, the plaintiff's damages theory is based on the decline in the value of the debtor company. In such cases, it may be appropriate to value the debtor company at two points (or more) in time. The multiple time period valuations are used to determine the difference (decline) in value allegedly caused by the defendants' actions. The appropriate valuation premise may change as conditions of the debtor company change. For example, at the first valuation date, the appropriate premise of value may be value in use as a going concern. However, due to the deteriorating conditions at the company, the HABU for the company assets at the second valuation date may indicate that the appropriate premise of value is value in exchange, on an orderly liquidation basis.

Technology company: In the bankruptcy of a technology company, the analyst was requested to measure economic damages resulting from the board of directors' alleged action—or more specifically, lack of action. The plaintiffs argued that the board should have liquidated the company at a certain point in time. Instead, the board allowed the company to continue operating, and, as a result, the company exhausted its resources. As part of the analysis, the analyst determined when to value the company as a going concern and when to value the company on a liquidation basis. The two types of analyses had to be performed at multiple points in time.

Conclusion. As illustrated in these case studies, no "off-the-shelf" valuation analysis fits all bankruptcy issues. In fact, numerous issues may be the focus of the valuation analyst's attention. These issues include which valuation methods to use, whether to value the company on a going-concern basis or on a liquidation basis, the specific debtor company assets to be valued, and the dates on which to value the debtor company.

Typically, the valuation analyst only considers information that is known or knowable, accounting for the company's existing conditions as of the date of the valuation. Case-specific circumstances may help determine how the analyst will address each of the issues discussed above.

Chapter 5. Dividend Recapitalizations: A New Market for Valuation Opinions[1]

By Patricia J. Luscombe, CFA, and Jeffrey A. McNamara

The 2010 Tax Relief Act extended the Bush era's maximum 15% tax rate for "qualified" dividends through 2012, eliminating the threat of a significantly higher dividend tax rate for two years. Nonetheless, stronger corporate balance sheets (fueled by dramatically improved profitability and cash flows) and accommodating credit markets continue to motivate boards of directors to consider the benefits of a dividend recapitalization. A "dividend recap," as it is known, is a technique where some or all of the proceeds of a new debt offering are dividended-out to the equity shareholders.

The use of dividend recaps grew more in the first quarter than ever before. Standard & Poor's Leveraged Commentary and Data (S&P LCD) reports that approximately $24.3 billion of debt was issued to pay dividends in first-quarter 2011 versus $9.4 billion in first-quarter 2010, representing an increase of 158% (see Exhibit 1). This sudden burst of activity is notable because the market for dividend recapitalizations was virtually nonexistent during 2008 and 2009; however, dividend-related transactions increased substantially in the second half of 2010. In fact, according to Thomson Reuters LPC, middle-market sponsored dividend recapitalization volume in fourth-quarter 2010 exceeded the volume of debt used to finance leveraged buyouts (see Exhibit 2). While some transactions in the second half of 2010 probably were motivated only by the threat of higher taxes, most market participants expect the volume of dividend recapitalizations to remain strong as the shareholders of private equity-owned portfolio companies use the technique to extract cash while they wait for improved financial results and a stronger economy before attempting to access the IPO market or to sell assets.

Although conditions might be ripe for a leverage-fueled dividend, boards of directors should engage in certain best practices to minimize the risk of subsequent claims in connection with a

1 Originally published in the June 2011 *Business Valuation Update*.

recapitalization that goes awry. Many states' corporation laws, including Delaware's, require that dividends be paid out of surplus, defined as the fair value of a corporation's total assets minus the fair value of its total liabilities, less the corporation's capital. (Capital is generally defined as no less than the aggregate par value of a company's stock.) For private equity-owned portfolio companies, boards of directors must demonstrate that the portfolio company has sufficient "surplus" to pay the dividend. Other states require not only that the dividend be paid from surplus, but also that the company have the ability to service its debts incurred in the recapitalization as these debts become due. If a company's financial performance deteriorates post-transaction to the point of insolvency, the dividend recapitalization can be "set aside" under fraudulent conveyance laws, and the corporate directors could be subject to personal liability. A fraudulent transfer occurs when a transaction results in the counterparty receiving a benefit at the expense of unsecured creditors, and the company: (i) at the time of the transaction is insolvent; or (ii) after the transaction either: (a) has unreasonably small capital to continue its business; or (b) is unable to repay its obligations as these obligations become due.

Therefore, many boards of directors hire an independent financial advisory firm to provide an opinion surrounding the recapitalization to assist them in the deliberation of whether to approve the dividend to shareholders. Such an opinion can serve multiple purposes. It can provide an independent and objective assessment of the company's value; it can assist in evaluating alternative scenarios; and, of course, it can be useful in defending against a lawsuit.

A few different types of opinions are requested of a financial advisor in connection with a dividend recapitalization. The first is a capital surplus opinion to determine whether the fair value of the aggregate assets exceeds the stated liabilities and identified contingent liabilities by an amount that is greater than the par value of the outstanding capital stock after giving effect to the payment of the dividend. This type of opinion is typically based on the company's going concern enterprise value as estimated using standard valuation approaches rather than book value as defined by accounting rules. In practice, standard valuation approaches and methods include the income approach and the market approach, including selected public company analysis and selected transaction analysis. Once the company's going concern enterprise value is determined, the pro forma debt to be incurred as part of the dividend recapitalization (as well as other stated and identified contingent liabilities) is estimated to determine the resulting equity cushion. The size of the equity cushion, as a percentage of enterprise value, is a useful indicator of the magnitude of the dividend recapitalization.

The second type of opinion is similar to a solvency opinion, in which it is determined whether: (i) the fair value of the company's total assets exceeds the sum of its total liabilities (and identified contingent liabilities) after giving effect to the payment of the dividend; *and* (ii) the company has the ability to pay its indebtedness as such indebtedness becomes due. This type of opinion applies sensitivity analysis and stress testing to determine whether a margin of safety exists if the company underperforms its projections. For example, a company's projected cash flows should be adjusted to account for "downside scenarios" that attempt to quantify the impact of various adverse developments in the company. In addition, analyzing the company's ability to pay its indebtedness as such indebtedness becomes due typically involves detailed credit analysis and a sophisticated understanding of today's complex fixed income markets to determine the company's ability to either repay or refinance its debt at maturity.

Finally, a financial advisor might be asked to provide a solvency opinion, which analyzes not only (i) and (ii) noted above, but also considers whether a company has sufficient capital to operate its business (i.e., "the reasonable capital test"). The reasonable capital test seeks to demonstrate whether a company will have a reasonable level of surplus capital following a dividend recapitalization. In practice, a financial advisor performs additional sensitivity analyses to ensure that the company has adequate equity, post-transaction, to support business and financial volatility.

Although specific circumstances and state corporation laws may dictate the type of opinion that is advisable or legally required for a proposed transaction, a valuation or solvency-like opinion will provide support to the board of directors approving a dividend recapitalization.

Exhibit 1. Dividend Financing Volume ($ in billions)

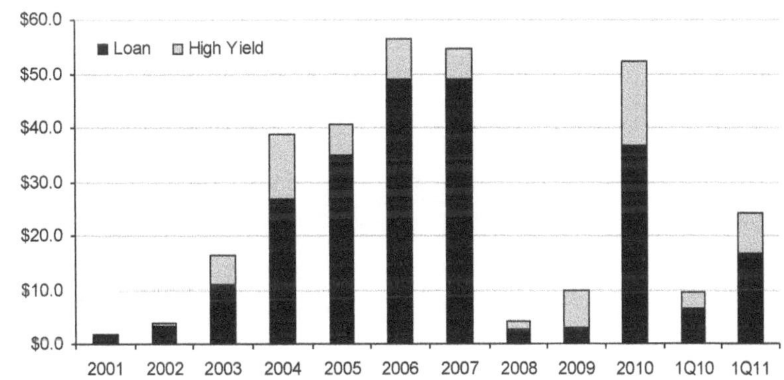

Exhibit. 2. Middle Market Volume, Dividend Recapitalization Vs. LBO Loans ($ in billions)

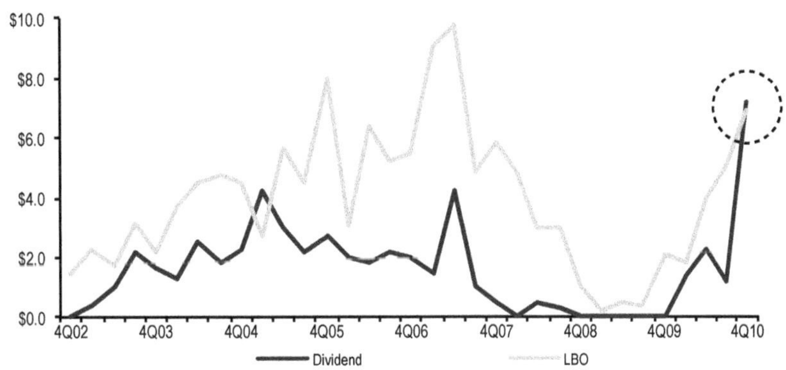

Note: 4Q10 includes completed and in process deals

Dividend recapitalizations can provide many benefits, including the ability of companies and private equity firms to "unlock" unrealized appreciation and to benefit from the tax shield attributable to the tax deductibility of interest payments on the newly issued debt. However, boards of directors should always follow best practices in order to reduce the risk of overleveraging a business and attracting litigation. Such best practices should include arranging for an independent financial advisor to assess the proposed transaction and its financial impact on the company.

Patricia J. Luscombe, CFA, *is a managing director in the Valuations and Opinions group at Lincoln International LLC. She can be reached at pluscombe@lincolninternational.com.* ***Jeffrey A. McNamara*** *is an associate at Duff & Phelps.*

Court Case Digests

Court Case Summary Table

Presented in order of State/Jurisdiction, then Case Name.

Case Name	Date		State/ Jurisdiction	Summary	Page
Lippe v. Bairnco Corp. (I)	1/28/03	United States Court of Appeals	Federal/2nd Circuit	Valuation 'Experts' Excluded as Unreliable Based on Numerous Errors in Methodology and Inability to Explain Conclusions	208
Lippe v. Bairnco Corp. (II)	3/14/03	United States Court of Appeals	Federal/2nd Circuit	Case Update—*Lippe v. Bairnco Corp.*	211
Lippe v. Bairnco Corp. (III)	4/9/04	United States Court of Appeals	Federal/2nd Circuit	2nd Circuit Affirms Application of *Daubert* in Fraudulent Conveyance Case	211
In re Pegasus Agency, Inc.	12/5/96	United States Court of Appeals	Federal/2nd Circuit	Proper Due Diligence Required for Reorganization Plan Confirmation	269
In re Stephen L. Vecchitto (II)	10/11/00	United States Court of Appeals	Federal/2nd Circuit	Stock in an Accounting Firm Valued at Zero	336
In re American Home Mortgage Holdings, Inc. (II)	2/16/11	United States Court of Appeals	Federal/3rd Circuit	3rd Circuit Confirms DCF to Value Mortgage Portfolios in Dysfunctional Markets	69
Kool, Mann, Coffee and Co. v. L. Coleman Coffey (II)	7/29/02	United States Court of Appeals	Federal/3rd Circuit	Discounted Cash Flow Method Used to Value Marina and Houseboat Rental Business	198
In re PWS Holding Corp.	9/18/00	United States Court of Appeals	Federal/3rd Circuit	Business Enterprise Valuation Showing Solvency Precludes Fraudulent Transfer Claims	282
In re Resorts International	6/30/99	United States Court of Appeals	Federal/3rd Circuit	Stockholder's Merger Price Recovery Reversed on Appeal	287
Trans World Airlines v. Trans World Airlines Official Committee of Unsecured Creditors	1/20/98	United States Court of Appeals	Federal/3rd Circuit	Fair Valuation Clarified for Bankruptcy Purposes	313
VFB LLC v. Campbell Soup Co.	3/30/07	United States Court of Appeals	Federal/3rd Circuit	Expert Valuations a 'Sideshow' Compared to Capital Pricing Markets	337
Heilig Meyers Co. v. Internal Revenue Service (In re Heilig Meyers Co.)	5/9/07	United States Court of Appeals	Federal/4th Circuit	Accounting Method Trumps Valuation in 'Clear Reflection of Income' Case	182
In the Matter of Elizabeth Ann Evert (debtor): Marsha G. Milligan, Trustee v. Elizabeth Ann Evert	8/6/03	United States Court of Appeals	Federal/5th Circuit	Property Equalization Payments Cannot Be Exempted in Bankruptcy	151
Sandra Davis v. Thomas Cullen Davis	2/5/97	United States Court of Appeals	Federal/5th Circuit	Exempted Property Not Immunized Against Alimony Arrearage	132
In re American HomePatient, Inc.	7/11/05	United States Court of Appeals	Federal/6th Circuit	Valuation Date for Rejection Damages in Bankruptcy	71
In re: CSC Industries, Inc. (Pension Benefit Guaranty Corporation v. Kathryn A. Belfance, Trustee)	11/17/00	United States Court of Appeals	Federal/6th Circuit	Unfunded Pension Claim Valued Using Prudent Investor Rate	127
In re Global Technovations, Inc. (II)	9/13/12	United States Court of Appeals	Federal/6th Circuit	6th Circuit Upholds Using Post Hoc Comparable Transaction	160
In re Structurlite Plastics Corporation: SPC Corporation v. Robert E. Griffith	8/25/98	United States Court of Appeals	Federal/6th Circuit	Previous Valuations Assist in Showing Debtor's Post-LBO Solvency	298
In re Valley-Vulcan Mold Co. (I)	8/19/99	United States Bankruptcy Court	Federal/6th Circuit	Solvency Opinions Admissible in Bankruptcy Court	334
In re Valley-Vulcan Mold Co. (II)	2/26/01	United States Court of Appeals	Federal/6th Circuit	Expert Testimony Using DCF Method to Determine Solvency Admissible	335

Case Name	Date		State/ Jurisdiction	Summary	Page
In re Wallace G. Wilkinson, Jr., debtor: Charles J. Lisle, Trustee v. John Wiley & Sons, Inc.	8/17/06	United States Court of Appeals	Federal/6th Circuit	Reasonably Equivalent Value Tested on Date of Transfer	350
Joseph D. Olsen, Trustee of Huntley Ready Mix, Inc. v. Gary A. Floit	7/14/00	United States Court of Appeals	Federal/7th Circuit	Value of Noncompete Agreement Considered in Bankruptcy Case	261
In re Prince	5/31/96	United States Court of Appeals	Federal/7th Circuit	Personal Goodwill Deemed Corporate Asset in Chapter 11 Bankruptcy Reorganization	278
United Airlines, Inc. v. Regional Airports Improvement Corp.	5/5/09	United States Court of Appeals	Federal/7th Circuit	Bankruptcy Court Cannot Just 'Split the Difference' in Divergent Discount Rates	326
In re Mary Beth Usery (Ewing B. Gourley v. Mary Beth Usery)	8/22/97	United States Court of Appeals	Federal/8th Circuit	The Same Capitalization Rate Must Be Used When Determining Actual Value and Value as Represented for Damages From a Fraudulent Business Sale	332
In re Susan E. Wick	1/9/02	United States Court of Appeals	Federal/8th Circuit	Stock Options Valued for Inclusion in a Bankruptcy Estate	361
In re Westpointe (II)	3/14/01	United States Court of Appeals	Federal/8th Circuit	8th Circuit Upholds Use of Preconfirmation Value	357
In re DAK Industries Inc.	3/19/99	United States Court of Appeals	Federal/9th Circuit	Company Found to Be Solvent Prior to Bankruptcy	128
In re Kim; Ardmor Vending Co. v. Kim	12/9/97	United States Court of Appeals	Federal/9th Circuit	Bankruptcy Court Erred in Undervaluing Appellant's Collateral	196
In re Integra Realty Resources, Inc.: Jeffrey A. Weinman v. Fidelity Capital Appreciation Fund	1/14/04	United States Court of Appeals	Federal/10th Circuit	Value of Recovery Under Sec. 550 May Be Greater Than the Value of the Asset Fraudulently Transferred at the Time of the Transfer	188
Pension Benefits Guaranty Corp. v. CF&I Fabricators (In re: CF&I Fabricators)	8/3/98	United States Court of Appeals	Federal/10th Circuit	Prudent Investor Method Used to Value Unfunded Pension Benefits Claim	273
In re Harper	8/18/93	United States Bankruptcy Court	Federal/ Arkansas	Valuing a Minority Interest in a Closely Held Family Corporation	175
In re: American Suzuki Motor Corporation	6/4/13	United States Bankruptcy Court	Federal/ California	What 'FMV'? Bankruptcy Court Restricts Car Dealer's Damages	73
Mercury Companies, Inc. v. FNF Security Acquisition, Inc. (In re Mercury Companies, Inc.)	3/31/14	United States Bankruptcy Court	Federal/ Colorado	'Reasonably Equivalent Value' Analysis Is Not a Dollars-and-Cents Issue	240
In re Oglesby	6/12/98	United States Bankruptcy Court	Federal/ Colorado	Bankruptcy Reorganization Uses Market Rates of Interest	259
In re Bartomeli	1/5/04	United States Bankruptcy Court	Federal/ Connecticut	Book Value in Financial Statements Not Materially False Though Company Has No Market Value	96
In re Colonial Realty Company; Hirsch v. Steinberg	9/9/98	United States Bankruptcy Court	Federal/ Connecticut	Stock Recipients Liable for Fraudulent Transfer Underpayment	122
In re Stephen L. Vecchitto (I)	3/30/99	United States Bankruptcy Court	Federal/ Connecticut	Can Debtor Transfer Valueless Stock?	336
In re Alta+Cast	3/2/04	United States Bankruptcy Court	Federal/ Delaware	*Software Company Value Based on Value of Wholly Owned Subsidiary Only*	63
American Classic Voyages Co. v. JP Morgan Chase Bank (I)	4/27/07	United States Bankruptcy Court	Federal/ Delaware	Valuation Turns on Reliability of Pre-9/11 Projections	64
American Classic Voyages Co. v. JP Morgan Chase Bank (II)	3/25/08	United States District Court	Federal/ Delaware	Bankruptcy Courts 'Required' to Reject DCF Analysis When Market Cap Data Are Available?	66

Case Name	Date		State/ Jurisdiction	Summary	Page
In re American Home Mortgage Holdings, Inc. (I)	9/8/09	United States Bankruptcy Court	Federal/ Delaware	Bankruptcy Court Chooses Between Market or 'Reasonable Valuation' of Troubled Loans	67
In re Capmark Financial Group	11/1/10	United States Bankruptcy Court	Federal/ Delaware	Valuing Director Guaranties in Bankruptcy: Using a Put Option Approach	102
In re Coram Healthcare Corp.	10/5/04	United States Bankruptcy Court	Federal/ Delaware	Too Many Adjustments Compromise Deloitte's Valuation	124
EBCI, Inc. v. America Online, Inc.	1/10/08	United States Bankruptcy Court	Federal/ Delaware	Proving Solvency When Internet Assets 'Disappear Overnight'	146
In re Hechinger Investment Co. of Delaware, Inc. (I)	3/28/04	United States District Court	Federal/ Delaware	Valuation Is Irrelevant to Establish Knowledge by Stranger to Indenture of Its Breach	179
In re Hechinger Investment Co. of Delaware, Inc. (II)	7/19/05	United States District Court	Federal/ Delaware	If Bankruptcy Is Not 'Clearly Imminent,' Corporation Must Be Valued on a Going Concern Basis	181
In re Lason, Inc.	10/15/03	United States Bankruptcy Court	Federal/ Delaware	Premise of Value Issue in Bankruptcy	206
In re Nellson Nutraceutical (I)	11/29/06	United States Bankruptcy Court	Federal/ Delaware	Expert Valuation Report Disqualified Under *Daubert* for 'Maverick' DCF Analysis	251
In re Nellson Nutraceutical (II)	1/18/07	United States Bankruptcy Court	Federal/ Delaware	Experts Left 'in the Dark' by Deliberately Manipulated Management Projections	253
Peltz v. Hatten	6/5/02	United States District Court	Federal/ Delaware	Bankruptcy Court Indicates Strong Preference for Market Approach, Price Per Subscriber Multiple	270
In re Spansion	4/1/10	United States Bankruptcy Court	Federal/ Delaware	Management Projections, DCF Discount Rate, and More Are Key to Bankruptcy Valuation	294
In re Tribune Co.	10/31/11	United States Bankruptcy Court	Federal/ Delaware	Tribune Bankruptcy Court Prefers Current Data to Fill Valuation 'Chasm'	315
In re UDC Homes, Inc.	12/6/96	United States Bankruptcy Court	Federal/ Delaware	Bankruptcy Expert Fees: UDC Homes	325
Whyte v. C/R Energy Coinvestment II, L.P. (In re SemCrud)	6/10/13	United States Bankruptcy Court	Federal/ Delaware	Bankruptcy Court Wary of Asset Approach in Solvency Analysis	346
In re Winstar Communication, Inc.	12/21/05	United States Bankruptcy Court	Federal/ Delaware	Analyst Convinces Court to Reject Stock Value as 'Fair'	363
Alberts v. HCA, Inc.	7/11/13	United States District Court	Federal/ District of Columbia	Trustee Claims Bankruptcy Court Flouted Valuation Rules	60
In re Greater Southeast Community Hospital Corp. (I)	1/2/06	United States Bankruptcy Court	Federal/ District of Columbia	BV Appraiser Challenged Under *Daubert* for Bias and Reliance on Third-Party Reports	164
In re Greater Southeast Community Hospital Corp. (II)	5/12/08	United States Bankruptcy Court	Federal/ District of Columbia	Bankruptcy Court Conducts Extensive Valuation Findings of Hospital in Fraudulent Transfer Case	165
In re Greater Southeast Community Hospital Corp. (III)	2/22/12	United States Bankruptcy Court	Federal/ District of Columbia	Bankruptcy Court Exposes 'Perils' of DCF Without Good Expert Evidence	171
Bakst v. United States of America (In re: Kane & Kane)	7/16/12	United States Bankruptcy Court	Federal/ Federal Circuit	Valuing Contingent Liability in Bankruptcy Precludes GAAP Standard	93
In re Chemtura Corp. (II)	4/19/11	United States Bankruptcy Court	Federal/ Federal Circuit	Valuing Two Tough Aspects of Damages: Pricing and Discount Rate	113
Daubert v. Merrell Dow Pharmaceuticals	6/28/93	Supreme Court	Federal/ Federal Circuit	Landmark *Daubert* Decision Develops New Standard for Admission of Expert Evidence	129

Case Name	Date		State/ Jurisdiction	Summary	Page
Holber v. M&T Bank (In re Scheffler)	6/5/12	United States Bankruptcy Court	Federal/ Federal Circuit	Cost Method 'Strikingly Inappropriate' to Value Technology	184
In re Jonatzke	8/24/12	United States Bankruptcy Court	Federal/ Federal Circuit	Flawed Expert Opinion Drastically Diminishes Plaintiff's Lost Profits	190
Kumho Tire Company v. Carmichael	3/23/99	Supreme Court	Federal/ Federal Circuit	Supreme Court Affirms 'Gatekeeper' Duty of Trial Courts for Expert Evidence	200
Monsanto Co. v. Roeder	12/14/09	United States Bankruptcy Court	Federal/ Federal Circuit	Bankrupt Farmer Gets Plowed by Another Patented Seed Case	245
Paloian v. LaSalle Bank	8/27/10	United States Court of Appeals	Federal/ Federal Circuit	DCF, Including Tax Affecting and Discounts, May Not Apply to Insolvency Opinions	265
In re Premier Entertainment Biloxi LLC	9/3/10	United States Bankruptcy Court	Federal/ Federal Circuit	Bankruptcy Court Prefers Adjusted Balance Sheet Test, Including FMV of Brand License	276
In re South Canaan Cellular Investments	1/6/11	United States Bankruptcy Court	Federal/ Federal Circuit	Should Neutral Appraiser Be Kept 'Blind' to Parties' Competing Valuations?	292
In the Matter of TCI 2 Holdings, LLC	4/12/10	United States Bankruptcy Court	Federal/ Federal Circuit	Competing Valuations of Trump Casinos Determine Fate, Feasibility of Restructuring	300
In re Texans CUSO Insurance Group	3/2/10	United States Bankruptcy Court	Federal/ Federal Circuit	Textbook Case of Proving Lost Future Profits Based on Past Finances of the Business	305
In re Washington Mutual, Inc.	9/13/11	United States Bankruptcy Court	Federal/ Federal Circuit	WaMu Bankruptcy Court Credits the More 'Complete' Valuation	353
In re White	3/4/10	United States Bankruptcy Court	Federal/ Federal Circuit	'Devastating' Cross-Exam in Shareholder Buyout Case Leads to Discredited Expert	359
In re Yellowstone Mountain Club, LLC	8/16/10	United States Bankruptcy Court	Federal/ Federal Circuit	Experienced BV Expert Manipulated by Resort Owner and Attorneys?	366
In re Young Broadcasting, Inc.	4/19/10	United States Bankruptcy Court	Federal/ Federal Circuit	'Levered' DCF for Bankrupt Business Fits the Facts but Falls to *Daubert* Standard	369
In re Certified HR Service Co.	9/25/12	United States District Court	Federal/ Florida	Expert Valuation More Credible and Critical Than Contemporaneous Market and Management Values	105
In re The Minnelusa Co.	9/29/94	United States Bankruptcy Court	Federal/ Florida	Share Value Can Consider Discounts, Says Court	244
In re TOUSA, Inc.	10/30/09	United States Bankruptcy Court	Federal/ Florida	Teams of Experts Help Court and Creditors Value Huge, Bankrupt Homebuilder	307
Vision-Park Properties v. Seaside Engineering	3/27/14	United States District Court	Federal/ Florida	Debtor's Challenges Justify Bankruptcy Court's Emergence Risk Premium	343
In re Leskosky; Tidwell v. Leskosky	12/17/02	United States Bankruptcy Court	Federal/ Georgia	Stock Valued as of Date of Petition in Bankruptcy Regardless of Potential Post-Petition Appreciation	207
In re Parnes	7/5/96	United States Bankruptcy Court	Federal/ Georgia	Ex-Wife, Creditors Allege Husband Knew Dental Practices Had Substantial Value When He Filed Bankruptcy	269
In re Bachrach Clothing, Inc.	10/10/12	United States Bankruptcy Court	Federal/ Illinois	Bankruptcy Court Discredits DCF as 'Easily Manipulated'	87
In re Doctors Hospital of Hyde Park, Inc.	3/2/07	United States Bankruptcy Court	Federal/ Illinois	Fraud-Infected Hospital Merits 'Tax Affecting,' High Risk Premium, and More	139
In re Edgewater Medical Center	8/15/07	United States Bankruptcy Court	Federal/ Illinois	Should Solvency Valuation Include Ongoing but Undiscovered Fraud?	149
In re Joy Recovery Tech. Corp.; Daley v. Chang	11/20/02	United States Bankruptcy Court	Federal/ Illinois	Experts' Testimony Scrutinized, Admitted Under *Daubert*; Court Uses Balance Sheet Test and Market Multiple Approach in Insolvency Analysis	192

Case Name	Date		State/ Jurisdiction	Summary	Page
In re Jumer's Castle Lodge, Inc.	5/11/05	United States Bankruptcy Court	Federal/ Illinois	Contested Valuation of One Asset Is Moot Where All Transferred Assets Provide Reasonably Equivalent Value	195
LaSalle Nat'l Bank Assn. v. Paloian	3/17/09	United States District Court	Federal/ Illinois	Expert Solvency Opinions Accused of 'Hindsight Bias'	202
Makula v. Sanwa Business Credit Corp.	8/7/97	United States District Court	Federal/ Illinois	Undervaluing Partnership Interest Comes at a Price	226
In re McCook Metals v. Lynch	1/14/05	United States Bankruptcy Court	Federal/ Illinois	Valuation Results in $2.7 Million Disgorgement	227
Mungo v. Taylor	3/7/03	United States District Court	Federal/ Illinois	Acceptance of Lower Valuation Based on Declining Profits Upheld	247
In re Nanovation Technologies, Inc.	5/17/07	United States Court of Appeals	Federal/ Illinois	Bankruptcy Trustee's Efforts to Go After Valuation Group Backfire	248
Scott v. Universal Fidelity Group	3/19/99	United States Bankruptcy Court	Federal/ Illinois	Net Worth	292
In the Matter of Baker	7/2/96	United States Bankruptcy Court	Federal/ Indiana	Going Concern Value Used in Bankruptcy Proceeding	92
Boyer v. Crown Stock Distribution, Inc.	2/17/09	United States District Court	Federal/ Indiana	Valuation Evidence Helps Support Trustee's Successful Claims	99
In re Civic Partners Sioux City, LLC	10/7/13	United States Bankruptcy Court	Federal/Iowa	Plan Confirmation Hinges on Property Valuation	117
Miller Bros. Coal v. Consol of Kentucky, Inc.	12/11/09	United States Bankruptcy Court	Federal/ Kentucky	Court Adjusts Discount Rate to Reflect Current Economic Risks	243
In re PieceGoods Shops Co.	10/10/95	United States Bankruptcy Court	Federal/ Maryland	Is Marketability Discount Offset by Possible Sale of Debtor?	275
In re Healthco International, Inc.; Brandt v. Hicks, Muse & Co., Inc.	5/17/96	United States Bankruptcy Court	Federal/ Massachusetts	Trustee Charges Directors, Financial Advisors, Others in Failed LBO	177
In re Global Technovations, Inc. (I)	3/31/11	United States District Court	Federal/ Michigan	'Most Reliable, Least Speculative' Valuation Prevails in Bankruptcy	158
Dietz v. Jacobs	3/21/14	United States District Court	Federal/ Minnesota	Court Admits Solvency Analysis Lacking Specific Valuation of Debtor	136
In re Westpointe (I)	5/26/99	United States District Court	Federal/ Missouri	What Valuation Methods Are Appropriate for a Going Concern in Bankruptcy?	357
Samson v. Western Capital Partners LLC (In re Blixseth)	3/28/13	United States Bankruptcy Court	Federal/ Montana	Court Credits Expert's Cash Flow Analysis in Solvency Determination	288
Kool, Mann, Coffee and Co. v. L. Coleman Coffey (I)	3/18/99	United States District Court	Federal/ New Jersey	Valuation Techniques for Misrepresented Businesses	197
Adelphia Recovery Trust v. FPL Group, Inc. (In re Adelphia Corp.)	5/6/14	United States Bankruptcy Court	Federal/ New York	Court Finds Facts Back Expert's Value-Per-Subscriber Metric	55
In re Boston Generating	12/3/10	United States Bankruptcy Court	Federal/ New York	Bankruptcy Expert Claims DCF Indicates Market Value Better Than the Market	97
In re Chemtura Corp. (I)	10/29/10	United States Bankruptcy Court	Federal/ New York	More Support for Using More Than One Method (DCF) in Current Valuations	109
In re Chrysler LLC	5/31/09	United States Bankruptcy Court	Federal/ New York	Fair Value at Crux of Chrysler Bankruptcy	115
In re DBSD North America, Inc.	9/30/09	United States Bankruptcy Court	Federal/ New York	Bankruptcy Court Rejects DCF for Troubled Company	132
In re Eastman Kodak Company	8/15/13	United States Bankruptcy Court	Federal/ New York	Court Bristles at Experts' Hasty Valuation of Debtor	142

Case Name	Date		State/ Jurisdiction	Summary	Page
In re Louis Frey Company, Inc.	7/28/06	United States Bankruptcy Court	Federal/ New York	New York Bankruptcy Court Confirms Valuation of Customer Lists, With High Praise for Valuator	217
In re Med Diversified, Inc. (I)	11/14/05	United States Bankruptcy Court	Federal/ New York	Report Is Inadmissible Where Purported Valuator Is Not Certified, Uses Incorrect Methodology, and Does No Independent Analysis	229
In re Med Diversified, Inc. (II)	8/2/06	United States Bankruptcy Court	Federal/ New York	BV on Trial in Bankruptcy? New York Court Excludes Appraisal as 'Junk Science'	231
In re Oneida Ltd.	8/30/06	United States Bankruptcy Court	Federal/ New York	Discovered Emails Plus a Contingent Fee Discredit Appraiser's DCF Analysis	263
Pereira v. Dow Chem. Co. (In re Trace Int'l Holdings, Inc.)	12/10/03	United States Bankruptcy Court	Federal/ New York	Inconsistent Legal Theory and Valuation Methods Cost Trustee Fraudulent Transfer	274
Pryor v. Tiffen (In re TC Liquidations LLC)	12/6/11	United States Bankruptcy Court	Federal/ New York	Certain Intangibles Only Have Value in Ongoing Business	279
In re Residential Capital, LLC	11/15/13	United States Bankruptcy Court	Federal/ New York	Creditors' Valuation Spoils Diminution in Value Claim	284
In re Spielfogel	7/28/97	United States Bankruptcy Court	Federal/ New York	Company Withholds Data From Minority Owner; Court Rejects Control Stockholder's Valuation	297
In re Terrestar Networks, Inc.	8/19/11	United States Bankruptcy Court	Federal/ New York	Security Interest Exists in Economic Value of FCC License	304
In re Tronox Inc.	12/12/13	United States Bankruptcy Court	Federal/ New York	Expert's Market-Based, 'Self-Contained' Solvency Analysis Crumbles	319
In re Village at Camp Bowie I, L.P.	8/4/11	United States Bankruptcy Court	Federal/ New York	Court Adopts Expert's Interest Rate, Based in Part on B/P Calculator	339
Antioch Co. Litig. Trust v. Morgan	4/7/14	United States District Court	Federal/ Ohio	Lost Value Opinion Using Untested Data Points Is No Go	76
In re Glueck	8/12/98	United States Bankruptcy Court	Federal/ Ohio	Market Rate of Interest Appropriate in 'Cram-Down' Case	162
Nelson v. Walnut Investment Partners, LP	7/13/11	United States District Court	Federal/ Ohio	Expert's 'Hyperbole' in Article Comes Back to Haunt Him in *Daubert* Hearing	256
Crane v. Morris (In re Morris)	12/17/03	United States Bankruptcy Court	Federal/ Oklahoma	Par Value Valuation Ruled Invalid but Not Grounds for Denial of Discharge	126
In re John Joseph Edwards	4/13/99	United States Bankruptcy Court	Federal/ Pennsylvania	Debtor Objects to Disposition of Assets	150
In re Frezzo	3/5/98	United States Bankruptcy Court	Federal/ Pennsylvania	Court Affirms Discounts and Hypothetical Capital Gains Taxes	157
In re Haskell Dawes, Inc.	8/28/96	United States Bankruptcy Court	Federal/ Pennsylvania	Largest Creditor Holds Up Debtor's Reorganization Plan a Year After Filing	176
In re Nesser; Boston Restaurants v. Nesser	3/7/97	United States Bankruptcy Court	Federal/ Pennsylvania	Court Determines Feasibility Requirements Not Met	258
In re Fairvue Club Properties	11/2/10	United States Bankruptcy Court	Federal/ Tennessee	Lender Uses Debtor's Own Appraiser to Show Plan Lacks Financial Feasibility	152
ASARCO v. Americas Mining Corp. (I)	8/30/08	United States District Court	Federal/ Texas	Case Considers Control Premiums, DCF Discount Rates, and More	79
ASARCO v. Americas Mining Corp. (II)	2/9/09	United States District Court	Federal/ Texas	May Plaintiff's Expert Assess Control Premium in Damages?	85
In Re: LMR, LLC	5/24/13	United States Bankruptcy Court	Federal/ Texas	Court Approves Debtor's 'Feasible, But Tight' Plan With 6% Interest Rate	213

Case Name	Date		State/ Jurisdiction	Summary	Page
In re Magna Cum Latte, Inc.	5/9/08	United States Bankruptcy Court	Federal/ Texas	Lost Profits Turn on Risk-Free vs. Risk-Adjusted Discount Rates	222
U.S. Bank N.A. v. Verizon Communications Inc.	1/22/13	United States District Court	Federal/ Texas	Expert's 'Unsupportable' Inputs Undermine DCF Analysis and Credibility	328
Villaje del Rio, Ltd. v. Colina del Rio, L.P.	6/8/09	United States District Court	Federal/ Texas	Cutting Costs on Expert Testimony and Appraisals Doesn't Always Pay Off	342
Waller v. Pidgeon	6/5/08	United States District Court	Federal/ Texas	Insolvency of Hedge Funds Turns on Book Value Versus 'Fair Valuation' of Debts	351
In re Lyall; Monticello Arcade LP v. Lyall	1/23/96	United States District Court	Federal/ Virginia	Should Lease Obligation Be Deducted From Value?	221
In re Flashcom, Inc.	12/4/13	United States District Court	California	GAAP 'Relevant' but 'Not Controlling' in Solvency Analysis	153
In re Mahoney	3/29/00	Supreme Court	New Jersey	Bankruptcy Court Determines Fair Market Value Under Pennsylvania Judgment—Court Details Claimant's Expert's Valuation Shortcomings	224
McDuffie v. O'Neal	8/12/96	Court of Appeals	South Carolina	Appeals Court Accepts Averaging of Two Experts' Values	227
Superior Offshore International, Inc. v. Schaefer	12/11/12	United States District Court	Texas	Expert May Use Public Information for Company Valuation	299

Court Case Digests

Presented in alphabetical order.

Adelphia Recovery Trust v. FPL Group, Inc. (In re Adelphia Corp.)

Citation: 2014 Bankr. LEXIS 2011
Date of decision: May 6, 2014
Country: US
State or Federal: Federal
State/Jurisdiction: New York
Court: United States Bankruptcy Court
Type of action: Bankruptcy
Judge: Gerber
Experts: Israel Shaked, Michael-Shaked Group (recovery trust); Ralph Tuliano, Mesirow Financial Consulting (defendants)
SIC: 4841 Cable and Other Pay Television Services (cable networks)
Key words: Comparable companies analysis, DCF, Discounted cash flow method (DCF), Fraudulent transfer, Market-Based Approach, Precedent transactions analysis, Projections, Redemption, Risk premium, Solvency, Stock Buyback, Value Per Subscriber Multiple, Weighted Average Cost of Capital (WACC)

Court Finds Facts Back Expert's Value-Per-Subscriber Metric

In the protracted bankruptcy proceedings of Adelphia, once one of the cable industry's biggest companies, a $150 million stock buyback gave rise to a recent finding that merits attention from valuation professionals. The Bankruptcy Court's ruling on the trustee's fraudulent transfer claim discusses the pros and cons of the methodologies the parties' experts used. Discounted cash flow analysis, comparable companies analysis, and precedent transaction analysis were all in play.

No value from stock buyback. In June 2002, Adelphia Communications, then one of the country's largest cable television operators, and some 230 subsidiaries filed for Chapter 11 bankruptcy protection. The company's financial trouble came to light earlier that year when it disclosed that it had over $2 billion in unreported debt related to loans to its controlling shareholders, the Rigas family. Thereafter, a special committee investigating related party transactions between Adelphia entities and the Rigases determined the loans exceeded $3 billion. Members of the family subsequently faced prosecution on securities fraud, wire fraud, bank fraud, and criminal conspiracy and various convictions.

In connection with the bankruptcy, the Adelphia recovery trust sued in federal court (S.D.N.Y.) to recover, as a fraudulent transfer, $150 million Adelphia paid in January 1999 to repurchase its own stock from the defendants. In 1995, Adelphia and the defendants—a group of related businesses with cable properties—entered into a series of transactions that resulted in the defendants' owning over 3.4 million shares of Adelphia's common stock. Less than four years later, the parties decided to end their relationship. One step in the process was the Jan. 28, 1999, stock buyback. A second step occurred eight months later that year and involved Adelphia's redeeming the defendants' one-third interest in a joint venture.

One question in this case was whether the two transactions were interdependent. As the court explained, if they were, "any excess value received by Adelphia on its second purchase could be regarded as consideration to offset any value deficiency with respect to the first." Ultimately, the court found the transactions were separate and Adelphia's stock buyback "was indeed without consideration." But these findings, in themselves, did not make the stock buyback avoidable, the court explained. Under the "traditional fraudulent transfer analysis," it still needed to determine whether Adelphia was insolvent at the time it bought back the stock or was rendered insolvent as a result of the transaction.

Trust's expert relies solely on DCF. Both parties offered expert solvency opinions. First, the experts determined the value of assets Adelphia had at the time of the transfer by computing the company's total enterprise value (TEV). Next, they ascertained the business's liabilities and subtracted them from the assets.

In terms of TEV, the experts' approaches differed considerably, as did the resulting values. Even though both experts recognized that performing a discounted cash flow analysis (DCF) in this case posed a challenge, the trust's expert ultimately staked his opinion on the DCF alone. The problem was the lack of accurate management projections. Any existing management forecasts in this case likely were based on fraudulent information and not a reliable foundation for the DCF. Neither were third-party industry analyst projections that likely were based on the company's inaccurately reported information.

The trust's expert tried to circumvent the issue by developing his own projections of the company's cash flow for the following 10 years. To start with, he created assumptions as to the factors that would inform the company's cash flow for the upcoming years using contemporaneous third-party analyses. The factors included penetration rates and growth rates, as well as revenue per subscriber, EBITDA margins, and capital expenditures. To arrive at present value, he applied a 15.08% discount rate, which he believed to be the company's weighted average cost of capital (WACC). The WACC assumed a debt risk premium of 6.79% and an equity risk premium of 3.95% (no other premia are stated) and grew out of the premise that "both lenders and shareholders require a higher rate of return on their investment in a fraud-plagued company than in a company that is law abiding."

He used the perpetuity method to calculate the terminal value. He said it was inappropriate to base the terminal on a multiple of final-year EBITDA, as is common, because doing so here would "introduce market-based analyses into his non-market-based methodology." Instead, he assumed that, after 10 years, Adelphia would grow in perpetuity at a rate of about 4%, considering 3% inflation and less than 1% subscriber growth. He concluded that the company's unadjusted TEV was approximately $2.5 billion.

The defendants' expert considered preparing projections for the company but decided he lacked the necessary reliable data. He considered the process "speculative" and declined to perform an independent DCF analysis but critiqued aspects of the other expert's approach.

Defendants' expert uses market-based methods. For his part, the defendants' expert performed a comparable companies analysis and a precedent transactions analysis to compute the unadjusted TEV. For the comparable analysis, he selected six companies, using only their cable components to compute multiples. For each of the companies, he calculated TEV based on the market value of equity and debt interests in the company but excluding cash and equity investments. He next performed a value-per-subscriber analysis—dividing the respective TEV by a company's reported number of subscribers—to determine each company's multiple, i.e., value per subscriber. The multiples ranged between $2,462 and $3,835. He explained that the value-per-subscriber multiple was "commonly used in the cable industry and provides a highly reliable indication of the value of Adelphia's cable business."

He decided that $3,024 was the multiple applicable to Adelphia, based in part on the company's relative upgrade status compared to the other six companies. Ultimately, he found that the value of the company's cable assets on a marketable, minority, basis was nearly $4.5 billion. He decided in this case a 25% control premium ($376.4 million) was appropriate because the stock prices for the comparable companies reflected minority interests, "and here there was a controlling interest." Under the comparable companies analysis, Adelphia's assets were worth over $4.8 billion prior to adjustments. Adding cash yielded a TEV of over $5 billion before adjustments, he concluded.

The trust's expert rejected the comparable companies approach because it required "a measure of historical or forward earnings for the subject company and the comparable companies." But in this case such data were unavailable considering the misrepresentations related to the company's financial performance. And, even though the expert agreed that the value-per-subscriber multiple was often used and often appropriate, he considered it inappropriate in this case because it did "not account for the differences between companies relating to upgrade status and profitability."

The defendants' expert also performed a precedent transaction analysis—an analysis that generates the value of comparable companies from purchase prices in past mergers and acquisitions. Three criteria guided the selection of the transactions: (1) choose only transactions involving target cable systems with more than 300,000 subscribers; (2) use transactions that occurred within six months of the Jan. 28, 1999, stock buyback; and (3) exclude pure "system swaps," i.e., one cable company trading in a set of systems with another. He decided that four transactions met the requirements, including one that was part system swap and part sale for cash. In that case, he said, the cash portion did yield a "highly reliable indicator of value." Again, his sole metric was the value-per-subscriber multiple. The resulting range was between $3,234 and $3,667. Considering Adelphia's relative upgrade status, he settled on $3,277. He arrived at a TEV of $4.8 billion. Adding the company's cash, the TEV was just over $5 billion, prior to adjustments.

The trust's expert rejected the precedent transaction method for the same reasons he rejected the comparable companies analysis.

Adjustments widen value gap. Both experts adjusted their TEV calculations to account for Adelphia's interest in related entities—two of them acquired around the time of the transfer. The most noteworthy was a January 1999 acquisition of a cable TV company for which Adelphia paid $135 million. The trust's expert assigned zero value to it. As he saw it, Adelphia issued its own stock in exchange for the assets. If the stock turned out to be worth less than the assumed value, the company would be liable for issuing fraudulent stock. The defendants' expert considered any such liability "highly uncertain and inherently speculative" on the transaction date and credited the entire $135 million. He pointed out that the company also had "speculative assets," but, as long as speculative assets and liabilities were treated in a consistent way, they would offset one another.

In January 1999, Adelphia also had a two-thirds interest in a partnership in which the defendants owned a one-third interest that they later in the year sold back to Adelphia (the redemption transaction). The trust's expert valued the company's two-thirds interest at twice the price at which Adelphia later redeemed the one-third interest. Consequently, he added $216 million to his valuation. The defendant's expert also doubled the value of the one-third interest, but, instead of using the actual price Adelphia paid, he used a valuation a different expert for the defendants had proposed. Because Adelphia only had a 50% voting interest in the partnership, he did not apply a control premium. He also added a 5% marketability discount. He concluded Adelphia's two-thirds interest was worth $318 million, which he included in his valuation.

After adjustments and based on the DCF alone, the trust's expert concluded the TEV was $2.8 billion. The defendants' expert, averaging the values he obtained from his two analyses and making adjustments, said the TEV was $6.7 billion. The trust's expert assumed the company's net debt was $3.7 billion, slightly more than the company had reported on its 1998 Form 10-K. The defendants' expert assumed net debt was approximately $3 billion.

As a result, the trust's expert concluded that at the time of the transfer the company was insolvent by $1 billion. In contrast, the defendants' expert determined it was still solvent by about $3.7 billion.

Expert fails to do 'sanity check.' The court found that both experts' analyses had weaknesses, but, in the final analysis, the defendants' expert's assumptions and methods were more persuasive. It said that its own calculation yielded a starting TEV of between $4.4 billion and $4.8 billion and an adjusted TEV in the range of $5.722 billion to $5.725 billion. And it found the company's liabilities at the relevant date were about $3.2 billion. Therefore, it concluded that Adelphia had a net worth of between $2.494 billion and $2.497 billion at the time of the stock repurchase. These figures were closer to the defendants' expert's determinations and led to the conclusion that Adelphia was solvent at the time of the transfer.

The court made the following observations about the expert testimony:

- The trust expert's reliance on the DCF alone was problematic and surprising. "The DCF works best (and, arguably, only) when a company has accurate projections of future cash flows; when projections are not tainted by fraud; and when at least some of the cash flows are positive." This case was deficient in all regards.
- The data the trust's expert developed to create his own projections to "craft" a DCF analysis were filled with "uncertainties." He formulated assumptions based only roughly on projections for the cable industry or the "typical cable company," and he selectively used assumptions from third-party analyses, raising questions as to "whether his analysis unduly deflated Adelphia's value." Specifically, he used capital expenditure assumptions from one analysis that projected extensive upgrades, but he did not use that analysis's revenue assumptions, showing an attending increase in revenue. Instead, he used the lower growth rate from another analysis.
- The trust expert's failure to use an alternative valuation methodology as a "sanity check" for the conclusions based on the DCF amounted to a "material deficiency in the quality of his analysis."
- Under the circumstances, the defendants' expert was "wise" to rely on the comparable companies and precedent transactions. His value-per-subscriber metric used one of the company's most reliable historical metrics because, by the time Adelphia had completed its efforts to restate its financials and had ousted the Rigases, its count of subscribers was among the most accurate financial data set down. Moreover, in the cable industry, the subscriber number is widely used in valuations for mergers and acquisitions. Also, given the narrow range of the comparable companies multiples, the court was "comfortable" that Adelphia would have been able to sell its assets "roughly" within this range.
- The defendants' expert failed to do a "sanity check" by developing his own DCF analysis and, critically, by considering Adelphia's market capitalization (MarketCap). According to the court, the expert valuation was 19% over market price. How Adelphia's valuation could exceed its MarketCap was difficult to see, the court said, especially because there had been as yet undisclosed fraud. But even if one applied a 19% discount and assumed the adjustments the expert made to his comparable companies analysis, Adelphia would have been solvent by over $3 billion.
- In terms of adjustments, the court disapproved of the trust expert's decision not to attribute any value to the company Adelphia bought in January 1999 for $135 million. "The outcome of litigation that was never brought is too speculative to justify disregarding the entirety of the value of [the acquired company]." At the same time, liability was not "remote." If the acquired company had sued, it probably could have established some fraud. The most likely possibility was that Adelphia at the time was overvalued but not worthless. The

difficult question, the court said, was whether to include the value "but with a haircut," i.e., a discount. Ultimately, since neither party argued for this approach, the court added $135 million to the assets.

- In terms of the second adjustment, the court agreed with the trust expert that the value of its two-thirds interest in one of the defendants' entities should align with the actual price Adelphia paid for the remaining one-third interest a few months after the stock buyback. Therefore, it included $216 million in its valuation.
- The defendants' expert produced a valuation that was "more closely tied to the market," offering a value that the company actually could get for its assets in a sale.

Conclusion. Besides finding that Adelphia was solvent at the time of the stock repurchase, the court determined the transaction did not leave the company with insufficient capital to keep operating and that it was not equitably insolvent. Accordingly, the trust's fraudulent transfer claim crumbled.

Alberts v. HCA, Inc.

Citation: 2013 U.S. Dist. LEXIS 96646
Date of decision: July 11, 2013
Country: US
State or Federal: Federal
State/Jurisdiction: District of Columbia
Court: United States District Court
Experts: Neil Demchick (trustee); Kevin Moss (defendants)
Judge: Lamberth

Trustee Claims Bankruptcy Court Flouted Valuation Rules

In his appeal, a trustee "strenuously" contested the Bankruptcy Court's decision to consider a $20.6 million capital transfer as a surplus rather than a necessary asset for operations when the court calculated the business enterprise value of a hospital under the income approach.

Recap. The case took root in 1998 when the debtor, a hospital corporation, bought a Chicago-based hospital from the seller, one of the world's largest private healthcare providers, for approximately $66 million to $68 million. (The Bankruptcy Court found that, of the $68 million the debtor transferred to the seller, $2 million was in exchange for its delay in closing; consequently, only $66 million was consideration for the asset). The debtor had relied for financing on a company that went bankrupt in late 2002; as a result, the debtor, itself, slid into Chapter 11 bankruptcy. In 2004, the trustee filed suit in Bankruptcy Court (Washington, D.C.) against the seller and affiliated companies and subsidiaries (the appellees) claiming the sale was a fraudulent transfer: The debtor did not receive reasonably equivalent value and was insolvent at the time of transaction. As a remedy, he requested recovery of the alleged excess purchase price.

In 2007, the Bankruptcy Court held a five-week bench trial, hearing expert testimony from both sides as to how to determine the hospital's fair market value at the time of transaction. It subsequently issued a 192-page decision against the trustee. To value the hospital, it first calculated its value under the cost approach at nearly $58 million. Next, it attempted to compute the value under the income approach using the discounted cash flow (DCF) method. However, it ran into a major problem with both experts' EBIT projections, finding "none of these projections offer a totally realistic picture of the reasonable anticipated future earnings" of the hospital. But instead of ruling there was no reliable valuation under the income approach, the court corrected projections the debtor's management team had prepared around the time of the transaction.

Importantly, in ascertaining the net cash flow of the hospital for each of the years in the projections, the court decided not to factor $20.6 million the debtor had acquired in net working capital into the net working capital projections. The record, it said, did not allow it to do so, and expert witnesses for both parties erred when they incorporated this amount into their net cash flow calculations. Instead, the court considered the $20.6 million as a nonoperating asset and added it to the $51.5 million it had computed under the income approach "as if normally capitalized." The two figures yielded a total business enterprise value of $72.2 million. In a final step, it decided to weigh the value stemming from the cost approach at 25% and the value resulting from the income approach at 75%. This reconciliation led to a final fair market value of $68.6 million and the Bankruptcy Court's conclusion that the debtor "received more than reasonably equivalent value from [the transaction], not less."

Capital transfer drives appeals. The trustee first challenged the court's findings in a post-trial motion, which the Bankruptcy Court, in another lengthy opinion, denied. Subsequently, the trustee appealed to the district court (Washington, D.C.) for review. In both instances, he homed in on the Bankruptcy Court's allegedly erroneous treatment of the $20.6 million capital transfer as surplus.

Double counting. Specifically, the trustee first claimed that the Bankruptcy Court's approach led to double counting. The court's net cash flow calculations, which it used to obtain the initial $51.5 million value as if normally capitalized, already included the $20.6 million, he argued.

The district court disagreed, adopting the Bankruptcy Court's response to the trustee's post-trial motion. The latter stated with emphasis that it first had valued the hospital's assets under an income approach as though the $20.6 million net working capital "*had not been* acquired" by the debtor. This scenario produced a value of $51.5 million. Next, it had asked "what would be added to the $51.5 million if, as occurred, the $20.6 million of net working capital had *also* been acquired" by the debtor. It concluded that the reasonable thing to do was to add the latter sum to the $51.5 million. In its DCF analysis, the court considered future accounts receivable on an accrual basis, following generally accepted accounting procedures; those future accounts receivable "*not* in existence on the transfer date were distinct from the $20.6 million that *was* in existence" on the sale date, the Bankruptcy Court pointed out. The trustee's assertion that the court's DCF calculation included the net working capital, related revenue, interest income, and expenses was "simply wrong."

For its part, the district court disposed of the trustee's argument in this way: "No matter how many times [the trustee] makes the argument, or how strenuously he presents it, there simply was no double counting."

'Inconsistent' approach. Second, the trustee argued that the Bankruptcy Court's approach was "inconsistent" with the opinions of experts from both sides and conflicted with "standard business valuation principles." Also, there was no evidence to allow the court to treat the $20.6 million as surplus, rather than as necessary capital to keep operations going. Witnesses for both sides had discussed how "strapped for cash" the hospital constantly was even with the working capital at issue.

The district court took a different view. For one, as a fact-finder, the Bankruptcy Court had discretion to credit or discredit expert opinions. And "just because the bankruptcy court disagreed with how experts *applied* the methodology to the facts of the case does *not* mean that the bankruptcy court made up its own unorthodox business valuation methodology," the reviewing court said.

Here, said the district court with approval, the Bankruptcy Court gave persuasive reasons for its approach. Specifically, it acknowledged that "theoretically" it could have included the $20.6 million net working capital in the income stream for its projections because "a reasonable purchaser would not expect to collect revenues from its post-transaction operations immediately" but would depend on the income stream from the net working capital until post-transaction revenue started to come in.

It also allowed for the argument that, if it treated the net working capital as a nonoperating asset, it should project no revenue for the hospital until the entity began to collect on its accounts receivables. But the Bankruptcy Court concluded that in the end neither approach was practicable because the record was wholly lacking in information with which to determine the average delay in the hospital's collection of accounts receivables.

Further, it found that, even assuming there was a reliable way to factor the $20.6 million into the income stream, the trustee had failed to show what the resulting value would be. The $51.5 million value as if normally capitalized would increase by $20.6 million, with an adjustment for the time value of money. The latter would reflect the dates of collection of the accounts receivables and the seller's guarantee related to the $20.6 million, as well as the dates of accounts payable included in the $20.6 million, but it would "be insufficient to have a meaningful impact on the outcome of this proceeding."

Moreover, the district court found that the trustee's claim about the hospital's shortage of funds had no merit because it concerned post-transfer financial struggles. A determination of whether a transfer was for reasonably equivalent value requires looking at the date of transaction. According to the district court, the Bankruptcy Court did not simply assume the hospital was fully capitalized notwithstanding the $20.6 million transfer. On the contrary, its projections assumed that a reasonable buyer would understand the need for injecting millions into working capital, and these assumptions underlay the Bankruptcy Court's valuation of the hospital as a going concern. "While there is no direct correlation between the length of an opinion and its soundness," the district court concluded, here the record showed that the Bankruptcy Court did not commit reversible error in its valuation of the hospital and its decision that the debtor received reasonably equivalent value.

In re Alta+Cast

Citation: 2004 Bankr. LEXIS 222
Date of Decision: March 2, 2004
Country: US
State or Federal: Federal
State/Jurisdiction: Delaware
Court: United States Bankruptcy Court
Type of action: Bankruptcy
Experts: Paul Maschmeyer (for Alta+Cast) Paul Hyde, EA, MCBA, BVAL, ASA (for Alta+Cast)
Judge: Walrath
SIC: 7372 Prepackaged Software (software publishing)
Key words: Bankruptcy, Liquidation value

Software Company Value Based on Value of Wholly Owned Subsidiary Only

One issue in this Chapter 11 bankruptcy case was the value of debtor's software company, Alta+Cast LLC. The value of the company, as stated in the debtors plan, was challenged on the grounds that it did not accurately reflect the liquidation value of the company and thus left Hays, an unsecured creditor and opposing party in this suit, without any compensation.

Valuation evidence. The debtor had two expert witnesses testify on its behalf. Hays did not present any expert testimony. Alta+Cast's two experts were a business appraisal expert, who, the court noted, was one of 44 Master Certified Business Appraisers in the country, and an expert on the costs and likely recoveries in a Chapter 7 liquidation. Although the court did not go into depth about the methods used by the business appraiser, it noted that it found both experts to be credible. Hays objected to the business appraiser because he was not an expert in the software industry. The court rejected this argument, stating, "One need not be an expert in a particular industry to provide a valuation of a company in that industry." The court noted that the business appraiser did take into account all relevant factors, including $5 million in contracts and the costs associated with fulfilling them, and properly valued the company (which had never been profitable) at the value of its wholly owned subsidiary, Health+Cast. The Chapter 7 expert testified as to the value of the company in the event that the Chapter 11 bankruptcy was converted into a Chapter 7 liquidation. The expert noted that the transaction costs incurred in a Chapter 7 liquidation would result in: (1) the Chapter 11 administration fees not being paid; and (2) the unsecured creditors, which had priority over Hays, not being compensated.

Bankruptcy court holding and rationale. The bankruptcy court dismissed Hay's objections and approved the Plan of Reorganization.

American Classic Voyages Co. v. JP Morgan Chase Bank (I)

Citation: 2007 Bankr. LEXIS 1394
Date of Decision: April 27, 2007
Country: US
State or Federal: Federal
State/Jurisdiction: Delaware
Court: United States Bankruptcy Court
Type of action: Bankruptcy
Experts: Perry Mandarino (plaintiffs/debtors) Brian Calvert (defendants/creditors)
Judge: Carey
SIC: 4725 Tour Operators

Valuation Turns on Reliability of Pre-9/11 Projections

For 15 years, American Classic Voyages Co. operated four cruise lines, three in inland U.S. waterways and one in Hawaii. Beginning in 1999, the company launched ambitious growth plans, funded by a $70 million secured line of credit from JP Morgan Chase Bank and others, reduced to $30 million in September 2000. The parties restated the loan facility again on Aug. 14, 2001, reducing it to $10 million while the lenders received a $30 million payment on the debt.

Tragedy strikes. The September 11th terrorist attacks devastated the U.S. tourism industry and, in particular, had a "profound effect" on American Classic Voyages, according to its CEO. Prior to 9/11, the company's vessels were fully booked through the end of the year. But immediately afterward, the company incurred significant costs and received no new bookings. Scarcely one month later, on Oct. 19, 2001, the company and its affiliates filed for Chapter 11 relief.

In bankruptcy, the debtors and their plan administrator (plaintiffs) sued to recover the $30 million loan repayment from JP Morgan and other banks (defendants) as a preferential transfer. To recover, the plaintiffs needed to show the collective companies were insolvent on Aug. 14, 2001, the transfer date. (Bankruptcy law presumes insolvency 90 days prior to filing, but, if the defendants introduced some evidence of solvency, then the burden of proof would shift back to the plaintiffs.)

All parties agreed that the company suffered "serious financial issues" as early as the start of 2001. But, while the plaintiffs tried to characterize these as a "downward spiral," a consequence of the too-costly growth initiatives, the defendants pointed to the company's financial recovery program to contend that the entire enterprise was a going concern right up until September 11.

Bank's expert relies on pre-9/11 projections. For example, prior to 9/11, capital markets were still financing the debtors and predicting "robust" prospects for the cruise industry generally. Moreover, just before the August transfer date, the debtors had prepared forward-looking projections (its Form 10-Q) that revealed no going concern issues.

The Bankruptcy Court agreed and reviewed the report by defendants' expert, which valued the company using a discounted cash flow analysis. Based on five-year management projections prepared as of July 31, 2001, the expert applied a 10.17% discount rate to his free cash flow calculations and used both the Gordon growth and exit multiples approach to establish a terminal value, ultimately concluding a range of enterprise value for the parent company between $805 million and $824 million. (He prepared similar analyses for the subsidiaries, with values that showed solvency.)

The plaintiffs criticized the expert's reliance on management's pre-9/11 projections as speculative and inconsistent with the debtors' historical numbers and 2001 performance, especially the financial "deterioration" brought on by overleveraging. Their expert report showed the companies' debts growing from $84.6 million in 1999 to over $577 million in 2001, while EBITDA declined from $18.1 million to a negative $22.2 million.

To counter these claims, defendants' expert testified that he'd reviewed management depositions and the detail level of the projections and found both to be reliable. In addition, as the debtors were in the midst of a major expansion, historical numbers were not sufficient to "bridge the gap to the future" for valuation purposes. The debtors had also implemented their financial recovery plan—and would have continued as a viable concern, but for the 9/11 attacks.

Court looks to more credible witness. The Bankruptcy Court agreed that "the unforeseen attacks of Sept. 11, 2001, dealt a fatal blow" to the debtors. The court also found the management projections to be sufficiently reliable when prepared.

The court also considered the parties' expert reports, and, while both were "valid," it found defendants' more credible, in large part due to his "extensive" (20-year) valuation experience and his adherence to accepted practices. (Plaintiffs' expert was a CPA and appropriately qualified but with "far less experience in performing solvency analyses.") Based on this evidence, the defendants successfully shifted the burden to plaintiffs to prove insolvency.

Plaintiffs' expert assigns 'no impact' to 9/11. In his primary report, plaintiffs' expert used an adjusted balance sheet approach rather than an income approach. (Although he agreed the latter was a "valuable technique," he "was not aware" of the July 2001 projections.) In calculating the "fair saleable value" of the companies' assets, he assigned no value to the ships under construction (due to risks related to ongoing litigation) and used post-petition sales of other ships to assess their value. (He claimed there were no sufficiently similar competitors to provide comparable asset values.) These values led him to adjust a June 30, 2001, balance sheet from over $852 million to $267 million; after subtracting $664 million in liabilities, he determined that the debtors were insolvent by nearly $90 million.

But it was clear to the court that plaintiffs' expert valued the debtors on a liquidation rather than going concern basis. "Moreover, he valued the main assets of the companies … based on transactions that occurred *after* the events of September 11 and *after* the October" bankruptcy filing. (court's emphasis) "He opined that the intervening events of Sept. 11, 2001, had no impact on valuing these assets because the opinion the court found inconsistent with the facts." Valuing the debtors on a liquidation basis also did not provide a "true picture" of their worth, and plaintiffs' claims were denied.

American Classic Voyages Co. v. JP Morgan Chase Bank (II)

Citation: 2008 WL 792773 (U.S. Dist.)
Date of Decision: March 25, 2008
Country: US
State or Federal: Federal
State/Jurisdiction: Delaware
Court: United States District Court
Type of action: Bankruptcy
Experts: Not specified
Judge: Farnan
SIC: 4725 – Tour Operators

Bankruptcy Courts 'Required' to Reject DCF Analysis When Market Cap Data Are Available?

This appeal of a bankruptcy case pits two common valuation approaches—the market capitalization method versus a discounted cash flow analysis—squarely against one another. When an "objective" value for a company is available by reference to its price in the public markets, are bankruptcy courts (and insolvency experts) compelled to use the market cap method rather than a DCF?

New precedent intervenes after trial. The original bankruptcy trial turned on whether the plaintiffs—a cruise company and their affiliates—were insolvent just one month after 9/11. Based on a discounted cash flow analysis by the defendants' expert, the Bankruptcy Court found that the plaintiffs were solvent. It also rejected the liquidation values offered by the plaintiffs' expert.

Meanwhile, one month before the Bankruptcy Court issued its final orders, but after the parties had already submitted their final briefs, the 3rd Circuit decided *VFB LLC v. Campbell Soup Co.* (2007).

That case upheld findings by the U.S. District Court that the public securities market provided the "most disinterested" if not "ideal data point" regarding the price of a publicly traded company at the valuation date. The District Court rejected expert DCF analysis, finding it flawed by hindsight and other "unreasonable" assumptions. "Absent some reason to distrust it," the court explained, "the market price is a more reliable measure of the stock's value than the subjective estimates of one or two expert witnesses."

The same court (U.S. Dist. Delaware) would also hear an appeal in the *American Classic* case—and plaintiffs in *American Classic* seized on the *VFB* decision as the basis for review. They claimed "it was error for the Bankruptcy Court to rely upon expert testimony regarding solvency that was premised on [DCF] methods, where … a public market existed for the [Debtors'] stock." The plaintiffs also reasserted their contention that the defendants' experts based their DCF analysis on unreliable management projections.

By contrast, the defendants argued that *VFB* does not create a bright-line rule that "market capitalization is the only accepted methodology for considering valuation in solvency disputes." Rather,

VFB recognizes that DCF is an accepted methodology. Further, defendants supported their expert's DCF analyses with SEC filings, management statements, and evidence of business dealings.

Valuation evidence consistent with market. While the District Court's discussion is brief, it confirmed the original findings of solvency. In particular, the Bankruptcy Court correctly credited the DCF analysis by defendants' experts over the liquidation value by the plaintiffs' experts. (Interestingly, the plaintiffs didn't appear to introduce evidence of the cruise company's declining stock prices until the appeal, contending that the common shares lost 94% of their value during the 18 months prior to the transaction date. However, it's not clear from the court opinion whether the precipitous drop in market value occurred as the result of 9/11 and events in the tourism industry generally, or from company-specific factors.)

The District Court also declined to adopt the plaintiffs' reading of the *VFB* decision:

> In *VFB,* the plaintiffs made no attempt to reconcile the disparity between the testimony of their expert witnesses and the objective value of the company at issue in the marketplace.... In contrast, the data and analysis accepted by the Bankruptcy Court in this case was consistent with the available marketplace data.

VFB does not "require" the solvency of a public company to be valued using a market capitalization method rather than a discounted cash flow analysis, it held. The defendants' additional evidence concerning the companies' business, including management projections, also supported the Bankruptcy Court's findings, which correctly discredited the plaintiffs' liquidation values. "In sum," the District Court said, it could find "no legal error in the Bankruptcy Court's use of the discounted cash flow analysis in the circumstances of this case."

In re American Home Mortgage Holdings, Inc. (I)

Citation: 2009 WL 2855888 (Bkrtcy. D. Del.)
Date of Decision: September 8, 2009
Country: US
State or Federal: Federal
State/Jurisdiction: Delaware
Court: United States Bankruptcy Court
Type of action: Bankruptcy
Experts: Dr. Ronnie Clayton (debtors); Robert Branthover (plaintiffs)
Judge: Sontchi

Bankruptcy Court Chooses Between Market or 'Reasonable Valuation' of Troubled Loans

Cases spawned by the economic crisis are starting to come in—and courts are straining to find guidance when the "nub of the question" is asset values, but current markets are disrupted or dysfunctional and "may not fairly reflect the potential sale price of [the] asset," as Delaware Bankruptcy Judge Christopher Sontchi explained in this case concerning a repurchase agreement of a troubled loan portfolio.

Repo participant accelerates loans. In August 2007—just before the credit markets cratered—a loan participant declared the debtors (American Home Mortgage Holdings) in default under their repurchase agreement, accelerating the obligation to redeem the entire mortgage portfolio. Five days later, the debtors filed for Chapter 11 bankruptcy and the participant claimed over $1.154 *billion* in damages.

The debtors contended no damages were due because the value of the loan portfolio exceeded the repurchase price—assuming Sec. 562 of the Bankruptcy Code permitted "commercially accepted" methodologies to determine value on the acceleration date (August 2007). By contrast, the repo participant argued that the only "commercially reasonable determinants" of value under Sec. 562 were the market or actual sales prices on the acceleration date. Because the market was distressed at that time and the loans suffered from a numerous deficiencies affecting salability, Sec. 562 required the court to measure damages "as of the earliest subsequent date ... on which there are commercially reasonable determinants of value," or no sooner than August 2008.

The court agreed that the Bankruptcy statute was ambiguous. Its legislative history indicated a strong preference for measuring damages on the acceleration date and discussed the circumstances when the market may not provide commercially reasonable determinants of value—but it was "silent as to what alternative methods, if any, may be used."

"In short, the court appears to be on its own," Judge Sontchi observed. The "most obvious" valuation method was to consult the market price, but, when this did not fairly reflect an asset's value, the court agreed with the debtors that Sec. 562's use of the word "determinants" (plural) suggested "that *any* commercially reasonable valuation may be used" as evidence of damages under a repurchase agreement after its rejection or acceleration. (Emphasis in the court's opinion) (Note: To help discern the value of mortgages in particular, the court also cited Prof. Aswath Damodaran's *Investment Valuation: Tools and Techniques for Determining the Value of Any Asset* (2nd ed. 2001).)

Valuation expert proves indispensable. To support their claims that no damages were due, the debtor's valuation expert conducted an extensive, loan-by-loan DCF analysis for all 5,600 mortgages in the portfolio, first by selecting an appropriate discount rate from the Federal Home Loan Mortgage Corporation's *Primary Mortgage Market Survey*. He then adjusted the interest rate to reflect the conditions of the mortgage market at the time of acceleration, including an estimated 50% delinquency rate. After applying the adjusted rates to the discounted cash flows for each individual mortgage, the expert concluded the portfolio was worth a total of $1.067 billion to $1.166 billion, depending on whether the servicing rights were retained.

Further, a DCF is appropriate "in all conditions," the expert testified, even when markets are dysfunctional, because it values the asset's continuing cash flows. Although the quality of the loans might affect their salability, he said, it would not affect their cash flows other than by possibly increasing delinquency rates, which he already accounted for by estimating 50% defaults. He also believed that value should not include speculation as to events subsequent to the acceleration date.

The repo participant failed to effectively contest the DCF methodology. "This is highly significant," the court said, "since the [applied] discount rate ... reflected, in part, the state of the mortgage market" on the acceleration date. Moreover, the repo participant's internally prepared market analyses—projecting a 92.5% recovery rate—lacked credibility because they were based on outdated assumptions and data and did not accurately reflect what the loans could have sold for in August 2007.

Finally, although the repo participant presented its own expert, who testified that the market value of the loan portfolio was at best 50 cents on the dollar and, at worst, only 10 cents, the court found his entire testimony irrelevant "because the debtors' proffered DCF was a commercially reasonable determinant of value." In sum, the court found the debtors' expert more credible, and, because the loan portfolio value exceeded its repurchase price on the measurement date, no damages were due.

In re American Home Mortgage Holdings, Inc. (II)

Citation: 2011 WL 522945 (C.A. 3 (Del))
Date of decision: Feb. 16, 2011
Country: US
State or Federal: Federal
State/Jurisdiction: 3rd Circuit
Court: United States Court of Appeals
Experts: Dr. Ronnie Clayton (debtors); Robert Branhthover (plaintiffs)
Judge: Sloviter

3rd Circuit Confirms DCF to Value Mortgage Portfolios in Dysfunctional Markets

The numbers in this bankruptcy case are staggering: In 2006, the debtors sold 5,700 mortgage loans worth $1.2 billion pursuant to a repurchase ("repo") agreement. Less than a year later, the debtors defaulted under the agreement and the participant accelerated the debtors' repurchase obligations, claiming over $478 million in damages under Sec. 562 of the Bankruptcy Code.

In particular, Sec. 562(a) provides that, if a participant accelerates a repo agreement, then damages are measured as of the acceleration date; if there are no "commercially reasonable determinants of value" available on that date, then damages are measured on the earliest subsequent date on which such determinants become available. The participant argued that Sec. 562 permits only the market or sale value to measure damages; since there was no active (or functional) market available on the 2007 acceleration date, then damages should be measured as of August 2008, the earliest date when it could have obtained a reasonable sale price for the loans.

In response, the debtors claimed that a commercially reasonable determinant of value—namely, the discounted cash flow (DCF) method—existed on the acceleration date. Under this method, the value of the loan portfolio exceeded the repurchase price and therefore no damages were due. The federal bankruptcy court (Delaware) agreed with the debtors, and the loan participant appealed to the U.S. Court of Appeals for the 3rd Circuit.

An issue of first impression. Although the amounts at stake were "dazzling" and the issue was one of "first impression" in the jurisdiction, the 3rd Circuit found that the issue came down to fairly routine statutory construction—namely, whether Sec. 562 permitted the use of any "commercially reasonable" valuation method to determine damages after the rejection and/or acceleration of a repo agreement.

The parties refocused their claims on appeal. The "centerpiece" of the participant's argument was that a market or sale price is the "only" reasonable determinant of value permitted by Sec. 562. Since all the parties (and the bankruptcy court) agreed that the secondary mortgage market was dysfunctional on the acceleration date, it would not have been reasonable to sell the portfolio at this time. Instead, the earliest possible resale date would have been August 2008. At that time, the loans would have been worth 10 cents to 50 cents on the dollar, according to the participant's expert, resulting in the $478 million deficiency (damages) claim.

The debtors agreed that reliance on market value was not "commercially reasonable" on the acceleration date but claimed that other "commercially reasonable determinants of value" were available at the time. In fact, its expert testified that the DCF methodology was "particularly apt" at valuing debt instruments such as mortgage loans because the owner holds the assets "for the cash flow, not for the distress sale in the market." To value the entire portfolio as of the acceleration date, the expert determined the DCF value of the individual mortgages, adjusting the individual interest rates to reflect market conditions and actual delinquency rates. Under this approach, the expert concluded the portfolio was worth $1.067 billion to $1.66 billion, depending on whether servicing rights were included. Since the entire range of value exceeded the repo price on the acceleration date, no damages were due.

Preventing a 'moral hazard.' The 3rd Circuit reviewed the parties' evidence as well as the bankruptcy court's reliance on the "first principles" of statutory construction. The appellate court agreed that the "primary purpose" of Sec. 562 was to preserve liquidity in the relevant assets and to align the "risk and rewards" associated with investing in them. Importantly, the statute seeks to avoid the "moral hazard" that would result if damages were measured at any other time than as of the acceleration date, such that the repo participant could hold the assets at little or no risk while the debtor became the insurer of the risk—despite having no management or control over the assets. Moreover, as the bankruptcy court noted:

> There is nothing in Sec. 562 that would imply a limitation on any methodology used to determine value, provided it was commercially reasonable. Indeed, the use of the word *determinants* suggests just the opposite—that *any* commercially reasonable valuation may be used.

The 3rd Circuit agreed with this reasoning, its concern with preventing a "moral hazard" as well as its confirmation that the DCF method fell within the statute's provision for "reasonably commercial determinants of value." It also found that the bankruptcy court had "homed in" on the intrinsic flaw in the participant's case, i.e., that it never intended to sell the loans and indeed had retained the portfolio as well as its income. Finally, it agreed with the debtors' arguments. By interpreting Sec. 562 to permit a valuation methodology other than sale value (in a dysfunctional market), the result is not to deprive the repo participant of damages but to confirm that it incurred none. "If Congress had intended §562 to be limited to market or sale price, it would have said so," the 3rd Circuit found, and sustained the bankruptcy court's orders expunging the loan participant's deficiency claims.

In re American HomePatient, Inc.

Citation: 2005 U.S. App. LEXIS 13800
Date of Decision: July 11, 2005
Country: US
State or Federal: Federal
State/Jurisdiction: 6th Circuit
Court: United States Court of Appeals
Type of action: Bankruptcy
Judge: Stafford
SIC: 3841Surgical and Medical Instruments and Apparatus
(except tranquilizer guns and operating room tables)
Key words: Bankruptcy rejection damages, Fair market value (FMV), Chapter 11 reorganization, Valuation date

Valuation Date for Rejection Damages in Bankruptcy

American HomePatient Inc. (AHP) entered into a credit agreement with certain of its secured lenders that included a warrant agreement that called for AHP to issue two series of warrants that, when exercised, would permit the warrant holders to purchase 3,265,315 shares (or 19.99%) of AHP common stock at an exercise price of $0.01 per share.

Thereafter, on July 31, 2002, AHP and its affiliates and subsidiaries filed for Chapter 11 relief, and their reorganization plan became effective on July 1, 2003. Under the plan, AHP and the other debtors were authorized to reject executory contracts within 10 days after the plan's effective date. Consequently, on July 11, 2003, the debtors filed a notice of rejection and a motion for an order authorizing them to reject the warrant agreement and to quantify the amount of any damages resulting from the rejection of that warrant agreement. They argued that the warrant holders' damage claim was $0.00 or, alternatively, at most $881,635.05.

The bankruptcy court, consistent with AHP's expert's testimony, set the price per warrant at $0.02692 (an estimate of the fair market value of shares on the date before the petition was filed), subtracted the warrant exercise price of $0.01 per warrant, then multiplied the difference by the number of warrants (3,265,315) held by the lenders, thus arriving at a damage figure of $846,369.85.

Valuation date. Experts for both sides testified that their rejection damage calculations were based on a prepetition, July 30, 2002, valuation date. However, the lenders later argued that the proper valuation date, instead, was July 11, 2003, the date the debtors filed their notice of rejection and motion for order authorizing them to reject the warrant agreement. Based on this date, the resulting damages would have been $6,987,774. Both the bankruptcy and district courts rejected this argument.

Holding and rationale. On further appeal, the 6th Circuit also rejected the lenders' position. The court noted that Bankruptcy Code section 365(g) provides that, upon rejection of an executory contract, the time of breach by the debtor is fixed as of the day "immediately before the date of the filing of the petition." The court also found that the language of section 502(g) of the Code, providing that a claim for rejection damages "shall be determined, and shall be allowed … as if such claim had arisen before the date of the filing of the petition" was clear. Reading the word "determine" to mean "fix the boundaries of," the court concluded that section 502(g) requires that damages be fixed as of a date "before the date of the filing of the petition." Indeed, consistent with § 365(g)(1), the court concluded that damages should be fixed as of the time of the deemed breach, which is "immediately before the date of the filing of the petition."

Finally, the court also observed that courts appear to be in general agreement that, when an executory contract is rejected, damages are fixed at or immediately before the date of the filing of the petition, not at some later time when an executory contract is, in fact, rejected.

Valuation Date for Determining Damages From Breach of an Executory Contract Considered

In *In re: American HomePatient, Inc.*, No. 04-5771 (6th Cir. July 11, 2005), the U.S. Court of Appeals for the 6th Circuit considered the proper date for calculating damages when an executory contract is rejected by a Chapter 11 debtor. Bank of Montreal, a creditor, entered into a credit agreement with American HomePatient, the debtor, under which the debtor transferred warrants for 3,265,315 shares of its common stock to Bank of Montreal. The warrants had an exercise price of $0.01 per share. In mid-2002, American HomePatient voluntarily filed for Chapter 11 bankruptcy protection. As part of its reorganization plan, the debtor rejected this contract with the bank on July 11, 2003.

The bankruptcy court calculated the loss from the contract as of the day before American HomePatient entered bankruptcy—July 30, 2002. Both parties presented expert testimony as to the value of the stock on that date. The court determined the damages under the intrinsic value method. The court concluded that Bank of Montreal had lost profits of $846,369.85. The bank appealed.

On appeal, the bank argued that the trial court erred when it estimated the damages as of the day before American HomePatient entered bankruptcy. It argued that the damages should be measured as of the day the contract was breached, July 11, 2003, and that, if that date was used, it suffered damages of $6,987,774.10. The 6th Circuit disagreed. The court concluded that, under these circumstances, the rejection of an executory contract is deemed to have occurred as of the day prior to the filing of the petition; therefore, the damages should be estimated as of the date of the deemed breach regardless of the actual date of the breach. The court reached this conclusion based on its statutory interpretation of 11 U.S.C. sec. 365(g)(1) and 502 (g) as well as case law from other jurisdictions that addressed this question.

In re: American Suzuki Motor Corporation

Citation: 2013 Bankr. LEXIS 2276
Date of decision: June 4, 2013
Country: US
State or Federal: Federal
State/Jurisdiction: California
Court: United States Bankruptcy Court
Experts: John W. Forehand, Joseph Roesner (dealer/complainant); Herbert Walter (debtor)
Judge: Clarkson

What 'FMV'? Bankruptcy Court Restricts Car Dealer's Damages

After the U.S. Suzuki distributor declared Chapter 11 bankruptcy, a Florida car dealership declined its offer to continue as a service and parts dealer with the debtor's successor and instead argued in Bankruptcy Court that it had a right to damages for breach of its dealership agreement and violations of a state dealer statute.

The debtor, a California corporation, was the sole distributor in the continental U.S. for the Japanese carmaker Suzuki. It sold most of its inventory wholesale through a network of independently owned dealerships, which, in turn, sold to retail customers. After it filed for Chapter 11 bankruptcy in November 2012, the company reached an agreement with almost all of its 220 dealers that allowed them to operate as a Suzuki parts and service dealer for another eight years with the successor owner.

A Florida Suzuki dealership, the claimant, did not join the umbrella agreement. In 1995, it had made a three-year contract with the debtor, which both sides subsequently extended by letter agreement for one year, through 1999. Even though the dealer never signed that letter, it adhered to its provisions for the next 12 years. In January 2013, the Bankruptcy Court (C.D. Cal.) authorized the debtor to reject its contract with the dealer under the Bankruptcy Code's section 365. In March 2013, the dealer tendered its inventory, parts, and tools to the debtor. Under the contract repurchase obligations, the debtor paid nearly $163,000 for eight cars in stock, nearly $24,600 for parts and accessories, and nearly $22,700 for special tools and data processing equipment, for a total of $210,250.

The dealer wanted more. It filed a claim in Bankruptcy Court (C.D. Cal.) asserting that the debtor's rejection violated a 2009 Florida dealer statute that required repurchase of the franchise at fair market value (FMV) as of 12 months before termination, as well as treble damages for violations of the state law; alternatively, it asked for past and future lost profits resulting from the debtor's breach of contract.

The debtor objected, noting it had met all its repurchase obligations for inventory and arguing that the dealer had no right to recovery under state law because the Bankruptcy Code preempted the cited 2009 state statute. In any event, the latter did not apply retroactively to the parties' 1995 agreement. Finally, even if the dealer could claim the FMV of the Suzuki franchise, the value its expert proposed was excessive.

Three problematic valuation methods. Both sides presented damages experts: the dealership two, the debtor one.

The dealer's first expert was the company's in-house counsel, whom the court declared an expert in valuing car dealerships. He stated that the company's FMV as of October 2011 was $330,000. He said he chose this particular date based on "his interpretation of property damages provided by Florida statute." He did not value the company based on the actual bankruptcy petition date, rejection date, or any date the company considered the termination of contract date. His valuation did not account for significant operations costs; he also stated he did not receive information on company sales in 2012 or 2013 and did not try to obtain these data.

As to lost profits, he stated that in 2011 there were 69 sales of new Suzuki cars and the average profit per vehicle was $531. He confirmed that, at the time of tender, in March 2013, the debtor repurchased eight cars. In terms of parts and accessories sales, he said the typical profit margin was between 65% and 70%.

The dealer's second expert calculated lost profits related solely to Suzuki parts and service sales for 3.5 years, the period the company solely had specified based on the original contract, not the one-year extension, through March 2016. By his calculation, lost profits yielded $294,200.

He explained he first had based his computation on "a regression analysis" of gross sales and service profits from January 2009 through November 2011, demonstrating a decline of sales and services net profits, combined with "a view of the average yearly service and parts gross profits for 2009 through 2012 minus the average 'Service and Parts Incremental Expenses' that were provided to him by [the company]." He concluded that net profits were $121,000; when he multiplied this amount by approximately 3.5 years, he arrived at net lost profits of $295,200.

On cross-examination, he admitted that he did not calculate the incremental expense figure but used the company's numbers. Had the company not provided the data, he said, he would have used an industry standard instead, which would have been "significantly higher." Specifically, net lost profits would have totaled only approximately $220,000.

The debtor's expert expressed doubts about the second expert's methodology and particularly questioned the "use, relevancy and meaning" of the regression analysis. He also explained that the so-called incremental expenses "severely understated the true expenses" the dealership incurred, pointing out that other divisions subsidized the company's Suzuki operations.

The debtor's expert himself presented "a calculus for determining [the dealer's] 'good will' immediately preceding Suzuki's bankruptcy." He said his methodology was "new and innovative" and that "he knew of no previous valuation of an automobile dealership that had utilized his methodology." He suggested the franchise's FMV was no more than $136,000.

Court favors traditional breach of contract damages. The purpose of contract rejection under § 365 was to enable the debtor to reorganize in a way that benefited the estate and its creditors, the Bankruptcy Court explained. Reorganization includes liquidation under Chapter 11. State law statutes, including the Florida statute at issue, protecting the economic interests of local car dealerships counteracted that purpose and were preempted by federal law, it stated. Moreover, in this case, the statute the dealer cited to support the repurchase of its Suzuki franchise at fair market value had no retroactive provision. In sum, there was no right to damages under the state statute, the Bankruptcy Court concluded.

But the court's earlier decision to allow the debtor to reject its agreement with the dealer did result in a breach of contract, the court continued. Accordingly, "the correct general practice is to utilize traditional breach of damage calculation, and when appropriate, liquidated damages provisions." It next assessed the expert testimony, pointing out weaknesses in all three opinions.

Dealer's first expert. The court quickly disposed of the $330,000 valuation the dealer's first expert—in-house counsel—proposed. Based on "stale and significantly incomplete financial information," it was devoid of "true economic analysis" that an expert would perform in an "actual" valuation. For example, the court said, the expert here never accounted for the fact that the dealer's other car line businesses subsidized most of the operations costs related to the Suzuki portions. It is "as likely as not" that without that subsidy Suzuki sales and service operations would have lost money during the years the expert reviewed. Also, he made no effort to value the company on any relevant date. And his own statements suggested that his activities, skills, and experience resembled those of a real estate broker who tried to determine "an appropriate listing price for a home being put on the market." Because of these defects, the court accorded no weight to that part of the opinion.

At the same time, it credited the expert's statements that the average profit was $531 per sale of a new Suzuki vehicle and that the typical profit margin for parts and accessories was between 65% and 70%.

Dealer's second valuation analyst. The future lost profits calculation related to parts and services had its own set of flaws, the court found. For one, the second expert failed to consider that the company carried a large variety of car brands and "might just as easily be able to redirect the work" of stocking Suzuki parts and repairing Suzuki vehicles into activities for other brands. Moreover, the company was "at liberty to contact the new distributor of Suzuki parts" and make a new contract, or it could buy them from other dealers, the court pointed out. In a footnote, it dismissed the expert's claim that the company would have had to pay "rack prices" had it bought from other dealers, saying it was common knowledge that dealers have reciprocal agreements. Also, he did not explore mitigation, and the 3.5-year multiplier for the claimed average lost profits (which the court discredited) was without support. All told, his methodology and calculation were "not completely sound" and deserved little weight.

Debtor's appraiser. The court also found the debtor expert's "self-designed" method to calculate the company's goodwill "unpersuasive and too innovative and new to be given any weight."

Ultimately, based on repurchase payments the debtor had already made, the court credited the dealer's first expert in awarded lost profits related to the sale of eight automobiles in the amount of $4,248, assuming a gross profit of $531 per car in 2011. This amount was "generous," it said, considering there was evidence that the dealer had few new Suzuki car sales and had factored in few expenses. Further, based on the $24,600 the company had received for parts and accessories, lost profits were about $17,200, that is, a 70% gross profit. This figure represented the highest amount the dealer's own expert derived. Because the dealer did not resell special tools and data processing equipment, there was no profit to attribute in this category.

Importantly, the dealer had no right to lost profits for future sales or services, the court noted. The company failed to offer credible evidence of its fair market value regardless of how one "parsed" the contract between it and the debtor in terms of time remaining. Since new Suzuki-made cars were no longer available in the U.S., it said, "a Suzuki car sales dealership is almost valueless." Ninety-seven percent of all Suzuki dealers agreed to continue their operations in parts and services with the debtor's successor, the court observed. Had this dealer also accepted the offer, "any lost profits, calculable or not at this time, would not be at issue." Nothing need have changed for the dealer, it concluded, granting only past lost profits.

Antioch Co. Litig. Trust v. Morgan

Citation: 2014 U.S. Dist. LEXIS 47740
Date of decision: April 7, 2014
Country: US
State or Federal: Federal
State/Jurisdiction: Ohio
Court: United States District Court
Type of action: Bankruptcy
Judge: Black
Experts: Mark A. Greenberg (plaintiff); unknown (defendants)
SIC: 2732 Book Printing
Key words: Damages, Daubert, Expert testimony, Lost value, Professional Fees, Waste

Lost Value Opinion Using Untested Data Points Is No Go

A recent bankruptcy-related case illustrates how an experienced valuator made himself vulnerable under *Daubert* by agreeing to be a conduit for information the client wanted to place in evidence without investigating the source material. If the court's exclusion did not sting enough, the expert heard the client argue to the court that it could show damages without him because the calculation required only "simple arithmetic," which the jury could perform on its own.

Bungled sales process. The debtor was a privately held company that produced bookplates, bookmarks, book covers, and calendars. By 2007, it experienced financial trouble and determined it needed outside money to meet its obligations. The company's board of directors (the defendants) hired a financial advisor to guide the 2007-2008 sales process. Two credible buyers presented letters of interest (LOIs) that the board and its legal and financial advisors reviewed in August 2007. The values ranged between $148 million and $185 million. But, after doing due diligence on the company, in October 2007 the prospective buyers withdrew, citing the company's declining financial health. In May 2008, there was an offer from a venture capital firm, J.H. Whitney, to buy the company's assets for $54 million in a "363" sale that required the company to file for bankruptcy and reorganize. Ultimately that proposition came to nothing, and other efforts to pursue a sale also failed. In November 2008, the company petitioned for bankruptcy.

As part of the bankruptcy filing, the company submitted a disclosure statement that referenced a valuation of the company between $31 million and $38 million. The disclosure statement cautioned that the estimate "does not necessarily reflect, and should not be construed as reflecting, values that will be attained in the public or private markets." The Bankruptcy Court did not adopt the valuation in any of its findings or its confirmation order.

The litigation trust sued the defendants (D. Ohio) on a number of theories, claiming they mismanaged the sales process and committed waste by employing various professionals without receiving value in return. The trustee demanded lost value and professional fees damages.

'No way to know.' To testify to both sets of damages, the trust hired a financial expert with decades of experience in business valuation, deal structuring, and financial and investment analysis, who had dealt with "363" sales. However, he was not a qualified damages expert and had never given testimony on damages. He admitted he was not familiar with any damages methodologies and said he did not use any method to calculate damages for this case. He opined that the defendants' conduct "caused the Company to lose the opportunity to realize between $20 million and $30 million in value, and to waste $6 million on professional fees."

As to lost value, he said he arrived at his range by using the $54 million from the Whitney LOI as a "top-end value" and the $31 million-to-$38 million range appearing in the bankruptcy disclosure statement as a "bottom-end value"—subtracting the latter from the former. He did not perform a formal business valuation and also did no independent analysis of the LOI. He did not contend that the $54 million offer was reasonable. Rather, he believed that when it came to the value of the company "the worst it would have been would have been $54 million if there wasn't anybody else stepping up to the option of the 363 sale." Whitney, he believed, had done "substantial due diligence," and its offer would have been a "stalking horse" that would have attracted other offers. At the same time, he conceded that "there's no way to know that." He also stated that a letter of intent was nonbinding and was not the equivalent of cash; he noted there was only one way to know a deal was done: "when the money is in the bank." And "more value is lost between the time there is a signed letter of intent and a closing than anyone ever cares to admit."

Although his report said that the amount of waste on professional fees related to the unsuccessful sales process was $6 million, he admitted in his deposition that he had not reviewed any information related to the professional fees. This figure, he said, was an estimate he had received from plaintiff's counsel; he did not know which professional received what part, if any, of the amount and indeed did not know what part of the $6 million estimate actually represented waste.

Plaintiff at oral argument on the *Daubert* motion admitted the figure stemmed from just adding up invoices and subsequently said it would not rely on the expert's testimony for this damages claim.

Blind reliance on sources. The defendants filed a *Daubert* motion to strike both parts of the expert's damages opinion, arguing he had lifted his base values from the work of others without establishing the reliability of the source material. He admitted to having no experience with the computation of damages and to using no methodology or reliable principles. Therefore, the testimony was unreliable. Also, the plaintiff failed to commit to a damages calculation in the pretrial stage and should be precluded from introducing it for the first time at trial.

The plaintiff countered that the expert had experience in dealing with the transactions at issue in the contested sales process. He was qualified to testify to the reliability of the Whitney letter. His testimony combined with the bankruptcy court record sufficed to establish lost value damages. The damages methodology he used was "simple arithmetic." Once the top and bottom values were in evidence, the jury could subtract the two numbers itself.

The court found the argument seriously flawed. As to methodology, the expert did not do any independent analysis of the $54 million figure in the Whitney letter. Even if an expert's opinion need not be based on first-hand knowledge and he or she need not have performed his own valuation of the company, the expert must establish that he drew on reliable sources. Regarding the top value he used, he never suggested that it was a reliable data point. Also, no Whitney representative was deposed to speak to the letter of intent. Therefore, it was hearsay. And, although an expert may rely on hearsay, "s/he cannot do so blindly," said the court. Regarding the bottom value, the valuation range included in the disclosure statement also was not reliable. "It is a document prepared, sponsored and filed by a party soliciting votes to accept or reject a reorganization plan," the court pointed out. Therefore, "courts do not look to values set forth by a plan proponent in a disclosure statement as admissible evidence." Accordingly, even if the court were to allow the plaintiff to prove damages by "simple arithmetic," without a damages expert, the plaintiff lacked reliable sources providing the requisite base values.

The court swiftly dismissed the expert's opinion about the $6 million professional fees figure, noting he performed no independent review of the payment records and invoices related to professional fees.

In conclusion, the court not only excluded the expert's damages testimony, but it also denied the plaintiff's last-minute request to show damages without an expert. The court's finding was the end of the case.

ASARCO v. Americas Mining Corp. (I)

Citation: 2008 WL 4009927(S.D. Tex.)
Date of Decision: August 30, 2008
Country: US
State or Federal: Federal
State/Jurisdiction: Texas
Court: United States District Court
Type of action: Bankruptcy
Experts: Navigant (plaintiff/debtor), Craig Pirrong (defendant)
Judge: Hanen
SIC: 1021 – Copper Ores

Case Considers Control Premiums, DCF Discount Rates, and More

By 2003, a century-old mining company had entered "the zone of insolvency," according to its valuation and legal advisors. Its most valuable asset: a 54% controlling interest in a Peruvian copper concern, which was worth between $600 million and nearly $1 billion. When its parent company decided to purchase the asset, those same advisors warned the board of directors that it would be difficult to justify the transaction "consistent with its fiduciary duty to protect all creditors" of the subsidiary. But the directors pressed forward with the sale, and the troubled subsidiary struggled for nearly two more years. In 2005 it declared bankruptcy, and as Chapter 11 debtor, it tried to recoup the sale of its "crown jewel" as a fraudulent transfer.

Valuation experts parse elements of purchase. In its 107-page opinion, the federal district court first examined the debtor's claims for constructive fraud—in particular, whether the debtor received "reasonably equivalent value" in exchange for its controlling interest in the Peruvian copper company. (The debtor also claimed actual fraud, which required a showing of actual intent to hinder or delay creditors.)

Both parties agreed that the parent company paid $765 million, composed of: (1) $450 million cash, used to pay down the debtor's revolving line of credit; (2) $50 million, to pay down "Yankee bonds" ($100 million of outstanding, unsecured bonds); (3) a promissory note payable for $123.25 million; (4) a guarantied promissory note for $100 million; and (5) a cancellation of $41.75 million in debt.

The debtor's expert concluded that the consideration was worth between $660.2 million and $726.6 million—prior to subtracting the negative, net economic effects of paying off the Yankee bonds, which reduced the value to between $611.2 million and $702.11 million. By contrast, the expert for the parent company valued the consideration at $720.3 million—without any reduction for the bond payoff. The court examined each element:

1. *Cash.* The parties—and the court—agreed that the $450 million cash paid to retire the revolving debt was worth $450 million.

2. *Yankee bonds.* The parent company claimed that the $50 million payoff of the Yankee bonds was worth $50 million to the subsidiary/debtor. The debtor's expert argued that, because

the bonds were trading below par, the court should discount their net economic benefit to the debtor. But the court held that the trading discount did not reduce the value of $50 million cash and credited the consideration accordingly.

3. *$123.5 million note.* The parent owed seven annual installments of $17.6 million to pay off the principal of the note. The debtor's expert estimated its present value between $78.6 million and $105.7 million; this essentially conformed to an analysis by Ernst & Young (E&Y), the debtor's advisors during the sale, which used a discount rate between 12.5% and 25%. The parent's expert used varying discount rates, however, ranging from 17.55% to 19.36%, based on a credit spread of 16.43%; he valued the note at $94.36 million. The court found this approach more reasonable, "somewhat buoyed by the fact that it falls within the center of the ranges found by [the debtor's experts]."

4. *$100 million note.* The debtor's expert relied on the E&Y analysis, which applied lower discount rates—10% to 12.5%—because the parent guaranteed the eight installment payments of $12.5 million, resulting in a present value for the note of $85.1 million to $91.4 million. The expert for the parent company examined its credit rating and prevailing market yields, determined a spread of 4.55% and discount rates of 5.68% to 7.99%, and valued the note at $99.8 million. But the court found his rates too low and valued the note at the higher end of the debtor's range, or $91.2 million. (The court didn't explain its reasoning—but its value falls almost midway between the experts'.)

5. *Debt forgiveness.* The parent company cancelled a $41.75 million past-due note from the subsidiary; its expert valued this debt forgiveness at $26.12 million, based on a renegotiation of the debt at 9.28% interest over an extended term. The debtor's expert claimed the value was worth up to 100% of the debt—and the court agreed, finding the situation analogous to the payment of the Yankee bonds. It was not appropriate to reduce the value of the debt cancellation based on the "mere possibility" of a renegotiation, it said, and valued this element at $475 million.

Overall, the court found that the debtor received $727.8 million in exchange for its stake in the Peruvian mining company. The next question became the value of this 54% controlling interest.

Public markets not always the most reliable measure. In addition to valuations by the parties' experts, the court considered the E&Y appraisals plus ones by Behre Dolbear and Houlihan Lokey (Houlihan), all conducted at the time of the sale. Each appraisal applied the three commonly accepted approaches for valuing publicly traded stock: (1) stock price valuation; (2) market multiples; and (3) discounted cash flow (DCF). In this case, the 54% interest was comprised of "Founders Shares" with enhanced voting rights. Additional founders owned enhanced shares (five votes per share), but all were thinly traded, less than 1% active in the open market.

The parent's expert believed that the stock's price on the day of sale was the best indicator of value, given the efficiencies of a "semi-strong" market, which factored in elements of control. But the debtor's expert did not believe the market for the Peruvian mining company was efficient, especially given a "serendipitously low" stock price on the day of sale. The debtor's expert also advocated a control premium.

Relying on Delaware law, the court recognized that the market price "may not always" represent the true value of publicly traded shares. And pursuant to a leading federal case (*Cammer v. Bloom*, D. N.J., 1989), it examined the Peruvian stock under several criteria, including average weekly trading volume, the number of securities analysts following the stock, and the company's public filings. At the time of the transfer, the stock was traded on the "extremely reliable" New York Stock Exchange—but its low trading volume and thin public float cut against the presumptive market efficiencies.

The debtor contended that a 20-, 30-, or 60-day trailing price would be more appropriate. "Mainstream valuation" practice used this approach to smooth out stock volatilities, their expert said. In fact, Ernst & Young had used a 60-day trailing average in addition to a single-day price in its analysis, and Houlihan used a 20-day trailing average of stock prices. Moreover, the stock on the day of sale reached its lowest price—$14.60 per share, compared to $15.00 and $16.00 per share in prior months. The court agreed with this approach, finding the stock sufficiently volatile to warrant using a trailing average, especially since the number of days selected resulted in similar pricing for the debtor's interest: $671 million for a 20-day average; $676 million over 30 days; and $678.8 million over 60.

Market price accounts for control? The debtor's expert urged the court to apply a 30%-to-40% control premium to the 54% Founders' stake. Houlihan had applied a 20% premium in its analysis, and E&Y had applied a 30% premium in its market approach. (Because investors knew the stock was "in play," E&Y did not apply a control premium in its stock valuation.) The debtor's expert adopted a 30% premium, based on 2002 Mergerstat data that showed 12-month median and average control premia in the mining industry of 25.9% and 39.5%, respectively.

The parent company argued that no premium was appropriate. Not only did the market price factor in control, but also an independent, third-party buyer could lose the enhanced voting rights associated with the 54% interest if the remaining founders acquired enough enhanced shares, with five votes per, to effectively obtain a controlling interest. Further, the Mergerstat data overvalued control because it did not consider synergies or account for negative premiums. If any premium was appropriate, it should be only 7% or 8%.

But the court found this range too low. A third-party buyer would pay a premium for the 54% controlling block, it said, despite the risk of the remaining founders buying a controlling share—which was "relatively low," given their lack of desire, means, or notice. Any distinction between synergies and control was misplaced because a buyer wouldn't "mechanically" separate the reasons for paying a premium, the court said. But a 30% premium was too high; E&Y had only used this in its market approach, and the debtor failed to convince the court that Mergerstat data should be added directly to the market price. Overall, the 20% control premium that Houlihan used in its contemporaneous analysis of the sale (and in a prior fairness opinion) was the more reasonable, the court said. Applying this to a 30-day trailing average, it valued the debtor's 54% interest under the stock valuation approach at $811.4 million.

Company-specific risk is key to market approach. The expert for the parent company rejected any guideline public company analysis, claiming that it was "highly unreliable as a standalone methodology," particularly if the information to conduct a "full-blown" DCF is available and the comparable mining companies weren't sufficiently similar to the Peruvian concern. However, the court noted that the expert had used market multiples in his DCF determination of terminal value; it also believed that a willing buyer would consider the market approach as a "sanity check" against a DCF and stock valuation. Moreover, the remaining experts had used the comparable company approach, as follows:

> After selecting five copper and mining companies, E&Y determined the debtor's interest in the Peruvian company was worth $644 million. To account for specific-company risk, it adjusted this amount downward by 30%, then applied the 30% control premium.

Houlihan used five of the same comparables plus an additional three but did not include the downward adjustment before adding a 20% control premium.

Behre Dolbear used market multiples of EBITDA and averaged its results with those from its comparable transactions and DCF analyses, before adding a 25% control premium without any downward adjustment.

The debtor's expert adopted the E&Y analysis, without the 30% downward adjustment.

In his DCF analysis, the expert for the parent company did not adjust his market multiples for a control premium or company-specific risk.

The experts also debated the mining risks in Peru—the debtor's expert believed the risks were low to moderate, while the expert for the parent company claimed that they were higher than those in any of the top 12 copper-producing countries during the relevant time period. Setting these arguments aside, the court didn't see sufficient objective evidence for applying the 30% downward adjustment. The comparable companies captured the risks in their betas and other numbers, and any further assessment seemed "arbitrary and speculative."

But the company numbers did not account for control. Relying on its stock price analysis, the court found an appropriate control premium to range between 20% and 30%. Using the equity that E&Y derived in its comparable companies approach, minus the downward adjustment, the court found the debtor's interest to be worth $890 million (20% control premium), $928 million (25%), and $965 million (30%). It briefly considered the comparable transactions approach but concluded (with most of the experts) that the available datasets were neither helpful nor reliable.

DCF turns first on copper prices. The court also agreed with the experts that, in this case, the DCF was the most reliable method for valuing the debtor's holdings in the Peruvian copper concern. The critical variables were the price of copper and the correct discount rate.

To determine the first, the court considered the prices used by valuation analysts at the time of the sale (2003), along with contemporaneous price forecasts by industry and financial analysts, the company's internal forecasts, and evidence from the trial experts. For instance, Behre Dolbear looked at 15-year forecasts that projected an average price of $0.96 per pound and concluded that the industry expected long-term prices to range between $0.90 and $0.95 per pound. It used three different prices ($0.85, $0.90, and $0.96) to conduct three different DCFs and considered the range of $0.90 to $0.92 per pound to be appropriate.

The debtor's expert looked at price forecasts from 2003 to 2007 and calculated the average of the median to be $0.95. During the relevant time period, the debtor was using a range of $0.90 to $0.92 for its internal forecasts, including a 10-year average of $0.91. In its 2001 and 2002 10-Ks, the debtor used $0.90 to value its copper reserves and long-term prices. Accordingly, the debtor's expert used $0.90 and $0.95 in its DCF analyses.

By contrast, Houlihan used a price of $0.85 per pound in its analysis at the time of the sale, but ultimately the court was convinced that $0.90 was the appropriate long-term price for copper, "especially as that was the price used internally by [the debtor.]"

Discount rates stir *Daubert* debate. "One of the most hard fought aspects of this trial was which discount rate should be applied and how it should be calculated," the court said, prompting the parties to file "dueling *Daubert* motions." (It dismissed both motions, saying the experts' use of different methods, Fama-French versus the capital asset pricing model (CAPM), went to the weight and not the admissibility of the evidence.)

Only the parent company's expert used the Fama-French method to calculate a discount rate of 13.4%. The remaining experts used CAPM to calculate discount rates that ranged from 9% (E&Y) to 10% (Houlihan). The Fama-French approach was primarily used by academics and resulted in a rate outside the range of the CAPM calculations, the court said. It found that a discount rate between 9% and 10% "would not be unreasonable" but that the 9% rate used by the debtor's expert and E&Y was "most appropriate" in valuing the debtor's interest.

After reviewing the expert's various DCF models, the court also decided that the debtor's expert presented the "most accurate model." Using this model and the 9% discount rate, and inputting the long-term copper price of $0.90, the court found the value of the debtor's interest to be $853 million. (The court also applied discount rates of 9.5% and 10% and found resulting values of $775.3 million and $708.3 million, respectively.)

The bottom line on reasonably equivalent value. To sum up the court's value determinations:

- Stock price approach: $811.4 million (30-day trailing average and 20% control premium);
- Market (comparable company) approach: $890 million (20% control premium, no company-specific risk premium); and
- DCF (income) approach: $853 million (9% discount rate, $0.90 long-term copper price).

The court found the result of the comparable company analysis to be outside the range of the other two methods and agreed with the majority of experts who used it only as a reasonableness check. It concluded that the debtor's 54% stake in the Peruvian copper company was worth between

$811.4 million and $853 million. Contrasting this against the debtor's receipt of $727.8 million from the parent, the court found the difference "not insubstantial." However, "percentage-wise," the numbers looked much closer: The consideration comprised approximately 85% to 90% of the value transferred, "well above the 70% rule" articulated by leading cases on reasonably equivalent value.

The court also considered the totality of circumstances surrounding the transaction. Although it lacked independence and arm's length, at the time of the sale, copper prices were only $0.71 per pound. In addition, the debtor's financial advisors (E&Y) provided an opinion that the sale was financially fair. "The law does not demand that a plaintiff receive an amount equal to the fair market value of the asset it transfers," the court said, "the consideration must only be *reasonably* equivalent." Given all the facts of the case, including "the lack of precision" inherent in valuing the mining company stock, the court found that the debtor received reasonable value in exchange for its stake.

Parent, directors still face liability. In the second half of its lengthy opinion, the court considered the debtor's claims of actual fraud and found that the parent company "entered into the ... transaction with the full knowledge that [the debtor's] creditors would be hindered or delayed as a result." It also found that the debtor was insolvent at the time of the transfer. Although the directors of the parent did not beach any direct fiduciary duties, they "aided and abetted" the subsidiary's directors by structuring the deal to deprive the "cash-starved" debtor of its most valuable asset. (Many of the directors sat on both boards.) The court denied the debtor's claims for punitive damages, but, given its favorable rulings on actual fraud and aiding/abetting, it directed the parties to address damages in further briefs.

The court also noted that the parties had already spent "millions of dollars" on the case, including fees for over 30 attorneys and experts. In an unusual step, it made additional, alternate findings on key rulings, anticipating review by the 5th Circuit court in an almost certain appeal.

ASARCO v. Americas Mining Corp. (II)

Citation: 2009 WL 890551 (S.D. Tex.)
Date of Decision: February 9, 2009
Country: US
State or Federal: Federal
State/Jurisdiction: Texas
Court: United States District Court
Type of action: Bankruptcy
Judge: Hanen
SIC: 1021 Copper Ores

May Plaintiff's Expert Assess Control Premium in Damages?

In the first round of the ASARCO litigation, the federal district court's decision voided the transfer of a controlling interest in a Peruvian copper concern. The parties exchanged the stock for reasonably equivalent value, so the court found no constructive fraud. It did, however, find actual fraud as well as fiduciary breach, thus setting the stage for this determination of damages.

A 'crown jewel' is taken. Plaintiff ASARCO was a wholly owned subsidiary of the Grupo copper mining conglomerate. Among its most valuable assets was ownership of roughly 54% of a Peruvian copper company, the interest enhanced by "founders'" stock with superior voting rights. By 2001, its financial condition became critical, its only options bankruptcy or sale of the stock. The parent company was also in dire straits and did not want to relinquish all control of this "crown jewel," so it caused the subsidiary to sell it to another related entity. (The boards of all entities were stocked with "loyal retainers," creating an integrated hierarchy within the Grupo corporate family.)

Nevertheless, the parent fell into Chapter 11 bankruptcy—as did the subsidiary and related entities. After the subsidiary successfully proved that the sale was fraudulent, it not only requested the return of the stock, plus dividends and interest, on behalf of its creditors in bankruptcy, but also a control premium for loss of the enhanced rights through the parent's post-transfer sales and dilutions. To calculate these damages, it multiplied the current market value of the stock by 20%, which was the control premium that the court had used in the liability proceedings to determine reasonably equivalent value.

The federal district court (S.D. Tex.) agreed that the appropriate remedy for actual fraud was the return of the stock, plus dividends and prejudgment interest. (This would also satisfy the breach of fiduciary duty and related claims). Still, the request for a control premium presented "the most perplexing problem." In finding that a 20% control premium was reasonable in the fraudulent transfer case, the court had reviewed copious evidence from multiple sources, including valuation experts.

Moreover, the 20% premium had two advantages that the court did not stress in its prior opinion. First, the control premium was derived in part from prospective appraisals, i.e., those made before the stock transfer took place. Consequently, they included the then-current forecasts regarding the copper market and did not include the "exponential" rise in prices that occurred soon after.

Second, "unlike the various retrospective opinions offered at trial," the court said, "[the control premium] was not biased by the lawsuit or by those advocating a certain position."

The parent company argued two reasons against simply "reversing the deal" and awarding the stock plus a premium:

1. All of the parties agreed that, given its financial condition, the subsidiary would have had to sell the stock "to someone, at some price"; and

2. The court already found that parent paid reasonably equivalent value (REV).

As to the second argument, during the liability proceedings, the court found that the 54% enhanced block of stock was worth between $811 million and $853 million. The parent paid $728 million, leaving the subsidiary with a deficit of $83 million to $125 million. Because of a number of variables—including the volatility of copper prices and the difficulty of precise valuation—the court also found that, legally, the consideration paid reached the level of REV, even without equating to fair market value. In the context of damages, however, the deficit proved much more pivotal, as it may have led directly to the subsidiary's bankruptcy and a creditor shortfall. The court could find no legal or equitable reason why its finding of REV in the first phase of trial precluded its award of a control premium during the second damages phase.

The control premium turns on actually having 'control.' The parent's second prong of attack was "much more compelling." Ultimately, the subsidiary's financial condition dictated that it would have had to sell its 54% interest, either to the parent or to another party, prior to bankruptcy or under judicial oversight. More importantly, given the restrictions placed on the stock at the time of the transfer, including its pledge to the subsidiary's secured lender, neither the subsidiary nor its remaining creditors could have gained or sold "control" of the stock.

Bankruptcy law dictates that the court should award damages sufficient "to make the debtor's estate/creditors whole." Because the evidence established that the subsidiary could not have maintained control of the 54% stock interest, "a control premium (or an amount representing that premium) would not have been available to [its] creditors" and was therefore not an appropriate element of damages in this case.

In re Bachrach Clothing, Inc.

Citation: 2012 Bankr. LEXIS 4807
Date of decision: Oct. 10, 2012
Country: US
State or Federal: State
State/Jurisdiction: Illinois
Court: United States Bankruptcy Court
Experts: Craig T. Elson (debtor); John D. Ciancanelli, Stan A. Murphy (defendants)
Judge: Hollis

Bankruptcy Court Discredits DCF as 'Easily Manipulated'

After more than 125 years in business, the owners of a family-run men's apparel business agreed to sell their stock to a private equity firm for $8 million, consisting of $4 million in cash and $4 million in a subordinated note. In connection with the proposed sale, the PE firm's financial advisor (KPMG) reviewed prior audited financials and found the target's historic book value was worth approximately $5 million, "substantially" more than the purchase price, noting in particular its $11 million in excess working capital and over $5.8 million in investment cash. After its own due diligence, the PE firm independently determined that the purchase price was "attractive," in large part due to the company's "strong base of assets" (inventory and accounts receivable), noting, in particular, the target's borrowing capacity of $7 million.

Minimal investment, maximum control. The PE firm structured the sale as a leveraged buyout (LBO), transferring the acquired stock to an affiliated entity, and then immediately replacing the target's board of directors with its own executives. The new entity then effectively caused the company to pay the $4 million cash due to the sellers by: (1) securing a $2 million bank loan, independently guaranteed by the PE firm; and (2) declaring a $2 million dividend. Notably, when they authorized the dividend, the new directors concluded the company was solvent.

Immediately after the acquisition, the PE firm appointed a new CEO, who lacked experience in men's retail but who began making substantial changes. For example, in a single month (May 2005), she marked down the company's inventory by $7 million, or more than 285% of the budgeted amount. Overall, the changes eroded $3 million in working capital, thereby reducing the company's borrowing base from $4.3 million to $1.3 million. At the same time, the company continued to pay the PE firm $400,000 in management fees plus the costs of the purchase, including attorneys' fees of over $800,000, which eventually amounted to over $3 million in extraordinary expenses.

To address the company's liquidity crunch, the PE firm announced it would make an additional $5 million equity investment in early 2006. A few months later, however, the firm began internally discussing the prospect of putting the company into bankruptcy. To effectively convert its investment into a secured claim, the PE firm caused its affiliated entity to execute a $5 million promissory note (including a repurchase of the $2 million bank loan made in connection with the original LBO) and then backdated the note by three months (or beyond the 90-day preference period). A few weeks later, the PE firm withdrew its funding, forcing the company to file for Chapter 11 protection.

According to the bankruptcy court (N.D. Ill.), the debtor "had a strong argument" to recharacterize the PE firm's secured claim as equity, yet, for various reasons, it "capitulated" and agreed not to sue its investors or their affiliates (demonstrating the investors' "continued control" over the debtor, the court said). Instead, the debtor sued its former owners to recover the purchase price as a fraudulent conveyance. To prove its claims under federal as well as state law, the debtor had to show the company was insolvent (or rendered insolvent) at the time of sale. To hold the individual sellers liable, it would also have to convince the court to "collapse" the several steps of the LBO into a single transaction as of the sale date.

Accordingly, the debtor's expert evaluated the company in the context of the sale as well as the structured LBO. In his report, he indicated counsel instructed him to rely on the combined action of both the sellers and the PE firm "to determine whether, *as a result of the LBO transaction*, [the company] was rendered insolvent." (emphasis by the court) To rebut these claims, the former owners—now the defendants—retained two experts, working together, to show the debtor was solvent at the time they transferred the company to the PE investors.

To calculate the company's enterprise value, all the experts considered a balance sheet approach, but the debtor's expert ultimately rejected the company's audited, consolidated balance sheet, prepared in connection with the sale, because he believed its reliance on historic book value did not reflect fair market values. By contrast, the defendants' experts used the audited book value as a starting point and then adjusted it downward by nearly $4.2 million to reflect "known market conditions." Under this analysis, they concluded the debtor was worth $9 million at the time of sale. The debtor's expert criticized this conclusion, saying it did not align with his discounted cash flow (DCF) analysis. In response, the defendants' experts criticized the debtor's expert for not even considering an asset approach.

Ultimately, all of the experts relied primarily on a DCF approach, but with widely divergent results. In particular, the debtor's expert determined the company was worth $1.1 million, but, after factoring in the $400,000 management fee to the PE firm, it was worth a *negative* $293,000, he said. Under their DCF analysis, the defendants' experts believed the company was worth just over $6 million. The experts' disagreement largely came down to how each calculated the weighted average cost of capital (WACC) under a CAPM approach, with the debtor's expert reaching a rate of 19.5% compared to the defendants' experts, who derived a 12.3% rate. In turn, this disparity stemmed from the experts' treatment of the following four inputs:

1. *Debt-to-equity ratio.* The debtor's expert chose not to consider the company's actual capital structure, believing this better reflected the view of a hypothetical purchaser. Instead, he used industry standards and the debt structure of comparable companies to establish debt-to-equity ratios for his WACC. However, the defendants' experts "insisted" that ignoring the company's actual capital structure was a mistake, particularly when its actual borrowing capacity at the time of sale made it a valuable prospect and its debt-to-equity ratio was well below that of comparable companies.

2. *Equity risk premium (ERP).* All the experts relied on Ibbotson's *Valuation Yearbook* to derive an equity risk premium, and all applied the arithmetic (rather than geometric) averages of historical

data. However, by using Ibbotson's longest data set (going all the way back to 1926), the debtor's expert derived an ERP of 7.2%. By contrast, the defendants' experts believed a shorter time period, going back only 50 years, more appropriately accounted for globalization and its effect on market trends. Using historical data from the prior 50 years, they arrived at a 5.6% ERP.

Notably, in their determination of ERP, all of the experts cited Prof. Aswath Damodaran's treatise on *Investment Valuation* (John Wiley & Sons, 2012), in which he notes that essentially half the users of an historical ERP rely on Ibbotson's entire data set (back to 1926), while the other half use a shorter period. Ultimately—as the defendants' experts pointed out—Damodaran recommends an historical ERP of no more than 5.5%.

3. *Size premium.* Once again, all the experts used Ibbotson's data to derive their respective size premiums. Although the company's market capitalization fit into three size categories—the micro-cap category (deciles 9 and 10), as well as 10 and 10b—the debtor's expert selected the smallest (10b) because the company was smaller than most in that subdecile and Ibbotson's indicated the 10b results were "statistically reliable." This led to a 9.8% size premium.

The defendants' experts believed the micro-cap category was more statistically reliable and a better fit for the company, particularly since Ibbotson's found that smaller apparel and accessory stores performed better than their larger-store counterparts. They also cited Damodaran's recommendation of 4% for small-cap stocks, ultimately arriving at 4.02% size premium for the subject company.

4. *Terminal value.* Using the Gordon growth model, the debtor's expert applied a 3% growth rate to his cash flow projections to reach his terminal value. The defendants' experts, on the other hand, used an exit multiple approach, applying a 6.5 multiple to projected EBITDA. They derived the 6.5 multiple from comparable companies, as well as comparable transactions, and believed the multiple was "conservative" because it fell within the lower quartile of comparable companies and none of the comparable sales involved a lower multiple.

The debtor's expert criticized the "hybrid" exit multiple approach, once again citing Damodaran's treatise and his warning that the use of multiples to calculate terminal value in a DCF results in a "dangerous mix of relative and discounted cash flow valuation." Moreover, the defendants' expert relied on companies with higher revenues and EBITDA margins than the subject, he said. Finally, he used the experts' exit multiple to "back solve" for an implied growth rate of 6.9%, which was more than twice the current economic growth rate.

In response, the defendants' experts explained that the company's lower margin (of 3%) could have yielded a much higher multiple than 6.5 "because there would be more room for growth." For example, one of his comparable companies had an even lower margin than the subject but reported a multiple of 86. By choosing the more "conservative" multiple of 6.5, the experts actually lowered their terminal value. As for the implied growth rate, by removing the management fees from the calculation, they reached a 5.5% growth rate, which was reasonable, assuming a GDP of 3% and inflation of 2.5%, they said. By comparison, the 3% growth rate that the debtor's expert proposed assumed that the company's future performance—notwithstanding its purchase by the PE investors at an "attractive" price—would lag the economy.

DCF versus 'the real world.' After valuing the company's assets (enterprise value) under the DCF approach, the experts valued its liabilities to reach an ultimate conclusion regarding solvency. Only the debtor's expert subtracted the full face value of the $2 million loan incurred at the time of sale as well as the $4 million repurchase obligation incurred by the PE firm's affiliate. But these contingent debts should have been substantially discounted, the defendants' experts claimed, because the PE firm (or its affiliates) were co-obligors on the loans.

After hearing all the evidence, the court found "no facts or real world evidence" to support the assertion of insolvency. The company had no long-term debt, was current on payables, and held substantial cash in excess of working capital. Moreover, the defendant sellers were not involved in structuring the LBO; nor did they take any part in deciding to take the "massive" inventory markdown after the sale or institute any of the changes that reduced revenues and accelerated liabilities.

In fact, the PE firm and its hand-picked CEO "created [the company's] liquidity crisis," the court said, and the investors' "refusal to provide further capital led to this bankruptcy." The sellers delivered "a solvent and properly capitalized company at closing," the court added, noting as well that any victory in this fraudulent conveyance action would effectively refund the investors their entire outlay. After "loading" the company up with debt and liabilities, the PE firm "brilliantly had two bites at the apple: big profits if it improved [the company's] performance and a refund if it failed."

Based on these facts, the court declined to collapse the sale of the company and the LBO into a single transaction, thereby "ending" the fraudulent conveyance case. Nevertheless (and presumably for purposes of any appeal), it considered the insolvency evidence, first in the context of the DCF method, generally. For example, even though the parties' experts relied on essentially the same data and analysis, the "striking" disparity among their conclusions "lends credibility to the concept that the DCF method is subject to manipulation," the court said, citing *In re Iridium Operating LLC*, 373 B.R. 283 (Bank. S.D. 2007). Indeed, the court reiterated *Iridium's* warning that:

> The DCF methodology has been subject to criticism for its flexibility; a skilled practitioner can come up with just about any value he wants. For this reason, it is important to validate conclusions reached using this methodology by comparing the results obtained when other accepted approaches to valuation are used.

In this case, the court found that "each expert generally selected parameters that pushed his valuation in the direction he wanted to go." In particular:

- The court dismissed the negative valuation by the debtor's expert, noting that his inclusion of management fees that were unique to the sale was inconsistent with his valuing the sale from the perspective of a hypothetical buyer.
- The debtor's expert should have used the company's actual capital structure, rather than an industry standard. "Regardless of who purchases a business, a company with actual leverage of 90% has to be worth less than a company with no debt," the court stated.
- In determining the equity risk premium, both experts should have used the geometric mean instead of the arithmetic mean, which the court found (apparently after its own

reading) Damodaran used to reach his historic ERP of 5.5%. Further, Damodaran indicates the "arithmetic average return is likely to overstate the premium" and that if "forced to choose" an ERP over the entire historic range of Ibbotson data, he would "go with 4.31%, the geometric average risk premium for stocks over Treasury bonds," but his preferred approach was "market neutral" and less than 3%.

- As a result, both experts overstated the ERP, the court found. However, the 5.6% by the defendants' experts was closer to Damodaran's estimates, while the 7.2% ERP by the debtor's expert was more than double the professor's preferred approach "and just not realistic."

- Regarding the size premium, the debtor's expert "did not pay particular attention to Ibbotson's point that the 10b decile might be less reliable," the court noted. Had he used the micro-cap category, his size premium would have been 4.0%—or less than half his selected rate of 9.8%. The defendants' experts, on the other hand, appropriately factored in industry-specific phenomena to "inform" their decision about the size premium. Their selection of 4.2% also coincided with Damodaran's recommended 4%.

- Similarly, their use of an exit multiple or "hybrid" approach in calculating a terminal value found support in Damodaran's treatise; their use of comparable company data as well as economic growth rates went beyond merely "consulting a book," the court said. "Again, real world information about the performance and sales of [comparable] companies informed [their] valuation of the terminal period," while the debtor's expert continued to "shuffle numbers in and out of formulas to get where he needed to go."

Overall, the defendants' experts provided "better reasoned" explanations for their DCF inputs, and their $6 million enterprise value was "more aligned with real world events or contemporaneous market data," the court held. In support, it cited (among other factors): the due diligence by both the PE firm and its financial advisor; the company's borrowing capacity as well as its working capital reserves; and the adjusted balance sheet test based on audited financials.

The court also found the debtor's expert "exaggerated" the company's liabilities, which he should have discounted due to the PE firm's co-obligation on the various loans. His "more glaring error," however, was to match any contingent liabilities against contingent assets, the court said, citing *Paloian v. LaSalle Bank, N.A.*, 619 F.3d 688 (7th Cir. 2011). In this case, for example, the PE investors "could easily pay … and ultimately paid" the bank in full by repurchasing the $2 million loan that the company originally incurred to pay the sellers. Moreover, if the $2 million loan had rendered the company insolvent, it could have pursued a claim against its directors for illegally declaring the $2 million dividend.

In sum, the failure by the debtor's expert to discount the contingent liabilities and his inflated WACC "doomed" his conclusions that the company was insolvent or rendered insolvent by the sale, the court held. The defendants were not required to prove solvency, "but they did so with [their experts'] analysis," and the court dismissed the fraudulent conveyance claims.

In the Matter of Baker

Citation: 78 AFTR2d Par. 965237
Date of Decision: July 2, 1996
Country: US
State or Federal: Federal
State/Jurisdiction: Indiana
Court: United States Bankruptcy Court
Type of action: Bankruptcy

Going Concern Value Used in Bankruptcy Proceeding

The U.S. Bankruptcy Court for the Northern District of Indiana considered whether a dentist's amended Chapter 13 should be confirmed. IRS allegedly held a $72,830 secured interest in the dentist, but 11 U.S.C. sec. 506 (a) secures the IRS's claim only to the extent of the value of the debtors' property. The debtors' proposed amended plan called for the IRS to be paid $18,300 over five years in satisfaction of the secured claim. The payments would have originated from the dentist's future earnings and the final payment would be made from the proceeds of the liquidation of the dental practice.

The IRS argued that the amended plan did not adequately consider the value of dentist's practice. The dentist argued that the highest value should not be used, when the best value can only be achieved through his post-confirmation efforts. Furthermore, the debtors contend that any value added after the confirmation date is not part of the subject collateral. In considering this plan and the value of the debtor's practice, the court looked to *In Re Maddox,* 194 B.R. 762, which states that "Section 506 (a) does not fix the measurement of 'value.' Rather … the value of the collateral must be determined "in light of the purpose of the valuation" and in light of "proposed disposition or use of such property.… Courts … have to determine value on a case by case basis, taking into account the facts of each case and the competing interests of the case."

The court received testimony from an uncertified appraiser who arrived at a liquidation value of $6,000 without receivables and a fair market value of $55,000 should the debtor dentist remain with the practice for a period of time after a sale. (No sale was contemplated at the time of trial). This expert valued the goodwill of the practice at $3.00 per active patient record and placed a liquidation value on each record of $1.00. The court considered this testimony, the age and health of the debtor, and found that the best value for the purposes of this reorganization was the going concern value of $50,000. Thus, the court refused to confirm the debtors' plan because it failed to provide for the distribution of property on account of the IRS's allowed secured claim, which this court set at $60,000, the value of the debtor's dental practice and personal property.

Bakst v. United States of America (In re: Kane & Kane)

Citation: 2012 Bankr. LEXIS 3223
Date of decision: July 16, 2012
Country: US
State or Federal: Federal
State/Jurisdiction: Federal Circuit
Court: United States Bankruptcy Court
Experts: Robert Zucker (plaintiff/trustee); James Reda and William Michaelson (defendant/government)
Judge: Kimball

Valuing Contingent Liability in Bankruptcy Precludes GAAP Standard

A father and son were the sole equity partners in a small personal injury firm in Florida. After many successful years representing primarily healthcare insurance firms, in 2008, the firm found itself subject to a state court judgment for over $2.7 million, based largely on claims that the partners had colluded with a large insurance company to reduce payments to attorneys representing medical providers.

While the judgment was on appeal, the law firm filed for Chapter 7 liquidation. The trustee brought this adversarial action against the U.S. government, claiming the law firm's payments of the partners' personal income taxes during the year prior to the bankruptcy petition (2008) amounted to fraudulent conveyances worth just over $727,000. In response, the government moved for summary judgment, arguing that it was a subsequent transferee who accepted the payments for value and in good faith. The trustee then filed its own summary judgment motion on all claims and, in addition, challenged both of the government's experts under *Daubert*.

Reasonable compensation at the core of reasonably equivalent value. To rebut the fraudulent transfer claims, the government offered two expert witnesses. The first would testify that the law firm debtor received reasonably equivalent value for the transfer/tax payments, in the form of the partners' services, and the second would testify that the debtor was solvent at the time of the payments. The trustee objected to both, the first on the basis of his qualifications and methodologies and the second on his misapplication of the law.

As to the first, the court found the expert qualified based on his 23 years' experience as a consultant on executive compensation. He'd also worked with small law firms, such as the debtor, focusing in particular on their productivity and pay concerns, for both partners and associates. Through his own firm, the expert had provided litigation advice in cases concerning attorney fees and had testified in at least one prior fraudulent conveyance case involving questions of reasonable compensation.

To determine the reasonableness of the partners' pay for their services in this case, the expert started with the 2009 Am Law 100 Survey, which presented data on revenues and compensation for the 100 largest law firms in the country. He then divided the aggregate partner compensation by gross revenues to determine a compensation ratio and concluded by comparison that the compensation to the partners in this case was slightly above median levels in 2007 but considerably below the median in 2008.

In determining whether the partners' services were appropriate in light of the compensation they received, the expert emphasized five factors:

1. The partners' contributions were vital to the success of the firm;
2. The partners had a combined 63 years of practice experience between them (45 years for the father and 18 for the son);
3. They both performed fundamental supervisory and managerial functions that were critical to the firm's profitability;
4. They both were responsible for developing the firm's business and client base; and
5. They were devoted full-time to the firm's success.

Based on his entire analysis, the expert concluded that the partners' services provided the law firm with a reasonably equivalent value in exchange for making the tax payments.

The trustee challenged these conclusions on several grounds. The expert's method was not subject to peer review or susceptible to a calculated error rate, the trustee said. Further, the expert could not reliably compare the debtor's small, Florida-focused, personal-injury practice to the Am Law survey, which looks at the 100 largest law firms in the country and depends on self-reported data.

The court disagreed, finding the expert "looked to a respected source to obtain baseline data for partner compensation in law firms." Even though the debtor was not among the "universe of firms" used to compile the Am Law survey, the expert had applied statistical analysis to relate the data to the debtor and presented his analysis in a "logical manner making all of his assumptions transparent." The trustee's objections went to the weight and not the admissibility of the expert's conclusions, and the court admitted his opinions on reasonably equivalent value.

Insolvency turns on contingent liability. Both the trustee and the government offered insolvency experts (but only the latter was subject to a pretrial *Daubert* motion). Based on the dates of the alleged fraudulent transfers and the timing of the partners' tax liabilities, both examined the debtor at two distinct points, April 2008 and September 2008, which they both agreed, as a practical matter, would provide representative snapshots of the debtor's net worth during the relevant time frame.

Predictably, the trustee's expert concluded the debtor law firm was insolvent on both dates and the government's expert concluded it was solvent. The disparity between the opinions turned entirely on their treatment of the state court litigation. Applying the GAAP standard for measuring contingent liabilities, the government's expert assigned it no value. The trustee's expert criticized this approach, claiming that it violated applicable precedent (11th Circuit), which precluded reliance on GAAP in fraudulent conveyance/bankruptcy cases.

The court agreed in part. The 11th Circuit has specifically addressed how to value contingent claims in cases such as this one by requiring bankruptcy courts to calculate their present value as "the expected cost of the liability times the estimated chance of it ever occurring." Unless either factor is equal to zero—that is, unless the liability is costless or the chances of it happening are negligible—the court should estimate the value of the contingent claim as "more than zero."

The government's expert explained his zero valuation of the contingent liability in this case by referring to the status of the state court litigation, which the law firm's attorneys had assured him (and the partners) would be overturned on appeal. Under GAAP, the expert said, a contingent liability is recorded only if: (1) a loss is probable; and (2) the amount of the loss "can be at least reasonably estimated." Even though the loss in this case might be quantifiable, its risk of occurring was only "reasonably probable," he said, which, under GAAP, meant something "more than remote but less than likely." Under these circumstances, the expert concluded that GAAP did not require recording any value related to the contingent claims.

However, for purposes of this bankruptcy proceeding, simply by admitting that a loss in the state court litigation was "reasonably possible," the expert had conceded the risk was "more than remote" or, to use the 11th Circuit's standard, "not negligible." Under this prevailing standard, the chance of the loss occurring was "not zero," the court held, and the expert was required to assign some value to the contingent liability. His failure to do so rendered his report irrelevant and inadmissible in this case.

Notably, the court did not agree with the trustee's sweeping argument that reliance on GAAP could never be appropriate in a fraudulent conveyance action. In those cases in which the likelihood of loss on a contingent claim is at least "probable," as GAAP uses that term, then GAAP would require the reporting of its value on a financial statement and this value might very well be relevant to a bankruptcy court's (and an expert's) insolvency analysis.

Professional standards in conflict with precedent, too. The government tried to argue that, because its expert was a CPA, he was bound to apply GAAP or would be subject to disqualification. Further, any objection to his application of the GAAP standard for valuing contingent claims went to the weight rather than admissibility of his opinion, and the jury should be allowed to compare the GAAP standard to the 11th Circuit's and make its own determination of value.

The government's argument "completely misses the mark," the court said. GAAP is the "industry standard" for purposes of preparing financial statements; the 11th Circuit precedent is the legal standard for valuing contingent claims in bankruptcy litigation. "An expert opinion based on a [professional] standard so completely at odds with the [law] is not a matter going to the weight of the evidence," the court said, and barred the government's insolvency expert from testifying at trial.

After losing this expert, the government claimed that the insolvency issue was still a matter of factual dispute, sufficient to preclude the trustee's motion for summary judgment at this stage of the proceedings. Indeed, the government intended to challenge the trustee's insolvency expert at trial, based on his methodology. In particular, the trustee's expert admitted that he'd never performed this type of analysis and had come into the case only after his colleague—the analyst who initially researched, prepared, and authorized the report—had lost his CPA license. At any rate, the government argued, the grant of summary judgment is inappropriate when the determination of critical factual issues turns solely on the proffered expert testimony.

In this instance, the court agreed. Although often helpful to a trier of fact, expert testimony is not required to make an insolvency determination, and thus, the government's loss of its expert did mean it had lost its case. The government should also still have an opportunity to challenge the trustee's expert at trial. For these reasons, the court declined to grant summary judgment on the trustee's insolvency claims or on its claims regarding reasonably equivalent value, for which the government's expert would still testify.

In re Bartomeli

Citation: 2004 Bankr. LEXIS 9
Date of Decision: January 5, 2004
Country: US
State or Federal: Federal
State/Jurisdiction: Connecticut
Court: United States Bankruptcy Court
Type of action: Bankruptcy
Judge: Weil
SIC: 1542 General Contractors - Nonresidential Buildings, Other than Industrial, Buildings and Warehouses
Key words: Bankruptcy, Book value, Fair market value (FMV)

Book Value in Financial Statements Not Materially False Though Company Has No Market Value

One issue in this bankruptcy case was whether the debtor misled the surety by listing book value of his construction business, Bartomeli Co., in unaudited financial statements. (Other assets and debts of the debtor as listed in the financial statements were also challenged by the surety.) Debtor listed the book value of the company as $267,520 on the financial statements submitted to the surety but then listed the market value of the company as "unknown" in his bankruptcy schedules. The surety argued that the schedules proved that the financial statements were "materially false." The court noted that book value and market value "are two different concepts." The fact that debtor could not determine market value as required in the bankruptcy schedules did not prove that his statement of book value in the financial statements was false. Accordingly, judgment was granted for debtor, and the debt owed to the surety was discharged.

In re Boston Generating

Citation: 2010 WL 4922578 (Bkrtcy. S.D.N.Y.)
Date of decision: Dec. 3, 2010
Country: US
State or Federal: Federal
State/Jurisdiction: New York
Court: United States Bankruptcy Court
Experts: Judah Rose (lenders)
Judge: Chapman

Bankruptcy Expert Claims DCF Indicates Market Value Better Than the Market

Over the last several years, low fuel prices, eroding demand, and a significant surplus of supply helped put Boston Generating—the third-largest fleet of power plants in New England—into $2 billion debt. Beginning in 2009, the company engaged in a restructuring process that eventually led to a heavily marketed sale for substantially all of its assets. In fact, the company signed an asset purchase agreement in August 2010 on one day and filed for bankruptcy protection for itself and its affiliates the next day.

Debtors were dying on the table? The debtors immediately sought authority to enforce the sale, which required court approval within 90 days. Based on the debtors' estimate, the net proceeds of the $1.1 billion cash transaction would pay nearly 99% of its secured first lien debt but none of its second lien or unsecured debt.

Not surprisingly, the second lien holders and unsecured creditors objected to the sale, claiming its terms did not satisfy Sec. 363 of the Bankruptcy Code (regarding preconfirmation sales). Specifically, well-established case law requires a court to consider several factors in relation to a Sec. 363 sale, including: (1) the proportionate value of the asset to the estate as a whole; and (2) the expected proceeds of a sale vis-à-vis an appraisal of the assets. In addition, the 2009 General Motors bankruptcy case suggests that courts consider whether the debtors can survive until confirmation, or was there a "material risk that, by deferring the sale, the patient will die on the operating table?" In this case, the value of the debtors' assets lay "at the very heart" of its determination, the bankruptcy court said.

The debtors pointed to several "data points" that indicated they were getting fair market value for their assets—primary among them the prepetition sale agreement, which represented the "highest and best offer after a robust, open, and fair process." An offer by the second runner-up also came very close to the winning $1.1 billion bid.

The second lien lenders offered the discounted cash flow (DCF) analysis by their expert, the managing director of an international energy consulting firm. Indeed, the court recognized him as a "leading expert on the energy industry generally and, in particular, on electric power." His valuation opinion was "detailed, thorough, and professional." The expert's DCF indicated the debtors' assets were worth $1.38 billion—or over a quarter of a billion dollars more than the proposed sale price.

Numerous critical assumptions underlay the expert's DCF analysis. For example, he estimated the discount rate using a capital asset pricing model (CAPM) with an implied weighted after-tax cost of capital of 10.4%. He also used the risk-free rate of return and estimated the nominal equity rate of return, the nominal debt rate of return, and debt-to-equity ratio. Other than the risk-free rate, which depended on U.S. Treasury prices, the remaining variables involved "substantial judgment," the court said, and "small changes in assumptions result in substantial differences in value."

The expert's DCF also used revenue projections that exceeded the debtors' own, particularly with respect to forecasted forward-capacity prices, which were currently low, reflecting low demand. Forward-capacity prices would not increase until demand increased and revenues equaled the cost of building a new plant, a point the lenders' expert referred to as the "equilibrium." He estimated that forward-capacity prices would increase from their current $3 per kilowatt month (with a corresponding 2011 projected EBITDA of $69 million) to approximately $16 per kilowatt month in 2018 (with a corresponding projected EBITDA of $283 million).

The key variable in determining the equilibrium was demand growth. The lenders' expert estimated that, for the years 2012-2014, demand would increase 2.8%. By comparison, federal industry regulators estimated demand would increase for the same period by only 1.2% to 1.6%. These "seemingly small differences cause multi-year shifts in the equilibrium date," the court pointed out. Shifting equilibrium by just one year, for example, changed the value of the debtors' assets by nearly $100 million.

The lenders' expert simply believed that the federal industry estimates were wrong because the regulators had historically underforecasted demand (and when their estimate proved incorrect, prices went even higher). By comparison, his forecasts had always been historically correct, he said. Increasingly onerous environmental regulation would also encourage the retirement of older polluting plants, including one owned by the debtors, resulting in decreased capacity, the expert said. Thus, a buyer of the debtors' assets will be able to influence market capacity and pricing.

Court believes the expert is wrong. In reviewing the expert's demand and price projections, the court found them too heavily contingent on a "wide range of factors, including regulatory reform, the timing of regulatory reform, demand for electricity (which is, in itself, contingent on broad economic factors), environmental regulation, retirement of competing plants, costs of plant operation, energy costs, construction costs, and other costs of new entry." His adjustments to these variables explained the quarter-billion-dollar gap between his DCF analysis and the debtors' proposed sale price. "Simply put," the court said, "[the expert] believes he is right and the market is wrong."

Case law and other authorities generally accept that—absent a clear showing of market failure—the behavior of the marketplace is the "best indicator of enterprise value," the court said. As the debtors' restructuring expert testified, "the market is very efficient ... as long as you go to a broad enough swathe of potential buyers, the market will tell you what the asset is worth."

The lenders' expert believed the market failure in this case came from its failure to understand or anticipate future regulatory changes. The sale occurred before market participants, especially the ultimate buyer, had time to properly consider pending regulatory reforms, he said. The debtors also failed to adequately disclose potential increased revenues due to the expedited reform process.

The court also disagreed with the expert on these critical points. The debtors provided all potential bidders with sufficient information regarding increased revenues that could result from anticipated reforms, and the sale participants were sophisticated and experienced investors in the industry. "Second, although armed with [their expert's] knowledge and expertise," the second lien lenders declined to participate in the sales process or top the winning bid, the court observed. Moreover, their expert's valuation was available during the sales negotiation, but the second lien lenders chose not to bring it forward until the "thirteenth hour," the court said, well after the bid deadline closed. The lenders "relentlessly complained" about the debtors' process, yet "it is worth noting how they chose to conduct themselves on this critical issue."

Finally—contrary to the expert's opinion—the court found there was no market failure in this case. The debtors' sale process involved "a multitude of steps, a bevy of professionals, and enormous amounts of information exchange and diligence, not to mention extensive litigation." Based on the entirety of the evidence, the court found that the market price, as represented by the sale transaction, was the best valuation of the debtors' assets. After consideration of additional factors, the court held that the transaction was consistent with the provisions of the Bankruptcy Code and 2nd Circuit precedent and authorized the sale.

Boyer v. Crown Stock Distribution, Inc.

Citation: 2009 WL 418275
Date of Decision: February 17, 2009
Country: US
State or Federal: Federal
State/Jurisdiction: Indiana
Court: United States District Court
Type of action: Bankruptcy
SIC: 3599 Industrial and Commercial Machinery and Equipment, NEC (other industrial and commercial machinery and equipment)

Valuation Evidence Helps Support Trustee's Successful Claims

Bankruptcy court voids $6 million paid for company as a fraudulent transfer, when valuation evidence shows it was worth no more than $4 million as a going concern at time of sale.

With annual net income of roughly $1.3 million at its peak in 1999, Crown Stock Distribution Inc. was a profitable company during the late 1990s. Just about this time—after his accountant reviewed the books and records and said its going concern value was worth between $2.3 million and $3 million—a buyer offered $2.4 million for the company.

Notably, the accountant questioned the company's viability at a purchase price greater than $6 million. In particular, the company lacked sufficient working capital to cover its $1.5 million liabilities.

Nevertheless, after his initial offer was rejected, the buyer agreed to purchase the company for $6 million, with $3.1 million down and a $2.9 million promissory note. He formed a holding company to acquire the assets and obtained appraisals of the company's real estate ($1.5 million) and its equipment ($406,000). He also agreed to assume its $1.5 million debt. However, the buyer did not receive a 1994 appraisal of the company at $1.2 million, which provided an annual 20% increase—and which would have roughly valued the company at $2.5 million the year prior to sale.

The deal closed in April 2000, with a bank financing the $3.1 million payment, secured by the company's assets, and minimal annual payments of $100,000 under the promissory note beginning a year later. The buyer tried to operate the company profitably, but, as his accountant predicted, its available capital could not service existing liabilities, including two payments on the note. By the third year, the company foundered and filed for bankruptcy. The trustee brought claims against the prior shareholders to recover the $3.1 million purchase price.

An attempt to characterize the sale as an LBO. The trustee first tried to persuade the court to treat the company's sale as a leveraged buyout (LBO). Although it was not a stock sale, the deal had common earmarks of an LBO; i.e., to make the purchase, the buyer received a loan, encumbering all the assets and delivering the proceeds directly to the shareholder/sellers. The court should collapse the entire transaction as if the lender transferred the funds directly to the selling shareholders, the trustee contended, which meant that the company received no value from the transaction, only new ownership.

The bankruptcy court rejected the theory, finding sufficient differences between the asset sale, which took place between two separate entities, and the typical LBO. Although the debtor ended up burdened with a "significant amount of debt," the court said, it also received some benefit from the transferred assets. Except for the primary owner/shareholder who negotiated the deal (and who knew about the prior appraisals), the court found no fraud on the part of the remaining shareholders. The company continued operations for nearly three years under its new ownership, including payments on the promissory note, and thus the court declined to collapse the sale and pull its value back into the bankruptcy estate.

The trustee pursued an alternative theory under the applicable fraudulent conveyance statutes, claiming that the debtor failed to receive "reasonably equivalent value" for its $6 million purchase of the company, when it was either insolvent or on the brink of financial failure. The defendants (sellers/former shareholders), tried to limit the trustee's proffered valuation evidence to his LBO "collapsing theory," but the court permitted its application to the fraudulent transfer claims.

In particular, the trustee stated before trial that it was presenting its valuation evidence to establish that the company was insolvent "on day one," that it was undercapitalized, and that the purchase price was too high. "The inadequacy of [the purchase price] is not the point of the valuation evidence," the trustee said. Instead, it would show that the sellers "gave nothing at all to the company" in exchange for the $6 million.

What the evidence showed. At trial, the trustee's valuation experts testified that, at the time of sale, the company's assets were worth only $3.25 million. (The appellate court opinion does not detail how the experts reached this conclusion, only that the bankruptcy court considered their "qualifications, background, experience, and expertise, as well as their valuation methods, the information they considered and had available to them, and the assumptions each expert made in formulating their respective opinions.") Based on this evidence, the bankruptcy court found that the fair market value of the company at the time it was sold "did not and could not have exceeded $4 million."

The defendants argued that the court should discount the $2.9 million promissory note from the purchase price because it was "essentially worthless," the debtor having received payments of only $200,000. The purchase price would have then been $3.3 million, well within the range of the company's value—but the court rejected this argument as well. The promissory note was an absolute as opposed to contingent liability, it said. The debtor booked it on its balance sheet and honored the obligation as long as it could. "The parties didn't discount the promissory note at the time of the transaction and the court shouldn't use hindsight to discount the note now."

Even if the debtor failed to receive reasonably equivalent value, the defendants argued that it was not insolvent at the time of the sale or holding such limited assets as to be "just short" of insolvency, especially since it continued to operate for nearly three years. However, the bankruptcy court refused to find the length of its post-sale operations determinative. The reason the debtor survived as long as it did "was through the financial equivalent of advanced life support," it said. Even though the new buyer may have had some impact on the company's demise, it was "doomed to failure."

In fact, the true cause of the debtor's financial distress was not what happened after the sale, but "the excessive purchase price paid to acquire the business" and its associated debt. Given the seller's access to the independent appraisal valuing the company at $2.5 million and his knowledge that the buyer would need sizeable financing, "there was no justification" for the $6 million purchase price.

Upon review of all the evidence, including the expert valuations, the bankruptcy court found that the debtor received less than reasonably equivalent value, and it voided the transfer as fraudulent. On review, the U.S. District Court (N.D. Indiana) affirmed the decision in all respects.

In re Capmark Financial Group

Citation: 2010 WL 4313046 (Bkrtcy. D. Del.)
Date of decision: Nov. 1, 2010
Country: US
State or Federal: Federal
State/Jurisdiction: Delaware
Court: United States Bankruptcy Court
Type of action: Bankruptcy
Experts: Dr. Timothy Luerhman and Edwin Litolff (debtors); Bradley Geer (creditors committee)
Judge: Sontchi

Valuing Director Guaranties in Bankruptcy: Using a Put Option Approach

Not many court opinions address the valuation of insider guaranties to secure company financing. One of the more interesting cases concerned an expert who valued director and shareholder guaranties by comparing them to the risks borne by an equity investor. In two successive decisions, the U.S. District Court (Maine) held that, although the expert applied reliable methodologies to value the guaranties by reference to the company's cost of equity, he failed to cite sufficient authority to support this approach, and the court struck the expert's evidence under *Daubert*. (The district court's initial opinion and its decision on reconsideration are available in *Baldwin v. Bader*.)

Billion-dollar bankruptcy settlement. Unlike the *Baldwin* court, which considered the value of insider guaranties in the context of dissenting shareholder claims, the federal bankruptcy court's main focus in *Capmark Financial* was whether a proposed plan of reorganization for the large commercial lender was financially feasible and fair. Basically, the proposed settlement would cash out 91% of a $1.5 billion loan from Capmark's secured lenders (including Goldman Sachs), which was made just 120 days before bankruptcy. In return, the lenders would release their liens on the underlying collateral, valued at $1.3 billion to $1.5 billion, according to the debtors, saving the estate over $300 million. In exchange for the lenders giving up 9% of their secured claim, the debtors also promised not to attack the loan as a fraudulent transfer.

The Official Committee of Unsecured Creditors objected to the proposal, claiming bankruptcy law does not permit preconfirmation payment of a secured claim from unencumbered cash, outside of the lenders' collateral. The committee also said the collateral "was not worth anywhere near" the asserted $1.3 billion to $1.5 billion, and the potential litigation against the lenders was valid and valuable.

In a 93-page opinion, the bankruptcy court focused on whether the value of the collateral left behind by the lenders equaled or exceeded the proposed cash payment. To do so, it examined three key transactions:

1. *2006 acquisition.* In March 2006, a group of four private equity investors acquired a controlling (78%) interest in the debtors from their parent company (GMAC) for $1.5 billion. As part of the transaction, the debtors also borrowed over $8.35 billion, secured by guaranties from nine of their subsidiaries.

2. *2007 offering*. Just over a year later, the debtors issued $2.55 billion in senior unsecured notes to investors, using the proceeds to pay off various obligations. Once again, the financing was secured by subsidiary guaranties.

3. *2009 restructuring*. As a result of the 2008 market turmoil, the debtors sought a "holistic restructuring" of their balance sheet. After months of "hard-fought" negotiations, they executed the $1.5 billion secured credit facility with their lenders, secured by their North American assets and guaranteed by subsidiaries.

After several months of difficult negotiations with their secured and unsecured lenders, however, the debtors filed for bankruptcy in October 2009, believing they could achieve restructuring only within the umbrella of Chapter 11 protections.

Expert's solvency opinions are key. To determine the fairness and feasibility of the proposed settlement in light of the committee's objections, the court considered evidence from the debtors' expert, a Harvard Business School professor with over 20 years' experience in business valuation and corporate finance.

The debtors' expert concluded that, at the times of the 2006 and 2007 transactions, the debtors and their subsidiaries were solvent, adequately capitalized, and able to pay their debts as they matured. Moreover, the debtors could have sold most or all of their assets to satisfy their own as well as the subsidiaries' liabilities. The expert's conclusions "were not close calls," he said.

Immediately following the 2009 refinancing, however, both the debtors and their subsidiaries were insolvent, the expert said. To confirm these conclusions, the expert used a discounted cash flow (DCF) analysis as well as a market approach (comparable companies) and an adjusted balance sheet approach. He also took "great pains to use conservative assumptions throughout his analysis and performed stress testing to ensure that his conclusions were correct and not biased," the court observed.

For example, as one cross-check of solvency, the debtors' expert evaluated the 2006 transaction and the related subsidiary guaranties. He likened the guaranties to put options and used standard option pricing models to reach a conservative estimate of value. This approach was consistent with the "majority practice in corporate finance courses," the expert said. It also coincided with FASB's Interpretation 45 (FIN 45), which requires listing guaranties on the balance sheet at their fair value at inception. The basic principle is that the beneficiary of the guaranty has the right to put the debt to the guarantor for the face value of the debt, even or especially if the value of the underlying assets declines below the stated debt. "And so that's exactly analogous to a put option," the expert explained.

Under this approach, he estimated the debtors would have to pay approximately $878 million to replace the guaranties with a put option at the time of the 2006 transaction, which was higher than the fair value of the guaranties. One reason for the higher replacement cost: the guaranteed debt allowed for additional financing advances. The guaranties were also contingent claims, and so it was appropriate to take into account various offsets to their face amount, the expert said. Finally, the debtors' collective assets amounted to roughly $1.37 billion, or more than enough to cover the guaranties. Even so, the expert also used "extra high" volatility estimates and average "tenure" estimates to make sure he reached a higher range of value for the guaranties.

In an interesting aside, the creditors' committee cross-examined the debtors' expert, seeking to demonstrate that, by using higher volatility figures, he reached a higher value for the replacement put option. But asset volatility is not readily ascertainable from capital market data, the expert responded. He used equity volatility measures, deriving an estimate that was even higher than the debtors' equity volatility expectations as of 2006. The court found this testimony logical and credible, sufficient to overcome the committee's objections and support the expert's solvency conclusions regarding the 2006 transaction.

Creditors' experts not as critical. In connection with the 2009 transaction, the creditors committee called an expert to testify that the debtors "did not receive anywhere near" equivalent value for the $1.5 billion security interest granted to the lenders. Further, the transaction reduced the unsecured creditors' recovery from 44.4% of their claims to 33%. The court found the expert credible but very limited in utility.

By contrast, the court considered testimony from the debtors' chief risk officer regarding the value of the assets granted as collateral in the 2009 transaction, which, under the proposed settlement, would revert to the debtors in exchange for the $1.1 billion cash payment to lenders. The pledged pool consisted of 127 distressed or nonperforming mortgage loans plus foreclosed real estate. Nevertheless, the pledged pool should result in recovery of $1.48 billion to $1.6 billion over the next three years, according to the debtors' CRO, based on historic recoveries, the debtors' projected recoveries, and asset-by-asset analyses, including strategies to monetize each asset and anticipated resolution date. As a result, the pledged pool exceeded the outstanding balance of the 2009 credit facility by $500 million and the proposed cash settlement by $625 million, the court found.

Interestingly, the debtors presented a real estate and restructuring expert from a national firm to perform an independent valuation of the pledged assets. Using the debtors' information and typical valuation methodologies for promissory notes secured by real estate, including the DCF and comparable transactions method, the debtors' independent expert found the outstanding balance of the secured credit was $1.10 billion as of October 2010—or roughly equal to the proposed cash settlement. The court found this evidence to have limited utility, however, based on three key points:

- First, instead of adopting the debtors' 12 risk ratings to the various asset classes, the debtors' independent expert applied a three-tiered system based on nominally different risk profiles and three separate discount rates.
- Second, the expert applied the discount rates to a different (and higher) unpaid principal balance than the one used by the debtors. Cross-examination revealed "material, unexplained discrepancies" between the portfolio that the expert used and the "real" pledged asset pool, in terms of both absolute asset size and quality, the court said. Importantly, the independent expert "did nothing to educate himself about [the debtors'] classification system ... and did not put any weight" on it during the valuation. He also moved 20 loans

characterized as nonperforming by the debtors to performing, thereby creating a portfolio "very distant from the reality of [the debtors'] loans," the court said.

- Third, the comparable transactions chosen by the debtors' independent expert were not particularly comparable to the loans in the pledged pool, and, in fact, many were of much higher quality. The expert also failed to consider and adjust for other significant differences, such as the weighted average life of the comparable loans, which was significantly longer than those in the debtors' pledged pool.

Further, the expert "misunderstood" the role of an expert witness, the court noted. He testified that it wasn't necessary to show all of the work performed to reach his conclusion but only his experience and credentials. Due to these "significant" problems, the court considered the evidence from the debtors' independent expert only as a "backup" or "stress tests" to the more credible testimony from the debtors' CRO.

Settlement tests the limits of bankruptcy law. The court conceded that the proposed settlement "certainly tests the limits of the authority to pay prepetition secured claims outside a plan." Nonetheless, the proposed plan did not violate the Bankruptcy Code, primarily because the value of the debtors' remaining collateral was "well in excess" of the cash pay-out to the secured lenders. The court also found the unsecured creditors were not harmed in any way by the settlement. "Indeed, just the opposite," the court said, and approved the plan as reasonable and fair.

In re Certified HR Service Co.

Citation: Sept. 25, 2012
Date of decision: 2012 U.S. Dist. LEXIS 136956
Country: US
State or Federal: Federal
State/Jurisdiction: Florida
Court: United States District Court
Type of action: Bankruptcy
Experts: Lawrence D. Morriss Jr. (trustee)
Judge: Marra

Expert Valuation More Credible and Critical Than Contemporaneous Market and Management Values

The debtor was a Florida-based company that processed payroll and other employee benefits, including workers' compensation claims, for small to midsized businesses. According to its filings with the SEC, the debtor's controlling shareholder was a Kentucky-based management company, which purportedly serviced the debtor's workers' compensation business pursuant to an exclusive risk management agreement.

Unscrupulous debtor acquires like company. As it turned out, the parent company had no daily operations, and the debtor's principals had set up their wives as executives and owners. From 2002 until early 2005, the principals also caused the debtor to transfer more than $130 million in cash to its parent, which left the debtor without any significant assets but with continuing contractual liability for all workers' compensation claims. When customers' payroll payments came in, instead of paying its outstanding workers' comp or other liabilities, the debtor would use the cash to fund new acquisitions or to pay off its parent, in what the trustee would later describe as a "Ponzi-like" scheme "because new entrance money was being used to pay old obligations, or no obligations at all: it was just being stolen."

In the meantime, the debtor looked to acquire a group of professional services companies held by America's PEO Holdings Inc. (APEO). Half of the company (50%) was in the hands of the president's wife, who was also the nominal CEO but had no substantive role in operations. The remaining shares were split between the CFO (30%) and another individual (20%). The parties eventually agreed to a purchase price of $17.5 million for APEO, including $1.1 million in cash and the remainder in promissory notes and stock. They closed the deal in November 2001.

Less than four years later, the debtor failed to pay more than $2.7 million in workers' compensation claims and filed for Chapter 11 bankruptcy. The trustee sought to avoid all of its transfers to its parent company as well as the APEO acquisition, particularly the $1.1 million cash payment to the president and his wife (the APEO defendants). To recover these amounts under federal bankruptcy as well as state law (Florida), the trustee needed to show the debtor was insolvent at the time of the $17.5 million purchase and in return received less than reasonably equivalent value from the defendants.

Only the trustee engages independent expert. To support his claims against the APEO defendants at trial, the trustee offered an independent valuation expert, who found the debtor was insolvent at all times during its operations. After transferring virtually all of its cash to its parent holding company, neither the debtor nor its parent retained sufficient assets to cover the outstanding workers' compensation liabilities.

Notably, the APEO defendants did not retain an expert to offer a solvency opinion regarding the debtor. Instead, both the president and CFO testified the debtor was "profitable" in the year following the acquisition (2002) and pointed to the company's form 10-K filed with the SEC. They also presented company financial statements from 2001 through 2003 that showed profits; in particular, they said the APEO acquisition reaped "synergistic values" for both parties, permitting the debtor to generate profits from acquiring the target's client base and helping the target by "fixing" its benefits liabilities.

However, further evidence from the trustee and its expert showed that the debtor simply "excised" its liabilities from its financial statements. In light of these facts, as well as the "Ponzi-like" scheme that had dominated the debtor's operations since its inception, the federal bankruptcy court adopted the insolvency findings by the trustee's expert. After further application of law, it permitted the trustee to avoid all of the debtor's transfers to the parent company.

As for the transfers to APEO, the expert applied the three traditional methodologies (income, asset, and market) to determine whether the target company had any value at the time of sale. Essentially, all three approaches "are trying to corroborate a value that is based on cash," he said, and, with APEO, neither its assets nor its earnings generated any cash flows for the business in 2000 or 2001. He also noted these specific points about the company:

1. Although it grew rapidly, managing gross payroll in excess of $20 million in its first year to over $113 million by 2001, the company's expenses grew at an even greater rate during the same time, resulting in negative earnings before taxes (EBIT), which led to its sale to the debtor;

2. In 2000, a major client had gone bankrupt, but the company was still liable for the client's $1 million in COBRA claims;

3. Banks declined to lend the company any money, citing insufficient collateral; and

4. By the time of the acquisition, the company had little business, and its equity shares were trading at $0.03 per share. Its year-end 2000 audited financials show liabilities exceeding assets by more than $1.9 million, indicating the company was insolvent.

"So when your assets are cash flowing," the trustee's expert testified, "when your earnings aren't cash flowing, and when your multiples in the market don't have a cash multiple, it's a negative value, or in the parlance for generally accepted valuation, it's a zero value."

In response, both the president and the CFO testified that the sale of APEO arose from arm's-length negotiations, assisted by attorneys. Further, the president testified that the parties relied on the following valuations to set the purchase price:

- An independent "strategic" appraisal that valued the target at $10 million;

- Comparable acquisitions that valued similar companies at $3,000 per serviced employee, which would have made APEO worth $30 million;

- A six-times multiple of EBITDA—the standard multiple in the industry—which would have made APEO worth nearly $18 million; and

- An offer from a third party to buy the company for $2 million.

The CFO testified that he believed the company to be worth at least $10 million at the time of the acquisition.

Notably, although the defendants relied on the "strategic" appraisal, they did not offer any of its authors as testifying experts. Neither did the appraisal explain why it omitted the target's $1.9 million in losses incurred in the year prior to sale. The president once again said "synergies" explained the omission in the appraisal as well as the year-end financials. Since the acquisition was going to "fix" the target's failing operations by eliminating the COBRA and other liabilities, its financial statements reflected value from a "marketing" standpoint. That is, "if somebody came along and helped us cure this problem" by purchasing the company, he said, then "this is what they would be left with."

Ipse dixit of insiders. After reviewing all of the defendant's evidence, the bankruptcy court noted there was no corroboration for the alleged third-party offer. The "strategic" appraisal served only as a business record; without any foundation for its authorship, it could not provide any reliable or credible evidence of APEO's value at the time of sale, particularly since it "ignored" the company's more than $1.9 million in claims-related losses. Similarly, the CFO offered no evidence to support his $10 million value for the company, and neither he nor the president had any "professional training or experience as a business valuation appraiser," the court noted.

Further, the president produced no support for the "synergistic values" the debtor would have received from its $17.5 million purchase. The target's COBRA and other liabilities were "real" claims that would have required "actual payment" in some form and at some cost to the debtor, the court said. Even if the alleged synergies of the acquisition could serve as some "yardstick" to measure reasonably equivalent value, the court lacked any reliable evidence to make such a measurement or calculate such a value.

In fact, none of the defendant's testimony was sufficient to rebut the "credible testimony" of the trustee's expert that APEO was essentially worthless at the time of sale. Its assets were not generating enough cash to support the business, the court found, and its year-end financials showed an excess of nearly $2 million in liabilities over assets. Moreover, according to the expert's testimony:

> APEO's actual negative EBIT and the projection of negative cash flow in 2001 are reasonable evidence that the value of APEO's assets would not satisfy its obligations, such as its trade and interest-bearing debts.

Accordingly, the best reasonable estimate of the value of APEO's assets at the time of sale was zero, the court found, and voided the sale as well as all of the cash transfers to the defendants.

Appeal also commends sole expert. The defendants appealed the bankruptcy court's decision to the federal district court (S.D. Fla.). Although they presented seven disputed issues, all were "variations of the same," the court said, namely, whether APEO had any value when the debtor purchased it for $17.5 million in 2001.

For instance, the appellants argued that the bankruptcy court gave "no weight" to either the testimony by APEO's managers or the strategic appraisal. They also reasserted the "arm's-length" nature of the transaction and its "synergistic" values.

In so doing, however, the appellants "simply seek to substitute their judgment" for that of the bankruptcy court, which undertook a "detailed analysis" of the evidence before coming to its conclusions, the district court said. Specifically, in reviewing that analysis, it affirmed that the strategic analysis lacked any foundation as evidence of value. Neither the APEO president nor its CFO had any valuation training or experience, and their explanations of "synergistic values" lacked credibility. In fact, given the target's clear financial troubles, only the debtor—with its Ponzi-like operations and "other questionable business practices"—could have possibly benefited from buying and operating APEO, the court said.

Finally, just because the parties went through all the "normal formalities" of negotiating and documenting their deal did not "constitute competent and credible evidence that APEO had value at the time to any but an unscrupulous company like [the] debtor," the district court said. The only competent evidence of value came from the "detailed" report by the trustee's expert, who outlined several salient points to support his arrival at a zero value for APEO. The bankruptcy court acted well within its discretion to accept the expert's report, and the court affirmed its findings as well as its avoidance of all transfers by the insolvent debtor.

In re Chemtura Corp. (I)

Citation: 2010 WL 4272727 (Bkrtcy. S.D. NY.)
Date of decision: Oct. 29, 2010
Country: US
State or Federal: Federal
State/Jurisdiction: New York
Court: United States Bankruptcy Court
Type of action: Bankruptcy
Experts: Lazard Freres (debtors); UBS (equity committee); and Houlihan, Lokey, Howard & Zukin (creditors committee)
Judge: Gerber

More Support for Using More Than One Method (DCF) in Current Valuations

The Chemtura Corp., a specialty chemical maker and its affiliates, filed for bankruptcy in March 2009—becoming the third major U.S. chemical manufacturer to succumb to the recession. A year later, the debtors proposed a plan of reorganization and settlement of claims. No creditors objected except the equity shareholders, who claimed it substantially undervalued the company.

The bankruptcy court held an independent valuation hearing, in which both the equity committee and the debtors presented expert evidence of total enterprise value (TEV), and the creditors presented a rebuttal expert to critique their approaches. The debtors' expert valued the company from $1.9 billion to $2.2 billion, with a midpoint at $2.05 billion, and the shareholders' expert concluded a range of TEV from $2.3 billion to $2.6 billion, with a midpoint at $2.45 billion. All the experts were from large investment banking firms, which played various advisory roles during the restructuring. In a 78-page opinion, the court discusses each expert's approach, their assumptions as well as their possible bias, to determine whether the debtors' TEV exceeded the value underpinning the proposed reorganization plan.

Adjustments to DCF for aggressive forecasts. To reach their respective total enterprise values, both the shareholders' and the debtors' experts used a discounted cash flow (DCF) analysis, with a similar range of discount rates, from 11.6% to 13.75%. Both relied on forecasts from the debtors' long-range plan (LRP), which assumed the national economy would recover to precrisis levels by 2011 and the company's earnings would grow during all five years of the forecast period. In their terminal value calculations, however, the experts differed significantly in selecting the earnings to which their multiples applied.

The shareholders' expert applied its multiples to the earnings for the final forecast year, to reach a DCF value between $2.47 billion and $2.9 billion. By contrast, the debtors' expert applied multiples of 6.5x to 7.5x from peer group averages and midcycle and normalized EBITDA to reach a TEV of $2.175 billion to $2.57 billion. The experts debated the extent of the debtors' cyclicality, with the shareholders' expert claiming that normalized earnings drove the present value down and the debtors' expert saying the final year forecasted EBITDA—which exceeded all historic levels—led to a significantly overstated value. The creditors' rebuttal expert agreed, believing the long-range forecasts were "overly" aggressive, based on unsupported assumptions of short-term economic growth, and requiring appropriate risk adjustments.

The court shared this skepticism regarding the company's and the country's growth. Although it might be more common to use final-year cash flow projections to calculate terminal value, it said, in this case, the slow economic recovery plus the cyclical nature of the debtors' business (or, at least, the seasonality of its customers for agricultural and pool chemicals) supported the use of adjusted cash flows. "Taking the business cycle into account makes for a better analysis," the court added, quoting Prof. Aswath Damodaran (NYU Stern School of Business) (*Ups and Downs: Valuing Cyclical and Commodity Companies*, 2009 ed.).

At the same time, the best normalization analysis would capture an entire business cycle—which the debtors' expert did not do, the court pointed out. Despite this flaw, it found the debtors' DCF analysis to be, on balance, more persuasive. If the economy were more stable, then it might consider the use of the final year's cash flows to be "perfectly ordinary, if not preferred." In the current economy, however, "relying on the very high terminal value in the last year of an admittedly aggressive string of growth projections is ... too aggressive," the court said. In addition, it was "troubled" that the shareholders' expert made no effort to "address cyclicality at all."

Market approach provides more than just a reality check. The court was also troubled that, unlike the debtors' expert, the shareholders' expert did not conduct a comprehensive analysis of comparable companies and comparable transactions to provide an independent value indicator but simply used the market approach merely to test the reasonableness of its DCF.

"That's disappointing," the court said, especially as it found the comparable companies analysis to be more meaningful in this case than either the DCF approach, which is generally susceptible to uncertain projections, or the comparable transactions approach, which can be subject to control premiums, synergies, bidding wars, and hostile deals. For these reasons, the court assigned the comparable companies approach the greatest overall weight in the case. In particular, it found the debtors' analysis had "substantial" weight, based on the following:

1. The debtors' expert examined 10 domestic comparables and five foreign because the latter operated in the same global markets as the debtors and were subject to similar tax and regulatory environments. In addition, 50% of the debtors' revenues came from foreign markets. Yet, despite including foreign comparables in his "sum of the parts" and comparable transactions analysis, the shareholders' expert left them out, here, further undercutting his criticism of the pool selected by the debtors' expert.

2. The shareholders' expert included two large multinational chemical corporations in his pool but excluded a smaller specialty chemical company, which effectively inflated the overall multiples. The debtors' expert excluded the large multinationals because their sales, earnings, and enterprise values "dwarfed" the debtors', but he included the smaller specialty company, which was more similar to the debtors in its size, product lines, and end markets.

3. Both experts conducted a "sum-of-the-parts" analysis, but the debtors' expert used the 2010 actual and projected numbers to derive its multiples and the shareholders' expert used the more reliable multiples derived from 2011 earnings forecasts.

In addition, both experts applied the comparable transactions approach. The debtors' expert reviewed 14 deals conducted between 2004 and 2010, worth between $1 billion and $10 billion. Given the material adversity caused by the global economic and capital markets crisis, however, the debtors' expert ultimately relied on only three transactions occurring after September 2008 (when Lehman Bros. collapsed). Using their mean EBITDA multiple of 6.2x as a midpoint, the expert determined the debtors' appropriate multiple range was 5.75x to 6.75x and applied this to Sept. 30, 2010, EBITDA to arrive at a range of TEV from $1.97 billion to $2.315 billion.

The shareholders' expert examined 19 deals, which all closed prior to September 2010 with a much wider range of value, from $290 million to $18.66 billion, and a mean EBITDA multiple of 9.7x. But he did not calculate a TEV range from these multiples; instead, he took its estimated TEV range for the debtors to back out EBITDA multiples of 6.9x and 7.9x. Since these back-calculated multiples were less than the 9.7x multiple for the comparable transactions, the shareholders' expert concluded his TEV estimates did not exceed the debtors' actual value.

Overall, the court found the shareholders' expert's heavy reliance on pre-Lehman transactions "was a serious flaw." Advanced economies are "fundamentally different today," the court observed, and "relying on multiples from a time period before the crash is inappropriate." It also found flaws with the comparables selected by the debtors' expert, noting that it included one with "dubious comparability" but omitted another that plainly should have been considered. However, with two post-Lehman comparables registering a 6.2x earnings multiple in the wake of the financial crisis, the court felt relatively comfortable in giving some weight to this methodology, especially since the upper end of the debtors' transaction analysis was still well below the shareholders' range of value under the DCF.

Market pricing and possible bias. If the court had to find a specific value for the debtors, it would have chosen an amount at the low end of the debtors' range, it said. But to confirm the proposed reorganization plan as fair and reasonable, it needed only to find that the debtors' TEV did not exceed the TEV underlying the plan, or $2.05 billion.

Based on all the expert evidence and analysis, "I so find," the court said. Market information also supported its decision. During its restructuring attempts, the debtors cooperated with the equity committee in trying to find a buyer for the company, contacting nearly 20 potential investors using the committee's $2.2 billion-to-$2.7 billion range of value. "But there were no takers, or offers, at that price or at any price that might ultimately lead" to such a value, the court said. Nor were any members of the equity committee—mostly hedge funds—willing to invest their own money into the debtors at that or even a lower price.

Moreover, under the proposed plan, the overwhelming majority of creditors and bondholders elected to take their recovery in cash rather than company stock. Once again, these stakeholders were highly sophisticated hedge funds and other "distressed debt" investors with the ability to dispose of stock. If they thought the plan undervalued the company, they would have "snapped up" the stock at the price offered by the equity committee, the court said. If they believed the valuation offered by the committee's expert, "they *really* would have snapped it up," it added, with emphasis. Their failure to do so and their preference for cash suggested they didn't believe the stock was worth as much as the shareholders contended.

The court also found "exceptional" instances of witness bias in this case. The opinions of all the experts were influenced to some extent by their prior activities with the debtor, the circumstances under which they testified, and inconsistent testimony. In particular, the equity committee's expert indicated a strong bias. To secure the engagement, he promised to be "aggressive in valuation" and to achieve "maximum value for the equity." The terms of his engagement agreement provided, in addition to a monthly fee, a hefty "transaction fee" that turned on his ultimate valuation of TEV.

Similarly, both the debtors' expert and the creditors' experts received million-dollar fees upon the consummation of a plan. Although these fee provisions are fairly common ways to incentivize the investment bankers—and, in this case, the court authorized their payment—the court couldn't ignore the fees when the same bankers testified, finding the payment terms "materially" and "adversely" affected the experts' credibility.

"Finally, failures by both [the debtors'] and [the shareholders' expert] to change the midpoint of their valuations after the passage of time and in the face of seemingly different circumstances tend to undercut the persuasiveness of each," the court held. For example, in June 2010, the shareholders' expert valued the debtors within the range of $2.2 billion to $2.7 billion, with a midpoint of $2.45 billion. Three months later, it issued its trial valuation opinion within a narrower range—$2.3 billion to $2.6 billion—but with the precise same midpoint. The debtors' expert likewise issued two separate valuations with the exact same midpoint, despite the company having achieved solid earnings in the interim coupled with the easing of uncertainty in national and global markets.

In both cases, the court found the coincidences were improbable, prompting it to be more "proactive in making [its] own valuation judgment rather than to accept [any] of the proffered ones." As a final matter, in addition to finding the proposed reorganization plan fair and reasonable, the court declined to disband the equity committee, leaving it intact to appeal this decision, if need be. Stay tuned …

In re Chemtura Corp. (II)

Citation: 2011 WL 1496327 (Bkrtcy. S.D.N.Y)
Date of decision: April 19, 2011
Country: US
State or Federal: Federal
State/Jurisdiction: Federal Circuit
Court: United States Bankruptcy Court
Experts: Unnamed
Judge: Gerber

Valuing Two Tough Aspects of Damages: Pricing and Discount Rate

Last year, the federal bankruptcy court approved the debtors' proposed reorganization plan of its billion-dollar chemical business. A few contested matters remained, including a $16.3 million claim against the debtors based on breach of contract to provide industrial heat and steam for chemical production.

Claims are barred. After an exhaustive review of the facts and applicable law, the bankruptcy court held that the plaintiff's claims were barred by the statute of limitations as well as a prior settlement and release. Given the "small" chance of reversal on appeal, however, the court needed to set aside a reserve based on an estimated value of the plaintiff's claims. In addition, the court ruled on two damages issues that would most certainly arise if an appellate court upheld the plaintiff's claims:

1. *Spot pricing vs. future pricing.* In assessing the fuel-costs component of the plaintiff's damages claim, the debtors' expert used the "spot market" price for natural gas as of the time of the bankruptcy filing, which he then held constant for all calculations from 2010 through 2016 (the end of the contract term). Spot prices were more appropriate, the debtors claimed, because they are more fixed and certain than future pricing, which are far more susceptible to market movements. In addition, contract law required the damages to be assessed as of the petition date. Using spot prices held the plaintiff's claims to no more than $7 million, the debtors concluded.

In his calculations, the plaintiff's expert used the pricing of future contracts for delivery of natural gas in the region (California/Nevada) available as of the petition date and through the contract term. Further, he used a different future price for each point at which a heat/steam installment was due under the contract. Using the futures market "generally reflects the … pricing at which a rational counterparty would be willing to sell natural gas to [the plaintiff] for future deliveries," the plaintiff's expert said, and the court agreed with this rationale.

"While it's true that the price of a futures contact is ultimately based on prediction, the future price captures the views of willing buyers and sellers in the marketplace as to what fuel prices likely will be in the future, at times which are relevant," the court held. In contrast, the use of spot pricing does not incorporate market participant views or any pricing predictions.

Moreover, future pricing was preferable in this case because: (1) the installment contract clearly revealed the particular dates for purchasing (and pricing) fuel; and (2) the future prices corresponded more closely to how much the plaintiff would have had to pay to "cover" the alleged cost of a contract breach, which was ultimately what any damages model should accomplish. Finally, although the debtors correctly stated that damages should be calculated as of the petition date, "this merely requires" selecting future prices on that date, the court explained, which was "precisely" what the plaintiff's expert did.

2. *Discount rate.* Not surprisingly, the plaintiff argued for applying the risk-free rate to discount future contract payments to their present value. Its expert used the "Ask Yield" rate for U.S. Treasury bills of corresponding maturities, producing a very low range of 0.048% to 2.9% for risk-free proxies. In particular, when asked why he chose the risk-free rate, the expert indicated that he was instructed to do so by plaintiff's counsel.

The debtors claimed that the risk-free rate failed to account for the specific risk factors accompanying the contract. Accordingly, their expert used the debtors' weighted average cost of capital (WACC), which captured the risk that the company might not be able to perform—a factor that any potential buyer of the contract's cash flow streams would consider. He proposed a discount rate of 11.75%, which represented the low end of the debtors' cost of capital and came from their trial expert on reorganization.

A 'Goldilocks' problem. The court agreed that a risk-free rate was too low—but it also found the debtors' proposed rate was "much too high." The debtors' WACC dealt with the company "as it had evolved," up and through bankruptcy, "and incorporated all of the risks that might affect the value of the company," the court noted. But only a "subset of those risks" would have affected the company when it originally entered the contract (via a predecessor) in 1991.

Instead, "case law and common sense" dictate a different result, the court said. In particular, it relied on *Teachers Ins. & Annuity Ass'n of America v. Ormesa Geothermal*, 791 F.Supp 401 (S.D.N.Y. 1991)—a case that neither party cited but the court found through its own research. There, the prevailing plaintiff argued for the risk-free rate ("as prevailing plaintiffs usually do," the bankruptcy court quipped), but the federal district court rejected that contention. From an economic standpoint, "the more appropriate choice is for the discount rate to reflect the same … risk as the alternate investment" that the plaintiff would have made, with an alternate obligor, "with similar [investment] characteristics," the *Ormesa* court held. Moreover, the cases cited by the debtor for applying the risk-free rate did not discuss *Ormesa,* leading the bankruptcy court to conclude that its sound economic analysis was similarly overlooked.

Accordingly, the court rejected both parties' proposals, ruling that the discount rate "must … correspond to the risk of nonperformance" at the time the parties originally entered the contract. Since neither party had offered this evidence, the court ordered them to "attempt to" agree on a discount rate, based on its ruling as well the principles set forth in *Ormesa* and other precedent. If they fail, "they can always come back to me," the court added, leaving the door ajar for more findings on the all-important discount rate in damages actions.

In re Chrysler LLC

Citation: 2009 WL 1507547 (Bkrtcy. S.D.N.Y.)
Date of Decision: May 31, 2009
Country: US
State or Federal: Federal
State/Jurisdiction: New York
Court: United States Bankruptcy Court
Type of action: Bankruptcy
Judge: Gonzalez
SIC: 3711 Motor Vehicles and Passenger Car Bodies (automobiles)

Fair Value at Crux of Chrysler Bankruptcy

When Chrysler, one of the world's largest automobile manufacturers and distributors, collapsed, the news was eclipsed only by the speed with which the U.S. Bankruptcy Court for the Southern District of New York considered a proposed sale of the debtors' assets. Much of the sale had been negotiated prior to filing the petition, but, within a month after seeking Chapter 11 protection, Chrysler and its affiliates agreed with Fiat, S.p.A. to these main terms:

- Chrysler would transfer most of its assets to an alliance entity (New Chrysler) in exchange for $2 billion cash and the assumption of certain liabilities;
- Fiat would contribute access to fuel-efficient technologies, global marketing and distribution networks, and substantial cost savings; and
- New Chrysler would issue membership interests, including 8% to the U.S. Treasury, 20% to Fiat (with the right to acquire an additional 31%); and 55% to an employees association (in a deal hammered out with union retirees).

The debtor also secured $4.96 billion in 60-day financing from the U.S. government with a promise of an additional $6 billion in senior secured financing to support New Chrysler's operations.

The sale would remit only 29 cents on the dollar. Certain secured creditors objected to the sale, claiming that it would strip and transfer their collateral for only 29 cents on the dollar to New Chrysler, to which it would be worth significantly more. In a three-day hearing, the court considered the proposed deal pursuant to Sec. 363(b) of the Bankruptcy Code, which authorizes the debtor to sell a major asset "out of the ordinary course of business and prior to acceptance and outside of any plan of reorganization." Applicable case law requires "a good business reason" to grant the sale and provides a nonexclusive list for courts to consider in making a 363(b) determination. Several factors turn directly on findings of value:

- The proportionate value of the asset to the estate as a whole;
- The amount of time elapsed since the filing of the Chapter 11 petition;
- The likelihood that a plan of reorganization will be confirmed in the near future;

- The effect of the proposed disposition on future reorganization plans;
- The proceeds from the sale vis-à-vis any appraisals of the property; and
- Any proposed alternatives of use, sale, or lease.

"And the factor which [is] most important," the court added, "whether the asset is increasing or decreasing in value."

Here, the debtors established a good business reason for the sale to go through, even during the early stages of its proceedings. "Notwithstanding the highly publicized and extensive efforts that have been expended in the last two years to see various alliances for Chrysler, the Fiat transaction is the only option that is currently viable," the court said. The only other alternative would be the immediate liquidation of the company.

"Further, the whole enterprise may be worth more than the sum of its parts" because of the available synergies among the parties. "Indeed ... the terms of the Fiat Transaction present an opportunity that the marketplace alone could not offer, and that certainly exceeds liquidation value." The government funding, for instance, was contingent on finalizing the sale quickly. If closing did not take place by June 15, 2009, then Fiat could withdraw its commitments.

An expert opines on fair value. Finally, the proposed asset sale did not constitute a *sub rosa* (under the table) plan of reorganization. "The Debtors are receiving fair value for the assets being sold," the court held. "Not one penny" was going to anyone other than certain priority lenders, who provided $10 billion to Chrysler in return for a first lien on substantially all of the company's assets. The debtors' valuation expert, the executive director of Capstone Advisory Group, provided unrebutted testimony that the $2 billion purchase price exceeded the value that the first lien lenders could otherwise recover in an immediate liquidation, which would net only $1.2 billion.

"[T]he true test of value is the sale process itself," the court observed. No other bidder besides Fiat had come forward. With no other alternative but liquidation, the first lien lenders had consented to the transaction. The debtors made a good business decision, and "[f]air value has been paid for the assets to be transferred." After considering all of the evidence in light of Section 363(b) requirements, the court granted the proposed sale of Chrysler in its entirety.

In re Civic Partners Sioux City, LLC

Citation: 2013 Bankr. LEXIS 4225
Date of decision: Oct. 7, 2013
Country: US
State or Federal: Federal
State/Jurisdiction: Iowa
Court: United States Bankruptcy Court
Type of action: Bankruptcy
Experts: Steven Shaykett (creditors); Fred Lock (debtor)
Judge: Collins
SIC: 6512 Operators of Nonresidential Buildings (except stadium and arena owners)
Key words: Chapter 11, Bankruptcy, Reorganization Plan Confirmation, Discounted cash flow method (DCF), Cramdown, Bankruptcy Code

Plan Confirmation Hinges on Property Valuation

After declaring Chapter 11 bankruptcy, the debtor, a developer, asked the Bankruptcy Court to confirm the latest version of its reorganization plan in a "cram-down" proceeding. Two key creditors objected, arguing that the plan rested on an improperly low valuation of the building complex that represented most of the collateral securing the claim. To resolve the issue, the court considered expert testimony on the value of the property.

Road to bankruptcy. In the early 2000s, Sioux City, one of the creditors involved in the case, invited proposals to revitalize a historic district. The debtor, a California real estate developer and his company, won the contract. The plan included building a movie theater complex with related retail spaces, including restaurants, bars, and similar services, as well as a hotel complex on an adjacent property. As part of the development agreement, the city offered cheap land and significant tax increment financing. The debtor received construction financing from a major bank, the other key creditor. The bank took a first mortgage and assignment of rents on the property in the amount of its loan whose principal sum was $5,625,000. Under the loan agreement, the city guaranteed the debtor's payments up to $300,000 per year to the bank. In addition, the debtor borrowed almost $2 million from the city. All parties agreed that the arrangement between the debtor and the city were subordinate to the debtor's obligations to the bank. The city had a second mortgage on the property.

The debtor only built the theater complex. It settled the city's claim that it had failed to perform on the hotel development. In 2004, it leased the theater space to a regional movie theater operator under an agreement that the tenant would pay "several categories of payments totaling $1.2 million in annual rent" and the debtor would fill up the vacant retail spaces with complementary tenants. Essentially, the theater operator was financing the debtor's whole project; its annual rental payment covered the debtor's debt service payments to the bank and the city. But construction on the site continued after the theater opened, and it had difficulty attracting moviegoers. Ultimately, its operator was unable to make even one full rent payment.

Relations between the debtor and the tenant deteriorated. The debtor never whipped the vacant retail space into ready-to-rent condition, and by 2009 it had decided not to put any more money into the project. Subsequently, an expert from the city testified about significant water and structural problems plaguing the building and requiring prompt fixing. Eventually, the debtor fell behind on its own payments to the bank, the city, and other lenders. Attempts among all the parties to restructure the entangled financial arrangements in mediation failed when the city decided not to support a proposed new arrangement because of the prior agreed-upon tax assessment and loan guarantees.

Among other things, the parties had contemplated an amended lease that lowered the annual rent payment to $900,000 to address the tenant's complaints, with one immediate $200,000 payment to make the new lease effective. Before it knew about the city's decision, the bank had taken steps to effect the loan modification for the debtor, and the debtor and the tenant had executed the amended lease. Once apprised of the city's decision, the bank cancelled its agreement and filed for foreclosure. The debtor initially adhered to the amended lease and collected on the $900,000 annual rent. But 12 days before declaring Chapter 11 bankruptcy, in April 2011, it reinstated the original lease, without obtaining the required consent from the bank. It never offered to pay the movie house operator back the $200,000 up-front payment or any of the $900,000 rent. For its part, the city sued the debtor for breach of contract based on its failure to pay on the city's additional loan. The debtor countersued and transferred all the actions to the Bankruptcy Court (N.D. Iowa).

Three reorganization plans. The debtor's first plan was based on reinstatement of the original lease. The debtor claimed that the tenant owed $3.2 million in back rent and it wanted equitable subordination of the creditors' claims. The bank called the plan "impossible to confirm," as it wrongly assumed that the tenant could afford to pay back rent or even was responsible for it and that the creditors did anything to justify equitable subordination.

Eventually, the debtor filed an amended plan that generated the same resistance from the creditors and the movie house operator. It contained a "new value" contribution from the debtor for $150,000, which the creditors found "woefully inadequate" to move the development ahead. In addition, it required reinstatement of the original lease, recovery of back rent, and equitable subordination.

When the lease issue took on urgency, the court ruled that the amended lease governed the case. Subsequently, the debtor filed a second amended plan—the subject of this case—under which it would continue to use the property that served as the bank's collateral. The latest plan sought to reduce the bank's secured claim and leave the city unsecured. At the same time, it contemplated full satisfaction of any smaller debt the debtor company's owner had guaranteed personally. Further, by way of a "new value" contribution in the amount of $150,000, the owner would keep an ownership interest in the reorganized business.

Not surprisingly, the bank and the city requested denial of the confirmation and dismissal of the case. Meanwhile, the movie house operator, satisfied about the lease ruling, backed off on most of its objections. In fact, at the time of the confirmation proceeding, its business was profitable. It was able to pay rent under the amended lease and wanted to stay in the space.

In response to the objections, the debtor asked for confirmation under the Bankruptcy Code's § 1129(b)(2) "cram down provisions."

Valuation of property. The bank and city's objection ultimately boiled down to one argument: that the plan was not feasible under the code's § 1129(a)(11). Specifically, it significantly undervalued the bank's secured claim. Proper valuation would leave the debtor unable to pay the secured claim in full as the applicable law required. (The bank submitted a total claim of over $6.2 million.) Also, the creditors argued, the plan was based on unreliable and unrealistic cash flow projections, and the debtor proposed to continue the same futile course with the same ineffectual management.

Because the bank had a first mortgage on the property and the property made up a large part of the total value of its security interest, valuation of the building was pivotal in determining the total value of the bank's secured claim. Both sides retained experts, who agreed that the discounted cash flow (DCF) method was the appropriate valuation technique but disagreed about variables that figured into the computation, including the length of time appropriate to measure cash flow and inputs for future cash flow.

1. *Debtor's expert.* Both experts used the seven years of annual rent that remained under the amended lease to project future cash flow. The debtor's expert used a 10-year holding period with a projected sale after 10 years. He said he believed the amended lease was substantially "above market" because it was paying off back rent from the original lease.

Fair market value rents would drop "precipitously," in Years 8 through 10. This decline in rent, in turn, would drive the property's resale value down sharply.

As comparables, he used an older movie theater project, as well as other commercial rent properties that did not function as movie houses.

He valued the property at $4.2 million, excluding repair-related deductions. As he saw it, no buyer would take the property without the requisite structural and drainage repairs, which amounted to $290,000, lowering the property's value to $3.91 million. He subsequently raised the repair costs by an additional $400,000 and decreased the property's value to $3.51 million.

2. *City's expert.* In contrast, the city's expert used a seven-year holding period with a projected sale after seven years. As he saw it, a prospective buyer would be more interested in the cash flow for the known and definite seven-year period than in adding three years of estimates. This was the most accurate forecast of how a buyer would determine value, he said. But he did give an estimate of Year 8 rent, which helped provide the proper reversion value for his calculation. For that value, he assumed the annual lease payment would be similar to the projections for the seven-year existing lease. But he applied a "generous discount" to account for the possibility—small, he believed—that the amount could drop after the seven-year period.

For comparables, he looked to one similar movie theater complex in Sioux Falls, S.D. This theater was geographically close to the one at issue; also both movie houses were similar in age and were part of economic development areas in their locations. They became the leading movie theaters in cities "that function as regional population centers." Moreover, he noted that, if the building's vacant spaces were improved to vanilla shell quality and the rent was lowered to $10 per square foot, the entire space could see full occupancy in three to four years. Avoiding a delay in building out the space, he believed, would improve the project's financial situation significantly. "[N]ewer dollars are worth more than future dollars."

He concluded the property was worth $5.54 million, including a downward deduction of $290,000 for the necessary repairs to the building. His valuation exceeded the debtor's appraisal by over $2 million.

3. *Court.* The court found several aspects of the debtor's valuation "entirely unpersuasive." For example, in assessing rent under the amended lease, the debtor's expert did not use a similarly situated movie theater. Even though he had more comparables than the competing expert, his selected properties were "less 'comparable.'" Moreover, he and the debtor strained to explain away the contradiction in the debtor's position as to the amended lease. On the one hand, the debtor had spent most of the case claiming that it had a right to reinstatement of the original lease, which provided for $1.2 million annual rent, and to $3.2 million in back rent under the original lease. On the other hand, its valuation expert testified that the amended lease was significantly above market value. "The Court finds those arguments hard to square."

All the evidence supported the city expert's central assumption that the current rents would continue. To show that the amended lease was near fair market value, he properly relied on a theater that was "a good comparable and good indicator of market value." Also, the theater operator had experienced an increase in revenue and had been able to pay the rent under the amended lease. If anything, the city expert's generous discount to account for a possible drop in lease payments may have produced too low an estimate. For these reasons, the court adopted the city expert's valuation.

However, it agreed with the debtor that the downward deduction for repairs should have been $600,000, not $290,000 as the city expert assumed. This modification resulted in a $5.23 million valuation for the property.

Effect of post-petition payments on secured claim. The bank received post-petition payments from the debtor because of its secured position. The parties reasoned these were appropriate because the case qualified as a "single asset real estate case" under the Bankruptcy Code, § 362(d)(3). In essence, the provision seeks to compensate secured creditors for the use of their collateral. (The court noted that none of the parties had ever asked it for a determination of whether the case indeed qualified as such.)

The valuation-related issue was how the payments affected the bank's secured claim. As the court noted, if the payments reduced the bank's secured portion of its claim, the amount the debtor had to pay in full to the bank would decrease, which would make the debtor's plan more feasible. Conversely, if the payments did not reduce the bank's secured portion but only the overall claim value, there would be no reduction in the amount the debtor had to pay, and the plan would be even less feasible. Courts have divided over the treatment of such payments: Some have added the post-petition rents to the secured portion and reduced the creditor's claim from the unsecured portion first; others have subtracted the payments from the secured portion and reduced it before affecting the unsecured portion.

Here the court concluded that the "addition approach" was more appropriate. In applying the approach, it found that the bank's post-petition security interest in rents increased its collateral, bringing the total value to over $5.5 million. This claim did not include any value the bank claimed for its security interest in "general intangibles," the court added.

The court's finding added yet another layer of support to its overall conclusion that the debtor's reorganization plan did not provide enough funds to fulfill its obligations. Under the plan, the debtor would likely "wind up in a future reorganization or liquidation," the court said.

Problematic cash flow projections. The court also agreed with the creditors' claim that there was no way that the debtor could pay off all its obligations over the life of the plan through its cash flow projections. For one, the projections were based on the undervaluation of the bank's secured claim. But other aspects of the projections were equally questionable.

Even though it was clear that the debtor needed to spend significant amounts of money immediately to turn the project around, until now, it had failed to put that value into it. Testimony showed that repair costs amounted to a minimum of $600,000 and certain defects demanded immediate attention. But the projections deferred most of the maintenance and repairs, without factoring in the greater future costs that would result from the delay. The projections also did not "realistically" address costs related to building out the vacant retail space. By the bank's "most persuasive" estimate, these exceeded $500,000. "That money simply does not appear in the near-term projections," the court found.

Repair and build-out costs were likely to rise above $1 million, said the court. But the debtor's plan only provided for a new value contribution of $150,000 augmented by $148,000 in the tenant improvement account. Even assuming all of these funds were available now, the debtor would still be short. The projections "simply reflect a hope that what did not work in the past will work in the future—without any new ideas or concepts for how that will happen," the court concluded, finding the debtor's reorganization plan not feasible and declined to confirm it.

In re Colonial Realty Company; Hirsch v. Steinberg

Citation: 226 B.R. 513, 1998 Bankr. LEXIS 1341
Date of Decision: September 9, 1998
Country: US
State or Federal: Federal
State/Jurisdiction: Connecticut
Court: United States Bankruptcy Court
Experts: Christopher Rahne, CPA, CFA (for trustee), Charles E. Coyne, Timothy J. Floyd, CPA, CVA (for Steinberg)
Type of action: Bankruptcy
Judge: Krechevsky
SIC: 8011 Offices and Clinics of Doctors of Medicine (except mental health specialists, HMO medical centers, and ambulatory surgical and emergency centers)
Key words: Discount for lack of marketability (DLOM), Fraudulent transfer

Stock Recipients Liable for Fraudulent Transfer Underpayment

The issue was whether the transfer of stock of Danbury Surgical Center Inc. (DSC) and Bridgeport Surgical Center Inc. (BSC) by debtors Jonathan Googel and Benjamin Sisti to the defendants Gerald Steinberg and Robert Simons were fraudulent transfers under Bankruptcy Code § 548(a). The transfer agreement recited the consideration as $100,000 for all of the stock. There was conflicting testimony regarding whether the release of debtors' liability on the centers' financing was part of the consideration and whether additional consideration was promised to be paid "after the debtors' financial troubles were over." At the crux of this issue was the value of the debtors' interests in the DSC stock at the time of transfer. The parties agreed that the value of the debtors' interests in the BSC stock was little or nothing at the time of transfer.

Trustee's expert applies DCF approach. The trustee provided the expert valuation testimony of Christopher Rahne, CPA, CFA, of BDO Seidman LLP. Rahne used the discounted net cash flow method to value the stock, projected net cash flows for three years, used the industry average capital structure of 24% debt and 76% equity, computed a discount rate of 17.5%, and determined thereby that the DSC's business enterprise value was $7,124,000. From this value he subtracted interest-bearing debt of $3,798,000, applied a 20% discount for lack of marketability, and applied an additional 5% discount for restrictions on voting rights. Based upon Googel and Sisti's ownership percentages of the total stock of DSC, Rahne concluded that each debtor's ownership interest was worth $349,100. Rahne further tested the validity of his valuation by comparing the results to the value of publicly traded surgical centers and to comparable centers that were traded within a reasonable period before the subject transfer.

Defendants' expert criticizes appraisal. Defendants provided the expert valuation testimony of Charles E. Coyne of Valuation & Financial Strategies LLC. Coyne did not independently appraise the value of the DSC stock but rather provided a critical review of Rahne's appraisal. Coyne's criticisms fell into three main areas. He testified that:

4. Rahne failed to fully consider the impact of the Connecticut economy, which was in a recession; The discount rate and weighted average cost of capital Rahne used did not account for

the "unsystematic risks" associated with valuing the future cash flows of a small, privately owned, highly leveraged business; and

5. Rahne's selection of a 20% discount for lack of marketability was too low—based upon a number of discount studies, a 35% discount for lack of marketability was appropriate.

Coyne recommended changes in the calculations and concluded that each debtor's ownership interest in DSC was worth $126,000. Coyne further testified that purchase of the DSC stock for investment purposes would be too risky if the purchaser was required to assume the centers debt.

Defendants' expert finds adequate consideration. Defendants also provided the expert valuation testimony of Timothy J. Floyd, CPA, CVA, of Andros, Floyd & Miller, P.C., who testified that certain provisions in the center's financing documents would further reduce the value of debtors' DSC stock. Based upon this reduction in value, Floyd testified that debtors received more than adequate consideration for their DSC stock.

Trustee did not prove actual fraud. The court concluded that the trustee had not proven his claim of actual fraud because the only evidence that additional consideration for the stock would be paid at a later date was the testimony of Googel. (It is of some interest that Googel testified by videotape due to his incarceration in federal prison for wire fraud, bank fraud, and impeding administration of IRS laws). The other badges of fraud were insufficient to allow the court to infer fraudulent intent.

Transfer constituted constructive fraud. Regarding the trustees constructive fraud claim, the defendants conceded that debtors were insolvent at the time of the transfer. Therefore, the trustee needed to prove that debtors did not receive reasonably equivalent value for their stock. Based upon the expert valuation testimony, the court concluded that the debtors indeed did not receive reasonably equivalent value for the DSC stock and the trustee could therefore avoid the transfer as fraudulent.

Court rejects defendants' testimony. First, the court rejected the testimony of Coyne and Floyd regarding the effect of the centers debt on the marketability and value of the stock. Second, the court generally credited the testimony of Rahne, the trustee's expert, but adjusted his valuation conclusion by applying the 35% discount for lack of marketability suggested by Coyne. Finally, the court rejected the defendants' contention that debtors received reasonably equivalent value because of their release from the center's financing. The court found, based upon the testimony of various witnesses, that the debtors' release from that indebtedness was unrelated to the stock transfer.

Court awards prejudgment interest. The court measured the trustee's recovery by taking the market value of the debtors' combined interests in the DSC stock at the time of transfer, $539,329, and subtracting the total consideration they received for the stock, $100,000, and concluded that the trustee was entitled to recover $439,329 from the defendants. The court also granted the trustee prejudgment interest from the date the complaint in this adversary proceeding was filed until the date of judgment.

In re Coram Healthcare Corp.

Citation: 2004 Bankr. LEXIS 1516
Date of Decision: October 5, 2004
Country: US
State or Federal: Federal
State/Jurisdiction: Delaware
Court: United States Bankruptcy Court
Type of action: Bankruptcy
Experts: Ewing Bemis and Co. (EB) (for trustee) SSG Capital Advisors (SSG) (for trustee), Deloitte & Touche (Deloitte) (for equity committee)
Judge: Walrath
SIC: 8082 Home Health Care Services
Key words: Bankruptcy, Earnings Before Interest, Taxes, Depreciation, Amortization, Guideline publicly traded company method, (EBITDA), Discounted cash flow method (DCF), Going concern, Comparable transactions method

Too Many Adjustments Compromise Deloitte's Valuation

The relevant valuation issue in this bankruptcy matter, in which the court confirmed the trustee's modified plan, was the value of Coram Healthcare Corp. and Coram Inc. (the "Debtors"), which would determine whether the trustee's plan was "fair and equitable."

Valuation evidence. Both parties provided expert testimony during trial and used the same methodologies: comparable public company analysis, comparable transaction analysis, and discounted cash flow analysis. However, as one might expect, their respective conclusions diverged substantially.

The court noted the key distinctions: "Deloitte [for equity committee] and EB/SSG [for trustee] included different assets in reaching their valuation conclusions, attached different weights to the three valuation methodologies, and took different positions regarding management's projections."

Did appraisers incorrectly rely on conservative, erroneous projections? The equity committee argued that EB/SSG artificially deflated debtors' value by relying on management's conservative projections. The equity committee argued that these projections were incorrect because they were not based on historical or industrial experience and the cash flow projections contained errors that resulted in a low discounted cash flow.

Additionally, EB/SSG did not conduct an independent review as to whether the projections were consistent with market projections or debtor's actual performance. EB/SSG's valuation was also criticized by the equity committee because their valuation methodologies varied from traditional methodologies as a result of their disregarding multiples that produced results that fell outside of their preconceived conclusions about the market. EB/SSG's valuation resulted in a going concern value of $220 million.

Too many upward adjustments by Deloitte? Deloitte's valuation utilized the "upside projections" prepared by EB/SSG. Deloitte adjusted EBITDA for charges that they did not consider to be regular.

In addition to making adjustments to EBITDA, Deloitte made significant adjustments to growth projections, cash flow projections, and management's established reserves. Deloitte determined that higher multiples were proper because debtors' value contained a "significant 'specialty pharmaceutical' component." Deloitte finally concluded that the going concern value of debtors was $279 million.

The trustee criticized Deloitte's valuation for numerous adjustments to management's projections and the utilization of inflated multiples. In addition, the trustee argued that Deloitte's characterization of the company as a specialty pharmaceutical company was inaccurate and that Deloitte's inflated projections did not take into account the "price pressures" inherent in the industry. The trustee also argued that the increase of the EBITDA by 40%, due to the multiple adjustments made by Deloitte, was improper.

Holding and rationale. The Bankruptcy Court discussed the motivation for the difference in valuations, "[W]e recognize each side's incentives to either overvalue or undervalue the Debtors." However, the court noted there are limits: "Although valuations are subjective, there are proper and improper methods of performing a valuation."

The court held, "After our review of the evidence, we cannot conclude that EB/SSG strayed from generally accepted valuation methodologies. While we agree that their numerical inputs … may have been conservative, the evidence does not establish that EB/SSG made inappropriate downward adjustments.… Accordingly, we do not find that the EB/SSG valuation is improper."

"After considering the competing valuations, the competing incentives of the parties, and the divergent evidence offered in support of the valuations we conclude that the value of the Debtors is less than $317 million." In a footnote, the court noted that "this figure is calculated by adding the going concern value of $220 million determined by EB/SSG, the $31.2 million in cash on hand, the $10 million in present value of the NOLs, and the value of the claims being released (less than $56 million)." In addition, the Bankruptcy Court noted why Deloitte's valuation was not adopted: "Deloitte took aggressive and optimistic views regarding the valuation and strength of the Debtors. Therefore, we do not find that the Deloitte valuation is an accurate reflection of the Debtors' value." The court adopted the valuation of EB/SSG and valued the debtor at $220 million.

Crane v. Morris (In re Morris)

Citation: 2003 Bankr. LEXIS 1732
Date of Decision: December 17, 2003
Country: US
State or Federal: Federal
State/Jurisdiction: Oklahoma
Court: United States Bankruptcy Court
Type of action: Bankruptcy
Judge: Michael
SIC: 1521 General Contractors—Single Family Houses
Key words: Bankruptcy, Shareholder agreement

Par Value Valuation Ruled Invalid but Not Grounds for Denial of Discharge

Debtor David Keith Morris operated a residential construction business called Grand Lake Builders, which he later incorporated as Grand Lake Builders Inc. (GLBI). He also held an interest in Grand Country Investments Inc. (GCI), together with his wife and sister-in-law. Morris was president of GCI, which was formed to do marketing of residential real estate.

Valuation evidence. The GCI shareholders entered into an agreement that provided that, if a shareholder filed bankruptcy, the remaining shareholders had the right to buy the bankrupt shareholder's stock at par value. The agreement also provided that, in the absence of a prior shareholder agreement on the per-share value of GCI stock, the value would be its par value, as stated in the aforementioned section.

The par value of Morris's GCI stock was $500, and he valued his interest in GCI on the bankruptcy schedules at $500. He also listed the value of GLBI on the schedules as $500.

Also in evidence were financial statements Morris had prepared for bank loan applications, which listed a value of $180,000 for his GLBI stock, and his tax returns showing GLBI inventory worth $128,000.

Earlier bankruptcy proceeding. In Morris's bankruptcy, the other shareholders sought to compel the trustee to abandon Morris's interest in GCI, claiming it was worth little to the estate. The trustee argued that he was not bound by the shareholder agreement and that the stock did have some value. The court found for the trustee.

In this subsequent adversary proceeding, two of Morris's creditors claimed that he submitted false oaths to the court that should preclude his debts being discharged. Namely, they contended that Morris made false statements when he valued his interests in GCI and GLBI at only $500 each.

Adversary proceeding findings and conclusions. The bankruptcy court found no merit in the creditors' argument. Regarding the GCI stock, Morris had no reason to know, when he submitted his schedules, that the court would later invalidate the shareholder agreement. Although the GCI valuation at par value was not binding in bankruptcy, the court said that it was "not done in bad faith or with the intent to defraud creditors, and does not constitute grounds for denial of Morris' discharge."

Regarding Morris's GLBI stock, the creditors claimed that the financial statements and tax return were evidence that the stock was worth far more than the par value listed in the bankruptcy schedules. Morris explained, however, that the $180,000 value was based almost entirely on goodwill, which was practically wiped out by a $171,000 prebankruptcy judgment against him. He also testified that the $128,000 inventory valuation included one "spec house," which was listed separately in the bankruptcy schedules. The court refused to find intent to defraud "from the mere fact that the [creditors] disagree with the Debtor's valuation."

In re CSC Industries, Inc. (Pension Benefit Guaranty Corporation v. Kathryn A. Belfance, Trustee)

Citation: 2000 FED App. 0393P (6th Cir.)
Date of Decision: November 17, 2000
Country: US
State or Federal: Federal
State/Jurisdiction: 6th Circuit
Court: United States Court of Appeals
Type of action: Bankruptcy

Unfunded Pension Claim Valued Using Prudent Investor Rate

The U.S Court of Appeals for the 6th Circuit considered whether the unfunded pension liability claim should be reduced to present value using the market rate or the prudent investor rate. CSC Industries had three defined benefit plans for its employees. The plans were governed under the Employee Retirement Income Security Act (ERISA) and insured by the Pension Benefit Guaranty Corp. (PBGC). The trustee and the PBGC disagreed over the calculation of the unfunded portion of the claims after the plans were terminated in the bankruptcy. PBGC argued that the plans should be valued using the market rate of interest pursuant to the federal regulations governing the termination of the plans. The trustee argued that the appropriate interest rate was the prudent investor rate. The bankruptcy court agreed with the trustee, and PBGC appealed.

The 6th Circuit agreed with the bankruptcy court. It found that, "while the *validity* of a claim might be a matter for non-bankruptcy law, bankruptcy courts have the statutory authority to determine the *allowability* and *amount* of the claim." (Emphasis in original) Therefore, it concluded that the bankruptcy court was within its discretion to treat PBGC's claims like any other creditors' claims, by reducing them to present value using the prudent investor rate. In reaching this decision, the 6th Circuit noted that it was not entirely persuaded by the 10th Circuit's decision finding that ERISA was subordinate to the bankruptcy code. See *Pension Benefit Guaranty Corp. v. CF&I Fabricators of Utah, Inc.*, 150 F.3d 1293 (10th Cir. 1998)

In re DAK Industries Inc.

Citation: No. 97-56375
Date of Decision: March 19, 1999
Country: US
State or Federal: Federal
State/Jurisdiction: 9th Circuit
Court: United States Court of Appeals
Type of action: Bankruptcy

Company Found to Be Solvent Prior to Bankruptcy

The United States Court of Appeals for the 9th Circuit determined whether a company was insolvent during the preference period. DAK Industries was a successful electronics catalog company. When it began to experience financial difficulties, it sought protection under Chapter 11. It operated as a debtor-in-possession (DIP) for another two and a half years, but then DAK filed for Chapter 7. The bankruptcy trustee filed suit to recover payments DAK had made to its creditors in the 90 days preceding its Chapter 11 filing. To successfully recover such payments, the trustee had to prove that DAK was insolvent during the 90-day period. The bankruptcy court found the trustee did not provide sufficient evidence to recover payments made to DAK's creditors. The trustee appealed.

On appeal, the district court affirmed the bankruptcy court's ruling. The 9th Circuit also reviewed the bankruptcy court's ruling. The Bankruptcy Code defines insolvency as "a financial condition such that the sum of such entity's debts is greater than all of such entity's property, at fair valuation." 11 U.S.C. § 101 (32). The 9th Circuit court stated that "'fair valuation' of a debtor's assets must begin with a determination of whether a debtor is 'a going concern' and end with the application of a balance sheet test to determine solvency."

The 9th Circuit found that DAK was a going concern during the preference period because it continued in business for two and a half years after its Chapter 11 filing. It then found that DAK was solvent after reviewing the experts' testimony from the bankruptcy court. The testimony from the creditors committee "focused on DAK's positive equity on a balance sheet basis," while the trustee's expert used a liquidation approach. The bankruptcy court accepted the testimony of the creditor's expert. Thus, the 9th Circuit affirmed the bankruptcy court's decision finding DAK was solvent during the preference period, denying the trustee and right to recover payments.

Daubert v. Merrell Dow Pharmaceuticals

Citation: 509 U.S. 579, 113 S.Ct. 2786 (1993)
Date of decision: June 28, 1993
Country: US
State or Federal: Federal
Court: Supreme Court
Type of action: Evidence
Judge: Blackmun

Landmark *Daubert* Decision Develops New Standard for Admission of Expert Evidence

In this case, we are called upon to determine the standard for admitting expert scientific testimony in a federal trial ...

So begins the landmark decision by the U.S. Supreme Court, which ended by promulgating a new "gatekeeping" function for federal judges and developing an evidentiary standard now known by a single name: *Daubert.*

Former standard was rigid, austere. The case originated in California, when two sets of parents sued Dow pharmaceuticals for marketing an antinausea drug that had allegedly caused birth defects in their children (one with the last name Daubert). The defendant drug company moved for summary judgment, submitting evidence from a credentialed medical expert who had reviewed over 30 published studies and found the drug posed no risk to developing fetuses.

In response, the plaintiffs enlisted eight equally established experts, who each concluded that the drug caused birth defects in humans based on in vitro and animal studies as well as the "reanalysis" of prior epidemiological (human statistical) studies.

The federal district court reviewed the pleadings under the then-applicable "general acceptance" rule; i.e., scientific evidence is admissible only if it is based on a principle or technique that is "sufficiently established to have general acceptance in the field to which it belongs." The rule was first articulated in *Frye v. United States*, a short, citation-free 1923 decision by the U.S. Court of Appeals for the D.C. Circuit (referred to since as the *Frye* standard).

In the *Daubert* case, the district court concluded that the plaintiffs' evidence did not meet the *Frye* standard because it was based on studies—including the experts' reanalyses—that had not met general scientific acceptance through peer review and publication. On appeal, the U.S. Court of Appeals for the 9th Circuit affirmed, citing the *Frye* standard. It also emphasized cases in which other courts had refused to admit reanalysis studies that had not been published or subject to peer review and were generated solely for use in litigation.

The plaintiffs petitioned the U.S. Supreme Court, which granted certiorari in light of "sharp divisions among the courts regarding the proper standard for the admission of expert testimony." Since the 1920s, a majority of federal courts had adopted the *Frye* rule but not without creating substantial controversy. Indeed, the "well-established" debate over *Frye*'s merits had "divided courts and commentators," the court explained.

Federal rules supersede *Frye*. In this case, the petitioners did not attack the content of the *Frye* standard so much as its continuing authority. They contended that the *Frye* test was superseded by the passage of the Federal Rules of Evidence (FRE)—and the court agreed.

In particular, Rule 401 FRE permits the admission of "all relevant evidence," defined as "that which has any tendency to make the existence of any fact that is of consequence to the determination of the action more probable or less probable than it would be without the evidence." "The Rule's basic standard of relevance thus is a liberal one," the court observed. In addition, Rule 702 speaks specifically to the admission of expert evidence, stating:

> If scientific, technical, or otherwise specialized knowledge will assist the trier of fact to understand the evidence or to determine a fact in issue, a witness qualified as an expert by knowledge, skill, experience, training, or education may testify thereto in the form of an opinion or otherwise.

Frye predated the Federal Rules by half a century, the court noted. Thus, the drafters of the Federal Rules could have incorporated the *Frye* standard into Rule 702—but they did not. "Nothing in the text of this Rule establishes 'general acceptance' as an absolute prerequisite to admissibility," the court said. Indeed, the rigid *Frye* rule would be at odds with the "liberal thrust" of the Federal Rules and their overall "relaxing" of the traditional barrier to opinion testimony. Accordingly, "that austere standard, absent from and incompatible with the Federal Rules of Evidence, should not be applied in federal trials," the court held, effectively banishing the *Frye* standard to the history books.

(*Note*: Pursuant to the court's *Daubert* holding, the *Frye* standard no longer applies in federal trials, but many states—including California, Florida, Illinois, Maryland, Michigan, Minnesota, New Jersey, New York, Pennsylvania, and Washington—still apply the *Frye* rule, and practitioners should always check the law applicable to their case when developing expert opinion evidence.)

New standard under *Daubert*. The Federal Rules may have displaced *Frye*—but they did not leave the admission of expert opinion evidence without limits. "Nor is the trial judge disabled from screening such evidence," the court noted. "To the contrary, under the Rules the trial judge must ensure that any and all scientific testimony or evidence admitted is not only relevant, but reliable." (In a footnote from Chief Justice Rehnquist, the court declined to define the by now familiar "gatekeeping function," believing the "better course" was to note the nature and source of the duty and let the courts develop what the role entailed.)

Rule 702 clearly contemplated some degree of regulation regarding the subject and theories about which an expert may testify, the court added. To qualify as "scientific knowledge," an expert's opinion must be derived by the scientific method; that is, it must be reliable. Further, Rule 702 requires the expert testimony to assist the trier of fact to understand the case; thus, it must be relevant.

(*Final note:* Rule 702 also applies to "technical or other specialized" expert testimony, but the court limited its discussion to scientific evidence because that was the nature of the expertise offered in this case. Six years later, it extended its *Daubert* ruling to "engineers and other experts who are not scientists" (including financial experts and business appraisers) in *Kumho Tire Co. v. Carmichael*, 119 S. Ct. 1167 (1999)).

"We are confident that federal judges possess the capacity to undertake this review" of reliability and relevance, the court stated. "Many factors will bear on the inquiry, and we do not presume to set out a definitive checklist." At the same time, the court cited four factors that would help trial judges to determine the admissibility of federal evidence under the new standard:

1. *Testing.* A key question is whether the expert's theory or technique can be (or has been) tested.

2. *Peer review and publication.* "Another pertinent consideration is whether the theory or technique has been subjected to peer review and publication," the court said. Publication is not a "sine qua non" of admissibility, nor does it necessarily equate with reliability—but it is a relevant consideration in assessing the scientific validity of an expert's methodology and opinion.

3. *Error rate.* Trial courts should also consider the known or potential rate of error of the expert's technique.

4. *General acceptance.* Finally, the court incorporated the general acceptance test into the reliability inquiry. "Widespread acceptance can be an important factor in ruling particular evidence admissible, and a known technique which has been able to attract only minimal support within the community ... may be properly viewed with skepticism." (internal citations omitted)

Dealing with 'shaky but admissible' evidence. "The inquiry envisioned by Rule 702 is ... a flexible one," the court emphasized. "Its overarching subject is the scientific validity and thus the evidentiary relevance and reliability of the principles that underlie a proposed submission." In an oft-cited phrase, the court added, "The focus, of course, must be solely on the principles and methodology, not on the conclusions they generate." Finally, the court allayed any concerns that the new rule will open the gates to "absurd and irrational pseudoscientific assertions." In yet another familiar, often repeated ruling, it held: "Vigorous cross-examination, presentation of contrary evidence, and careful instruction on the burden of proof are the traditional and appropriate means of attacking shaky but admissible evidence."

To summarize the court's ruling: "General acceptance" is no longer a necessary precondition to the admission of scientific evidence under the Federal Rules. Instead, the Rules—in particular, 702—assign the trial judge the task of ensuring that an expert's testimony "both rests on a reliable foundation and is relevant to the task at hand," the court held. Accordingly, it vacated the prior evidentiary rulings and remanded the case for findings consistent with the new *Daubert* standard.

Sandra Davis v. Thomas Cullen Davis

Citation: No.95-11112
Date of Decision: February 5, 1997
Country: US
State or Federal: Federal
State/Jurisdiction: 5th Circuit
Court: United States Court of Appeals
Type of action: Bankruptcy

Exempted Property Not Immunized Against Alimony Arrearage

A divided U.S. Court of Appeals, 5th Circuit considered a bankruptcy court's refusal to grant turnover relief of Thomas's exempted property in satisfaction of Sandra's nondischargeable, prepetition claim for $250,000 in alimony, child support, and maintenance under 11 U.S.C. 522(c). The parties were divorced in 1968, and he was required to pay her alimony, child support, and maintenance. He ceased making payments to her in 1979 after he filed for Chapter 7 relief. He exempted unencumbered property valued at $500,000 from the bankruptcy estate according to the state homestead exemption laws. She was refused relief on the grounds that the bankruptcy code was preempted by the state homestead exemption law. *In re Davis*, 170 B.R. 892,898 (Bankr.N.D. Tx. 1994).

The appellate court reviewed the legislative and case history of sec. 522 (c), and determined that "The [bankruptcy] code uses state exemption laws only as a means of identifying and quantifying the property that the debtor may exempt under federal law from the bankruptcy estate. *Owen v. Owen*, 500 U.S. 305.... By the same token, federal law determines whether property is exempted and immunized against seize and sale for pre-bankruptcy debts. 11 USC Sec. 522." The appellate court concluded that she was entitled to proceed against his otherwise exempted property in order to satisfy the alimony arrearage and may do so by ordinary legal proceedings.

In re DBSD North America, Inc.

Citation: 2009 WL 3491060 (Bankr. S.D.N.Y.)
Date of Decision: September 30, 2009
Country: US
State or Federal: Federal
State/Jurisdiction: New York
Court: United States Bankruptcy Court
Type of action: Bankruptcy
Experts: Nabholz (creditors), Henkin (debtors)
Judge: Gerber

Bankruptcy Court Rejects DCF for Troubled Company

The debtors are a next-generation mobile satellite service provider, planning to offer wireless communications throughout North America. Since 2004, they have been developing a full-scale hybrid system, utilizing both satellite and land-based systems, for which they required a great deal of capital.

They also obtained significant financing: over $51 million in a secured, "first tier" lending facility and $752 million in secured, second lien notes, plus $211 million in unsecured debt.

The debtors successfully launched a satellite in 2008 but were unable to lease their broadcast spectrum to third parties or find additional sources of operational revenues without substantial cost (estimated $300 million to $1.5 billion). They continued to "burn cash," and in May 2009 they declared Chapter 11 bankruptcy, seeking to restructure their approximately $800 million in outstanding liabilities.

Prearranged plan. Within two months, the debtors filed a proposed plan to deleverage by exchanging 95% of their stock for the $752 million in second lien notes, effectively "cramming down" on two classes of objecting creditors: DISH Network, which purchased the $51 million first-tier debt at par value, and SPRINT/Nextel Corp., which held $2 million of the unsecured claims. Valuation of the debtor proved pivotal to the federal bankruptcy court's consideration of the proposed reorganization plan. Any "cram down" must comply with the Bankruptcy Code's feasibility and fairness requirements and provide any dissenting creditors with the "indubitable equivalent" of their secured claims.

Both the debtors and DISH Network retained experts to determine the debtors' total enterprise value (TEV). Both experts applied the same three methods but with varying assumptions and weightings, creating a wide, multi-billion-dollar spectrum of value as follows:

1. *Guideline comparables analysis.* Both experts used the same two publicly traded companies in the mobile satellite systems industry (SkyTerra and TerreStar). In calculating the comparables' TEV per megahertz-population (MGh POP), both experts reviewed their book and market values, but the creditor's expert rejected the book value as unreliable. Using only a market value of the comparables, he estimated the debtors' TEV between $530 million and $560 million. Using both the market and book values of the comparables, however, the debtors' expert calculated a much broader range of value for the debtors of $380 million to $650 million.

2. *Comparables transactions analysis.* Both experts examined sales of broadcast satellite spectrums. The debtors' expert analyzed transactions since 2001, finding three recent spectrum sales (2006, 2007, and 2008) similar to the debtors'. Because the debtors would have to launch a second satellite to realize full comparability, their expert deducted this cost, reaching a valuation range of $850 million to $3.1 billion.

By contrast, the creditor's expert used a single FCC auction in 2006. He adjusted the price for perceived changes in spectrum values since that time, based on an average 85% decline in market price for the two comparables in his guideline company analysis (Sky Terra and TerraStar). He also deducted the cost of building a second satellite and securing five years of additional funding, concluding that the debtors were worth between $140 million and $215 million.

3. *DCF analysis.* The debtors' expert used cash flow projections from its proposed business/reorganization plan, which assumed the debtors would build the second satellite, establish its hybrid network, and secure capital investment of $1.5 billion along with necessary short-term financing.

The expert calculated a terminal value using an EBITDA multiple between 6.0x and 6.5x, derived from the median 2009 and 2010 TEV/EBITDA multiples of wireless, satellite, and competitive local exchange industries. After applying discount rates between 22% and 24%, the debtors' value ranged between $570 million and $900 million.

The creditor's expert used the 2010-2013 financial projections from the debtors' bankruptcy disclosures—all of which were negative cash flows—and used the average TEV/MGh POP multiple derived from guideline company analysis to calculate the terminal value. Because negative projections aren't as uncertain as positive ones, he used a risk-free rate to discount the cash flows under one scenario and a 25% discount rate in the second scenario. He applied a 25% discount rate to the terminal values in both scenarios, thereby calculating a range of DCF values between $70 million and $100 million.

Court finds serious flaws. "I had serious problems with the use of DCF analysis by each expert," the court said. The debtors' expert used a DCF approach "even though the debtors could not expect to achieve the projected cash flows without major capital expenditures—possibly as much as $1.5 billion." Under current facts, this assumption was "unrealistic" and "unjustifiably skewed [the expert's] valuation to the high extreme."

At the same time, the creditor's expert unrealistically assumed a continuous stream of negative cash flows. Although some negative yearly projections might be plausible, "I have difficulty seeing how a stream of *totally negative* cash flows could provide a basis for valuation," the court said, with emphasis. "It seems extraordinarily unlikely to me, if not remote, that anyone would pay to secure … uniformly negative cash flows." Such a purchaser would have to be looking at asset values, perhaps, "but would not be buying it for the privilege of taking an unrelenting stream of losses." Moreover, the creditor's expert heavily weighted this approach (40%), skewing his overall valuation to "the low extreme."

As a result, the court rejected the DCF analysis outright and requested supplemental valuations from both experts with new weightings based solely on the comparable companies and transactions analysis. Both experts—and the court—agreed that it was appropriate to allocate the weightings previously assigned to the DCF analysis on a pro rata basis according to the weightings of the two alternative methods, thereby maintaining what the experts considered to be their relative reliability.

Comparables are truly comparable. Of the two, the court found the comparable company analysis to be the most reliable method. Both experts used the same two companies, which had assets directly comparable to the debtors' and operated in the same segment of the satellite communications industry, under the same regulatory and capitalization requirements. Significantly, this method produced the "smallest valuation differences" between the experts, the court noted, amounting to a mere $45 million in their mean values.

Of the two experts, only the debtors' used the book and market approaches—and, because the comparables' stock was trading at a significant discount at the time of valuation and the market as a whole was uncertain, he weighted the book and market values equally. The court found this method and reasoning persuasive. By contrast, "I find that [the creditor's expert's] sole reliance on the market value of the comparable companies made his valuation unduly subject to trading discounts at the time of valuation."

As for their comparable transactions analysis, the court found both experts marked by "indicia of unreliability." By using several spectrum transactions, the debtors' expert produced an "extremely broad" and "less useful" value range. At the same time, by using only a single transaction with substantial adjustments to reflect the volatility of the comparables, the creditor's expert also produced an unreliable range of value. Although the court did not find the adjustments improper, it hesitated to give the same high weighting to the transactions approach (66.7%) that the creditor's expert did, agreeing more with the low weighting (5.3%) that the debtors' expert assigned.

In fact, because the debtor's expert gave a substantially higher weighting to the comparable company analysis than the creditor's expert (94.7% versus 33.3%), the debtors' expert ultimately persuaded the court to adopt his overall valuation as the "best assessment" of the debtors' total enterprise value. Thus, the court found that the value of the reorganized debtors' business was in the range of $492 million to $692 million, providing the first-tier secured lender (DISH Network) with liens on assets worth six to nine times the amount that it would be owed under the proposed plan of reorganization. "That leads me to find, and I do find, that the First Lien Lender's principal and interest will be safe over the next four years," the court held, in particular because the debtors would be significantly deleveraged and its primary asset—the satellite spectrum rights—was bound to increase in value.

Liquidation value also has consequences. The debtors' expert also provided a liquidation value for the debtors. He used the bankruptcy sales of comparable mobile satellite system providers to express a recovery rate as "fixed assets as a percentage of transaction value," finding a median rate of 16.3%. Applying this to the potential sale of the debtors' assets, the expert estimated a net liquidation value of between $113 million and $153 million.

The court accepted the undisputed liquidation value, finding that its consequences were "very different for each of the two objectors to confirmation." At any value within the liquidation range, the first-tier lender (DISH) would receive payment in full on its secured claims. "By contrast, at any valuation within that range, Sprint [the unsecured lender] would get nothing in a liquidation," the court stated.

Accordingly, and based on all findings of law and fact, the court concluded that DISH would receive the indubitable equivalent of its claims under either a Chapter 11 reorganization scenario or a Chapter 7 liquidation scenario. Further, "it appears that Sprint is the only unsecured creditor that has rejected the plan and objected to confirmation," the court noted. But ironically, under the proposed plan, Sprint would receive some return on its unsecured claims (4% to 46%, depending on future equity distributions), while under liquidation it would receive zero. Thus the cram-down plan was in the best interest of all creditors, the court held, and it otherwise complied with the feasibility, good faith, and fairness requirements of the Bankruptcy Code.

Dietz v. Jacobs

Citation: 2014 U.S. Dist. LEXIS 37144
Date of decision: March 21, 2014
Country: US
State or Federal: Federal
State/Jurisdiction: Minnesota
Court: United States District Court
Type of action: Bankruptcy
Experts: Arthur C. Cobb (solvency-defendants); unknown (trustee)
Judge: Ericksen
SIC: 3732 Boat Building and Repairing (boat building)
Key words: Solvency Analysis, Discounted cash flow method (DCF), Balance Sheet Approach, Daubert, Fraudulent transfer, Preferential Transfer, Bankruptcy Code Section 547b, Bankruptcy Code Section 548, AICPA SSVS No. 1

Court Admits Solvency Analysis Lacking Specific Valuation of Debtor

In a bankruptcy proceeding, the trustee filed a pretrial *Daubert* motion attacking the adjusted balance sheet and discounted cash flow analyses that the defendants' expert submitted to show solvency. As the court considered the arguments, it discussed the significance that the AICPA's valuation standards assume in a solvency analysis.

The debtor, a parent company and numerous subsidiaries, manufactured marine yachts sold to various dealers. On June 1, 2009, the companies filed for Chapter 11 bankruptcy, which subsequently became a Chapter 7 bankruptcy. The appointed trustee brought suits against various individual defendants to avoid preferential and fraudulent transfers under the Bankruptcy Code's Sections 547 and 548. Ultimately, the consolidated case wound up in federal district court (D. Minn.) for a jury trial.

Balance sheet a 'starting point.' To succeed under either Section 547(b) or Section 548, the trustee had to show that the debtor was insolvent at the time of transfer.

The defendants' expert was a CPA who concluded that during the relevant period—two years before bankruptcy—the parent company was a going concern and its assets were greater than its liabilities. His primary solvency analysis took an adjusted balance sheet approach. In his report, he explained that he started with the company's balance sheet as of May 30, 2009, which, he said, complied with GAAP. He acknowledged that GAAP-conforming balance sheets "do not include all assets, property, and liabilities, debts, and do not include assets at fair valuation." He called them a "starting point."

He then adjusted the numbers in two asset categories: (1) land, buildings, and operating equipment; and (2) trade names, trademarks, and intellectual property. Specifically, he added over $21.5 million to the first category and approximately $142.6 million to the second category to "reflect their 'fair' rather than 'book' value," he explained. Under the bankruptcy schedules, the company's liabilities exceeded its assets by over $68.2 million as of the petition date. Owing to the adjustments, the expert's analysis showed that assets exceeded liabilities by nearly $95.9 million.

The expert's report also noted that for the other categories the "fair value is estimated to be the reported value." And it included a separate section discussing "Unreported Liabilities" but did not state a definitive figure for those items. Moreover, even though the analysis focused on the May 30, 2009, balance sheet, the report stated that in general the company's assets decreased and its liabilities increased from June 2006 to June 2009. It concluded that, since the company was solvent on May 30, 2009, it likely was solvent during the relevant prior years.

In the report's brief section called "Valuation," there was scant reference to a discounted cash flow (DCF) analysis. Without providing specific numbers or inputs, the expert concluded that "representative estimates of prospective cash flow" indicated an equity value for the parent company of approximately $50 million as of May 30, 2009. In his deposition, the expert declared he developed numerous projections "that varied by the top line revenues" and he discussed several considerations (missing from the court's opinion). He did not remember what discount rate he had used.

Regarding the solvency of the related debtor entities, the report listed the subsidiaries' reported numbers for stockholder equity and intercompany balances for 2008 and 2009. In his deposition, the expert admitted he only "generally" analyzed the entities' solvency situation but said the numbers showed that the entities' assets exceeded the liabilities. In his words, "as went [the parent company], I believe so go the subsidiaries."

Vital DCF information missing. The trustee filed a *Daubert* motion to preclude the expert from testifying on solvency. Although the trustee did not challenge the expert's going concern analysis, he claimed that the valuation part of the analysis was unreliable and thus inadmissible.

1. The adjusted balance sheet analysis was deficient for two reasons:

(a) *Violation of SSVS No.1.* The trustee contended that the expert's approach did not meet the professional standards of the American Institute of Certified Public Accountants (AICPA). The standards (SSVS No. 1) require a financial expert to reach a "conclusion of value," which the defendants' solvency expert did not do. Specifically, he did not reach "a specific conclusion about the amount by which he believed" the parent company's assets exceeded its liabilities but only concluded that they exceeded them.

The court saw this issue differently. Here, the expert was not on the case to provide a valuation opinion for the parent company but to determine solvency under the Bankruptcy Code. Although the AICPA's standards list bankruptcy as one situation in which a valuation may occur, they do not indicate that solvency determinations under the Bankruptcy Code must result in a definitive valuation number, the court pointed out. The trustee failed to cite any other authority to the contrary.

Here, the court observed, the defendants' expert took the position that the "magnitude of excess" resulting from his two adjustments made other variations immaterial and allowed him to conclude that the company was solvent. The court agreed that there were weak areas in the report, but they did not render the testimony inadmissible. Rather, they were targets for cross-examination. For example, the report stated that for the other categories the reported values equaled the fair values but did not explain why; it also did not give a determinative number for the unreported liabilities.

(b) *Improper use of book values.* Next, the trustee claimed the expert used book value rather than fair market value because he only adjusted two asset values.

The court disagreed. True, the expert only performed two adjustments, but he analyzed the other categories and concluded that the reported values represented the fair value, said the court. Even if his conclusions were open to challenges, his opinion was admissible.

2. Details about the DCF were too sketchy.

The trustee claimed the expert failed to provide any of the numbers he used for his DCF analysis or data sources that resulted in his finding that the parent company's equity value was at least $50 million.

The court explained that a DCF analysis required:

> [E]stimating the periodic cash flow that a company will generate over a discrete time period, determining the "terminal value" of the company at the end of the period, and discounting each of the cash flows and terminal value to determine the total value as of the relevant date.

Here, said the court, the expert's report lacked the projected periodic cash flows, the terminal value, and the discount rate that led the expert to his conclusion. At his deposition, the expert could not recall the discount rate he had applied. His actual calculations were not available anywhere. According to the court, the trustee had no opportunity to explore and counter the specifics of the expert's analysis. It went on to say that "the omission cannot be overlooked," particularly since the expert claimed the DCF analysis stated the company's value as of the date that the company was poised to file for bankruptcy.

Accordingly, the court precluded the expert from discussing the DCF analysis and his conclusion resulting from it.

3. Missing solvency analyses for subsidiaries.

The trustee also objected to any statements regarding the solvency of the related debtor entities because the expert did not analyze those businesses separately from the parent company.

The court agreed that a particularized analysis was appropriate under the Code's provisions for preferential and fraudulent transfer claims and under case law: "Moreover, a parent company's solvency does not necessarily imply solvency of its subsidiaries."

Here, the defendants' expert admitted he only "generally" analyzed the solvency situation of the subsidiaries and his report only quoted financial statement numbers without any explanation as to why it was unnecessary to make further adjustments. Also, the defendants failed to show that the solvency of the parent company implied the solvency of the subsidiaries.

Therefore, the court also precluded the expert from testifying on solvency as it related to the subsidiaries.

In re Doctors Hospital of Hyde Park, Inc.

Citation: 2007 Bankr. App. LEXIS 605
Date of Decision: March 2, 2007
Country: US
State or Federal: Federal
State/Jurisdiction: Illinois
Court: United States Bankruptcy Court
Type of action: Bankruptcy
Experts: Scott Peltz and Michael Lane (Trustee) Thomas Blake (lender)
Judge: Schmetterer
SIC: 8011 Offices and Clinics of Doctors of Medicine (except mental health specialists, HMO medical centers, and ambulatory surgical and emergency centers)

Fraud-Infected Hospital Merits 'Tax Affecting,' High Risk Premium, and More

The history of Doctors Hospital in Chicago was short and dark: James Desnick, M.D. purchased the property in 1992 for $2.4 million and became the sole shareholder and a director of Doctors Hospital, a Subchapter S corporation, as well as a controlling shareholder in various entities that owned and operated the hospital's real estate, leases, and other assets.

The hospital's revenues were largely derived from federal reimbursements, and court testimony would later reveal—and local news services report—that hospital employees passed out cigarettes and cash to addicts and the homeless in return for their submission to unnecessary hospital tests, stays, and other Medicare/Medicaid reimbursables. Fined over $30 million for federal healthcare fraud, the hospital declared bankruptcy in April 2000 and closed its doors. To avoid a civil indictment, Dr. Desnick settled with the government for $14 million—but two high ranking executives served lengthy prison sentences for fraud, racketeering, and tax charges.

Trustee seeks to avoid $60 million. In its opinion, the Bankruptcy Court takes over 60 pages, one chart, three diagrams, and an index of key players to help explain the complex, fact-intensive financing of the debtor. In essence, in 1997, the hospital secured a $50 million operating loan with its real estate, equipment, accounts receivables, and certain intangibles (the securitization assets). As further security, the hospital assigned all rights to various lease payments to a bank, secured by a guaranty (the Guaranty), which was later assigned to another bank and trust. But, as the court put it, "the loan was primarily intended for the benefit of Dr. Desnick," whose dealings cast a dark shadow over the financial facts.

When Doctors Hospital declared bankruptcy, the bank asserted a $60 million claim against the estate based on the Guaranty. The Trustee countered that all lease payments were avoidable as fraudulent transfers; or, in the alternative, that any lease payment exceeding fair market value was recoverable. The primary issue for determination was whether the debtor was solvent in 1997, at the execution of the Guaranty. Under the applicable federal "balance sheet" test, a debtor is insolvent if the sum of its debts exceeds its property, at a "fair valuation." Thus, despite several years of staying in operation, the Trustee needed to show the debtor had been insolvent in 1997, while the bank attempted to prove solvency.

Trustee uses *Med Diversified* expert. In an interesting twist, the Trustee had retained Scott Peltz (currently with RSM International, Chicago) as its expert. Peltz, a healthcare insolvency expert, had also appeared in the *In re Med Diversified* bankruptcy proceeding but was disqualified by the bankruptcy court (E.D.N.Y) primarily for his lack of business valuation credentials. (The *Med Diversified* court also disqualified the report by Robert Cimasi, a highly credentialed healthcare valuation expert, in a decision that arguably attacked the BV profession as much as any individual practitioner.)

Presumably, the August 2006 *Med Diversified* case was reported after the trial in *Doctors Hospital* but before the parties presented their final written arguments—because in its post-trial brief, the bank raised for the first time an objection to Peltz based on the *Med Diversified* disqualification.

The court denied the objection based largely on the belatedness of the motion but also added—in language that will reassure the many appraisers alarmed by *Med Diversified*—that this "isolated" decision did not diminish the force of Peltz's opinions in the *Doctors Hospital* case. Nor did it disparage his qualifications as an insolvency expert who'd appeared "in numerous other cases, including a previous case before this Court."

However, the court also found that any lack of business valuation certification was not an issue in the *Doctors Hospital* case as it had been in *Med Diversified*. This leaves the door open for parties to challenge purported experts in the valuation context for lack of specific BV credentialing, education, and court experience.

Discounted cash flow method not appropriate. Given the hospital's history of fraud and inability to reach forecasted results, both the Trustee and the bank's expert agreed they could not use a discounted cash flow method to calculate the hospital's 1997 "fair enterprise value." Instead, they both used a capitalization of normalized cash flow method. As for market approaches, the bank's expert rejected both the guideline company and guideline transactions method for lack of comparables, while the Trustee's expert used these approaches solely as a reality check, along with a sensitivity analysis.

Both experts also used the capital asset pricing model (CAPM) to determine an appropriate capitalization rate, and, as their methods were very similar, the bank's expert adopted the Trustee's weighted average cost of capital (WACC) data, with the exception of the company-specific risk premium. This, along with different normalization assumptions and valuation calculations, distinguished the two experts—and determined the outcome of the case:

1. *Tax affecting.* The Trustee's expert analyzed the hospital as a "regularly taxable corporation," using a 40% corporate rate to reduce its 1997 and 1998 net incomes. Even if, as a Subchapter S corporation, the hospital did not directly pay federal corporate taxes, he argued that most pass-through entities set aside sufficient distributions to cover the shareholders' tax liability, thereby effectively paying a corporate tax.

The bank's expert did not reduce the hospital's cash flows for federal taxes, claiming there had never been any distributions to cover the controlling shareholder's (Desnick's) income tax liability.

Moreover, the hospital had never paid any taxes except for minor state replacement and sales tax, and evidence suggested that any potential acquirer of the hospital would be a nonprofit or another S corporation.

However, the court accepted the Trustee's deductions for corporate income taxes, finding support from an unnamed book by "two experts in business valuation" who opined that "C corporation valuation methods may be used for valuing controlling ownership interests in S corporations." As the subject of the insolvency analysis was a 100% interest in the debtor, "tax-affecting the hospital as a C corporation was appropriate," the court said, making the somewhat opaque observation that valuation implied a "theoretical buyer, regardless of the nature of the buyer."

2. *Company-specific risk premium (CSRP).* The bank's expert had selected a CSRP of 5%, based on the related party transactions between the debtor and the controlling shareholder and his associated entities. Normalization adjustments to historical financial performance had already accounted for other risks, he said, including federal fraud, poor management, and unreliable financials, and he'd already incorporated a size adjustment. Lastly, industry factors (such as Medicare fraud investigations) were also "baked into" the beta factor affecting the equity risk premium.

The Trustee's expert disagreed, saying federal fraud investigations focused on specific targets and the associated risks had not been "baked into" the industry beta factor, and he cited market evidence in support. Moreover, in unrelated litigation (between the various creditors), a financial expert for the bank had testified that Doctors Hospital was "atypical," given its reliance on federal reimbursement, and "would need to be capitalized at the highest end of any survey of acute hospitals." That deft use of prior sworn testimony and market research persuaded the court to adopt the 10% CSRP of the Trustee, calling it "conservative."

3. *Contributions from the owner.* To reach a finding of solvency, the bank's expert had also added $18 million to each of the debtors' fiscal years 1997 and 1998. Apparently, these amounts represented the original Medicare/Medicare fraud assessments for these years but not the eventual $14 million settlement between the owner and the government. The expert characterized these as "contingent payments," testifying that a putative purchaser would have made similar capital contributions, but the court found that such a theory "defied common sense."

First, the debtor had no contractual obligation to receive such payments and thus would have no claim for the same from any future purchaser. Second, the fraud liabilities didn't even exist in 1997 and 1998; the $14 million settlement was negotiated after the debtor's bankruptcy—and it was negotiated purely for the owner's benefit; the debtor received no value.

Finally, adding a "nonexistent contribution" from the owner to the debtor's assets contradicted the expert's methodology, which normalized cash flows into perpetuity; the assumption that the owner (or any putative owner) would consider making such contributions indefinitely was not supported "by evidence or logic," the court said. Even if the capital contributions came from a potential buyer, "they are still not part of the fair value of the Doctor's Hospital equity."

4. *Alleged fraudulent earnings.* The bank's expert also added back to net income $4.5 million in fraudulent earnings that were supposedly "booked" in 1997. But there was little evidence the debtor had written off these earnings, and the add-back made no sense when viewing the debtor as a whole, as its fraud was systemic, carried over from year to year. A $4.5 million accounting for fraud was also a "best case scenario," according to an auditor's report, while the "worst case" was $29 million—and that was for just Medicare upcoding.

5. *Excessive lease payments.* According to a real property appraisal, the debtor's lease payments exceeded fair market rentals. Relying on this opinion, the Trustee's expert deducted the excess value as debt; specifically, he capitalized the excess as an additional, nonoperating liability, using the interest rate "implicit in the income stream"—i.e., the rate applicable to the loan (9.6%) serviced by the lease payments.

The bank's expert made no adjustment to rent expense for fair market value; he also disagreed with the discount rate, arguing the Trustee's expert should have used the higher (17.5%) rate of his WACC calculations. But the WACC rate contained a large element of equity return, and using it to discount a debt cash flow "would be simply wrong," the court said.

Solvency and salvaging. In light of these findings and more, the court concluded that Doctors Hospital was insolvent in 1997. It voided the Guaranty and allowed the Trustee to recover all proceeds from the sale of the securitization assets, as well as excess lease payments—thus ending the short, unhappy life of Doctors Hospital with some redemptive light. (According to the latest reports, the University of Chicago purchased the hospital at auction in September 2006 and is considering demolishing the property to develop a hotel/convention center.)

In re Eastman Kodak Company

Citation: 2013 Bankr. LEXIS 3325
Date of decision: Aug. 15, 2013
Country: US
State or Federal: Federal
State/Jurisdiction: New York
Court: United States Bankruptcy Court
Experts: Maulin V. Shah, Elise Neils (shareholders); David S. Kurtz (debtor)
Judge: Gropper

Court Bristles at Experts' Hasty Valuation of Debtor

Shareholders of Kodak objected to the company's reorganization plan and asked the Bankruptcy Court to appoint an equity committee to represent their interests. They presented opinions from two experts arguing that Kodak had underestimated its fair market value, which Kodak challenged. In its *Daubert* ruling, the court took umbrage at the little amount of time and effort the experts gave to complex valuations, finding each analysis was rushed and lacking the intellectual rigor experts in the field apply or should apply.

Incredulous at drop in value. In January 2012, Kodak (the debtor) filed for Chapter 11 bankruptcy. In response, a group of shareholders filed a motion for the appointment of an official equity committee, which the company, the U.S. trustee, and the unofficial unsecured creditors' committee opposed. In denying the request, the court (Bankr. S.D.N.Y.) found that there was adequate representation of the various interests and only a small probability that the shareholders had a right to a "meaningful distribution."

The bankruptcy proceedings moved along; Kodak abandoned its dedicated capture devices business and, after much effort, managed to sell its digital imaging patent portfolio for $527 million. This amount was much less than the $2.2 billion to $2.6 billion Kodak had expected to collect at the beginning of the case. Further, in a settlement with its largest creditor, Kodak sold it the personalized imaging and document imaging businesses for $650 million. Some 13 months later, the company was headed toward a hearing on its reorganization plan. Its first amended disclosure statement of June 2013 confirmed the futility of the shareholders' expectation of a distribution.

Specifically, projections and cash flow forecasts set the company's enterprise value as of fall 2013 at $498 million. According to the company's financial experts, the statement accounted for payment toward administrative, priority, and secured claims and estimated the recovery to unsecured creditors would be at 4% to 5%, or approximately $70 million. This amount was "at least $2.4 billion less than the midpoint of aggregated estimated general unsecured claims and retiree settlement unsecured claims against [Kodak]." This valuation "was the result of hundreds of hours of work by recognized professionals," one financial expert testified at a subsequent hearing.

For their part, a number of shareholders regrouped and renewed their demand for an equity committee, presenting expert reports and other documentary evidence in support. Kodak filed a pretrial *Daubert* motion to exclude most of the evidence and all of the expert testimony. Following a hearing, the court issued this decision.

Allegations of undisclosed value. To bolster their claim that the reorganization plan was "not fair and equitable" to them, the shareholders had to show that Kodak understated its reorganization value by over $2 billion. To do so, they first presented one expert who computed the alleged undisclosed value in Kodak's patent portfolio and a second expert who spoke to the undisclosed value of the Kodak brand. The court considered the testimony in turn.

1. *Patent portfolio value.* The first expert was a law graduate who, in 2009, after one year of practicing, founded a business providing intellectual property (IP) advisory and research services.

He performed a discounted cash flow (DCF) analysis and, in a three-page letter to the shareholders in June 2013, said he believed "the intrinsic value of Kodak's US patent portfolio to be $1.6 billion to $2.5 billion." He premised his analysis on the fact that in June 2013 Kodak had slightly more than 8,500 U.S. patents in force, with an average remaining term of 8.177 years. Then he went on to claim that the annual patent revenue was in a range of $250 million to $350 million. He admitted that these statements drew on a Jan. 23, 2012, "Public Lender Presentation" Kodak had made and also on publicly reported licensing figures the company had published in recent years.

As to the patents, an expert for the creditors' committee, which aligned itself with Kodak, stated that Kodak's settlement with its largest creditor actually reduced the number of worldwide active patents to 7,000 and active U.S. patents to 4,400. Moreover, Kodak had granted licenses to "virtually all" of the retained patents to a consortium that participated in the sale of the digital imaging patent assets. There was evidence that any unlicensed patents were essential to maintaining the company's core business following reorganization and consequently were not for sale or licensing. Also, the company's most up-to-date public financial 2013 statements projected 2013 revenue from IP to be only $35 million, not $350 million.

In response, the shareholders' expert admitted he had not reviewed the most recent financial information and said he was aware of the 2013 asset sales. Regardless, he did not revise his forecasts of future patent revenues. As he saw it, Kodak had a sizeable patent portfolio remaining and *in the past* (his emphasis) had stated it had generated over $3 billion in licensing revenue. It had failed to account for $2 billion in revenue, he maintained. Kodak "clearly understands the nature of patent licensing and enforcement, given its track record in the past of obtaining over $3 billion in revenue."

The Bankruptcy Court found his testimony highly problematic. "Whatever the strength of his background, he spent only five hours and his firm spent a total of ten hours on valuing Kodak's patents," it pointed out. His contradictory attitude deserved special mention: On the one hand, he admitted at the hearing that his firm would need 5,000 hours to do a full analysis of the value of the patent portfolio; on the other hand, he "did not take the position that he could not provide any opinion testimony until such analysis had been performed." His opinion rested on assumptions "that have no validity whatsoever." His speculation as to the company's past revenues from patent licensing may have "encouraged" shareholders to believe "that Kodak could not conceivably have fallen as far and as fast as it did," said the court. But it was not "useful or admissible" as to the estate's current value.

2. *Brand value.* The second expert had "substantial" experience in valuing brands and in testifying as an expert. She said she used the "relief from royalty" method to determine the "proportion of future cash flows that are attributable to the brand—the present value of the post-tax royalties that are held to represent the value of the brand today." She began by looking at company revenues and evaluated brand strength by establishing a range of "similar" royalty rates the business would have to pay if it did not own the brand; she then discounted the future revenues and considered the net present value of post-tax royalties to be the "brand value." Her starting point was Kodak's projections of 2014 revenues of $2.6 billion, she said. She also reported that in 2007 the Kodak brand was worth almost $3 billion; this figure represented 35.1% of the total enterprise value of $8.5 billion; by her account, in 2008, the brand was worth almost $2 billion, which amounted to 40.2% of the total enterprise value of nearly $5 billion.

At the hearing, the expert admitted that she had lacked the time and information she normally required to perform a thorough analysis. For example, she did not interview Kodak's management or determine the effect of Kodak's settlement with its largest creditor under which Kodak would grant a perpetual license for its products.

Again, the court homed in on the fact that the expert or her colleagues only "spent a grand total of six hours" before she submitted a "preliminary brand valuation" at 3:00 a.m. on July 26, 2013. The expert's "admitted inability to perform an analysis with the same information she would ordinarily use" makes her valuation inadmissible, the court said. But even if the expert could have learned the basic facts about Kodak's present financial situation, her valuing the brand for the purpose of determining whether the shareholders could expect any meaningful recovery was a "useless exercise." The expert admitted that brand value was not "a separate item of value in excess of the total equity of an enterprise." The fact that the Kodak brand was worth $1 billion or more years ago when the company was a leader in the business was meaningless, said the court, because reliable expert testimony showed that its total equity today was less than $500 million, "resulting in a wholly insolvent debtor." Although some shareholders might refuse to accept this value, they failed to disprove it, the court concluded.

Value added from net operating losses? Finally the shareholders argued that Kodak's reorganization plan "unnecessarily" gave up $2.6 billion in net operating losses (NOLs) because it represented a change in ownership for tax purposes. Avoiding the loss of the NOLs would create $760 million in new value and raise the reorganization value to $1.2 billion, they believed. However, one of Kodak's experts stated that the creditors, whose rights to the NOL benefits trumped those of the shareholders, recognized that a change in ownership was "inevitable." The creditors were not willing "to leave enough equity in the hands of the existing shareholders to avoid the loss of the NOLs," he said.

The court acknowledged that the shareholders had reason to press the tax issue, "but there is nothing in the Bankruptcy Code that requires the result that they desire." What's more, they failed to explain how the preservation of the tax attributes would increase the reorganization value—or that they could expect a distribution based on that level. To benefit from the NOLs, a reorganized debtor must have income to offset, the court pointed out. In sum, the shareholders failed to show that Kodak was solvent and that an equity committee was appropriate.

EBCI, Inc. v. America Online, Inc.

Citation: 2008 Bankr. LEXIS 38
Date of Decision: January 10, 2008
Country: US
State or Federal: Federal
State/Jurisdiction: Delaware
Court: United States Bankruptcy Court
Type of action: Bankruptcy
Experts: Robert Hutchings (AOL)
Judge: Walrath
SIC: 5945 Hobby, Toy, and Game Stores

Proving Solvency When Internet Assets 'Disappear Overnight'

How can an Internet toy company be a solvent, going concern right before Thanksgiving—and be bankrupt within 45 days, just after Christmas, with nothing left but liquidation value in the new year?

That's the tough question the expert in this bankruptcy case had to tackle. In 1999, the toy company (eToys) paid America Online (AOL) $7.5 million to provide online advertising services for three years at a total cost of $18 million. After the first year, AOL failed to perform, and, on Nov. 15, 2000, the parties amended their agreement. AOL would provide ads for the next two years, for which eToys paid $750,000 without further obligation.

High hopes for the holidays. At the time of the amendment, everyone—eToys as well as its investors and industry experts—expected the company to have a "tremendously successful" holiday season. During the prior year, eToys had expanded its warehouse operations, moved into new headquarters, increased full-time employees by over 300%, and doubled its customer base. An IPO in May 1999 had raised $175 million. The company raised another $145 million by issuing unsecured convertible notes in December 1999 and $100 million in a preferred stock offering in June 2000. On Nov. 15, 2000—the same day as its amended agreement with AOL for advertising services—eToys secured $40 million in revolving credit.

But then came a "disastrous" holiday retail season. By Dec. 31, 2000, the company began conserving cash and hired an investment banker to look for buyers. Several expressed interest, but none followed through, and, in February 2001, eToys fired all its employees, closed operations, and filed for Chapter 11 bankruptcy. Two days later, AOL terminated their agreement. During bankruptcy, eToys sought to recover both the payments to AOL and the termination of the agreement as fraudulent transfers.

AOL focuses on adjustments to book value. To recoup the payments to AOL, eToys had to prove that it was insolvent on the date of the amended agreement—Nov. 15, 2000—and that any transfer was "for less than reasonably equivalent value."

It retained an expert, who used a going concern (as opposed to liquidation) premise of value based on the following factors:

1. eToys' capital investments during the relevant period;
2. Its access to capital and credit;
3. Its employment base;
4. Its customer base;
5. Lack of any fraud or mismanagement; and
6. Managers' and investors' expectations.

AOL's expert also used the standard "balance sheet test" to show solvency, adjusting to the book value of eToys' assets to reflect their market value. For example, he increased the value of its inventory by 21% but reduced the book value of goodwill from $124 million to zero and decreased property and machinery by 33%. He also included the value of licensed software, which eToys used in its operations. The expert did not adjust eToys' liabilities nor did he include the company's preferred stock, which its balance sheet listed as a $37 million debt.

Based on those adjustments, AOL's expert calculated that eToys' assets were worth approximately $302 million, excluding the value of the intangibles, and approximately $545 million inclusive. Under the balance sheet test, he believed that eToys' assets exceeded its debts by $15 million to $258 million, and the company was solvent on Nov. 15, 2000. The expert also considered eToys' ability to pay its debts ("cash flow test") and whether its capital was sufficient to fund operations ("capital adequacy test") to confirm that the company was solvent at the date of its agreement with AOL.

eToys could have used an expert. eToys declined to obtain an expert, arguing that the company (as well as the Internet industry) simply "collapsed by the end of 2000." Even AOL's expert admitted that eToys was insolvent by that time. Since "nothing unforeseen happened between November 15 and Dec. 31, 2000," it was "common sense," eToys claimed, to conclude that the company was bankrupt on both dates. Thus liquidation was the appropriate premise of value to measure insolvency.

Alternatively—even if eToys was a going concern at the time of the transfer—AOL's expert made inappropriate adjustments to the book value of eToys' assets. In particular, he should have valued inventory at wholesale, and he shouldn't have valued its intangibles based on market capitalization—because this value "disappeared overnight" when the company collapsed. The licensed software had no value, eToys claimed, and the preferred stock was an ongoing debt.

The court rejected this analysis. "eToys' condition was fundamentally different on November 15 and Dec. 31, 2000," it said, citing all the factors that AOL's expert considered in his adoption of the going concern premise. At the time of the transfer with AOL, the company was still selling its inventory at retail and still using its software. Bankruptcy law also permitted the court to consider eToys' market capitalization in valuing its intangible assets.

'True' market value trumps GAAP. Further, even though eToys did not carry the value of intangibles on its balance sheet, the balance sheet test in bankruptcy is based on a "fair valuation" of assets rather than generally accepted accounting principles (GAAP). The test may include values "not used to prepare a typical balance sheet," the court said, citing legal precedent as well as Shannon Pratt (*Valuing a Business*, 4th ed., 2000).

"GAAP does not deal with the true market value or assets or the determination of" a company's legal liabilities, the court added. Although GAAP treats redeemable preferred stock as a liability, SEC regulations do not. In addition:

> Just as GAAP rules regarding the book value of assets do not determine their fair market value, similarly GAAP rules for treating debt as equity and vice versa are not relevant to determining whether they are truly debt or equity.

Instead, the facts and circumstances determine the "true" nature of the item—and, in this case, the preferred stock was payable at eToys' discretion. Given its "dire" financial condition, the company probably would not have paid the debt (in fact, its plan of reorganization canceled it). Given the value conclusions by AOL's expert under the balance sheet test—as well as his conclusion under the alternate cash flow and capital adequacy tests—the court found eToys solvent as of the transfer date.

Liquidation value appropriate for agreement. eToys also claimed that AOL was liable for the value of their original agreement (as amended). Because the company paid $8.25 million but received only $3.75 million in services when AOL cancelled, eToys was entitled to the remaining $4.5 million.

The court disagreed. The parties may have agreed on pricing but not on the value of the advertising services. In fact, the agreement had no value to eToys by the time AOL terminated; ads for its website were worth nothing when the company was no longer running. eToys contended that it could have sold the agreement for some value as part of its general asset liquidation in bankruptcy. But the court rejected this, too, noting that, under applicable law, the contract was unique to the parties and unassignable.

Even if eToys could have assigned the rights to receive AOL services, AOL's expert valued these between $16,500 and $38,500, based on the prices eToys realized in its asset liquidation. eToys tried to assert that liquidation value wasn't appropriate, but it lost this final argument as well. Despite its Chapter 11 filing, eToys was clearly liquidating, and the totality of circumstances led the court to conclude that, on the termination date, the value of the agreement was "de minimus."

In re Edgewater Medical Center

Citation: 2007 Bankr. LEXIS 2696
Date of Decision: August 15, 2007
Country: US
State or Federal: Federal
State/Jurisdiction: Illinois
Court: United States Bankruptcy Court
Type of action: Fraud
Experts: John Hartwig and Patrick McNally (plaintiff/debtor)
Judge: Black
SIC: 8062 General Medical and Surgical Hospitals

Should Solvency Valuation Include Ongoing but Undiscovered Fraud?

Appraisers are well acquainted with the prohibition against including hindsight in the valuation of a business interest. But what about a current condition—present at the time of valuation—but unknown to all but company insiders, such as a pervasive accounting or Medicare fraud? This case examines both elements in the bankruptcy context and makes an interesting distinction between fraud that conceals insolvency and fraud that causes it.

$13 million Medicare fraud. In 1994, the principal owner of a hospital corporation and related holding company (which owned the hospital's real estate assets) sold most of his interest to a non-profit company, doing business as Edgewater Medical Center (EMC). The holding company retained ownership of certain properties adjacent to the hospital, and, two years later, in 1996, granted EMC a 10-year lease and option to purchase the adjacent properties.

In 2001, EMC stopped paying rent and ceased operations and presumably filed its Chapter 11 proceedings; the court opinion does not specify the precise timing of the bankruptcy. It does note that the owner of the real estate holding company (the same one who sold the hospital operations to EMC) was charged with Medicare fraud, breach of fiduciary duty, and other claims. After lengthy trial proceedings—and fines/forfeitures of $13 million—the owner abruptly fired his lawyers and left the country.

In this next phase of proceedings, EMC attempted to recover the substantial (nearly $18,000 per month) rental payments made pursuant to the lease/option agreement with the holding company as fraudulent or preferential transfers. Both claims depended on EMC proving that it was bankrupt at the time of the transfers.

Fraud was pervasive but hidden. Neither party disputed that the Medicare fraud took place during the relevant valuation period. At trial, however, the defendant holding company claimed that EMC was solvent during the time, because—pursuant to the definitions under both the federal Bankruptcy Code and the local (Illinois) Uniform Fraudulent Transfer Act—its assets exceeded its debts. Evidence showed that EMC held a "strong cash position" at the time of the transfers (over $29 million in cash and investments).

EMC didn't directly challenge this valuation evidence. Instead, it presented credible expert testimony that, had the ongoing Medicare fraud come to light in 1996, federal reimbursements would have ceased and the debtors would have been bankrupt. To advance its argument, EMC cited a New York bankruptcy case in which a debtor's insolvency was hidden behind false accounts receivable and other financial misrepresentations.

In theory, the court agreed. Whether valued on a going concern or liquidation basis, EMC was insolvent if the effect of the Medicare fraud was included in its valuation. But it distinguished the New York precedent. In that case:

> [T]he company actually was insolvent. It only *appeared* to be solvent because it was 'cooking the books.' In the case at bar, the debtor [EMC] *might* have been rendered insolvent *if* the Medicare fraud had been uncovered.

Further, in the case of falsified accounting records, there was no need to incorporate any hypothetical fines, penalties, or cessation of payments to make a finding of insolvency. "But that is exactly what [EMC] is asking the court to do here." To find insolvency, the court would have to disregard the company's actual cash position and speculate on what would have happened had the government discovered the Medicare fraud. The court declined to do so and found that EMC was solvent at the time of the transfers because its assets "clearly outweighed" its debts.

In re John Joseph Edwards

Citation: 1999 Bankr. LEXIS 401
Date of Decision: April 13, 1999
Country: US
State or Federal: Federal
State/Jurisdiction: Pennsylvania
Court: United States Bankruptcy Court
Type of action: Bankruptcy
Judge: Sigmund
SIC: 5541 Gasoline Service Station (gasoline station with convenience store)

Debtor Objects to Disposition of Assets

The main issue in this bankruptcy case (third and final opinion on the matter) is the objection of debtor, Edwards, to the disposition of his assets by the Chapter 7 Trustee. The case thoroughly discusses his objections and the judge's decisions.

In the Matter of Elizabeth Ann Evert (debtor): Marsha G. Milligan, Trustee v. Elizabeth Ann Evert

Citation: No. 02-50411 (5th Cir.)
Date of Decision: August 6, 2003
Country: US
State or Federal: Federal
State/Jurisdiction: 5th Circuit
Court: United States Court of Appeals
Type of action: Bankruptcy

Property Equalization Payments Cannot Be Exempted in Bankruptcy

The U.S. Court of Appeals for the 5th Circuit considered whether a promissory note executed in connection with a divorce settlement agreement could be exempted in a bankruptcy proceeding under sec. 522 (d)(10)(D) as "alimony, support, or separate maintenance." In 1999, the debtor and her former spouse divorced in Texas. During the marriage, the debtor's former spouse operated a business, which along with the marital home, was one of the two major assets in the divorce. The husband retained the business (having equity of $230,000) while the debtor retained the home (having equity of $100,000). To equalize the property distribution, and under that heading in the divorce decree, the husband executed a promissory note having a face value of $65,000, carrying 8% interest, and payable monthly. Under a separate section of the divorce instrument, the wife received $1,350 in spousal support. The spousal support was nonassignable and subject to modification under certain circumstances.

In 2001, the debtor sought Chapter 7 bankruptcy protection. She declared the note an exemption for "alimony, support, or separate maintenance" under section 522. The trustee challenged that exemption. Because there was no law directly addressing this type of exemption, the bankruptcy court looked to the corresponding section on dischargeability of obligations arising from divorce instruments. See sec. 522 (a)(5). Under this section, the court looked past the labels given to the payment by the parties and the divorce court and considered the payments under a variety of factors (known as the *Nunnally* factors). Those factors included disparity of earnings between the divorcing parties, relative business opportunities, their physical condition, their educational background, future financial needs, benefits each party would have received had the marriage continued, and fault for the breakdown of the marriage. Applying those factors, the bankruptcy court concluded that the note could be exempted under sec. 522 (d)(10)(D). The trustee appealed.

The 5th Circuit initially noted, "The threshold question is whether the same approach this circuit has used for determining what constitutes alimony in the context of dischargeability under 11 U.S.C. § 523 (a)(5) should apply to exemptions under 11 U.S.C. § 522 (d)(10)(D)." However, it declined to directly answer the question. Rather it looked to the specific facts of this case. It stated:

> We hold only that, at least for the purposes of section 522(d)(10)(D), where in the agreed divorce decree there is 1) also a meaningful separate alimony provision, 2) the obligation in question is described as being part of the property division, 3) the label given to the obligation in question is matched to its actual characteristics, and 4) the evidence does not suggest the parties

> conspired to disguise the true nature of the obligation in order to subvert the bankruptcy or tax laws, there is no ambiguity necessitating the use of the *Nunnally* factors to essentially work backwards to determine the nature of the obligation.

Thus, the 5th Circuit reversed the bankruptcy court's decision permitting the exemption of the note in light of the fact that the divorce instrument clearly showed that the note was part of the parties' property settlement and the divorce instrument separately provides for nontrivial alimony.

In re Fairvue Club Properties

Citation: 2010 WL 4501959 (Bkrtcy. M.D. Tenn.)
Date of decision: Nov. 2, 2010
Country: US
State or Federal: Federal
State/Jurisdiction: Tennessee
Court: United States Bankruptcy Court
Experts: Andy Hinds (debtors); Miles McDonald and Andrew Cantor (lender)
Judge: Paine

Lender Uses Debtor's Own Appraiser to Show Plan Lacks Financial Feasibility

The owner of two semiprivate golf clubs pledged to do "whatever it takes" to pull his properties out of bankruptcy. He and his management team put together an optimistic reorganization plan, which exceeded even his appraiser's projections, based on increasing membership, reducing tee times, and "any other necessary step" to make the plan work, the owner said. The primary secured lender objected to the plan, however, claiming it was neither financially feasible nor fair.

In particular, the owner projected annual cash flows approaching nearly $2 million, when the clubs had never posted more than $1 million per year at any point in their operating history, the lender said. In fact, 2007 was the last positive cash flow year for the clubs. In addition, the owner's revenue projections were substantially higher than those forecast by its own business appraiser—whom the lender called as its own witness at the confirmation hearing.

In his original report to the debtors, the business appraiser had valued the clubs under the capitalization of income approach at $7.7 million. In addition to considering the clubs' historic revenues and expenses, he considered those of comparable clubs in the area as well as general market trends in the golfing industry. Based on these three components, the appraiser developed revenue projections, discounted to present value, which were 14% to 23% less than the owner's projections in the plan, or between $300,000 and $500,000 per year. His three market comparables all had positive cash flows of only $360,000, the appraiser noted—and, compared to the debtors, they were all more established operations and none were in bankruptcy.

The bank also called its own expert appraiser, who said the owner's projections were unrealistic primarily because they called for increased membership and golf rounds beyond the clubs' capacity. The bank's expert also agreed "90%" with the financial projections by the debtors' appraiser and said that any lender considering the owner's projections would be a "default waiting to happen." Finally, a third, a turnaround expert, analyzed the owner's projected revenues, income before capital expenditures, membership, and golf rounds played and concluded the debtors would experience cash flow shortfalls in all the years of the proposed plan.

Hope and effort are not enough. The court had no doubt that the owner was committed "to trying to successfully reorganize these debtors." Unfortunately, it also found that the projections by all three experts proved more persuasive as to what the business could achieve. "Hope and effort alone cannot make the debtors' projections attainable," the court said, and rejected the plan as unrealistic, without a reasonable framework or assurance of success.

In re Flashcom, Inc.

Citation: 2013 U.S. Dist. LEXIS 171266
Date of decision: Dec. 4, 2013
Country: US
State or Federal: State
State/Jurisdiction: California
Court: United States District Court
Type of action: Bankruptcy
Experts: David Hahn (trustee-appellant); Randy Sugarman (defendants-appellees)
Judge: Olguin
SIC: 4813 Telephone Communications, Except Radiotelephone (resellers)

GAAP 'Relevant' but 'Not Controlling' in Solvency Analysis

After an Internet business collapsed, the bankruptcy trustee unsuccessfully sued its venture capital investors and directors over a $9 million transfer to one of the company's founders. The Bankruptcy Court found that the trustee failed to prove insolvency, by relying on a problematic valuation. The expert who performed it failed to value the business as a going concern and slavishly followed generally accepted accounting principles in analyzing assets and liabilities. The trustee attacked the ruling in an appeal with the district court.

Interlocking transactions. In the late 1990s, a wife and husband formed an Internet service provider that resold digital subscriber line (DSL) service to consumers and businesses. Several venture capital (VC) funds invested $15 million to buy preferred stock and obtained the right to appoint three of the company's five-member board of directors; the husband and wife occupied the other two seats. When the majority of the board decided the wife's management style interfered with customer, vendor, and strategic partner relations, she demanded a substantial amount of money in exchange for her withdrawal. Eventually, she threatened litigation against the company, the VC investors, the directors, including the husband, and management. To raise money and resolve all disputes with the wife, the VC funds arranged for another round of financing. They committed to buying $5.7 million in Series B shares but insisted that settling matters with the wife was vital to proceeding with the financing. They also made bridge loans in the amount of $9 million to the company, as short-term working capital to keep operations going before the financing.

Ultimately, the investors, the company, and the wife executed a stock purchase agreement under which the company would repurchase some of the wife's common stock for $9 million. Relatedly, under a settlement and release agreement, the wife would abandon her claims against the various parties. The $9 million transfer, in turn, was conditioned on the company's ability to raise at least $40 million through a Series B offering. This condition was satisfied. On Feb. 23, 2000, the company raised $84 million in an offering that actually was oversubscribed; the same day, it bought out the wife by way of a $9 million wire transfer and reaped $75 million in proceeds. Subsequently, it even contemplated an IPO but was unable to secure additional financing. Ultimately, the economic downturn contributed to its filing for bankruptcy at the end of 2000.

Going concern or barely standing? The bankruptcy trustee pursued various legal strategies and theories to recover the $9 million from the VC funds and directors, the defendants-appellees. In a pretrial motion in Bankruptcy Court (C.D. Cal.), she argued that the transaction was a constructive fraudulent transfer because the company received nothing in return for the redemption of the wife's stock in exchange for the $9 million payment.

The Bankruptcy Court disagreed, finding that the transfer left "no negative effect" on the company's estate. It was appropriate to consider the entire context in which the transaction occurred. Without the wife's relinquishing all claims against the company, investors would not have completed the Series B financing. The wife, however, would not have released the company without receiving a $9 million payment for her stock. In the final analysis, the company benefited from the exchange by securing $75 million of new financing and an end to the threat of litigation.

At trial, the trustee tried to avoid the $9 million transfer by showing that the company was insolvent at the time of the transfer, February 2000. Both parties presented valuation experts to shore up their arguments.

The company's expert determined that the company was worth approximately $400 million on a going-concern basis just prior to the transfer. The calculation included $21.9 million for subscriber contracts as of the transfer date based on book value. He explained that, if the company had put up its subscriber contracts for sale at that time, the market would have considered them "very valuable" and "there would have been a bidding war to purchase [the] contracts."

In contrast, the trustee's expert said he had not valued the company "as an entire entity on a going-concern basis." In determining assets and liabilities, the expert believed the $5.7 million of funds from the investors should not be treated as assets under generally accepted accounting principles (GAAP) because they had not closed at the date of transfer. At the same time, he testified that at that date it was more likely that 100% of the legally committed Series B proceeds would be received than the projected 90% of the company's accounts receivable that he did include as assets in his solvency analysis. He also counted $6.7 million in bridge loans as a liability, even if they were not absolute, because "liabilities include debts that are contingent or disputed." Further, relying on the opinion of the trustee's subscriber valuation expert, he determined the contracts would only generate approximately $3.3 million in an orderly sale.

The Bankruptcy Court gave numerous reasons why the company should be valued as a going concern, including: (1) it was able to raise $84 million in an oversubscribed Series B financing; (2) its vendors were willing to extend it substantial credit; (3) investors seemed uniformly optimistic about its prospects; and (4) it received 1,500 new orders for subscriber lines each week.

It discredited the trustee expert's valuation, finding it should have counted the $5.7 million in Series B proceeds as an asset because the "investors were contractually committed to fund their obligation to purchase Series B shares, and [the company] would have had a claim against these investors if the payment was not made." At the same time, the valuation incorrectly included $6.7 million in bridge loans as a liability. Under controlling case law, "[t]o determine a contingent liability, one must discount it by the probability that the contingency will occur and the liability will become real." In this case, the promissory notes for the loans stated that they automatically would convert to equity once the company received at least $30 million in Series B proceeds. There was an "extremely low" probability that the company would have to pay for the notes," the court found. The trustee's expert had failed to consider this eventuality in his analysis. As for the value of the subscriber contracts, the court noted that the trustee's expert relied on a subscriber valuation expert who by his own admission had not considered all of the testimony key members of the company's management and board had given. Further, other trial witnesses described his data as unreliable compared with the data the competing subscriber valuation expert used.

Adopting the company expert's valuation, the Bankruptcy Court found the company was solvent on the date of transfer.

Subscription value dispute. The trustee next appealed the Bankruptcy Court's decisions with the district court (C.D. Cal.). First, the trustee argued error as to the ruling that there was no fraudulent conveyance.

The District Court dealt with that claim quickly. At issue in the case was an "integrated transaction," whose effect was a net financial gain for the company of $75 million in new equity, it said. Consequently, the company did not receive less than a reasonably equivalent value in exchange.

Second, the trustee challenged the Bankruptcy Court's insolvency ruling, homing in on three errors. Were it not for these errors, the Bankruptcy Court "would have had no choice but to conclude" that the company was insolvent at the transfer date, the trustee contended.

At the outset of its analysis, the district court noted that a "fair valuation" in the context of the Bankruptcy Code involves a two-step process: First, the court determines whether the debtor company was a "going concern" or "on its deathbed." Second, the court values the debtor's assets based on the status it assigned in the first part of its analysis. If it designated the company as a going concern, it determines the fair market price of its assets; if it finds that the company is barely alive, it determines the liquidation value.

Here, the Bankruptcy Court correctly held that the company should be valued as a going concern. Because the trustee's expert "declined to provide a [going concern] valuation," the $400 million valuation the company's expert presented was uncontroverted evidence and by itself "enough for the court to conclude that the Trustee did not meet her burden" of showing insolvency, the reviewing court concluded.

Next, the district court addressed the three errors the trustee alleged.

1. Under the GAAP, it was error to include cash—specifically the $5.7 million in Series B funds—as an asset because it arrived after the $9 million transfer to the wife.

The reviewing court found no error. "GAAP is not controlling in determining the fair market value of assets or the insolvency of the debtor," it said. To find otherwise "would make accountants and the board which promulgate GAAP the arbiters of insolvency questions." But the Bankruptcy Code "clearly" left the decisions to judges. Moreover, no rationale existed "why judges should not be allowed to consider subsequent events … in valuing assets and determining liabilities." Here, the Bankruptcy Court correctly found that the investors had a contractual obligation to buy Series B shares. "In any event, the Series B proceeds arrived two days later." Also, the trustee's expert testified to the strong likelihood that 100% of the Series B proceeds would be received as opposed to only 90% of accounts receivable, which he designated as assets.

2. It was error not to count debts—that is, the bridge loans, which the company owed at the transfer date—as liabilities. Even if the loans were not an absolute liability, they were a contingent liability, which "must be reduced … to its present or expected amount before a determination on insolvency can be made."

According to the reviewing court, the Bankruptcy Court correctly assessed the probability—extremely low—that the liability would become real by looking at the provisions in the related promissory notes. Accordingly, it properly determined not to include them as a liability in its analysis.

3. It was error to value the DSL subscriber contracts in place, not as if sold.

"Book value does not necessarily prove fair market value," the district court acknowledged, but nonetheless "is competent evidence." Here, the company's expert testified to the high value the contracts would have held in the market had they been offered for sale at the time of transfer. His statements suggested that the contracts were valued as if sold, said the court. Also, statements from the trustee's contracts valuation expert and other witnesses supported the Bankruptcy Court's decision not to give great weight to the much lower estimate the trustee's valuation assigned to the contracts.

For all these reasons, the district court affirmed the Bankruptcy Court's ruling.

In re Frezzo

Citation: 217 B.R. 985, 1998 Bankr. LEXIS 224
Date of Decision: March 5, 1998
Country: US
State or Federal: Federal
State/Jurisdiction: Pennsylvania
Court: United States Bankruptcy Court
Type of action: Bankruptcy
Judge: Raslavich
SIC: 2873 Nitrogenous Fertilizers
Key words: Bankruptcy, Income approach

Court Affirms Discounts and Hypothetical Capital Gains Taxes

In a motion before the bankruptcy court, Chapter 7 trustee, Gloria Satriale, sought leave to sell debtor's 50% interest in a mushroom composting company to debtor's brother, James Frezzo, who also had a 50% interest in the company known as Frezzo Brothers. The motion was opposed by the debtor, claiming the price of $1,290,000 was insufficient.

During the course of her duties as trustee, Satriale was approached by James Frezzo, who offered to purchase the subject shares for $1,000,000. Lacking an appraisal, Satriale declined to immediately act on the offer. She instead requested James Frezzo obtain an independent appraisal at his expense. James Frezzo retained Stephen J. Scherf, CPA, ABV, CVA, with Miller Tate & Co., to perform the valuation.

Expert employs income and asset approaches. In reaching his opinion of value, Scherf employed both the income approach and an asset-based approach. His income approach produced a value for the 50% interest of $1,290,000, versus his asset-based approach, which produced a value of $1,285,000. Rather than splitting the difference, Scherf adopted the higher of the two values.

The court noted that the objectors did not quarrel with Scherf's income approach, given the fact he used the company's audited financial statements. The financial statements reflected an erratic stream of earnings and sizable losses for the current period. Scherf used a capitalization rate of 25.1% to reflect the high risk factors facing the company and also to reflect that the company was in a declining industry.

Objectors offer little evidence. The objectors maintained that the interest in question was worth $2,500,000, even though they did not offer expert testimony or evidence to support their assertion. Specifically, the objectors challenged the independence of the valuation report, claiming that it was a transparent guise by James Frezzo, who sought to capitalize on the adverse circumstances.

Minority and marketability discounts approved. However, the court further noted that, ceteris paribus, Scherf himself would have arrived at a value of $2,049,913 for the 50% interest, before accounting for his 10% discount for lack of control, and 30% for lack of marketability. Regarding the discounts, the court stated, "Intuitively, this Court finds nothing inherently objectionable in the reasons for the two discounts ... they are factors routinely applied by experts in deriving estimates of values. The particular percentages applied by Scherf in this instance produced a significant adverse monetary effect, but given the circumstances, they might arguably be defended as conservative."

Reduction for taxes appropriate. Regarding Scherf's asset-based approach, Scherf deducted a hypothetical capital gains tax of 35% for a sale of the company's assets. The court stated, "A reduction for potential taxes is certainly appropriate. Indeed, the Chester County Special Master himself specifically indicated [that] he too, would reduce the value of Frezzo Brothers, Inc., for potential income taxes, and that he would further reduce it for transaction costs as well, should sale of the company's assets be necessary to realize their cash value."

The court concluded that, in light of the evidence presented, James Frezzo's purchase offer satisfied the fair value test. Motion granted.

In re Global Technovations, Inc. (I)

Citation: 2011 WL 1297356 (E.D. Mich.)
Date of decision: March 31, 2011
Country: US
State or Federal: Federal
State/Jurisdiction: Michigan
Court: United States District Court
Experts: Jeff Risius (appellants); Van Conway (debtor)
Judge: Battani

'Most Reliable, Least Speculative' Valuation Prevails in Bankruptcy

In the first phase of these proceedings, the bankruptcy court found that the debtor became insolvent after acquiring the American division of a Japanese automotive technology company, in large part because the parent company had covertly directed its subsidiary to overstate its 12-month trailing EBITDA by $2 million.

The court also discredited the seller's valuation expert for using the subsidiary's inflated earnings projections in his solvency analysis, preferring instead the debtor's expert, who used the seller's historic 12-month trailing earnings. The bankruptcy court deemed this method "the most reliable and least speculative" means by which to evaluate the target company's "reasonably expected future performance." Based on this evidence, the court concluded that the target company was worth only $6.9 million (compared to the original $25 million purchase price), and, after the acquisition, the debtor's liabilities exceeded its assets by $12.2 million. The court avoided the transaction as a fraudulent conveyance, and the seller appealed.

Present value of promissory note. In particular, the appellant argued that the evidence failed to satisfy two prongs of the applicable fraudulent conveyance law (Florida). That is, the debtor received "reasonably equivalent value" when it purchased the Japanese subsidiary, the appellant claimed, and the acquisition did not render the debtor insolvent. Further, the bankruptcy court erred by permitting the debtor's expert to supplement his report after disclosure deadlines had passed.

1. *Reasonably equivalent value.* In the original transaction, the debtor paid for the subsidiary with $13 million in cash and $12 million in promissory notes. At trial, the subsidiary's expert reduced the face value of the notes to $8.6 million, based on the market rate of interest for comparable unsecured debt. The court adopted his opinion regarding the value given in the transaction but declined to adopt the expert's ultimate solvency conclusion. "There is no requirement that the trier of fact must adopt an expert's opinion in its entirety," the appellate court said, in confirming the ruling. "Specifically, the discount rate to be applied to unsecured debt is not inextricably tied to [the debtor's] solvency." Further, there was no finding below that the debtor was insolvent when it executed the notes (only that it became insolvent as a result of the purchase.)

As to the value the debtor received in the sale, the bankruptcy court relied on the debtor's expert to find that the equity value of the subsidiary amounted to $6.9 million. The appellants maintained that this value ignored the "pre-transaction" projections of benefits that the debtor would receive, such as new business, exclusive distribution rights, access to trademarks and technology, a $3 million cash closing fee, and maintaining its stock exchange listing.

The bankruptcy court acknowledged that synergies and similar "non-stock" benefits factor into an assessment of "reasonably equivalent value." Since, in this case, the value of the subsidiary's stock constituted a mere 53% of the debtor's cash payment, "the value of all the benefits to [the debtor] becomes critical and demonstrates why bankruptcy courts [must] examine all aspects of the transaction and carefully measure the value of all benefits and burdens to the debtor, direct or indirect." According to the appellants, the debtor frustrated the bankruptcy court's inquiry by failing to provide any evidence of the nonstock benefits it received.

The bankruptcy court noted some value in the debtor avoiding delisting on the American Stock Exchange. Other than that, however, it found the net value of any nonstock benefits to be zero, not only because the debtor suffered economic damages from acquiring the inflated target, but also because any nonstock benefits were "highly speculative and in fact … unachievable." In making this finding, the bankruptcy court did not impermissibly rely on hindsight, the appellate court said (noting that the "critical time" for assessing reasonably equivalent value is at the time of the transfer). In fact, the bankruptcy court correctly found that the target had assessed these indirect benefits as of the date of the closing, based on information known only to its management.

Further, as the debtor's expert showed, the immediate cash drain on the debtor following the acquisition undermined any value of nonstock benefits. The bankruptcy court did not err by crediting this expert over the seller's, the appellate court held, which also credited the debtor's expert with a more "substantive analysis, inasmuch as [he] admitted that he would not have wasted his time" on the representations made by the target's management.

Finally, the appellate court conceded that the debtor's expert failed to observe Rule 26 requirements by submitting a supplemental solvency analysis past the disclosure deadlines. Instead of striking the expert's evidence, however, the bankruptcy court ordered the debtor to pay the costs associated with redeposing the expert. Since this relatively lesser sanction did not prejudice the debtor's opponent, the appellate court affirmed.

In re Global Technovations, Inc. (II)

Citation: 2012 U.S. App. LEXIS 19209
Date of decision: September 13, 2012
Country: US
State or Federal: Federal
State/Jurisdiction: 6th Circuit
Court: United States Court of Appeals
Experts: Van Conway (debtor); Jeff Risius (defendants)
Judge: Boggs

6th Circuit Upholds Using Post Hoc Comparable Transaction

This multilevel litigation began in bankruptcy court. The debtor, which had acquired the American division of a Japanese automotive technology company for $25 million—$13 million in cash and $12 million in short-term promissory notes—sued the seller, claiming the purchase was a fraudulent, avoidable transaction.

Actual vs. projected earnings. At trial, experts for both parties used the comparable transactions method to calculate the fair market value (FMV) of the target company. Based on four transactions, the plaintiff's expert developed an earnings multiple, which, when applied to the target's 12-month trailing EBITDA, yielded an FMV of $6.9 million. He also valued the promissory notes at face value. He further stated that the economic value of the indirect benefits that the debtor allegedly received from the acquisition was zero. Further, he did not discount the notes because they were short term (three years).

On cross-examination, the expert discussed any risk of hindsight in his calculation of the multiple as well as his determination of EBITDA. He acknowledged that the target's actual earnings after the Aug. 31, 2000, closing date "are not to be used unless again you would have predicted those results based on information you would have known." As for using comparable transactions that took place after the closing date, he said it was acceptable to use those that occurred within a reasonable range of time. "Otherwise you'd never be able to use this method." Any expert who prepares a valuation after the event could benefit from hindsight, but this in itself did not skew the calculation because the selected transactions took place around the time of the event.

By contrast, the defendants' expert used the target's projected EBITDA for 2000, including his own projections for the target's performance after the closing date to arrive at an equity value of $45 million. As for valuing the promissory notes, he applied a discount based on the market rate of interest for comparable unsecured debt to arrive at a value of $8.6 million. He also provided a separate opinion that the acquisition did not cause the debtor to become insolvent.

The bankruptcy court discredited the defendants' expert for using "unreasonable" projections. Relying on the debtor's expert's opinion, it concluded that the target company was worth only $6.9 million and that, after the acquisition, the debtor's liabilities exceeded its assets by $12.2 million.

At the same time, the court accepted the $8.6 million discounted value that the defendants' expert assigned to the promissory notes. But it largely dismissed the defendants' claim that the debtor received many indirect benefits from the acquisition, such as its ability to maintain its stock exchange listing, access to substantial credit, and access to the defendants' trademarks and technology. The only such benefit to the debtor was its temporary ability to avoid being delisted from the exchange, the court found. Most of the indirect benefits had a net value of "zero or less."

Finding that the debtor paid $21.6 million but received equity worth only $6.9 million, the court concluded the debtor did not receive a "reasonably equivalent" value. (Applicable Florida law presumes that, if a debtor receives 70% or less of the value it gives, it has not received "reasonably equivalent" value.) The court also found the debtor became insolvent as a result of the acquisition.

The defendants challenged the bankruptcy court's findings in federal district court. For one, they claimed that the debtor did receive "reasonably equivalent value" when it purchased the target. In terms of the value the debtor gave, the bankruptcy court erred when it adopted the reduced value the defendants' expert had assigned to the promissory notes but declined to adopt the expert's conclusion as to solvency. "There is no requirement that the trier of fact must adopt an expert's opinion in its entirety," the district court stated, finding no error. As the district court saw it, there was no inextricable link between the discount rate applied to unsecured debt and the debtor's solvency.

Next the defendants argued that, by adopting the $6.9 million value the debtor's expert assigned to the target, the bankruptcy court disregarded the indirect benefits that accompanied the transaction. Had it assessed their value, the target's overall value would have met the 70% mark. The district court, however, found the bankruptcy court did analyze their values. But with the exception of the delisting, it determined the other benefits to be "highly speculative" and their value to be "less than zero," considering the economic harm the debtor incurred in acquiring the target. The bankruptcy court did not err when it credited the debtor's expert's statements that the cash drain on the debtor following the acquisition undercut whatever value resided in those benefits. For all these reasons, the district court affirmed.

And one more thing. The defendants next appealed to the U.S. Court of Appeals for the 6th Circuit, raising almost the same issues: (1) the debtor failed to prove the value of *all* the economic benefits it received from the transaction, direct as well as indirect; (2) the bankruptcy court relied on hindsight when it determined the value of the target's stock; and (3) the debtor failed to prove the value of its promissory notes. The 6th Circuit revisited the claims:

1. *Indirect benefits:* The Court of Appeals found that the bankruptcy court heard extensive and sufficient testimony on whether these benefits had any value to the debtor and upheld its conclusion that only one, the avoidance of delisting, had any tangible value; the rest had "minimal" value. Moreover, even if the promissory notes had a zero value, reducing the purchase price to $13 million, the defendants failed to show that the value of the indirect benefits was sufficient to reach the critical 70% level.

The 6th Circuit also affirmed the bankruptcy court's decision not to require the debtor's expert to prove the value of the indirect benefits. While it acknowledged the general requirement that the plaintiff calculate the value of indirect benefits, it found that this case fell under the established exception to the rule. Specifically, the bankruptcy court had sufficient evidence from witness testimony to conclude the value of the nonstock benefits was negligible.

2. *Hindsight value:* The defendants next raised a new challenge, claiming the debtor's expert used improper hindsight when—in calculating the FMV under the comparable transactions method—he used a transaction that occurred after the valuation date to select a multiple. "The methodology centers on transactions that are similar in nature," the 6th Circuit observed, and there is no precedent that precludes an expert from examining a post hoc transaction simply "because to do so would draw on hindsight." The record showed that the debtor's expert expressly stated during cross-examination that he was not relying on hindsight, the Court of Appeals found. Furthermore, the bankruptcy court was fully cognizant of the expert's valuation method and "of the potential problems with using hindsight to determine [the target's] value." Accordingly, the bankruptcy court did not err when it adopted the debtor's expert's FMV for the target.

3. *Promissory notes:* Not only did the debtor's expert fail to value the promissory notes, the defendants claimed, but the bankruptcy court erred by adopting their expert's discounted value for the notes without also accepting his FMV and solvency conclusions.

The 6th Circuit found the record clearly showed the debtor's expert valued the short-term notes at face value. Furthermore, a bankruptcy court need not credit all aspects of an expert's testimony; accordingly, in this case, it did not err by accepting the discounted value of the notes by the defendants' expert while disregarding his ultimate conclusions. Nor did any bankruptcy rule require discounting promissory notes in a fraudulent transfer case in which their acquisition helped render the debtor insolvent, the court held, and affirmed all aspects of the lower courts' decisions.

In re Glueck

Citation: 223 B.R. 514, 1998 Bankr. LEXIS 1020
Date of Decision: August 12, 1998
State or Federal: Federal
State/Jurisdiction: Ohio
Court: United States Bankruptcy Court
Type of action: Bankruptcy
Judge: Calhoun

Market Rate of Interest Appropriate in 'Cram-Down' Case

The key issue in this case is setting the appropriate interest rate to establish present value in a "cram-down" situation under 11 U.S.C. 1325(a)(5)(B). In a "cram-down" situation, the bankruptcy court, in effect, forces the creditor to accept a new loan for the property rather than allowing the creditor to repossess the secured property.

Debtors propose 10% rate. Debtors, Derrill and Leslie Glueck, filed for relief under Chapter 13 of the Bankruptcy Code on March 19, 1998. In the plan of reorganization, debtors proposed a 10% rate of interest per annum for the secured claim.

The creditor claimed that the proposed cram-down interest rate was insufficient to provide a market rate of interest and believed, instead, the original contract interest rate of 22.95% should be paid on the secured amount. A witness for the creditor testified that, based on the debtors' credit history, the appropriate interest rate would be in the range of 18.95% to 24.95%.

In analyzing this case to determine the appropriate interest rate, the court refers to *Memphis Bank & Trust Co. v. Whitman* 692 F.2d 427 (6th Cir.1982). In this case, the court stated that it would be inappropriate to arbitrarily establish an interest rate for cram down under 1325(a)(5)(B), but instead "bankruptcy courts should use the current market rate of interest used for similar loans in the region … and the most equitable rate to establish in this type of situation is the prevailing market rate of interest on similar types of secured loans at the time of allowance of the creditor's claim and the confirmation of the plan in bankruptcy with a maximum limitation on such rate to be the underlying contract rate of interest."

Current market rate prevails. In this case, the debtors presented no testimony or evidence concerning the market rate of interest that was available for borrowers with similar credit histories but simply proposed an arbitrary interest rate of 10%. Referring to the *Memphis* case, the court determined that such an arbitrary figure was unacceptable. The only evidence that was submitted as to the current market rate of interest was that provided by the lender's expert.

The court decided that the appropriate interest rate for the secured loan is 18.95%. They justified the lower interest rate based on the reduced risk associated with debtors' payments to the Chapter 13 trustee, and discharge of debts on completion of their Chapter 13 plan.

Decision consistent with prior cases. This conclusion is consistent with previous rulings in many other cases, such as *Rankin v. DeSarno, General Motors Acceptance Corp. v. Alphonso Jones,* and *Green Tree Financial Servicing Corporation v. Ruben R. Smithwick, Jr.,* all discussed in Chapter 19, "Cost of Capital in the Courts'" in *Cost of Capital—Estimation and Applications* by Shannon Pratt.

In re Greater Southeast Community Hospital Corp. (I)

Citation: 2007 Bankr. LEXIS 1
Date of Decision: January 2, 2006
Country: US
State or Federal: Federal
State/Jurisdiction: District of Columbia
Court: United States Bankruptcy Court
Type of action: Bankruptcy
Experts: Neil Demchik (plaintiff/Trusttee)
Judge: Teel
SIC: 8062 General Medical and Surgical Hospitals

BV Appraiser Challenged Under *Daubert* for Bias and Reliance on Third-Party Reports

It's been nearly five years since the Greater Southeast Community Hospital Corp. (GSCH) filed for Chapter 11 protection. In 2004, the Bankruptcy Court for the District of Columbia confirmed the debtor's reorganization plan, by which the "Reorganized Debtors" succeeded to the operations and the preconfirmation creditors succeeded to a Liquidating Trust. But the bankruptcy battles didn't end, and in 2005, nearly a third of the court's published opinions (five out of 16) were related to the GSCH litigation—for which the Trustee received $1 million to cover some of the expense, including this most recent adversarial proceeding.

BV expert challenged as unreliable, biased. Judge S. Martin Teel Jr., who has presided over the *GSCH* bankruptcy since the beginning, provides none of the facts but only the procedural disposition of this latest hearing, in which the defendants sought to preclude the Trust's expert from testifying at trial pursuant to the Federal Rules of Evidence and the U.S. Supreme Court standards set forth in the *Daubert* and *Kumho Tire* decisions.

Specifically, defendants claimed the expert, Neil Demchick, CPA, CBA, CIRA, CVA (Invotex Group; Baltimore, Md.), was neither qualified nor independent, as he'd relied on third-party appraisals to prepare a net asset valuation, and his income approaches were allegedly biased and based on flawed methodologies.

But a review of his "extensive" background in business valuation quickly led the court to qualify Demchick as capable of offering "expert net asset valuation and solvency opinions." And though Demchick had apparently conceded his lack of qualification to perform real estate or equipment appraisals, all he needed to show was the "requisite knowledge, skill, experience, training, or education to competently render a net asset valuation opinion based on the opinions of others."

It is permissible for BV analysts to rely on third-party reports, the court said, "so long as those appraisals are of the type experts in the field of business valuation would reasonably rely on."

Allegations of bias more troubling. The defendants also complained that, since Demchick had acted as a "virtual member" of the Trust's legal team by recommending the adversarial suit, he was "biased and cannot be trusted to offer an objective and reliable expert opinion." The court simply deferred these allegations to trial, when they would factor into the weight of Demchik's opinion, not its credibility.

However, the defendants had also accused Demchick of "selective reliance on data favorable to the Trust's litigation position." In particular, when valuing the improved real estate, he had allegedly excluded the one appraisal that contradicted the Trust's claims. This "self-serving determination" of reliability constituted an "impermissible weighing of the evidence," according to defendants, sufficient to warrant its exclusion.

Judge Teel disagreed and permitted Demchick to offer his report, with this warning:

> As the finder of fact, I will address at trial whether the reasons asserted by Demchick for disregarding the [appraisal] are sufficiently logical and persuasive to conclude that an expert in [his] field would reasonably *not* rely upon the [appraisal]. (emphasis added)

Although experts are "virtually always" required to make certain threshold determinations regarding which data to consider or reject, "nevertheless, an expert's selective exclusion of only that data which is unfavorable to his client's litigation position warrants close scrutiny by the Court," and any expert should be prepared at trial "to address what objective criteria he relied upon in making such determinations."

In re Greater Southeast Community Hospital Corp. (II)

Citation: 2008 WL 2037592
Date of Decision: May 12, 2008
Country: US
State or Federal: Federal
State/Jurisdiction: District of Columbia
Court: United States Bankruptcy Court
Type of action: Bankruptcy
Experts: Neil Demchick (plaintiff), Kevin Moss (defendants)
Judge: Teel Jr.
SIC: 8062 General Medical and Surgical Hospitals

Bankruptcy Court Conducts Extensive Valuation Findings of Hospital in Fraudulent Transfer Case

More than five and a half years since the Greater Southeast Community Hospital Corp. (GSCH) filed for Chapter 11 protection—and 16 months after trial in January 2007—the Bankruptcy Court for the District of Columbia (Judge Teel Jr.) issued its nearly 200-page opinion.

Two years after filing for relief, the trustee of the healthcare corporation (GSCH, through a subsidiary formed expressly for the asset purchase of Reese Hospital), which had purchased the hospital (Reese) in question, filed suit to recover more than $68 million transferred for the purchase—a value the court had previously determined. The trustee alleged the transfers were fraudulent under both federal and state (Illinois) fraudulent transfer statutes. After numerous pretrial motions, hearings, and "memorandum decisions" (including a *Daubert* challenge to the trustee's valuation expert, Neil Demchick [Invotex Group; Baltimore, Md.]), this most recent opinion focuses primarily on one issue: "whether the debtor made the transfer ... without receiving a reasonably equivalent value in exchange." To recover, the trustee had to show that the corporation: (1) had not received reasonably equivalent value for the transfers; and (2) the corporation was insolvent (or became insolvent) on the date in question—Nov. 12, 1998.

To define "reasonably equivalent value" under the fraudulent transfer statute, the court had to "determine the value of what was transferred and to compare it to what was received." To accomplish this, the court undertook a lengthy, thorough consideration of the fair market value (FMV) of the "thing received," namely, the Reese hospital.

Market approach: a lack of true comparables? The court first examined the applicability of the market approach. Demchick conducted an exhaustive search of over 300 transactions and found that there were inadequate comparable transactions to calculate a market value for Reese; similarly, he determined there were insufficient guideline companies to compare with Reese. Therefore, he did not offer a value using the market approach.

In contrast, the defendants' valuation expert, Kevin B. Moss, provided a market approach value range of between $74 million and $90 million. Moss used transactions of companies with positive EBITDA margins, even though Reese had negative EBITDA on the date in question. Moss also selected seven publicly traded companies to use as guideline comparables in his calculations, with revenue ranges from $585 million to $20.6 billion (in 1998, Reese had revenues of $150 million).

The court held that the market approach could not lead to an "accurate or reliable" value for Reese. Ross's selected transactions were not "truly comparable," according to the court, and the seven companies chosen were "not even remotely comparable to Reese" because they were diversified companies with nonhospital operations. Further, the court stated their revenues were significantly higher than Reese's and they had positive EBITDA compared with Reese's negative EBITDA and operating losses at the time of the transfer.

Cost approach: includes three sets of assets. Turning its attention to the cost approach, the court determined that the proper measure of value under this methodology was "going concern" value, as opposed to liquidation value—despite the trustee's assertions that Reese was already "on its deathbed" at the time of the transfer. The court included three sets of assets in its calculations:

- Real property;
- Equipment; and
- Net working capital.

Combined, the court arrived at a total value under the cost approach of approximately $57.99 million—$25.3 million of which was attributed to real estate. The value of the hospital's equipment was $12 million, an amount that the parties had predetermined based on "existing equipment appraisals" and confirmed by both experts as being "appropriate." The final component of the cost approach calculation was net working capital, which the court found to be approximately $20.68 million, based on the closing statement for the purchase of the hospital.

Income approach: a six-step process. The court acknowledged the use of both the discounted cash flow (DCF) method and the capitalized returns method under the income approach but accepted that the DCF is recognized by "many authorities [as] the most reliable method."

Applying the DCF method, the court articulated a six-step analysis to arrive at the hospital's "enterprise value":

1. Project earnings before interest and taxes (EBIT);
2. Calculate net cash flow;
3. Determine the weighted average cost of capital (WACC);
4. Ascertain a terminal value for the hospital;
5. Determine present value of the projected net cash flows and projected terminal value; and finally
6. Add the nonoperating and excess assets purchased.

Projected earnings. To project anticipated future earnings from Reese, the court was presented with multiple sets of projections. One set was prepared by outside valuation consultants in early 1998—prior to the hospital's purchase. While the court found these "the most objective," they were nonetheless "hopelessly outdated" and disregarded by the court.

Another set was prepared by a vice president of the corporation and were based on the "financial model" of the 1998 projections but completed closer to the date of the purchase (the Reese Projections). Further, these projections included "Strategic Assumptions" that centered around an expected increase in productivity and volume at the hospital, as well as an increase in physicians, and operational changes. While more specific than the 1998 projections, the court found the Reese Projections premised upon revenue increases or operational plans that would go into effect after the date of the transfer and would be difficult to implement. Further, the projections failed to take into account a "severe downturn in revenue at Reese Hospital in 1998" and instead predicted an increase in revenue to prepurchase levels. Accordingly, the court called the assumptions "unreasonable" and the set of projections based upon them as "flawed in their inception."

Finally, the court reviewed the projections of the trustee's expert, Mr. Demchick. Demchick had prepared two "very different" sets of projections: one that assumed the hospital would return to 1996 levels of performance after one year (the "Turnaround" scenario) and a set that predicted reaching the revenue figures projected by the Reese management team after a one-year "delay" (the "Strategic Growth" scenario). The court found his Turnaround projection "highly unlikely" and did not accept it. The court found his Strategic Growth scenario to be "rooted in a sound premise" but executed "in a very poor fashion." The court ultimately rejected Demchick's projections.

Finding that there were "no credible projections from which it [could] derive a business enterprise value," the court made a series of adjustments to the Reese Projections that related primarily to the time period it would have taken for certain of the "Strategic Assumptions" to be achieved.

Net cash flow. Both experts provided projections of depreciation and amortization (D&A) in their respective analyses. The defendants' expert, Moss, adopted the Reese management team's 1999 projected D&A of $9.06 million as his own, while Demchick projected D&A of approximately $5.9 million. Finding an "absence of any evidence" to account for such a deviation, the court adopted Moss's D&A figure.

Demchick based his net working capital projections on "the [hospital's] historic average of net working capital required as a percentage of total net revenue." Moss, in contrast, used a percentage of total net revenue based on the median level of guideline companies. The court noted that Moss provided "no explanation" as to which companies he used as comparables and that Demchick's figures more accurately captured the "idiosyncrasies" of Reese Hospital.

Both experts also projected capital expenditures to be made from the date of purchase through 2002. Demchick's projected capital expenditures totaled approximately $40.74 million for the five-year period; Moss's total was $37.53 million. The court found neither expert's projections reasonable and based its own calculations on the Reese Projection's "Strategic Assumptions," which themselves totaled $44.2 million—although with modifications that delayed or outright removed certain hospital acquisitions and projects. Those modifications lowered the court's projection of capital expenditures to approximately $33.74 million for the years in question.

The court combined all of the findings, as well as the projected income tax rate, to arrive at its ultimate net cash flow figures for the five-year period, which totaled approximately $7.43 million.

Weighted average cost of capital (WACC). With the hospital's "business enterprise value" being determined and not simply its "equity value," the experts considered both the cost of equity and the cost of debt when arriving at a WACC.

The experts again took divergent approaches in calculating a proper discount rate. Demchick used the build-up method, while Moss chose the capital asset pricing model (CAPM). The court found that the build-up method was the most appropriate under the circumstances "because the companies used by Moss as guidelines for his CAPM method [were] not truly comparable to Reese."

The court adopted a 5.46% risk-free rate based on the 20-year U.S. Treasury Bond's yield to maturity in place at the time of transfer. The court also found Demchick's equity risk premium of 7.8% to be correct in calculating the discount rate, which was based on data from Ibbotson Associates' *Stocks, Bonds, Bills and Inflation 1998 Yearbook.*

Next, an industry risk premium adjustment to the sum of the risk-free rate of return and equity risk premium (or "average market return") had to be made. Moss did not provide such a premium adjustment in his CAPM analysis; accordingly, the court adopted Demchick's proffered 3.63% adjustment. The average market return must also be adjusted for "a risk premium relating to the size of the company that is being valued," the court continued. The court determined that Reese properly fell within Ibbotson's 10th decile and therefore adopted the 5.36% size premium.

Finally, the court made its adjustment for risk factors specific to the hospital. Moss used a 23% premium, which was indicative of a "higher probability" that Reese would fail to meet certain management projections. Demchick used a company-specific risk premium of 12%, which "reflects his modification to those [Moss's] projections by delaying revenue growth and expense reductions over the course of one year." The court adopted a slightly higher premium than Demchick's—13.5%—which reflected the court's finding that 18 months, rather than the one year projected by Demchick, was a more likely term for Reese to reach projected revenue levels.

In determining the cost of debt, the court adopted the 7.3% pretax figure used by Moss, which was based on Moody's Baa corporate bond rate on the date of the transfer, rather than the 12% offered by Demchick. Demchick's cost of debt was based on the interest rate charged by one of the financers of the Reese purchase, which the court characterized as "an error."

Finally, the court adopted Demchick's debt-to-equity ratio of 43.1% debt to 56.9% equity, based primarily on the fact that Moss relied on "comparable company research" without any specific reference. Therefore, the court found an appropriate WACC of 19.36% from the date of transfer through 2001 and 18.14% for 2002.

Terminal value. While there can be several methods by which to estimate the terminal value of a business, Moss used a market multiple method and arrived at terminal value by multiplying the terminal EBITDA by a market multiplier of five, which Moss described as a "cleaner depiction of value."

The court disagreed, finding the Gordon growth model was the "most often used" method and "most appropriate method" in this particular case. The court did, however, acknowledge that the market multiple method can prove useful as a "sanity check" against a Gordon growth model-derived value. The court divided the terminal net cash flow for the year 2002 (approximately $12.87 million) by "the discount rate less long-term growth" (WACC of 18.14% minus presumed long-term growth of 5.31% to arrive at a rate of 12.82%) to arrive at a terminal value of approximately $100.39 million.

Present value of net cash flow and terminal value. Moss used a midyear discounting method, which the court found appropriate. That determination, in turn, required the court to "alter" its calculation of the terminal value because the Gordon growth model's assumption that cash flows are received at year's end "is inconsistent with the preceding mid-year discounting technique." This "modified Gordon Growth Model" calculation raised the 2002 terminal value to $109.11 million, which, when discounted to present value, was reduced to $54.73 million. Net cash flow for the five-year period was discounted to arrive at a present value of negative $3.22 million.

Nonoperating and excess assets. The ultimate step in determining final business enterprise value of Reese Hospital under the income approach, the court noted, is "to add the non-operating and excess assets purchased … in exchange for the [transfers]." Both experts focused primarily on projected, hypothetical sales of "surplus" land on the hospital campus, which the court found "erroneously swelled" the value of the hospital. The court further found that the approximately $20.68 million in net working capital should have been considered by the experts but wasn't. Accordingly, the court added this figure into its calculations.

Based on the summation of the present value of the net cash flows for the five periods (negative $3.22 million), the present value of the terminal value ($54.73 million), and working capital ($20.68 million), the court calculated Reese's total business enterprise value to be approximately $72.19 million.

Reconciliation: income approach 'heavily favored.' Having determined a value of approximately $57.99 million under the cost approach and $72.19 million using the income approach, the court—in its final analytical step—sought to "reconcile" its findings. The court found that:

> It is appropriate to give greater weight to [the court's] income approach determination than to [the court's] cost approach determination precisely because a hypothetical purchaser would reasonably expect to earn income based on the hospital's operation rather than accumulate wealth through the acquisition of its assets.

With that in mind, the court made an ultimate determination of value "heavily in favor of the income approach"—three-to-one, in fact—to reach a final FMV of Reese Hospital of $68.64 million (($57.99 million × 0.25) + ($72.19 million × 0.75)).

Not only did GSCH receive reasonably equivalent value as a result of the transfers, "if anything," the court suggested, the evidence showed that it had "received *more* than reasonably equivalent value," and the transfers could not have been fraudulent. Accordingly, the court had no need to rule on the issue of the debtor's solvency and rendered judgment in favor of the defendants.

In re Greater Southeast Community Hospital Corp. (III)

Citation: 2012 Bankr. LEXIS 618
Date of decision: Feb. 22, 2012
Country: US
State or Federal: Federal
State/Jurisdiction: District of Columbia
Court: United States Bankruptcy Court
Experts: Neil Demchick (plaintiff); Kevin Moss (defendant)
Judge: Teel Jr.

Bankruptcy Court Exposes 'Perils' of DCF Without Good Expert Evidence

The Greater Southeast Hospital Corp. filed for Chapter 11 bankruptcy protection nearly a decade ago. Since then, the major controversy has focused on the debtor's prior purchase of a hospital for $68 million back in 1998, which the trustee tried to recover as a fraudulent conveyance under federal as well as state law (Illinois).

But first, the trustee's valuation and insolvency expert had to survive a *Daubert* challenge. And then, after a trial in 2007 and a delay of over a year, the bankruptcy court denied the trustee's claims, ruling that the debtor received "reasonably equivalent value" in exchange for the $68 million purchase price. To support this conclusion, the court conducted its own discounted cash flow (DCF) analysis, based largely on the parties' expert valuations, and ultimately concluded that the hospital was worth approximately $68.6 million on the transfer date.

In this latest filing, the trustee moved the court to reconsider its findings, asserting four major flaws in the court's DCF analysis.

Net working capital counted twice. Since the original closing statement for the purchase of the hospital showed approximately $20.7 million in net working capital, the court added this amount at the end of its calculations, on a dollar-for-dollar basis. The trustee said this was double counting because the court had already included the net working capital, which consisted largely of uncollected accounts receivables, in its net cash flow calculations.

On review of its income approach, however, the court explained that it specifically excluded the net working capital amount from its calculations because it lacked any evidence on the record regarding the hospital's historic collection rates. As a result, the court could only factor net working capital *requirements* into its cash flow calculations on an accrual basis (in accordance with GAAP). "Such future accounts receivable, *not* in existence on the transfer date, were distinct from the [$20.7] million that *was* in existence," the court emphasized.

In other words, the court's discounted cash flow model was based on accruals of amounts that would be owed for future patient services and for operating revenue generated by other post-transfer events, and those amounts were unrelated to the $20.7 million in working capital transferred on the sale date.

At the same time, the court didn't ignore the $20.7 million in net working capital but added the full amount as a final step because it "stood to reason" that this reflected an additional and separate asset, acquired by the debtor. Given this treatment, its DCF analysis theoretically should have projected no revenue "whatsoever" for the acquired hospital until it began collecting on its accounts—but this approach was not feasible, given the parties' failure to produce any evidence regarding collection rates. The trustee tried to argue that this wasn't the case, but, even on its motion to reconsider, the trustee did not provide any analysis that factored the $20.7 million into the court's income stream calculations. "There was no double counting," the court said.

Similarly, the court recognized that it did not discount the $20.7 million to present value but once again faulted the trustee (and its expert) for failing to provide "any evidence that would permit an adjustment for the time value of money." In any event, any such adjustment would not have materially altered the ultimate finding of reasonably equivalent value, the court held.

Finally, the trustee said the court should not have added the $20.7 million figure on a dollar-for-dollar basis (citing Jay Fishman et al., *PPC's Guide to Business Valuation* (18th ed. 2008) ("Public markets recognize when a company has excess assets ... although investors *usually* do not build the amount into the price dollar-for-dollar"). (emphasis by the court) In this case, however, the net working capital did not resemble the typical nonoperating because any costs of collecting the amounts had already been attributed to expenses associated with the hospital's collections department. Thus, the asset was more like excess cash, with no liquidation costs, and it was appropriate to value it on a dollar-for-dollar basis, the court held, in dismissing the trustee's first argument.

Fair market value should have included marketability discount. As a second matter, the trustee argued the court should have applied a discount for lack of marketability (DLOM) to its income approach valuation (once again citing Fishman, et al., as well as Shannon Pratt, et al., *Valuing a Business* (4th ed. 2000)).

These authorities, however, address the value of an ownership interest in a company, the court said, and not the value of "a set of assets purchased by a company." Estate tax cases frequently address (and apply) marketability discounts in the former context by determining the amount that a decedent could have sold its shares in a nonpublic company. In contrast, a fraudulent conveyance action simply asks whether the debtor paid too much for the assets it acquired. The question is how much the acquired assets were worth, not what shares in the acquirer could be sold for.

In this case, it didn't matter what amount a shareholder might have obtained if it attempted to sell its interest in the hospital corporation after the purchase. "After all," the court said, "a publicly traded company could have purchased the [acquired] assets," and its resulting aggregate market value "would not be affected by an illiquidity discount." For purposes of fraudulent conveyance law, the acquired assets shouldn't have any different value to the debtor than they would have to "a hypothetical purchaser that was a publicly traded company," the court said. A party who sells assets to a privately owned company (as opposed to a public company) "ought not to be penalized."

In any event, the seller in this case was a publicly held company, with "excellent accounting systems in place" along with the ability to respond to the debtor's request for financial information prior to sale. "Such superior information systems of a publicly traded company versus a private company are a critical reason why shares of a closely held company require a discount for illiquidity," the court said (once again citing Pratt, et al.). For all these reasons, it rejected the trustee's second argument for reconsideration.

Wrong projections used to calculate professional fees. The trustee argued that the court miscalculated the amount of variable professional fee expenses (i.e., payments for nonemployee doctors). But once again, the court attributed any error to the evidence presented at trial (or the lack thereof).

In particular, it noted that there were only two sets of projections on the record, one that provided a breakdown of how the management team derived its figures for the professional fee expenses and a second that "simply stated a naked amount." In its original DCF calculations, the court rejected the projections that "failed to show their work" and were speculative, even though they were made closer to the sale date. Instead, it used the projections that were slightly older but articulated an "operational formula" for calculating these fees as a function of inpatient services. Based on its growth assumptions, the court was able to project these inpatient services and their associated expenses, which seemed to make better sense from "an operational standpoint," it said, and were not clearly erroneous.

However, even if the court accepted the trustee's argument that it should have used the "naked" projections of professional fee calculations, which would have reduced its overall valuation by nearly $13.4 million, the other assumptions it made (in the trustee's favor) effectively negated this reduction. For instance, in its DCF, the court had assigned no value to the possibility that the hospital would renegotiate its contracts with a major HMO provider (Humana) for more favorable reimbursement rates, even though a hypothetical purchaser would have "likely" assigned some value to this opportunity and even though evidence at trial suggested renegotiated rates might rise by 15%. (The court admitted that it had improperly relied on contrary testimony at trial, which suggested the hospital would not be able to achieve such rates; the testimony was later shown to be improper hindsight, based on events taking place after the sale date.)

On reconsidering this evidence, the court found that a hypothetical purchaser would have ascribed a 50% likelihood of renegotiating a 15% increase in the Humana rates. Based on its DCF projections, the value of that 50% chance would have equaled nearly $21.7 million in additional revenues (even a 30% chance would have boosted revenues by more than $13 million). This possible $21.7 million increase in revenues—even accounting for the time lag in its collection—"dwarfs" the $13.4 million that the trustee wanted to add in connection with variable profession fees, the court said.

In sum, if the court accepted the trustee's position regarding what a hypothetical purchaser would determine regarding professional fees, it would also have to accept the probability-adjusted value that the same hypothetical purchaser would ascribe to renegotiating the Humana rates, which would result in an even higher value for the hospital than the $68.6 million under the court's DCF valuation. For these reasons, the court dismissed the trustee's third challenge.

D&A expenses were projected into perpetuity. In its fourth and final argument, the trustee said the court miscalculated the depreciation and amortization (D&A) expenses to determine its terminal value. Specifically, the court determined that one-time depreciation for capital expenditures in 1999 (the year following the sale) extended into perpetuity rather than substantially expiring after five years (in 2004). After adjusting for this alleged error, the trustee reduced the court's value by $7.75 million.

At trial, however, the trustee's insolvency expert identified 2002 as the year of "stabilized operations" and the basis for calculating a terminal value, the court said. The trustee did not contend at trial (and neither did the expert's report) that, based on a decrease in D&A expenses after 2002, "a later year should be used for calculating a terminal value," the court said, and it was improper to inject a new issue in these post-trial proceedings.

Even if its expert erred at trial, the trustee said, the court could simply amend what amounted to a "common and easily correctible error" (once again citing Fishman, et al. for the proposition that future depreciation expenses cannot exceed capital expenditure estimates into perpetuity). However, any error arose from the trustee's "failure to present evidence or argument alerting the court that in performing a valuation, it ought to take into account the fact that depreciation and amortization after 2002 would decrease," the court said. An error in his expert's report would not have been binding on the trustee at trial, it added, but the trustee bore the burden of raising the point in the original proceedings and not belatedly in post-judgment motions.

Addressing post-2002 depreciation would be "opening a can of worms," the court said, not only because it was too late, but also because the trustee's post-trial submissions contained several errors and omissions regarding depreciation expenditures. Even if the court were inclined to grant reconsideration of this particular issue, an appropriate reaccounting of the D&A expenses would reduce the court's overall valuation of the hospital from $72.1 million (under the income approach) to just about $63.5 million. This reduced value still only represented a shortfall of 6.68% from the original purchase price of $68 million, the court held, which was not enough to alter its ultimate findings, especially given the applicable standard of value.

The issue in fraudulent conveyance cases is "not whether fair market value was received," the court reiterated, "but whether reasonably equivalent value was received." In other words:

> Fraudulent conveyance law does not posit perfect knowledge on the part of a hypothetical purchaser of a business, but asks instead whether the *actual* purchaser and the seller acted in a way that was designed and intended to achieve a just result from the perspective of the *actual* purchaser's creditors, and did not result in the actual purchaser's paying an amount so disproportionate to the fair market value of the property that it shocks the conscience of the court. (emphasis added)

Moreover, a good-faith purchaser, after due diligence, can ascribe a "wide range of value" to a target business, especially one as "complicated as a hospital," the court said. Its purchase does not later amount to a fraudulent conveyance simply because "some assumption it made … proves wrong." Nor does a court's subsequent determination of fair market value, alone, "provide the answer as to whether reasonably equivalent value was received."

Instead, to determine reasonably equivalent value, courts will typically look to the following factors:

- The arm's-length and overall "reasonable" nature of the transaction;
- The good faith and experience of both parties; and
- The due diligence by the purchaser in pursuing the purchase.

Lack of expert evidence left court at peril. In this case, the court found evidence supporting all three factors. In addition, it noted "the large degree of uncertainty" regarding what assumptions a hypothetical purchaser would have made in acquiring the hospital "and thus the large degree of uncertainty regarding the true fair market value" of what the debtor received in the transaction. The court also found the trustee failed to provide "reliable expert testimony with which to fix the fair market value" of the hospital; in fact, the record suffered from a "lack of any expert valuation testimony by anyone having expertise in hospital operations."

Moreover, the court admitted its own lack of expertise, both in the industry and in making "appropriate assumptions (regarding such matters as the discount rates) in performing a discounted cash flow analysis." Nevertheless, given the dearth of reliable evidence, the court attempted "with much trepidation" to calculate its own DCF, even though such an approach was "fraught with peril." As the plaintiff in these proceedings, however, the trustee bore the burden of proof and suffered the consequences of any doubts that resulted from lapses in the evidentiary record, the court held, and denied the motion to reconsider.

In re Harper

Citation: 157 B.R. 858
Date of Decision: August 18, 1993
Country: US
State or Federal: Federal
State/Jurisdiction: Arkansas
Court: United States Bankruptcy Court
Type of action: Bankruptcy
Judge: Mixon

Valuing a Minority Interest in a Closely Held Family Corporation

The valuation of a minority interest in a closely held family corporation was in question in this bankruptcy case. The debtor and his wife owned approximately 25% of the outstanding stock of P.L.R. & M. Inc., an S corporation. The debtor's father and siblings owned the balance of the stock; however, no shareholder owned a majority of the outstanding shares. Farm Credit, a major creditor, objected to the confirmation of the debtor's Chapter 12 plan, claiming that the plan vastly undervalued the debtor's interest in the P.L.R. & M. stock. James S. Schultze, of Schultze-Maechling & Associates Inc., provided a valuation for the debtor, primarily based upon a review of tax returns and real estate appraisals. Schultze applied a 10% discount for lack of marketability, a minority discount of

25%, and a 20% discount for restrictions on corporate borrowings and transfer of shares, for a total discount of 55%. Kenneth L. Thomas, CPA, then of Farm Credit, now with CPA Associates, P.A., determined the stock's value on behalf of Farm Credit based on an income approach and stated that no discount should be applied to stock in a family owned corporation. The court found Schultze's testimony more persuasive than that of Thomas. It first stated that Farm Credit's argument was unreasonable. Although no one shareholder owned a controlling interest, the court concluded that a hypothetical purchaser would realistically assume that the family members would vote together to create a majority interest against any unrelated shareholder. Thus, it held, the discounts applied by Thomas were appropriate, especially in light of discounts applied in other cases.

In re Haskell Dawes, Inc.

Citation: 199 B.R. 867, 1996 Bankr. LEXIS 1080
Date of Decision: August 28, 1996
Country: US
State or Federal: Federal
State/Jurisdiction: Pennsylvania
Court: United States Bankruptcy Court
Type of action: Bankruptcy
Judge: Sigmund
SIC: 3552 Textile Machinery

Largest Creditor Holds Up Debtor's Reorganization Plan a Year After Filing

Debtor is in a conflict with its largest creditor over confirmation of a plan of reorganization a year after filing. The court states:

> While we are not prepared to conclude that a reorganization is not possible for this Debtor, we must sustain the Stenberg objection insofar as it contends that the plan is not fair and equitable because equity is retaining its interests while unsecured claims are not being paid in full.... We have focused our analysis on the Debtor's effort to come within the "new value exception" to the absolute priority rule.

The court's analysis of this issue is very instructive for anyone involved in a proposed plan of reorganization.

In re Healthco International, Inc.; Brandt v. Hicks, Muse & Co., Inc.

Citation: 195 B.R. 971, 1996 Bankr. LEXIS 553
Date of Decision: May 17, 1996
Country: US
State or Federal: Federal
State/Jurisdiction: Massachusetts
Court: United States Bankruptcy Court
Type of action: Bankruptcy
Judge: Queenan
SIC: 5047 Medical, Dental, and Hospital Equipment and Supplies (medical, dental, and hospital equipment and supplies sold via retail method)
Key words: Bankruptcy

Trustee Charges Directors, Financial Advisors, Others in Failed LBO

In this action, the Chapter 7 bankruptcy trustee brings the complaint against "65 defendants and the entire class of selling stockholders, virtually anyone who had anything to do with the LBO ... defendants are the buyer, financing banks, debenture holders, directors, officers, controlling shareholders, financial advisors, lawyers and accountants."

The decision abstracted herein involves only rulings on motions to dismiss certain counts. We include it because of the court's language regarding the obligations of certain parties, especially the company's directors and financial advisor.

'Lurid picture of greed.' The decision states, "The Trustee paints a lurid picture of greed and breach of duty causing the collapse of a sizeable company.... Prior to its demise, Healthco was a major distributor of dental supplies, equipment and services ... throughout the United States, Canada and Western Europe."

On June 18, 1990, Healthco retained Lazard Freres & Co. (Lazard), a New York City investment banker. "Lazard ... searched for a 'white knight' who would rescue management from a looming proxy contest ... soon centering its efforts on the eventual buyer, Hicks, Muse & Co. (Hicks, Muse), which specialized in leveraged buyouts."

'Ignoring all evidence ...' "Ignoring all evidence that Healthco was currently operating at a loss, Hicks, Muse prepared financial projections on the assumption that there would be no material adverse change in Healthco's condition after December 29, 1990.... By letter dated March 26, 1991, Lazard opined to Healthco's board that the proposed cash consideration of $15 per share to be paid to Healthco's stockholders 'is fair, from a financial point of view, to such stockholders.'"

"The LBO closed on May 22, 1991, effective as of April 30, 1991. Shareholders and option holders were paid $141,509,000. Fees paid to professionals and advisors, including Lazard, totaled $18,806,000." (*13.3% of the deal value!*)

Transaction left Healthco insolvent. "The net effect of the transaction was that Healthco was left insolvent and with unreasonably small capital."

"Hicks, Muse, the financing banks, Healthco's directors, and Lazard all exchanged and received financial analyses projecting the post-LBO profitability of Healthco. These projections were unreasonable and unrealistic."

Conflict quashes business judgment rule. "It is hornbook law that a corporate director owes the corporation fiduciary obligations of care and loyalty. The protection afforded a director by the business judgment rule disappears when the person has a personal interest in the transaction."

"In discharging their duty of care owed the corporation, directors normally need be concerned only with the interest of stockholders. What is good for stockholders is usually good for the corporation. That was not the case with this LBO. Although the shareholders fared quite well, Healthco was left terminally ill. When a transaction brings a corporation to insolvency or the brink of insolvency, the rights of creditors become paramount. In those circumstances, the corporation may, through a creditor representative, recover damages from the derelict directors."

While there are far more counts in the case than we can summarize in this abstract, a particularly interesting one is "aiding and abetting breach of fiduciary duty." The court stated, "The complaint asserts Healthco's directors breached their fiduciary obligations and that Lazard in its capacity as financial advisor to the company cooperated in the breach. A party who knowingly participates in a breach of fiduciary duty is liable to the beneficiary of the duty."

Trustee says financial advisor derelict. "The Trustee alleges, based on the information Lazard knew or should have known ... that Lazard was derelict in its contractual obligations when it failed to advise Healthco against effecting the transaction and, indeed, encouraged it.

"Nor is there any merit to Lazard's argument that its obligations were confined to issuance of a fairness opinion and finding a buyer. Lazard's agreement of engagement does not even mention a fairness option. And it provides in broad terms that Lazard was to act as Healthco's 'exclusive financial advisor.' Lazard agreed, among other things, to 'consider the appropriateness of various financial and acquisition alternatives' and 'to evaluate any transaction....' The complaint alleges Lazard 'played a substantial role in negotiating and formulating the LBO' and that it knew, or should have known, the transaction would leave Healthco insolvent and with unreasonably small capital. Lazard's compensation was largely based upon the total consideration payable in the LBO. Lazard cannot limit its LBO-related activities and obligations to the issuance of a rather innocuous fairness opinion."

In re Hechinger Investment Co. of Delaware, Inc. (I)

Citation: 2004 U.S. Dist. LEXIS 5537
Date of Decision: March 28, 2004
Country: US
State or Federal: Federal
State/Jurisdiction: Delaware
Court: United States District Court
Type of action: Bankruptcy
Experts: Dr. Israel Shaked (for Hechinger Liquidation Trust)
Louis Paone, Robert Rock (for BankBoston Retail Finance, Inc. and General Electric Capital Corp.)
Judge: Robinson
SIC: 5211 Lumber and Other Building Materials Dealers
(home center stores)
Key words: Breach of contract, Secured transaction, Discounted cash flow method (DCF), Earnings Before Interest, Taxes (EBIT), Earnings Before Interest, Taxes, Depreciation, Amortization (EBITDA), Comparable company multiple (CCM), Adjusted balance sheet valuation method, EBITDAR

Valuation Is Irrelevant to Establish Knowledge by Stranger to Indenture of Its Breach

The issue in this case was whether an acquired company was worth more or less than a loan amount covered by an indenture's negative pledge—if the company had a value less than the loan, the negative pledge would have been breached.

Facts. In 1992, Hechinger Co. (Hechinger) entered into an indenture that contained a clause restricting future secured debt (the "Negative Pledge"), which covered Hechinger's operating assets and property. The indenture contained a purchase money exception and a refinancing exemption to the Negative Pledge.

In 1997, through a series of complex transactions, Hechinger merged with Builders Square Inc. (Builders Square). As part of the merger, a group of lenders led by The Chase Manhattan Bank (the "Chase Group") loaned $243 million to a Hechinger subsidiary, Hechinger Investment Co. of Delaware (HICD), to which all of Builders Square operating assets had been transferred. This amount was used to finance the merger and to refinance an existing credit facility in the amount of $89,599,034.08.

Bankboston Retail Finance Inc. and General Electric Capital Corp. (collectively "defendants") then refinanced the loan, becoming HICD's senior lenders. Thus, if Builders Square was worth less than $153,400,965.92, the loan would have breached the Negative Pledge (arguably entitling Hechinger's unsecured creditor Hechinger Liquidation Trust (plaintiff) to an equitable lien in its property as against defendants).

Valuation evidence. The plaintiff's expert, Dr. Israel Shaked, used both a comparable company multiple (CCM) analysis and a discounted cash flow (DCF) analysis to conclude that Builders Square was worth less than $153 million. Using the CCM analysis, adjusted for competitive ranking and interest-bearing debt, Dr. Shaked concluded that Builders Square had an equity value ranging between negative $374 million to negative $60 million, with a negative value of negative $73.2 million.

For this analysis, he identified four comparable companies and three indicators of value based upon the companies' financial data for the 12 months preceding the 1997 transactions, including EBIT (earnings before interest and taxes); EBITDA (earnings before interest, taxes, depreciation, and amortization); and EBITDAR (earnings before interest, taxes, depreciation, amortization, and rent). Using DCF to value Builders Square as an ongoing concern, he determined that Builders Square had a negative equity value in excess of negative $500 million.

Defendants' first expert, Louis Paone, performed a CCM analysis, DCF analysis, and a merger and acquisition analysis (M&A analysis). Under his CCM analysis, Paone testified that Builders Square had a value of between $350 million and $410 million. Unlike Dr. Shaked, he did not utilize historical EBITDA and EBIT but instead used revenue, adjusted assets, and projected EBITDA in his analysis.

Under the M&A analysis, Paone testified that Builders Square had a value of between $430 million and $500 million. Finally, using his DCF analysis, Paone testified that Builders Square had a value of between $420 million and $480 million.

Defendants' second expert, Robert Rock, testified that Builders Square had a net asset value of $258 million using an adjusted balance sheet valuation method, for which Rock relied on the audited financial statements of the company and the audit statements of its auditors.

Trial court findings and rationale. The court first noted that the purpose of the valuation was to determine whether the Negative Pledge clause had been breached and whether defendants, who were strangers to the indenture, had notice of its breach. The court concluded that, while Dr. Shaked's analysis might have been appropriate to establish a breach as between the parties to the indenture itself, it did not satisfy plaintiff's burden with respect to a stranger to the indenture.

Accordingly, the court reasoned that, even if the court were to find that Dr. Shaked's analysis was legally and factually the best valuation methodology and, therefore, the Negative Pledge was breached, his analysis was legally irrelevant to whether defendants had knowledge of the breach. It was uncontroverted that, post-merger, Hechinger valued Builders Square's net assets and liabilities at $260 million under GAAP fair market value standards for purchase accounting, as well as that an independent audit confirmed the post-merger valuation. In the absence of a showing of fraud or bad faith, the court ruled that it would be contrary to principles of equity and law to impair the status of a secured creditor by determining that the valuation methodology used by the parties to the 1997 transactions was unreasonable or improper. (For these reasons, the court denied plaintiff's requested equitable lien).

In re Hechinger Investment Co. of Delaware, Inc. (II)

Citation: 2005 U.S. Dist. LEXIS 14386
Date of Decision: July 19, 2005
Country: US
State or Federal: Federal
State/Jurisdiction: Delaware
Court: United States District Court
Type of action: Bankruptcy
Experts: Dr. Israel Shaked (for liquidation trust)
Judge: Robinson
Key words: Bankruptcy, Insolvency, Going concern basis

If Bankruptcy Is Not 'Clearly Imminent,' Corporation Must Be Valued on a Going Concern Basis

In June 1999, Hechinger Co. and its affiliates (Hechinger) filed for bankruptcy protection under Chapter 11 of the Bankruptcy Code. This followed the acquisition and subsequent combination of the assets of Builders Square Inc. (Builders Square) with Hechinger by Leonard Green & Partners L.P. (Leonard Green) in September 1997 ("the Transaction").

The liquidation trust asserted, inter alia, that Hechinger was insolvent at the time of the Transaction or was rendered insolvent as a result of the Transaction, and that certain of its directors knew or should have known of Hechinger's insolvency. The trust asserted that, by virtue of Hechinger's insolvency, the directors owed to Hechinger and its creditors a duty of undivided loyalty in managing and supervising the business affairs of Hechinger, including the duty to preserve and maximize the value of Hechinger's assets for the benefit of such creditors and that the directors breached this duty.

To determine whether Hechinger was insolvent or in the vicinity of insolvency, the trial court first noted that the definition of "insolvent" is a "financial condition such that the sum of [a corporation's] debts is greater than all of such entity's property, at a fair valuation." The Bankruptcy Code does not, however, mandate what constitutes a "fair valuation." Nonetheless, the court ruled that, in the context of determining insolvency under the Code, where bankruptcy is not "clearly imminent" on the date of the challenged conduct, assets should be valued on a going concern basis. Moreover, the court noted that, because valuation is, to a great extent, a subjective exercise dependent upon the input of both facts and assumptions, the court will give deference to "prevailing marketplace values," rather than to values created with the benefit of hindsight for the purpose of litigation.

Finding that bankruptcy was not "clearly imminent" in September 1997, as it could not be disputed that Hechinger continued to operate and satisfy all of its obligations to its creditor constituency for well over a year subsequent to the Transaction, the court held that the assets of Hechinger should be valued on a going concern basis. In this regard, the court found that, despite thousands of pages of exhibits, it was unclear whether any party conducted such an analysis:

> For instance, plaintiff relies on the expert opinion of Dr. Israel Shaked. Dr. Shaked's expert report comprises an exhaustive recitation of data that allegedly was known or knowable at the time of the transaction.... However, none of the data in the report is specifically referenced to any of the exhibits, and Dr. Shaked's actual valuation analyses (as opposed to his conclusions) are contained on a one page summary of data attached to his report.... It is plaintiff's burden to prove that the Director Defendants owed a duty to the creditors by proving that Hechinger was operating in the vicinity of insolvency. There are genuine issues of material fact in this regard.

Accordingly, the court refused to grant summary judgment on this issue and left it for trial.

Heilig Meyers Co. v. Internal Revenue Service (In re Heilig Meyers Co.)

Citation: 2007 U.S. App. LEXIS 11052
Date of Decision: May 9, 2007
Country: US
State or Federal: Federal
State/Jurisdiction: 4th Circuit
Court: United States Court of Appeals
Type of action: Bankruptcy
Experts: Ernst & Young (debtor/taxpayer), Theodore Barnhill Jr. (IRS)
Judge: Wilkinson
SIC: 5023 Home furnishings (merchant wholesalers except those selling via retail method)

Accounting Method Trumps Valuation in 'Clear Reflection of Income' Case

In this 2-1 decision, the 4th Circuit held that a mark-to-market valuation of a company's consumer debt portfolio pursuant to *Internal Revenue Code* §475(b) must meet the "clear reflection of income" requirements of IRC §446(b). Put another way, "where ... the accounting method at issue essentially consists of a determination of market value, §446(b) applies to that determination."

IRS disallows $46 million tax deduction. The tax issue arose in the Chapter 11 bankruptcy of various Heilig-Meyers companies, which sold home furnishings through installment credit plans. For their taxable year ending in February 1997, the debtors had elected §475's mark-to-market accounting method, which permitted a fair market valuation of the retail accounts at year's end to calculate a tax gain or loss. (Congress later eliminated the §475 election for "nonfinancial customer paper," effective in 1998.)

Debtors hired an accountant from a national firm to prepare the appropriate valuation study, using the discounted cash flow method to determine the fair market value of the 1997 accounts receivable. In estimating the future cash flows, the analyst reduced their face value by: (1) a 3% servicing cost; (2) anticipated customer defaults; and (3) projected taxes on the income stream. In addition, she estimated the weighted investment returns related to seven consumer credit card companies to arrive at a weighted average cost of capital (WACC) of 11%.

From that rate, the analyst derived discount rates of 8% for current receivables, 15% for those 61 to 120 days old, and 22% for those aged 121 to 180 days. Applying these, the fair market value of the accounts receivable came to $1,027 million. As the stipulated book value of the accounts was $1,073 million, the debtors recognized a loss (and a tax deduction) of approximately $46 million, which they carried back to the 1994 tax year.

The IRS questioned several aspects of the valuation methodology, including the estimated servicing costs and the reduction for taxes. The Service also found debtors' discount rates "excessive and unfounded," allowing too much risk for potential customer defaults. The Service applied a risk-free discount rate of 6.5% (the rate of 18-month Treasury securities in 1997) and recomputed the fair market value of the accounts receivable to $1,049 million, resulting in a loss/deduction of nearly $24.3 million—and a disallowance of over $21.6 million. After the debtors filed for bankruptcy, the Service sought to recover over $4.8 million in tax underpayments and penalties.

Debtors' analyst relies on 'expert judgment.' At trial in bankruptcy court, the IRS presented a new valuation of the receivables by a finance professor, who calculated a DCF using a range of discount rates from 6.2% to 7.3%, applying the lower rate to accounts maturing earlier and the higher rates to those maturing later. This expert also criticized the debtors for estimating cash flows on a pretax basis, using an inappropriate WACC, and failing to provide quantitative support for the choice of the three discount rates (8%, 15%, and 22%).

The debtors admitted the underlying records for the accounts receivables were no longer available. The expert also conceded that her report failed to explain the choice of seven consumer credit card companies for the WACC determination or her selection of the three discount rates; at trial, the analyst defended these choices based on her "judgment as a valuation expert."

Finally, the expert's 3% estimate of servicing costs was contradicted by the debtors' SEC Form 10-K, which claimed they could not accurately estimate such costs. Despite problems with the IRS valuation as well, the court found that the debtor's valuation method failed to clearly reflect income under §446(b) and accepted the Service's calculations of the 1997 tax loss. An appeal to the District Court upheld the application of §446(b), finding further that the debtors bore the burden to show the IRS assessment was "clearly unlawful."

The devil in the 'valuation details.' On appeal to the 4th Circuit, the debtors argued that the dispute was really a "valuation" case as opposed to a "method of accounting case" and the court should sustain their valuations because the underlying methodology was sound.

But the majority disagreed, citing the rule that "the reporting of income under Section 475, *inclusive of the valuation requirement subsumed therein,* is a method of accounting" (court's emphasis), and that method of accounting must "clearly reflect income" under Section 446(b).

This conclusion does not portend, as debtors claimed, that "the Service will attempt to bring every valuation dispute within the compass of §446(b)." A valuation that does not constitute the "core" of an accounting method will not raise §446(b) requirements. But where a taxpayer's failure to assess market value correctly is essentially a failure to execute the appropriate accounting method,

§446(b) will apply. "To hold otherwise would be to allow taxpayers to subvert the entire aim of §446 merely by confining the devil to the details."

> [T]he taxpayer may not avail itself of an accounting method, the entire substance of which consists of accurately determining market value, only to implement it in a way that does no such thing.

Once the bankruptcy court had rejected the debtors' method as failing to clearly reflect income, "it was not the court's task to determine *de novo* whether the Commissioner's method" did. Unless the IRS interpretation is clearly unlawful or arbitrary, a court must defer to its method of calculating fair market value.

Dissent would have permitted a trial. A strong dissent (by Judge Neimeyer) pointed out that, in the precedent relied upon by the majority, the taxpayer's accounting method had violated IRS regulations. But here, the parties agreed on the appropriate accounting method (mark-to-market) as well as the appropriate valuation method (discounted cash flow). Their valuations were within 2% of one another, only because they disputed the appropriate risk premium rate. That "narrow" valuation issue should have been resolved by a neutral fact finder:

> Under the majority's view, the taxpayer never receives a trial on the fact of the appropriate risk premium by which to discount the book value of its accounts receivable. Rather, the majority upholds the IRS's post-trial declaration that the selection of a particular risk premium is a method of accounting within the IRS's regulatory purview.... Thus, the IRS may always decree that the taxpayer's position on valuing accounts receivable fails to clearly reflect income and ... is subject to recomputation ... under §446(b) without a trial.

The IRS's authority does not "reach down to this level of detail," the dissent concluded, "and it should not." Given this "due process" characterization of the case—and the millions of dollars at stake—an appeal to the U.S. Supreme Court may be the debtors' next step.

Holber v. M&T Bank (In re Scheffler)

Citation: 2012 Bankr. LEXIS 2568
Date of decision: June 5, 2012
Country: US
State or Federal: Federal
State/Jurisdiction: Federal Circuit
Court: United States Bankruptcy Court
Experts: David Weinberg (trustee); Damon Neagle (defendant)
Judge: Fehling

Cost Method 'Strikingly Inappropriate' to Value Technology

In this Chapter 7 bankruptcy case, the trustee attempted to avoid two mortgage loans, secured by the debtor's residence, in the aggregate amount of $650,000. In any other case, the question of whether the debtor received reasonably equivalent value in exchange for the liens on his house would not typically give rise to a business valuation. But here, the issues turned on a family business, a "battle of experts" over the value of failed technology, and the loss of an entrepreneurial dream.

A spiral into 'financial oblivion.' Back in 2005, the debtor worked for his family's business, a firm that supplied equipment to the high-speed printing and reprographic industry. Much of his time and effort went into developing a robotic "stacking" technology, which, at first, drew a great deal of interest from the trade. The business sold its first three units for just about $1 million apiece and received seven additional orders—but its overall costs of production always exceeded the sale price by hundreds of thousands of dollars per unit. As the federal bankruptcy court noted in its review of the facts, "this was not a good way to stay in business."

Indeed, initial outlays on the new technology forced the family business to exhaust its available capital and open a new line of credit. By 2006, it decided to staunch the "river of red ink" associated with the "money-losing stacker," the court said. The son, however, still wanted to pursue his "dream" of making the technology profitable and started his own company with the blessing of his family and the unfettered right to use the technology. At the same time, he felt "morally responsible" for the financial drain on the family business and promised to repay its development costs. None of these transactions were ever reduced to writing, that is, the son's spinoff never included a documented purchase of the stacker technology, and his agreement to repay the family business was verbal and entirely voluntary.

In an effort to replace its depleted capital, the family business acquired two loans from M&T Bank totaling $650,000 in April 2007. In June, the son guaranteed the loans, secured by mortgages on his primary residence. Importantly, the son did not specifically pledge the stacker technology as collateral. However, more than a year and a half after guaranteeing the loans—and presumably to tie the value of technology to the transfers—the family business issued a highly restricted (nonexclusive, terminable-without-cause) license to the son's business, permitting him to use the stacker technology as of or around the time of the guaranties.

The son "never had a chance," the court noted. Saddled with monthly debt payments in addition to a product that continued to sell at well below production costs, his business "lost ever more money, spiraling into inevitable financial oblivion." In 2009, the business closed and the son filed his Chapter 7 petition. His home was valued at $350,000 but was encumbered by a primary mortgage loan as well as real estate taxes and the $650,000 lien to M&T Bank, for a total of $775,000 in debts.

Two very different approaches to valuing the technology. To defend against the trustee's fraudulent transfer claims, the bank maintained that the son received reasonably equivalent value in exchange for guaranteeing the loans—to wit, the transfer of the stacker technology via the 2008 licensing agreement, which by its terms was made retroactive to July 1, 2007.

As a preliminary matter, the court noted that the terms of the licensing agreement were not effective as of 2006, when the son originally spun off his business and was given "absolute, unrestricted" use of the technology. Nor was the license effective in April/June 2007, when the family firm took out the two loans and the son executed his guaranties. Moreover, pursuant to the loan agreements between M&T Bank and the family business, the latter pledged "general" categories of collateral, including "general intangibles"—which very well could have included the stacker technology.

Evidence suggested that, back in 2006, the family business wanted "no part of" the technology and "dumped it," the court said, but then tried to take it back with an "onerously one-sided" and "long-after-the-fact" licensing agreement, which purported to transfer technology "that may have been pledged to M&T as collateral."

These factors strongly influenced, but did not ultimately control, the court's findings regarding the value of the technology license. For that, it turned to the "battle of the experts" and their "very different approaches" to valuing the assets.

1. *Trustee's expert.* The trustee offered the managing director of a well-known regional financial advisory and counseling firm, with advanced academic degrees and credentials in finance, restructuring, and distressed business valuations. Despite a 25-year career and previous appearances in bankruptcy court, the expert conceded that he had never testified solely to the value of a technology license and had written only one prior report valuing a general intangible (a brand name). He also did not know how the stacker technology worked and had no legal training pertaining to technology assets. Based on these lapses, the defendant argued he was not qualified to testify in this case.

However, the expert's last comment on cross-examination persuaded the court otherwise. Although he might not know much about the legal or technical aspects of the technology at issue, "he knows about the economic value of any asset, including intangibles, significant to a business," the court said, and admitted his testimony.

To calculate the economic value of the stacker technology and the licensing agreement, the trustee's expert reviewed the tax returns and other financial information pertaining to the son's business, including summaries of its hard and soft operating costs as well as any revenues generated by sales. He also looked at general information about the printing equipment industry. At no time from its inception in 2006 through the timing of the loan and guaranty agreements (April/June 2007) did the business have any value, the expert concluded. No matter how many stackers it sold, it had never historically made a profit and never would make a profit, he said, assigning the firm a value of zero at all relevant times.

The expert also reviewed the technology license, finding it "restrictive, punitive, and deprivative." Beyond these negatives, he also believed the technology was subject to the general pledge of intangibles by the family business to the bank. "The only value (such as it was) that the debtor enjoyed from the technology license was fulfillment of his aspiration to use the technology to run his own business," the court said, summarizing from the expert's testimony. Yet, if he had been successful, the licensing agreement left him no protection against his family's business "unilaterally and for no cause terminating the technology license and enjoying the fruits of his labor."

Further, any value that might be attributed to the license was as of its effective date, July 1, 2007, or two months after the effective date of the loans and the debtor's guaranties. "The time for any valuation, therefore, expired before the technology license came into existence," the court explained. Interestingly, it also noted that the trustee's expert did not expressly say in his direct testimony (although it could be inferred) that the value of the licensing agreement was zero.

However the defendant remedied this omission on cross-examination, when counsel prompted the plaintiff's expert to testify that, in appraising the son's business, he was referring to "the value that would be embedded in its equity by virtue of having access to the technology license." But the value of the stacker technology was worthless to the company, he added, and, due to its deprivative nature, he accorded no value to its license on the open market at any of the relevant times.

2. *Defendant's expert.* By contrast, the defendant presented a local attorney with a practice in intellectual property, whose career also involved the valuation and sale of "numerous" IP assets. (Although the court opinion does not say, it doesn't appear that the plaintiff challenged these credentials.)

To value the stacker technology, the defendant's expert used two approaches. Under the cost method, he analyzed the original costs to develop the technology by the family business, estimating these amounted to at least $440,000. He also used a "capitalization of hypothetical income approach," under which he assumed an 8% annual profit on sales of the stacker units as well as a 10-year useful life. To reach these figures, he reviewed the *Quarterly Financial Report of the U.S. Census Bureau*, in particular, the average pretax profit margins for manufacturers of electrical equipment, appliances, and components.

One expert opinion credible, the other 'absurd.' After reviewing all the facts and opinion evidence, the court commended the trustee's expert for the "clear, succinct, and credible" presentation of his opinion that the son's business and the stacker technology never had any value at any times applicable to the trustee's claims.

By contrast, the court "could not avoid believing that the defendant's expert would have grasped any approach he could find to establish some value in the stacker technology." Further, the "absurdity" of his statements pertaining to its value under the cost approach were "stunning." Perhaps, as a method to value tangible assets, such as a constructed building, the cost approach could provide an accurate measure. But applying it to a unique intangible asset such as the stacker technology—or one developed by Apple or IBM, for that matter—was a "strikingly inappropriate methodology" to determine its market value, the court said.

Similarly, the defendant's expert appeared to have pulled the figures for his "hypothetical" capitalization of income approach "from thin air." He looked to the economics of a "wholly unrelated industry and ignored the actual, terrible absence of profit from selling every one of the stackers at a huge loss," the court said. "He believes the technology had value simply because it worked and because [the debtor's company] had buyers." No witness ever testified that the stackers could now (or soon or ever) be sold at a profit, the court added. In fact, the evidence showed that the more stackers the company made and sold, "the more money it lost and would lose."

Accordingly, the court rejected the testimony of the defendant's expert as incredible and adopted the opinion of the trustee's expert. It also examined the terms of the licensing agreement and found a different "twist" from either interpretations advanced by the parties or their experts. However valueless the stacker technology might be, the family realized that it would be lost upon the collapse of the son's business. After conferring with patent counsel to develop the one-sided terms, the family imposed the licensing agreement on the son to "completely redo and revise the unwritten, unqualified, unlimited transfer of the stacker technology" in 2006, the court said. The family "wanted a way to take the technology back."

As a result, the debtor accurately claimed in his bankruptcy schedules that the value of his defunct business was zero. If the stacker technology were truly worth the $440,000 to $793,000 the bank claimed, then it might very well be a substantial asset. But "where then is this ... technology?" the court asked. If the family business does not have it, "then who does?" The record did not reflect any investigation or action by the trustee along these lines, but further consideration "might be appropriate," the court reflected.

In the meantime, the trustee had successfully proven the debtor's guaranties and related grant of liens in his residence were constructive fraudulent conveyances under applicable law, the court held, and avoided the same.

In re Integra Realty Resources, Inc.: Jeffrey A. Weinman v. Fidelity Capital Appreciation Fund

Citation: No. 99-1547 (10th Cir.)
Date of Decision: January 14, 2004
Country: US
State or Federal: Federal
State/Jurisdiction: 10th Circuit
Court: United States Court of Appeals
Type of action: Bankruptcy

Value of Recovery Under Sec. 550 May Be Greater Than the Value of the Asset Fraudulently Transferred at the Time of the Transfer

The U.S. Court of Appeals for the 10th Circuit considered the recovery of the value of an asset that was fraudulently transferred under sec. 550 of the Bankruptcy Code when the asset increases in value following the transfer. Integra Realty Resources Inc. in the late 1990s was publicly traded on the New York Stock Exchange. In 1988, it held a 90% interest in ShowBiz, which operated themed pizza restaurants and Tex-Mex restaurants. At that time, Integra was experiencing cash flow problems. To alleviate some of its problems, it spun off ShowBiz in a tax-free transaction. Each Integra shareholder received 0.429 shares of ShowBiz, which would then be listed on the NASDAQ exchange. The Integra shareholders were notified in the spinoff that the ShowBiz shares or the value thereof may be surrendered to a bankruptcy trustee in the event that Integra was not able to rectify its cash flow situation. The spinoff transaction occurred in 1989. On its first day of trading, ShowBiz closed at $5.50 per share, while the value of Integra dropped by $3.13 per share. Integra's fortunes did not improve, and it filed a voluntary Chapter 11 bankruptcy in 1992. During the same period, ShowBiz's fortunes increased. By the time of the bankruptcy, ShowBiz stock traded at $101.25 (adjusted for splits).

Under Integra's 1994 reorganization plan, all claims regarding the ShowBiz spinoff became the property of a trust for the benefit of the unsecured creditors. Weinman is the trustee of the unsecured creditors' trust. He brought suit against the recipients of the ShowBiz stock in the spinoff. Those shareholders received class certification, and Fidelity, a mutual fund company that received the largest distribution of ShowBiz stock from the spinoff, was named lead defendant. Weinman sought to recover the stock or the value thereof under sec. 550 of the Bankruptcy Code. He argued that the spinoff was a fraudulent transfer under the Texas Fraudulent Transfer Act. Fidelity and Weinman settled the claim. Under the settlement agreement, the recipients of ShowBiz stock were required to pay the unsecured creditors' trust a maximum of $7 per share of ShowBiz stock they received in the spinoff. The settlement was confirmed by the bankruptcy court and the district court. Several receiptants of the ShowBiz stock appealed the confirmation of the settlement.

On appeal, they argued that the settlement was not fair, reasonable, or adequate. They specifically argued that the value of the ShowBiz stock could not be more than $5.50 per share, its market price at the time of the spinoff. The appellate court noted that the bankruptcy trustee may recover the transferred asset or the value thereof, if the court so ordered, under sec. 550 of the Bankruptcy Code; however, "value" is not defined nor does sec. 550 indicate when the "value" is to be determined. It further noted that case law has established that the trustee may recover the market value of the property transferred at the time of the transfer, less any consideration received, under sec. 550 in a falling market. *Hirsch v. Steinberg (In re Colonial Realty Co.),* 226 B.R. 513 (Bankr. D. Conn. 1998). It further noted that there was little case law discussing the value of the transferred property for sec. 550 purposes when the market for the property rises following the transfer. However, it stated, "As the *In re Colonial* court recognized, 'the proper focus in [sec. 550(a)] actions is not on what the transferee gained by the transaction, but rather on what the bankruptcy estate lost as a result of the transfer.'" The 10th Circuit rejected that guidance. It stated, "Rather than *In re Colonial*'s rule, we believe the only generally applicable rule in regard to sec. 550(a) valuation is that 'the time at which the value is measured depends upon the circumstances in each individual case.'" It then considered the evidence of value in this matter. It noted that the value of ShowBiz stock ranged from $5.50 per share to $101.25 per share and that the lower court could have ordered either the return of the ShowBiz stock or any value of that stock within that range if the spinoff had been found to be a fraudulent transfer. Thus it concluded, "The only way to determine precisely what the outcome would have been was to litigate the case to conclusion (which, we note, defendant class members had the option of doing by opting out of the settlement). We therefore conclude that the terms of the settlement limiting the Trustee's recovery to the lesser of $7 per share or the amount for which the stock was ultimately sold, are not inherently unfair." Thus, it affirmed the lower court's decision to confirm the settlement.

In re Jonatzke

Citation: 2012 Bank. LEXIS 3882
Date of decision: August 24, 2012
Country: US
State or Federal: Federal
State/Jurisdiction: Federal Circuit
Court: United States Bankruptcy Court
Experts: Eric Fudo (plaintiff)
Judge: Shefferly

Flawed Expert Opinion Drastically Diminishes Plaintiff's Lost Profits

In 2004, the defendant went to work for the plaintiff, an automotive supplier using a unique laser process to make prototypes. A year later, after he had been terminated, he opened a competing business. The plaintiff sued in state court, claiming theft of trade secrets. The parties eventually settled, but the defendant defaulted on the $3 million agreement. Soon afterwards, he filed for Chapter 7 bankruptcy. The plaintiff subsequently sought to enforce the state court's $3 million consent judgment as a nondischargeable debt in the bankruptcy case.

In pretrial rulings, the bankruptcy court accepted the state court's determination of liability but held that it was not bound by the $3 million judgment. Since the plaintiff never had to prove its damages in the prior proceeding, the court directed it to do so here. Accordingly, the plaintiff retained an experienced accounting and financial expert, who calculated its cumulative losses in four areas:

- Lost profits from 2005 through 2007 of $1.25 million;
- Price erosion during the same period of $350,000;
- Combined lost profits and price erosion from 2008 to 2012 of $1.91 million; and
- Out-of-pocket expenses of $800,000.

In making his determinations, the expert relied almost exclusively on information provided by the plaintiff's founder and reviewed only limited information from the defendant's company. He used a "but for" method to quantify the plaintiff's damages, comparing the plaintiff's actual sales to those it would have made but for the stolen trade secrets, and estimated damages under all four scenarios totaled $4,764,639.

Time and again, expert accepted plaintiff's assertions. The court assessed the expert's testimony as to each of the four determinations and discounted all but one:

1. *Lost profits from 2005 through 2007.* To calculate these amounts, the expert reviewed the defendant's sales, converting the defendant's pricing method to conform to the plaintiff's, and then quantified the sales that the plaintiff lost to the defendant, minus any related expenses. He applied a 20% discount rate to account for the plaintiff's size and uncertainty in making what could be "volatile"

sales. At the same time, he added a statutory interest rate to account for an expected court judgment or payment.

The court found two significant flaws in the analysis. First, the expert admitted to having accepted management assumptions without question. And second, he performed "a zero sum analysis," assuming that every sale by the defendant's business was one less sale that the plaintiff would have made, but without confirming so by talking to the defendant's customers or reviewing documentation. By contrast, the court accepted the expert's 2005 and 2006 calculations because—in addition to the plaintiff's bald assertions—the expert relied on documented financial records. These included tax returns that demonstrated the defendant's business grew considerably in 2006 and a project management report that showed it made sales primarily to the plaintiff's customers in 2005 and 2006. The defendant also admitted that, in 2005, no other automotive suppliers were capable of competing with the plaintiff. Together, these facts provided a "sufficient foundation for [the expert's] estimate of [the plaintiff's] lost profits through 2006," the court held.

By 2007, however, the industry had picked up on the plaintiff's trade secrets. Other companies started to bid on the same projects as the plaintiff, and at least one hired away an employee who knew of the trade secrets. Consequently, the court found support for only $400,000 in lost profits for November 2005 through December 2006.

2. *Price erosion.* To arrive at the claimed $350,000 for these damages, the expert calculated the difference in the plaintiff's prices from before November 2005 with those afterward and then applied a 20% discount rate. Yet the expert never performed an independent pricing study to determine trends or influencing facts/data in the automotive industry. Once again, he based his estimate on the plaintiff's assertions that the defendant's theft alone caused its prices to erode. "That conclusory statement does not provide a reliable foundation for [the expert's] opinion," the court found.

3. *2008-2012 combined lost profits.* Similarly, the court dismissed this estimate as speculative, based on the expert's unverified assumption that there would be no competitors other than the defendant's business while it existed and even after it folded in 2010. As the court saw it, even assuming there were no other competitors, there was no evidence to support the expert's assumption that the plaintiff's products enjoyed a five-year life cycle.

4. *Out-of-pocket costs.* The expert's $800,000 calculation accounted for the additional, incremental advertising, marketing, and other professional fees that the plaintiff allegedly incurred due to the defendant's theft. However, this estimate essentially "regurgitated" the plaintiff's statement of these expenses without any supporting evidence. "In sum, just because [the plaintiff] paid out lots of money during its [state court] litigation," the court said, "does not by itself mean that [it] was entitled to recover all of those payments" as damages.

In conclusion, after subtracting the amount the defendant already paid under the parties' settlement agreement, the bankruptcy court awarded actual damages plus attorneys' fees of approximately $276,000 and determined that the amount was nondischargeable.

In re Joy Recovery Tech. Corp.; Daley v. Chang

Citation: 286 B.R. 54, 2002 Bankr. LEXIS 1307
Date of Decision: November 20, 2002
Country: US
State or Federal: Federal
State/Jurisdiction: Illinois
Court: United States Bankruptcy Court
Type of action: Bankruptcy
Experts: Scott Peltz, CPA, Martin W. Terpstra, CPA, CFE (for Daley), James F. Schultz, CPA, CVA, Kenneth S. Pinsky, CPA (for Chang)
Judge: Schmetterer
Key words: Bankruptcy, Capitalization rate, Discount rate, Earnings Before Interest, Taxes, Depreciation, Amortization (EBITDA), Fair market value (FMV), Company-specific risk premium

Experts' Testimony Scrutinized, Admitted Under Daubert; Court Uses Balance Sheet Test and Market Multiple Approach in Insolvency Analysis

Facts. This was an adversary proceeding related to the Chapter 11 bankruptcy of Joy Recovery Technology Corp. The trustee charged Chang—chairman of the board, director, and shareholder—with fraudulent transfer for selling his 50% stock interest to Young—president and shareholder—in a leveraged buyout (LBO) that left the company insolvent.

***Daubert* hearings.** The parties offered expert witnesses. Chang moved in limine to bar trustee's experts, and trustee sought to bar testimony by Chang's experts. *Daubert* hearings were held, and all experts were allowed to testify.

Chang's first motion sought to bar the testimony of Scott Peltz, the trustee's key solvency expert, on three grounds: (1) Peltz's testimony constituted improper legal conclusions; (2) Peltz lacked credibility because he was a de facto contingent witness; and (3) Peltz's testimony was not consistent with business valuation techniques employed by professionals in his field.

Chang first argued that Peltz offered impermissible legal conclusions because he referred to the Illinois Fraudulent Transfer Act (IUFTA) in his written report and lifted language directly from the statute. The court held that:

> Although Peltz organized the disputed section of his report to correspond to subsections of the IUFTA, the actual analysis was consistent with principles of accountancy. Peltz gave his opinion on whether Joy was rendered insolvent as a result of the Young-Chang transaction, but his conclusion was based on applying accounting rules to Joy's financial reports.... The mere fact that Peltz's report referred to relevant portions of the IUFTA did not render it an impermissible legal conclusion.

Chang also argued that Peltz should not be allowed to testify because he was a de facto contingent witness, that is, the trustee ran out of money to pay his fees and owed him an undisclosed sum. Peltz admitted that he would not be paid unless the trustee prevailed. The court distinguished between state ethical rules—which prohibit attorneys from using contingent fee experts—and evidentiary rules, which say nothing about contingent witnesses.

Chang has not offered any authority for the proposition that contingent fee experts are incompetent to testify in federal court or that evidence obtained from such witnesses is inadmissible. Merely showing that Peltz may have an incentive to exaggerate his testimony is insufficient to bar that testimony. Moreover, the court is unwilling to sanction Joy's creditors by barring evidence from their key witness because the [trustee] ran out of funds to pay him. However, the court is mindful of the fact that Peltz had an incentive to shade his testimony in favor of the Trustee, and this was a consideration in the assessment of his credibility, though not dispositive.

Finally, Chang objected that Peltz committed numerous computational errors, showing that he did not follow the "general standards of others in his field." The court found that the alleged errors were actually conclusions based on assumptions Peltz made. "Accounting is not an exact science. Accountants are therefore required to make judgments about how to communicate financial information. A *Daubert* hearing is not the time to fully test the validity of those assumptions." The court concluded that Peltz "employed the methodology used by accountants engaged in business valuation," and that his assumptions were "certainly not so inappropriate as to render his testimony speculative."

Chang's second motion in limine sought to bar the testimony of Martin Terpstra on the grounds that his testimony was speculative and therefore irrelevant. The trustee employed Terpstra to evaluate the Young-Chang transaction, and Terpstra determined that the most appropriate treatment was as a stock redemption. Chang argued that there was no foundation for this, based on a statement in Terpstra's own report that the facts did not support "any one particular accounting treatment." The court reasoned that Terpstra did not state that he had inadequate data to determine how to classify the transaction, rather that he gave his professional opinion as to the best way to record the transaction, in light of conflicting data.

The trustee sought to bar the testimony of Chang's experts, James Schultz and Kenneth Pinsky. Trustee argued that Schultz's testimony should be barred because he had never testified in a bankruptcy case or because he was not published and had worked primarily as an estate tax consultant. The court held that none of those reasons were sufficient to bar testimony under *Daubert* and admitted both expert's opinions.

Valuation evidence. One of the issues was whether the LBO made Joy insolvent. Under the Bankruptcy Code, a debtor is insolvent if "the sum of the debtor's debts is greater than all of the debtors assets at a fair valuation." The court first determined that the valuation should be on a fair market value basis, rather than a liquidation basis, because the company was not "on its deathbed." Thus, the court did not consider Peltz's liquidation analysis done for the trustee.

Both primary experts, Schultz and Peltz, used the weighted average cost of capital to determine the discount rate. Their calculations were as follows:

Peltz: (1 + growth rate) (income) - (long-term debt + short-term debt)
= Enterprise Value Cap rate (growth rate - discount rate)

Shultz: (1 + growth rate) (income) - (long-term debt)
= Equity Value Cap rate (growth rate - discount rate)

Peltz concluded that Joy had an enterprise value of $2.345 million against liabilities of between $3.714 million and $3.988 million. Thus, he found Joy was insolvent after the LBO to the extent of between $1.369 million and $1.643 million.

The differences between the two expert's opinions were substantial. Schultz argued that Peltz's cap rate was too high because he used a specific company risk factor of 10%, compared with 2% used by Schultz. Schultz also claimed that Peltz incorrectly used a debt-to-equity ratio of 2 to 1, resulting in a 17% cap rate versus Schultz's 11.1% cap rate. These two differences alone accounted for a $1.2 million reduction in Joy's value in Peltz's calculations. Moreover, Schultz alleged that Peltz understated the base income stream by $190,000 per year, which would have increased Joy's value by $1.7 million (using Schultz's 11.1% cap rate). Schultz also accused Peltz of improperly including short-term debt in the formula and further asserted that Peltz erred by not adding the alleged $1.8 million receivable from Young as a nonoperating asset.

Bankruptcy court findings. The bankruptcy court said that, although some of the foregoing criticisms had merit, the LBO still made Joy insolvent, even if the court used Schultz's capitalized earnings number. Schultz concluded that Joy's post-LBO equity value was $2,669,530. Joy, however, had liabilities of between $3.714 million and $3.988 million. Applying the balance sheet test for insolvency, the company was insolvent by more than $1 million even using Schultz's analysis.

The court also said that Joy was insolvent after the LBO using a second solvency test: the market multiple approach performed by Schultz. He multiplied EBITDA by 4.5 to derive the value of Joy's assets after the LBO and then subtracted long-term debt to reach "net worth." The court disapproved: "It is inappropriate to use a term that implies a balance sheet analysis to a projected income stream, since doing so connotes a false sense of precision." The court also was troubled that Schultz used a single sales transaction not comparable to Joy to derive the 4.5 multiplier, rendering Schultz's calculation "of questionable value."

Notwithstanding these concerns, the court stated that this method still resulted in Joy's insolvency after the LBO. Schultz concluded that Joy's value was $5.1 million. He then deducted long-term debt of $2.6 million, resulting in a valuation of $2.4 million, which was inadequate to offset liabilities over $3 million. According to the court, the only way Joy could be found solvent after the LBO was if the $1.8 million "receivable" from Young were added in as a nonoperating asset, thus raising Joy's fair market value to $4.2 million. Given that the receivable was "mostly illusory"—since Young likely could not have repaid the loan—the court said it could credit the receivable at no more than $400,000, increasing Joy's total invested capital value to $5.7 million. After deducting long-term debt of $2.6 million, a $3.1 resulting value would be insufficient to offset liabilities between $3.7 million and $3.9 million.

In re Jumer's Castle Lodge, Inc.

Citation: 2005 Bankr. LEXIS 843
Date of Decision: May 11, 2005
Country: US
State or Federal: Federal
State/Jurisdiction: Illinois
Court: United States Bankruptcy Court
Type of action: Bankruptcy
Experts: Douglas Nelson (for creditors), Jay Seaton (for transferee defendant)
Judge: Altenberger
SIC: 7011 Hotels and Motels (hotels, except casino hotels, and motels)
Key words: Bankruptcy, Reasonably equivalent value

Contested Valuation of One Asset Is Moot Where All Transferred Assets Provide Reasonably Equivalent Value

One of the issues in this Chapter 11 bankruptcy case was whether James Jumer, as principal stockholder of the debtor corporation, Jumer's Castle Lodge (JCL), had caused JCL to fraudulently transfer assets. As to one of the transferred assets, the creditors argued that JCL did not receive reasonably equivalent value because Jumer's valuation of the asset (a hotel property) at $4,500,000 was inflated and allowed Jumer to siphon off $2,400,000 from JCL. Specifically, the creditors contended that the asset was only worth $2,100,000 at the time of the transfer, based on an appraisal by Douglas Nelson.

In response, Jumer contended that JCL did receive reasonably equivalent value because his valuation of the asset at $4,500,000 was appropriate, as it was done by Jay Seaton, a certified appraiser.

The bankruptcy court did not have to assess the relative merits of the disparate valuations because it determined that, even using the creditors' lower valuation, JCL received reasonably equivalent value for all the assets transferred to it, including the disputed hotel property. In other words, the court decided that the debtor (JCL) received more than it gave to the transferee (Jumer), even using the creditors' lower valuation of the transferred asset.

In re Kim; Ardmor Vending Co. v. Kim

Citation: 130 F.3d 863, 1997 U.S. App. LEXIS 34370
Date of Decision: December 9, 1997
Country: US
State or Federal: Federal
State/Jurisdiction: 9th Circuit
Court: United States Court of Appeals
Experts: Robin D. Rix
Type of action: Bankruptcy
Judge: Tashima
SIC: 7211 Power Laundries, Family and Commercial
Key words: Fair market value (FMV)

Bankruptcy Court Erred in Undervaluing Appellant's Collateral

Debtors Peter and Un Kim filed a Chapter 13 bankruptcy plan treating appellant Ardmor Vending Co. dba Great Northern as partially secured ($34,000) and the Ardmor Profit Sharing Plan as wholly unsecured. At the time of filing, the Kims owed Great Northern approximately $98,000, secured by the dry cleaning equipment and the lease of the business premises. The Kims also owed Ardmor approximately $10,000, secured by the equipment. Also under the plan, the Kims would assume the lease and continue to operate the business. The bankruptcy court confirmed the plan, and the Bankruptcy Appellate Panel affirmed the bankruptcy court's findings.

Collateral worth more as turnkey business. Appellants appeal the plan confirmation and at issue before the Court of Appeals is the method of valuation of appellants' collateral, given their security interests in both the equipment and the lease of the Kims' dry cleaning business. Specifically, appellants argued that the Kims had undervalued the collateral by valuing the equipment and the lease separately, as opposed to valuing the two together as a "turnkey" business.

Fair market value is proper standard of value. The Appeals Court, citing Section 506 of the bankruptcy code, stated, "The value of a secured creditor's interest 'shall be determined in light of the purpose of the valuation and of the proposed disposition or use of such property....' Thus, when the debtor retains property subject to a lien, the proper valuation is fair market value, not foreclosure value." As a result, the Appeals Court reversed the bankruptcy court's ruling, stating that the bankruptcy court erred in valuing the equipment and lease separately. The bankruptcy court committed further error by accepting the off location valuation (not in use value) of the equipment, when in fact the valuation should have been based on the equipment's worth on location.

Broker estimates business worth $165,000. The Appeals Court also noted that the bankruptcy court gave no consideration to the most relevant evidence before it: Robin D. Rix, an agent who specializes in the sale of dry cleaning businesses, estimated the value of the Kims' business to be $165,000. Rix had also previously listed the Kims' business for sale.

On remand, the Appeals Court ordered the bankruptcy court to redetermine the value of the equipment and lease as a turnkey operation.

Going Concern Is Standard of Value When DIP Operates the Business

In re Peter Kim, Ardmor Vending Co. v. Peter Kim, No. 97-55298, Dec. 9, 1997, the U.S. Court of Appeals for the 9th Circuit consider the confirmation of Kim's Chapter 13 reorganization plan. Kim operated a dry cleaner. Ardmor held a secured interest in the equipment and lease of Kim's business. The plan allowed for the continued operation of the business but valued the equipment "off location" or liquidated. The plan also placed a zero value on the lease because it provided for above-market rent. Ardmor appealed. It claimed that the assets were undervalued, and the equipment and lease should be valued as a "turnkey" package or going concern.

The 9th Circuit reviewed the bankruptcy code, which requires the value of a secured interest to be determined "in light of the purpose of the valuation and of the proposed disposition or use of such property." 11 U.S.C. 506(a). "Thus, when the debtor retains the property subject to a lien, the proper valuation is fair market value, not foreclosure value." *In Taffi v. United States (In re Taffi),* 96 F.3d 1190 (9th Cir. 1996). The 9th Circuit found that the bankruptcy appellate panel's valuation was "based on its finding that [Ardmor's] security interest did not amount to a turn-key operation; thus, the appellants did not have the right to sell the lease plus the equipment as a package." The 9th Circuit found this clearly erroneous because "selling the equipment alone, and then selling the lease, as vacant premises with no improvements and no equipment, is impractical and would not maximize the value of the collateral." Thus the 9th Circuit reversed and remanded the plan for a revaluation of the collateral as a turnkey package.

Kool, Mann, Coffee and Co. v. L. Coleman Coffey (I)

Citation: 233 B.R. 291, 1999 Bankr. LEXIS 443
Date of Decision: March 18, 1999
Country: US
State or Federal: Federal
State/Jurisdiction: New Jersey
Court: United States District Court
Type of action: Bankruptcy
Experts: Robert Malinowski, Thomas Millon (for debtor) James Graves (for Coffee)
Judge: Gindin
SIC: 7999 Amusement and Recreation Services, NEC (canoe, pleasure boats, bicycles, motorcycles, moped, go carts, etc. rental)

Valuation Techniques for Misrepresented Businesses

Buyers purchased a marina business under fraudulent misrepresentation. The Bankruptcy Court held they were entitled to recover, based on fraud theory, the difference between the value of the business as it had been represented and the actual value at the time of sale. The case includes an extensive discussion of valuation techniques for misrepresented businesses.

Kool, Mann, Coffee and Co. v. L. Coleman Coffey (II)

Citation: No. 01-4052 (3rd Cir.)
Date of Decision: July 29, 2002
Country: US
State or Federal: Federal
State/Jurisdiction: 3rd Circuit
Court: United States Court of Appeals
Type of action: Bankruptcy

Discounted Cash Flow Method Used to Value Marina and Houseboat Rental Business

The U.S. Court of Appeals for the 3rd Circuit considered the valuation of a claim in bankruptcy stemming from the sale of a business. Coffey sold his Kentucky marina and houseboat rental business to Kool Mann, an equipment leasing business. The business sold in a 1985 stock sale for $5 million—$1 million down, five annual principal payments of $150,000 plus interest at 0.5%, and a balloon payment of $3.25 million. Additionally, the parties entered into a side agreement that permitted Kool Mann a reduction in the purchase price for any capital gains tax savings.

Shortly after the sale, Kool Mann determined that Coffey had misrepresented the cash flow of the business. It additionally contested its assumption of the business debt. Kool Mann then stopped paying for the business. Coffey brought suit for payment. Kool Mann countersued for fraud in connection with the sale. It also filed for bankruptcy. Coffey filed a proof of claim with the bankruptcy court. The cases were consolidated before the bankruptcy court, which ordered interest payments to continue through trial.

The bankruptcy court then set about estimating the value of Coffey's claim. The bankruptcy court determined that Coffey committed fraud in connection with the sale by inflating the business's revenue. After correcting the cash flow for the misrepresentations, the bankruptcy court determined the true value of the business. The bankruptcy court used a multiple of cash flow methodology, based on estimates of the business's future houseboat rentals and other business activity. It determined that the company had a true value of $2.5 million. It then reduced that amount by $236,566.22 for the tax savings side agreement, it converted the interest payments to principal payments, and it determined that the parties' purchase agreement did not call for the assumption of debt. Thus, it reduced the filed figure by $1.2 million, the amount of the assumed debt, and determined Coffey's claim had a value of $26,915.78 after deductions. Coffey appealed to the district court.

The district court reversed, it concluded that the bankruptcy court incorrectly valued the claim. It "expressed concern about the methodology used by Kool Mann's expert because it was 'based upon hypothetical cash flow projections bearing little or no relationship to the actual facts pertaining to this particular business.'" The district court further found that the bankruptcy court erred in reducing the claim by the amount of the tax savings agreement because the benefits of the tax savings agreement to Coffey had not come to pass. It also found that the bankruptcy court erred in permitting a reduction for the assumed indebtedness of the business. Thus, the district court remanded.

The bankruptcy court revalued the claim. It received expert valuation reports that determined the true amount of the cash flow. It recast the business's financial documents to the tune of $1.4 million for assets listed but not accounted for, the overstatement of profits and the omissions of miscellaneous business expenses. The bankruptcy court determined that the free cash flow was $188,848 in 1985. It then applied a multiple of cash flow method. Under this method, the court valued the business as of 1985 by projecting the cash flow over 15 years into the future using a 7.5% growth rate and discounting to present value using 18.5%. It determined that the business had a true value of $2.28 million. It then reduced that value by the amount of tax savings ($236,566.22), the down payment ($1 million), and the amount of the interest payments that it recharacterized as principal payments ($291,784). It declined to reduce the amount of the claim by the amount of debt Kool Mann assumed in connection with its acquisition of the business. It valued Coffey's total claim at $1.051 million. Both parties appealed to the district court. The district court affirmed the bankruptcy court on all the contested issues except the reduction for the tax savings agreement, which it reversed. Both parties appealed to the 3rd Circuit.

Coffey argued before the 3rd Circuit that the bankruptcy court erred in determining the true value of the business at the time of the sale. Coffey specifically argued that the bankruptcy court was precluded from utilizing the cash flow method by the district court's first decision. The 3rd Circuit found that the district court did not preclude the use of this method but made a statement of opinion regarding its use. The 3rd Circuit then noted, "According to Kool Mann's expert, the rates and time frame utilized were industry standards in valuing a company like … [the one at issue here], an assertion which was not disputed by the Coffeys' expert." It further noted that various courts had reached conflicting decisions regarding the propriety of the cash flow method. However, it stated, "The particular facts of this case, which involve the extremely difficult task of valuing the stock of a company which is privately owned and not traded on a public exchange, favor the use of such methods which take into account the expected value of the company's future performance." Thus, the 3rd Circuit affirmed the use of the discounted cash flow method. In doing so, the 3rd Circuit corrected an error it found in the application of the bankruptcy court's discounted cash flow method. Correcting for that error reduced the true value of the business to $1.766 million.

The court then considered the various deductions from that value. It affirmed the reduction for the interest payments made by Kool Mann in 1986 of $291,784, which the bankruptcy court recharacterized as principal payments in light of the fraud ruling.

The court next considered the decision not to set off the true value of business by the amount of the business's indebtedness. The 3rd Circuit affirmed. In doing so, it stated, "Indeed, by purchasing … [the business's] stock, and not just its assets, Kool Mann agreed to pay a particular price for … [the business] as a whole— its assets and liabilities."

The 3rd Circuit lastly considered the tax savings credit. The tax savings agreement permitted Kool Mann to set off a capital gains tax credit of $236,566 against the $3.25 million balloon payment. The 3rd Circuit then determined that after deductions for the down payment and the interest payments from the true value, Coffey would be due a balloon payment of $474,847. It determined that, as a result of fixing the balloon payment amount, the tax savings credit, as agreed to by the parties

($236,566.22), must then be deducted from that amount. One judge dissented to this portion of the majority's decision. The judge concluded that Kool Mann was not entitled to a deduction for the tax savings agreement because Coffey had not realized any savings as a result of the capital gains tax treatment of the sale as contemplated by this side agreement.

The 3rd Circuit thus redetermined the true value of the business. It then made various deductions from that value to determine the value of Coffey's claim. It determined the value of that claim to be $238,280.78.

Kumho Tire Company v. Carmichael

Citation: 526 U.S. 137, 119 S. Ct. 1167, 1999 U.S. LEXIS 2189
Date of Decision: March 23, 1999
Country: US
State or Federal: Federal
State/Jurisdiction: Federal Circuit
Court: Supreme Court
Type of action: Evidence
Judge: Breyer
SIC: 3011 Tires and Inner Tubes

Supreme Court Affirms 'Gatekeeper' Duty of Trial Courts for Expert Evidence

In this product liability case, the trial court ruled that the expert testimony of the plaintiffs' tire failure analysis expert was inadmissible because it was not reliable. The trial court applied the *Daubert* factors in reaching this ruling.

11th Circuit rules *Daubert* doesn't apply. Plaintiffs appealed, and the 11th Circuit Court of Appeals reversed the trial court's ruling, stating that:

> A *Daubert* analysis applies only where an expert relies "on the application of scientific principles," rather than "on skill- or experience-based observation.

Supreme Court reverses 11th Circuit. Defendant petitioned the Supreme Court for certiorari, asking it to determine whether the trial court may apply the *Daubert* analysis and factors in determining the "admissibility of an engineering expert's testimony." The Supreme Court agreed to hear the case because of uncertainty among the appellate courts as to the application of *Daubert* to nonscientific expert testimony.

***Daubert* factors may be considered in making reliability determination.** The Supreme Court held that a trial court may consider the following factors if they bear on the court's determination of reliability and relevance of expert testimony:

- Whether a "theory or technique … can be (and has been) tested";
- Whether it "has been subjected to peer review and publication";

- Whether, in respect to a particular technique, there is a high "known or potential rate of error" and whether there are "standards controlling the technique's operation"; and
- Whether the theory or technique enjoys "general acceptance" within a "relevant scientific community."

The Supreme Court did not, however, state that these factors must be applied rigidly. Rather, the rule from *Daubert* must be applied flexibly:

> [T]he trial judge must have considerable leeway in deciding in a particular case how to go about determining whether particular expert testimony is reliable. That is to say, a trial court should consider the specific factors identified in *Daubert* where they are reasonable measures of the reliability of expert testimony.

Daubert Is Applied to All Expert Testimony

In *Kumho Tire Co., Ltd. v. Patrick Carmichael, etc.* 119 U.S. 1167 (1999), the Supreme Court of the United States determined how *Daubert v. Merrell Dow Pharmaceuticals, Inc.*, 509 U.S. 579 (1993), applied to the testimony of experts who are not scientists. The 11th Circuit concluded that *Daubert* applied only in the context of scientific testimony rather than "on skill or experience based observation." The Supreme Court found that the gatekeeping function imposed on the trial court by Fed. Rul. Evid. 702 and 703 as clarified by *Daubert* applied to all expert testimony "whether the testimony reflects scientific, technical or other specialized knowledge."

The Supreme Court further considered whether all the *Daubert* factors must be met in order for the testimony to be admissible. Here, Kumho Tire "asked ... whether a trial judge ... may consider several more specific factors that *Daubert* said might 'bear on' a judge's gate-keeping determination." These questions included whether a technique had been tested and whether it was subject to peer review or publication. The Supreme Court found that the application of the *Daubert* factors must be considered on a case-by-case basis. It further stated that "we can neither rule out, nor rule in, for all cases and for all time the applicability of the factors mentioned in *Daubert*, nor can we now do so for subsets of cases categorized by category of expert or by kind of evidence. Too much depends upon the particular circumstances of the particular case at issue."

The court reversed the 11th Circuit's decision. It stated that "the trial court must have the same kind of latitude in deciding how to test an expert's reliability, and to decide whether or when special briefing or other proceedings are needed to investigate reliability as it enjoys when it decides whether that expert's testimony is reliable." It further noted that the trial court's reliability determinations are reviewed under the abuse-of -discretion standard. Justice Scalia, concurring but writing separately, noted, "It is [the trial court's] discretion to choose among reasonable means of excluding expertise that is fausse and science that is junky."

LaSalle Nat'l Bank Assn. v. Paloian

Citation: 2009 WL 721510 (N. D. Ill.)
Date of Decision: March 17, 2009
Country: US
State or Federal: Federal
State/Jurisdiction: Illinois
Court: United States District Court
Type of action: Bankruptcy
Experts: Michael Lane and Scott Peltz (trustee) Thomas Blake (defendant bank)
Judge: Pallmeyer
SIC: 8062 General Medical and Surgical Hospitals

Expert Solvency Opinions Accused of 'Hindsight Bias'

When last we visited the Doctor's Hospital Chapter 11 proceedings the bankruptcy court had found, among other issues, that:

- The Medicare-fraud riddled hospital was insolvent at all times between August 1997 and April 2000, when it filed for bankruptcy; and
- The hospital's 1997 guaranty and security payments to LaSalle National Bank were void as fraudulent transfers for less than equivalent value.

The bank appealed to the U.S. District Court (N. D. Ill.), claiming that the bankruptcy court impermissibly relied on expert evidence when contemporaneous market data were a better indication of solvency values. The bank also alleged that experts improperly relied on "hindsight bias" regarding the fraud and other factors.

Two qualified experts teamed up on the insolvency opinion. Much of the bankruptcy's findings regarding insolvency came from two qualified experts: one certified in healthcare valuation, the other a CPA and turnaround consultant. Together they prepared a joint report on behalf of the bankruptcy trustee showing that the debtor/hospital was insolvent from the date of its loan from the bank (August 1997) to its financial failure nearly three years later. They used three tests to show insolvency:

1. Fair market balance sheet, viewing the hospital as a going concern and capitalizing its normalized cash flows;
2. Adequacy of capitalization; and
3. Ability to repay debts.

The bankruptcy court relied primarily on the first method to find insolvency, but it also concluded that the hospital lacked adequate capital and was unable to pay its debts as they came due. The court also identified a number of other factors that compromised the hospital's financial integrity:

- The hospital earned 85% to 89% of its revenue from Medicaid and Medicare, compared to average hospitals in the region, which derived about 50% of revenues from federal reimbursement.

- Its supply of hospital beds exceeded demand by 37%. In addition, the average patient stay was significantly higher than other hospitals in the same market, and, because federal programs reimburse on a per-case rather than per-patient basis, the hospital incurred higher costs for the longer stays.

- The Balanced Budget Act of 1997 (BBA) would reduce federal reimbursements substantially, up to $5 million for the hospital.

- Federal investigations into Medicare/Medicaid fraud led the bank to obtain a Coopers & Lybrand report in 1997, which showed the hospital could lose from $4.6 million (best case) to $29 million in revenues.

- In 1999 and 2000, the hospital was assessed $19.4 million in fraud fines, both of which were paid by the owner, largely from funds loaned by the bank.

Did the experts indulge in bias? The bank argued on appeal that the trustee's experts "indulged in improper hindsight bias," assuming facts that would not have been known or knowable to a willing, hypothetical buyer as of August 1997:

> Expert testimony is often prepared many years after the events at issue, and the temptation to indulge in hindsight bias may be greater where the absence of an actual buyer requires a certain amount of speculation concerning what a "hypothetical buyer" would have known at the time.

The bank cited the following examples of "hindsight bias" in the experts' report:

- They reduced the hospital's net income as of September 1997 by some $3 million to adjust for certain settlements related to the fraud investigations, which were not booked until 1999-2000;

- They used an inflated 10% company-specific risk premium (CSRP);

- They refused to add back $4.5 million in fraud payments that the hospital supposedly wrote off in 1997;

- They improperly concluded that a hypothetical buyer would have deducted the above-market rents that the hospital paid to its parent corporation; and

- They failed to consider contemporaneous market data that better reflected the hospital's financial condition.

On the latter point, the bank claimed that there is a "growing body of law favoring contemporary market evidence over post facto expert testimony prepared in anticipation of litigation."

For instance, in *VFB LLC v. Campbell Soup Co.,* 482 F.2d 624 (3rd Cir. 2007), the 3rd Circuit found that "[t]he public trading market constitutes an impartial gauge of investor confidence and remains the best and most unbiased measure of fair market value and, when available to the court, is the preferred standard of valuation."

In considering these arguments, the federal district court acknowledged "a preference for contemporaneous market evidence." However, this is "by no means a requirement, and even where available, contemporaneous data does not preclude a court from assigning greater weight to expert testimony." In this case, the bankruptcy court used "the generally accepted approach" of basing its determination on "seasoned appraisals [and] expert testimony." The experts were highly qualified to testify about the numerous regulatory and market factors that ultimately led to the hospital's demise.

For example, in adjusting the hospital's net income by roughly $3 million in 1997, the experts relied on government settlement documents that estimated the hospital's fraudulent earnings per year. They then multiplied that number by a percentage representing the total settlement amount divided by the total fraudulent activities. As their report explained, "the prospective net income that [a hypothetical third-party buyer could expect to receive] would not include earnings from these activities."

Although the bank argued such adjustments were improper, its own expert made similar adjustments based on the 1997 fraudulent earnings but to a lower degree. Despite the disagreement on the amount, the rationale behind such reductions was "unmistakable," the court said. "[B]oth sets of experts believed some reduction was warranted based on known future liability for the [fraud] violations." The bankruptcy court simply found the trustee's experts more credible in light of their "experience and expertise in valuing similar entities." It also relied on the 1997 Coopers & Lybrand report, which a hypothetical buyer would have to consider, including its projection of potential liability ranging from $4.6 million to $29 million for the hospital's fraud. "Far from ignoring this kind of contemporary data, both the trial court and [the trustee's] experts used it to support their conclusion[s]."

Did the experts inflate the CSRP? In calculating the CSRP, the trustee's experts looked not only at the hospital's fraud, but also at the depth of its management and the effect of the BBA. By contrast, the bank's expert—who was not a healthcare specialist—looked only at the hospital's transactions with related entities to assess a 5% CSRP. The remaining risks were "baked into" the hospital's beta and its size premium, he said.

The trustee's experts disputed the "baked in" assumption, explaining that the government's fraud investigations focused on select targets, so that any risks were specific to the hospital—which also suffered because of its disproportionate reliance on federal reimbursements. The hospital's equity risk premium did not account for the remaining risks, they said, such as its potential to lose $5 million because of the BBA. "Given this evidence and the numerous other company-specific risks unrelated to the impact of the BBA, the bankruptcy court reasonably concluded that [the trustee's] experts were, if anything, conservative in choosing a 10% risk premium."

Similarly, the argument that the experts should have added back the $4.5 million into the hospital's 1997 net income was "a non-starter," the district court said. Any evidence that the hospital wrote off this amount to account for fraudulent earnings was "sparse at best," as the hospital's financial statements did not refer to the $4.5 million until 1999. Moreover, "revenues generated through prolonged, systematic fraud cannot typically be accounted for in a one-time adjustment, as billing irregularities are rarely limited to a regular, twelve-month cycle," the court said. Given the range of potential liability that the Coopers & Lybrand report predicted, a $4.5 million add-back would be "absurd" from the perspective of a hypothetical buyer.

Finally, the court considered the normalization of the hospital's above-market rent, which resulted in a $31.5 million adjustment, the experts' single-largest deduction to the hospital's enterprise value. This amount should be reduced by $10.7 million, the bank claimed, and equal to the income tax deductions that a hypothetical buyer could take for rent expense. However, federal tax law prohibits deductions for amounts above fair market value, the court observed, in dismissing this argument. It also found that the expert's treatment of the above-market rent as "debt" for purposes of the insolvency opinion (and calculation of the discount rate) was appropriate.

Did the experts improperly tax affect? Even though the hospital was a Subchapter S corporation, the trustee's experts applied a 40% corporate tax rate on its 1997 income, reducing it by $2.2 million. Treating the hospital as a C corporation was "standard when valuing a controlling interest in an S corporation," they said, citing a book by two valuation experts (unnamed in the court's opinion).

"How to address the effect of taxation in valuing a Subchapter S corporation is a contentious issue among experts in the field of valuation," the court observed. It also criticized the bankruptcy court somewhat, which found:

> It is not logical to suggest that a buyer would pay substantially more for [the hospital just because the buyer is an S corporation. The object of an insolvency analysis is to determine the value of [the hospital] to a theoretical buyer, regardless of the nature of the buyer.

"This may be an overstatement," the district court acknowledged; "the nature of the buyer, theoretical or not, would appear to be significant to determining [the hospital's] value from that buyer's perspective." An S corporation might not pay substantially more—but a C corporation would almost certainly account for its tax liability in purchasing the hospital.

The court declined to reweigh the evidence, however. The bankruptcy court's conclusions did not rest on the logic of what an S corporation buyer would pay but on the expert testimony, supported by "external expert authority" that the dispositive factor in valuing an S corporation was the 100% ownership interest.

Overall, the bankruptcy court did not apply improper hindsight bias in making its insolvency determination, nor did it err in valuing the hospital as an S corporation to reach that conclusion, and the district court affirmed its findings.

In re Lason, Inc.

Citation: 2003 Bankr. LEXIS 1324
Date of Decision: October 15, 2003
Country: US
State or Federal: Federal
State/Jurisdiction: Delaware
Court: United States Bankruptcy Court
Type of action: Bankruptcy
Judge: Walrath
SIC: 7374 Computer Processing and Data Preparation and Processing Services

Premise of Value Issue in Bankruptcy

The issue in this Chapter 11 bankruptcy is whether the secured creditors would receive more under a liquidation of the debtors' businesses under Chapter 7 than they would under the Chapter 11 plan.

One of the secured creditors, Ark 2000-1 CLO, Limited and Patriarch Partners LLC (Ark), argued that certain funds in escrow should be released to it because the Chapter 11 plan did not meet the best interest of the creditors test. This test is applied by conducting a hypothetical Chapter 7 liquidation, then comparing the proceeds of that liquidation sale to what the secured creditors will receive under the Chapter 11 plan.

Premise of value. One of the disagreements between the parties that is relevant to this issue was the appropriate premise of value to be applied in determining what the debtors' businesses would be worth in a liquidation setting. Ark argued that debtors' businesses should be valued on a going concern basis because they could be sold by the trustee in an orderly fashion. Debtors argued that the appropriate premise of value was liquidation value because the conversion to Chapter 7 would significantly reduce the value of the businesses.

The bankruptcy court agreed with the debtors because "debtors' business is a service business, largely dependent on customers and key employees." Other evidence before the court support this conclusion, such as testimony that debtors' had already lost many customers and that many other customers had made contingency plans to replace debtors with a different company in the event of liquidation. Without these customers, the value of debtors' businesses would be significantly reduced.

Valuation evidence. The debtors' expert witness opined that liquidation value of debtors' businesses and other assets that comprised the collateral of the secured creditor's was worth $75 million to $83 million.

Ark's expert witness opined that the going concern value of the restructured company was between $79 million and $111 million.

Bankruptcy court findings. The court rejected the testimony of Ark's expert because he had no experience with Chapter 7 liquidations. Debtors' expert, on the other hand, "was an investment banker with significant experience in 'distressed sales.'"

The secured creditors were to be paid $90 million under the Chapter 11 plan. Accordingly, the court found that the plan did meet the best interest of the creditors test because, even at going concern value as opined by Ark's expert, the creditors would receive more under the Chapter 11 plan.

Editor's Note: The court incorrectly used the term "standard of value," so we have substituted the correct term, "premise of value," in the abstract.

In re Leskosky; Tidwell v. Leskosky

Citation: 287 B.R. 295, 2002 Bankr. LEXIS 1444
Date of Decision: December 17, 2002
Country: US
State or Federal: Federal
State/Jurisdiction: Georgia
Court: United States Bankruptcy Court
Type of action: Bankruptcy
Judge: Hershner
Key words: Bankruptcy, Fair market value (FMV)

Stock Valued as of Date of Petition in Bankruptcy Regardless of Potential Post-Petition Appreciation

The issue in this bankruptcy matter was the proper date for valuing stock that the debtor claimed as exempt. The debtor listed the value of the stock at $10 in his claim for exemption. The stock was in a company that was in Chapter 11 bankruptcy. If the company came out of the bankruptcy successfully, the value of the stock might increase significantly. On the other hand, the debtor's interest in the stock could be wiped out in the company's bankruptcy and become worthless.

The trustee argued that the amount of the exemption should be limited to the stated value of $10. He also argued that the court should adopt a "wait and see" approach to valuation and that, as trustee of the debtor's Chapter 7 case, he would be entitled to any post-petition appreciation in the value of the stock.

The bankruptcy court disagreed. The court held that the fair market value of any property claimed as exempt is determined as of the date of filing of the bankruptcy petition. Although this creates a potential windfall for the debtor if the property appreciates in value, this is the valuation scheme created by the bankruptcy code and by which the court is bound.

In this case, the trustee offered no evidence that the stock was worth more than the amount claimed by the debtor on the filing date of the petition. Therefore, the stock was valued at $10 and the exemption granted.

Lippe v. Bairnco Corp. (I)

Citation: 288 B.R. 678, 2003 U.S. Dist. LEXIS 1133
Date of Decision: January 28, 2003
Country: US
Federal or State: Federal
State/Jurisdiction: 2nd Circuit
Court: United States Court of Appeals
Type of action: Bankruptcy
Experts: Thomas E. Dewey, Jr. (for Lippe), Jocelyn D. Evans (for Lippe)
Judge: Chin
SIC: 2821 Plastics Materials, Synthetic and Resins, and Non-vulcanizable Elastomers

Valuation 'Experts' Excluded as Unreliable Based on Numerous Errors in Methodology and Inability to Explain Conclusions

In this bankruptcy adversary proceeding , the trustees as plaintiffs sought to prove that the defendants—Bairnco Corp., Keene Corp., and the individual managers of the companies—had engaged in a series of fraudulent conveyances among subsidiaries to protect assets from the reach of asbestos claimants.

Plaintiffs offered the testimony of two experts, Thomas E. Dewey Jr. and Jocelyn D. Evans, to prove that newly created subsidiaries did not pay "fair consideration" for the assets they purchased from Keene Corp., one of the subsidiaries of the holding company Bairnco Corp. Plaintiffs also offered the testimony of a third expert who was to testify regarding fraudulent intent.

Defendants filed a motion to exclude the testimony of all three experts. After thoroughly reviewing the reports and depositions of the experts, the court ruled that the testimony of all three was inadmissible under the *Daubert* standard. Only the testimony and exclusion of the valuation experts is discussed in this abstract.

***Daubert* standard explained.** Before ruling on the motion to exclude, the court thoroughly discussed the *Daubert* standard as it applies to experts offering business valuation testimony.

First, the expert's testimony must be reliable:

> [T]o be reliable, expert testimony must be based on sufficient facts or data and it must be the product of reliable principles and methods properly applied. The trial court's task is to make certain that an expert, whether basing testimony upon professional studies or personal experience, employs in the courtroom the same level of intellectual rigor that characterizes the practice of an expert in the relevant field.

Second, the expert's testimony must be relevant; that is, it must assist the trier of fact in determining the facts that are at issue in the case. "An expert's role is to assist the trier of fact by providing information and explanations; the expert's role is not to be an advocate."

Expert lacks reliability. Thomas Dewey, an investment banker, offered valuation reports and was deposed regarding the value of the subsidiary companies involved in the alleged fraudulent transactions. The trial court found that Dewey's report and deposition testimony did not have a reliable foundation and discussed just some of the problems with his valuations.

First, Dewey did not use the discounted cash flow (DCF) method, even though the court said that it is recognized as "the most reliable method for determining the value of a business." Instead, he relied solely on the comparable companies method. When questioned about this during his deposition, Dewey could not explain why he did not do a DCF analysis.

Second, Dewey did not offer his opinion as a range of values but rather as a single number. The court cited a case and several treatises in support of its conclusion that a range of values is more appropriate because "fairness is a range, not a point."

Third, Dewey did not rely on accepted business valuation principles and methods. The court quoted several excerpts from his deposition testimony indicating that he did not keep up with business valuation literature or otherwise educate himself regarding what others in the field were doing. As an investment banker, he testified that he did things the way he had done them for 40 years and didn't care what others did. Accordingly, his methods could not be tested or compared with any accepted standard.

Fourth, Dewey could not explain his analysis or how he reached many of his valuation conclusions. The court again quoted from his deposition testimony. One example of his inability to explain his own analysis was his statement that he used a 19x price-to-earnings ratio in one valuation "but he had 'no idea where the 19x multiple came from.'"

Fifth, Dewey applied control premiums (varying from 41.8% to 58.4%) but was "unable to provide any concrete basis for his decision to apply a control premium ... [or] for the amount of the control premium he applied." In fact, he testified that there were no facts to support his application of a control premium and that the use of the premium was "entirely theoretical" based on the *assumption* that if the company changed hands it would be at a premium.

Sixth, Dewey failed to consider and make adjustments for certain variables between his subject company and the comparable companies. The court noted that:

> Companies are not completely comparable merely because they are in the same industry, and often factors such as product and geographic markets, size, growth rates, profit margins, and other industry and economic considerations warrant adjustments.

In addition to not making such adjustments, Dewey could not explain why he chose the comparables that he chose and rejected others that appeared comparable.

Inexperienced expert rejected. Jocelyn Evans, a finance professor, also offered valuation reports and was deposed concerning her opinion as to the value of several of the subsidiaries, as well as her valuation of Keene. The trial court also discussed Evans' report and deposition testimony and found that it was also unreliable.

First, Evans made the same error as Dewey in applying substantial control premiums on a theoretical basis. Notably, however, she did not apply a control premium in her valuation of Keene, citing a lack of factual evidence to support such a premium. The court noted that:

> Lower values [for the subsidiaries] would support plaintiffs' claims as plaintiffs contend that Keene's worth was less than the probable cost of its liabilities. In contrast, for the valuations of Keene's businesses that were sold, higher values are necessary to support plaintiffs' claim that the assets were transferred for less than fair consideration.

Evans' selective use of control premiums appeared designed to support the "desired" results rather than a reliable valuation.

Second, Evans did not develop her own selection of comparable companies but rather relied upon the list of comparable companies supplied by plaintiffs' attorneys. She did not analyze the companies to determine whether they were truly comparable or make any adjustments.

Third, Evans deposition testimony revealed that she was uncertain about the accuracy of her conclusions and analysis. She repeatedly stated that she didn't know why she had made a certain calculation or reached a certain conclusion and would have to go back and "rethink my rationalizations." She also testified that she had no business valuation experience and that this was her first valuation engagement.

Trial court excludes experts. The trial court ultimately concluded that the reports and testimony of Dewey and Evans were not reliable and would not assist the trier of fact. The court noted that, in a close case, expert testimony should be allowed so that the trier of fact can determine its weight. "This, however, is not a close case." The court found that:

> The opinions of Dewey and Evans are [not only] "shaky," but that the opinions are so unreliable—"so unrealistic and contradictory"—as to suggest bad faith or, at a minimum, as to constitute an "apples and oranges" comparison. I am convinced that Dewey and Evans had only one goal in mind—to come up with conclusions that would support plaintiffs' positions in the case, and they were determined to get to that point anyway they could. I conclude that Dewey and Evans are unlikely to "assist the trier of fact" because their opinions are speculative and conjectural, their opinions are not based on sufficient facts or data but instead are based largely on their own say-so or on unfair and one-sided interpretations of the available data, they do not apply reliable principles and methods in a fair and reliable way, and they make no effort to account for major variables that one would expect to have an impact on their conclusions. Taken together, these flaws and failings go far beyond weight.

Accordingly, the testimony of both experts was excluded.

Lippe v. Bairnco Corp. (II)

Citation: 249 F. Supp. 2d 357, 2003 U.S. Dist. LEXIS 3861
Date of Decision: March 14, 2003
Country: US
State or Federal: Federal
State/Jurisdiction: 2nd Circuit
Court: United States Court of Appeals
Type of action: Bankruptcy
Judge: Chin

Case Update—*Lippe v. Bairnco Corp.*

Following exclusion of plaintiffs' witnesses, the court denied plaintiffs' motion to substitute a new valuation expert or submit a supplemental expert report, finding that defendants would be severely prejudiced.

The court granted defendants' motion for summary judgment based on the evidence before it, which did not include any valuation expert for plaintiffs. Plaintiffs failed to provide any "concrete evidence" in support of their fraudulent conveyance claim.

Lippe v. Bairnco Corp. (III)

Citation: No. 03-7360 (2nd Cir. 2004), unpublished
Date of decision: April 9, 2004
Country: US
State or Federal: Federal
State/Jurisdiction: 2nd Circuit
Court: United States Court of Appeals
Type of action: Bankruptcy
Attorneys: Jennifer Cowan, Murray E. Abowitz, Michael S. Chernis, Nicole L. Vander Voort, David R. Gross, Caroline Luckenbach, Irwin J. Sugarman, Charles F. Rysavy, Mary Morabito Rosewater, Pranita Raghavan, Alissa Pyrich, Robert D. Carroll, David K. Momborquette, John H. Hall, Stanley J. Levy, Steven Klugman, Sean R. Kelly, J. Paul Oetken
Experts: Thomas E. Dewey, Jr. Jocelyn D. Evans
SIC: 5033 Roofing, Siding, and Insulation Materials (merchant wholesalers except those selling via retail method)

2nd Circuit Affirms Application of *Daubert* in Fraudulent Conveyance Case

The U.S. Court of Appeals considered whether the district court erred when it did not admit Lippe's valuation experts into evidence, when it failed to permit Lippe to add a new valuation expert after their initial experts were not admitted, and when it dismissed their fraudulent conveyance claims against the defendants. In the 1970s, Keene Corp. (Keene), a conglomerate, owned a company that manufactured asbestos insulation. In the 1980s, Keene, through a drop down merger, became a subsidiary of Bairnco Corp. (Bairnco), and began to divest itself of several of its businesses through cash transactions. Fairness opinions were obtained in connection with the divestitures. During the 1970s through the 1990s, Keene was named in asbestos-related lawsuits. In 1993, Keene filed for bankruptcy. The plaintiffs are trustees of an asbestos-related creditors' trust. The plaintiffs brought suit against Keene, claiming that the divestiture transactions occurred at less than fair value and were therefore avoidable.

The plaintiffs filed the fraud actions in 1996. They retained two valuation experts in 1998, whose reports were completed by 2001. The plaintiffs' first expert valued the divestitures using a comparable companies approach, and the second expert used a comparable companies and discounted cash flow approach. Both experts also applied control premiums in their analyses. The experts were deposed in 2002. Thereafter, the defendants moved to exclude the experts under *Daubert*. The court did not hold a separate *Daubert* hearing on the defendants' motion but made its decision based on the record before it, which exceeded 900 pages and included the experts' opinions and their deposition testimony.

The district court determined that both experts' analyses were flawed. It pointed out several deficiencies in their analyses. The deficiencies the court found in the first expert's analysis included the failure to explain why a discounted cash flow valuation was not performed as a check against his comparable companies valuation; failure to explain the assumptions used in his valuation including the selection of p/e multiples, the selection of comparable companies and income projections, failure to account for differences between the comparables and the subject companies, and the large number of admitted mistakes in his valuation. It found that the deficiencies in the second expert's analysis included the failure to select her own comparables (she utilized comparables suggested by plaintiffs' counsel), failure to account for variances between the subject company and the comparables, and failure to explain why her market and income approach valuations arrived at different conclusions. Additionally, both experts failed to adequately explain how they selected the control premium applied in their analyses. Thus, the district court granted the defendants' motion to exclude the experts.

The plaintiffs then offered the court a substitute valuation expert. The district court declined to include that expert in the evidence because it concluded that the plaintiffs were on notice for several years that their experts' conclusions contained numerous flaws. Thus, the district court concluded that it would be unfair to permit the plaintiffs to include a substitute expert at this late juncture. The district court then dismissed the action because the plaintiffs had no evidence supporting their claim that the divestitures occurred at a price below fair value. The plaintiffs appealed.

In this unpublished opinion, the 2nd Circuit affirmed the district court's determinations in their entirety. It found the district court properly determined that the plaintiffs' experts' opinions contained significant flaws, which made them unreliable under Fed. Rul. Evid. 702. In reaching this decision, the Circuit Court pointed to numerous situations where the experts failed to explain their assumptions and reasoning.

It further affirmed the district court's decision not to hold a separate *Daubert* hearing with regard to the experts. In reaching this decision, the court noted that the district court has broad latitude in deciding how experts should be tested. It concluded, "Given the amount of information upon which the district court made its decision, it did not abuse its discretion by denying a hearing."

The 2nd Circuit further concluded that the trial court did not err when it declined to permit the plaintiffs to include a substitute valuation expert after the district court's *Daubert* determination. It noted, "Although plaintiffs were long on notice of defendants' criticisms of ... [the experts'] reports, plaintiffs decided not to respond to those criticisms until the district court finally excluded the evidence as unreliable." It then ruled, "As the district court well documented, plaintiffs had a full and fair opportunity to develop and defend their choice of experts. That they failed in that endeavor does not entitle them to begin anew."

The 2nd Circuit then affirmed the district court's ultimate conclusion dismissing the fraudulent conveyance claim. It noted that since that claim rested on the opinions of the experts that were excluded, the plaintiffs had no admissible evidence showing that the divestitures occurred at less than fair value. It further noted that this was especially true in light of the fairness opinions obtained in connection with the divestitures that took into account the future value of the divested companies.

In Re: LMR, LLC

Citation: 2013 Bankr. LEXIS 2127
Date of decision: May 24, 2013
Country: US
State or Federal: Federal
State/Jurisdiction: Texas
Court: United States Bankruptcy Court
Experts: None (debtor); Byron Hinton (creditor)
Judge: Mott

Court Approves Debtor's 'Feasible, But Tight' Plan With 6% Interest Rate

The debtor, a hotel owner and operator, slid into bankruptcy, but it subsequently achieved what the court called "a remarkable turnaround" thanks to the burgeoning local hotel market. As a result, it asked the Bankruptcy Court for permission to "cram down" its reorganization plan on the objecting creditor.

Revenue increase throughout bankruptcy. The debtor was a limited liability company that in 2007 purchased a hotel in Austin, Texas. Besides cash equity contributions from its four members, it used a bank loan to finance the remaining $3.9 million of the purchase price. The hotel secured the loan. The loss of its Best Western franchise in 2010, the protracted conversion to another franchise, and the lingering national recession led to a severe decline in revenue. The creditor, a private equity distressed debt investor, acquired the loan in mid-2012 and posted the hotel for foreclosure as soon as it matured in September 2012. To preserve the hotel, the debtor filed Chapter 11 bankruptcy a month later.

Since then, the business's circumstances have improved markedly. Gross income was at a low, $919,000, in 2010 but increased to $1.12 million in 2011 and $1.14 million in 2012. The debtor projected net revenue (after occupancy taxes) of about $1.25 million in 2013. It credited the upturn to the improving local economy and Austin's ability to stage well-known cultural and sports events, including South by Southwest, that attract leisure travelers on a budget, in addition to businesspeople—both of whom were target customers for the debtor.

One of the debtor's witnesses, a hotel broker and consultant with experience in selling and financing hotel real estate, testified to the connection between the strength of the local economy and the hotel market, citing the *Texas Hotel Performance Factbook*. The latter provided statistics for the ZIP code in which the hotel operated that confirmed that, in the last quarter of 2012, the debtor's revenue increased 19.1% and its room occupancy by 12.5% compared with the same quarter of 2011. This witness also said that the hotel's 2013 revenues year-to-date compared to 2012 were up 16.5% and its revenue per available room per day (RevPar) was up by 8%.

No 'true interest rate expert.' In January 2013, the debtor, wanting to continue hotel operations, proposed a plan for reorganization to which the creditor objected. All other creditors and interest holders were in favor of approval. A plan confirmation hearing followed. The debtor showed it had made three adequate protection payments of $23,750 each and was prepared to make the impending fourth one. Its members also planned to make a $200,000 equity infusion, providing the business with nearly $474,000 in cash on hand and $70,600 in escrow for upgrades and repairs, as well as payment of the annual property taxes.

Assuming the creditor had a secured claim of $3.2 million, the debtor planned to make 59 monthly payments amortized over 25 years at 6% interest, with a balloon payment of the remaining amount of the secured claim in the 60th month, in five years. To the extent the creditor had an unsecured claim, the debtor planned to pay it in 60 equal monthly installments, also with a 6% interest. The creditor would retain its lien on the hotel, as well as other collateral to ensure payment of its secured and unsecured claims. The debtor projected to have at least $118,000 cash on hand at the end of the plan's five-year term.

The creditor contended, among other things, that the plan was not feasible because the debtor could not meet its projections, the $200,000 in member contributions was speculative, and it lacked the funds to make upgrades and repairs. Importantly, the proposed 6% interest rate was below market interest rate and failed to meet the Bankruptcy Code's § 1129(b)(2) "cram-down provisions."

It presented a licensed real estate appraiser (the only one testifying at the hearing), who used both the comparable sales and income approaches to value the hotel at $3.2 million as of October 2012, the bankruptcy filing date. Specifically, in terms of comparables, he considered one sale from 2010, three sales from 2011, and one sale from 2012. He used $358,400 as net operating income. Institutional investors, he said, would not be interested in the hotel; smaller investors that might consider acquiring it would not be interested in the restaurants' business. Consequently, he excluded any rental income the debtor was receiving from the two restaurants on its property. He recognized there currently was a "good" market for Austin hotels but claimed there was no major change that made him reconsider his earlier appraisal. Yet, when pressed at the hearing, he admitted that hotels in the city had risen in value during the past seven months.

The court noted that neither side presented a "true interest rate expert." The debtor's hotel broker and financing witness said that loans that had an 80% debt-to-100% value ratio (80/20 loans) currently had an interest rate between 4.5% and 5.25%. The debtor's proposed 6% rate was a "premium" over the market, he maintained. He admitted there were no loans with a 100% debt-to-100% value ratio (1/1 loans) or greater in the current market.

The creditor's appraiser confirmed both of those statements. He added that any loans with a 1-to-1 ratio or greater would only be from a high-risk lender that would charge more than 6% interest.

A representative of the creditor who had financing experience confirmed that there was "absolutely no market for income producing real property." He added that obtaining such a loan would require tiered financing from a hard money lender, which would consist of a "mezzanine" debt with a 15%-to-17% return and/or an equity participation requiring a percentage return in the mid-to-high-20% range.

Same interest rate for secured and unsecured claims. The U.S. Bankruptcy Court (W.D. Tex.) first determined the value and amount of the creditor's secured and unsecured claims. As to the value of the collateral, i.e., the hotel, it noted that the only probative evidence was the real estate appraiser's $3.2 million valuation, dated October 2012. But this value did not reflect the improved market and the corresponding increase in the value of the hotel. Normally, it said, a court would reduce the value of the secured claim by the amount of outstanding property taxes on the hotel—$68,000; but in this instance it decided not to do so because "there can be no real dispute based on the record" that the value of the hotel had increased by at least that amount since the appraisal. Therefore, the secured claim was for $3.2 million and the unsecured claim for a little over $520,000, considering the debtor's protection payments.

Secured claim. Next the court considered the plan's feasibility under Sect. 1129(b)(2), which was known as a "cram down" in bankruptcy parlance, it said. The provision applied here because the creditor, which held both secured and unsecured claims, rejected the plan. Specifically, the issue became whether the debtor's proposed 6% interest rate was sufficiently high to yield the creditor at least the "present value" of its secured claim.

The court first looked to the U.S. Supreme Court's decision in *Till v. SCS Credit Corp.*, 541 U.S. 465 (2004), a Chapter 13 bankruptcy case that nevertheless has guided most bankruptcy courts in their feasibility analysis under Sect. 1129. Under the "*Till* formula approach," the court looks to the national prime rate and then adds a supplemental "risk adjustment." In this context, the court dismissed the creditor's suggestion that the debtor had the burden of presenting a "true interest rate expert" to prove a cram-down interest rate.

"It is fair to say," it stated, that "courts almost invariably conclude that efficient markets are absent in a Chapter 11 case." Based on the opinions of the parties' financial consultants and the appraiser, this was certainly the case here, it concluded. All agreed there was no 1/1 loan to be had in the current market, "which is what the Debtor's Plan effectively proposes." To obtain this type of loan required "the kind of tiered financing that have led other courts to conclude that no efficient market exists for the cramdown loan."

The national prime rate, which had not changed in years, was 3.25% at the time of the hearing, the court found. For the upward risk adjustment, courts typically consider factors such as the circumstances of the bankruptcy estate, the nature of the security, and the duration and feasibility of the reorganization plan and generally have approved of an upward adjustment of 1% to 3%, the Bankruptcy Court remarked.

In this case, the circumstances of the estate had "dramatically improved" since the bankruptcy filing, "as the Debtor started with a negative cash position that has now grown to over $300,000 in cash on hand." At the same time, the creditor's collateral, the hotel, was appreciating in value as independent statistics and credible testimony about Austin's hotel market and economy and the excellent location of the hotel showed. Its value would rise through the plan, the court concluded, considering the owners' cash equity infusion for upgrading the property. The owners also personally guaranteed the debt, and there was insurance for the hotel.

The debtors' plan was "feasible, but tight," particularly when it came to the balloon payment due in five years, the court stated. Its revenue projections were conservative and the projected expenses were "realistic and reasonable," aspects that further reduced the risk. In an earlier hotel case, the same circuit had approved a plan with a 5% cram-down interest rate. Given the circumstances of this case, a 2.75% upward adjustment was sufficient to ensure at least the "present value" of the secured claim. If anything, the court said, this rate was "on the higher side of the 1% to 3% general range."

Unsecured claim. Because the objecting creditor also had an unsecured claim, the court scrutinized the debtor's plan for repayment of that debt using the same formula approach. That the debtor's plan provided the creditor with the same risk adjustment—6% interest rate—for both types of claims "may, on its face, appear to ignore that unsecured debt may be inherently riskier than secured debt," the court observed. It added that an unsecured creditor often had a better chance of repayment if the debtor survived rather than its being forced to liquidate. If there were liquidation, the creditor likely would foreclose on the hotel and receive no more than the $3.2 million value its own appraiser determined for the hotel—meaning little or nothing of the $520,000 unsecured claim.

For various reasons, in this case the unsecured claim had "less risk and more protection than most unsecured claims." The court pointed out that the debtor did not try to "strip down" the lien to secure only the secured claim, although courts have permitted lien stripping in Chapter 11 cases. Also, if the debtor defaulted in its payments of the secured or unsecured claim, the creditor had state law remedies to enforce its lien rights. Further, the creditor actually benefited from having an unsecured claim. Total monthly payments on both claims would be approximately $30,700. If the creditor only had a secured claim of $3.8 million, it would receive only about $24,600 a month because of the 25-year amortization. All the factors suggested there was not enough risk to require a cram-down interest above 6%.

Finally, the court observed that the formula's starting point, the national 3.25% prime rate, already accounted for some degree of risk. "Although this Court will not go [as far as] starting its upward risk adjustment from the Treasury Bill rate, it merely serves to demonstrate that [the creditor] is receiving over a 5% upward risk above a truly riskless rate on its unsecured claim. Because the debtor also met the other plan confirmation requirements, in this instance it "actually succeeded" in its unusual attempt to cram down both secured and unsecured claims, the Bankruptcy Court concluded.

In re Louis Frey Company, Inc.

Citation: 2006 Bankr. LEXIS 1523
Date of Decision: July 28, 2006
Country: US
State or Federal: Federal
State/Jurisdiction: New York
Court: United States Bankruptcy Court
Type of action: Bankruptcy
Experts: Michael Aronow (Trustee)
Judge: Bernstein
SIC: 7334 Photocopying and Duplicating Services (except quick printing)

New York Bankruptcy Court Confirms Valuation of Customer Lists, With High Praise for Valuator

Within a week of one another, two bankruptcy courts in New York issued separate opinions regarding critical valuation issues. Interestingly, the judges share the same last name—but, fortunately for business appraisers, they did not share the same outlook on the credibility of the BV profession, its data, and its methodologies. It's worthwhile to compare the *In re Med Diversified* decision by Judge Stan Bernstein, Eastern District of New York, to this comprehensive, well-substantiated opinion by Chief Judge Stuart Bernstein in the Southern District of New York.

Defendant destroyed the debtor. The first half of this opinion summarizes how the defendant, a public company and leading U.S. provider of reprographic services for architectural and engineering firms, entered into a management agreement with the debtor/plaintiff, a long-time (30-year) provider of reprographics to the East Coast. But after taking charge of the financially distressed, privately held company, the defendant abruptly shut it down, misappropriated its confidential customer information, improperly diverted the debtor's business, and destroyed its ability to operate. The second half of the opinion addresses damages for breach of fiduciary duty, breach of contract, and related claims.

The debtor and its secured lender each offered an economic damage expert; of these, the court found the report for the Trustee by Michael Aronow, MBA, CPA, ABV, CVA (Eisner LLP, New York City) to be the most credible, "and his methodology the most rigorous." Aronow divided his damage calculation into two categories: the Primary Component, consisting of the 15 customers that the defendant had taken and the Remainder Component—the customers who remained with the debtor but whom it could no longer service.

Aronow calculated the Primary Component by measuring the benefit to the defendant of the diverted customers, which consisted of the increase in its enterprise value (EV) attributable to the incremental earnings from these customers. The first step: Start with the stipulated net sales to these customers over the relevant time period, or $5.768 million. Next, deduct the sales to customers who left the defendant, for a net sales figure of $5.405 million.

As net sales don't translate directly into net profit, Aronow calculated the defendant's historic profit margins for these customers (28.7%) and subtracted the estimated, variable selling and administrative costs (9.8%) to arrive at the incremental EBIT percentage of 18.9%—which yielded $1.022 million in net sales.

Arriving at EBIT multiple. Next, Aronow estimated the defendant's EV by calculating the value of its membership units, using $5.55 per unit (the average weighted exercise price for options granted to key personnel). He multiplied this by the number of units outstanding in the company's 2003 financial statements to arrive at an aggregate fair value estimate of $196,956,000. To this, Aronow added long-term debt, capital leases, and preferred stock ($385,131,000) and subtracted cash and cash equivalents ($173,150,000) to derive an EV, as of the valuation date (year-end, 2003) of $564,772,000.

From here, Aronow calculated the defendant's EBIT multiple to be 9.1. (To be conservative, he had ignored the extinguishment of a $15 million debt, which would have artificially inflated the EBIT multiple). He then multiplied the estimated incremental EBIT ($1.022 million) by the multiple to conclude that the defendant's EV increased by $9,300,000 due to its appropriation of the debtor's 15 customers.

The court adopted all of Aronow's methodology and figures—with the exception of the 2003 year-end financials. The defendant had produced more current data at trial, through the testimony of its CFO, who used this information to recalculate Aronow's margins and ratios. (The court denied the Trustee's "belated" attempt to strike the CFO's "valuation testimony"; it's unclear what would have been the effect of a timely motion.) Using Aronow's methodology, the CFO arrived at a damage figure of $8.164 million, which the court adopted as the "Primary Component" of damages.

Secondary calculations also carry the day. To estimate the amount that a competitor would have paid for the Remainder customers, Aronow first calculated the net sales attributable to these customers, factoring in the debtor's overall decline in financial condition/sales. (The court rejected the defendant's argument that the debtor would have gone out of business and lost these customers anyway; the debtor was distressed but still a viable concern.) He subtracted actual sales to reach an adjusted net sales figure of $11.507 million. To avoid double counting , Aronow subtracted the net sales from the customers taken by the defendant, to reach net sales of $6.102 million.

To compute what a buyer would have paid for the business, Aronow calculated a weighted-average gross profit margin of 30.3% from the debtor's financials; he then estimated the incremental EBIT, adjusting the figure to account for estimated incremental costs, backing out certain expenses that a strategic buyer would most likely not incur, and adding back in a bad-debt expense. Subtracting this figure (25.4%) from the gross profit margin, he estimated an incremental EBIT multiple of 4.9%. Applying this multiple to $6.102 million net sales gave an incremental EBIT of $299,000. As service businesses are commonly sold based on a multiple of EBIT, Aronow used 3.75 (taken from a letter of intent between the parties, who once contemplated a sale). Applying this multiple to $299,000 resulted in a value of $1.121 million, or "the amount that a strategic buyer would pay for the remaining business."

But he wasn't done yet: Aronow discounted this figure by 20% to reflect the inherent risks and uncertainty associated with the use of projected and admittedly limited financial information, yielding Remainder damages in the amount of $897,000.

Lender's expert took market, income approaches. On behalf of the secured lender, Sam Rosenfarb CPA, CVA, CBA, CFE (Rosenfarb Winters LLC, New York City), approached the debtor as a business consisting of nine customers that the defendant had stolen. (The opinion does not clarify why Rosenfarb used only nine out of the stipulated 15.) Using the market approach, he concluded that the debtor could have been sold for $1.62 million on the valuation date; under the income/capitalization of earnings approach, the debtor was worth $1.49 million to a potential buyer.

Additionally, Rosenfarb valued the diverted customers based on certain ratios extracted from the debtor's records and the defendant's public information. Starting with the same net sales figure, he estimated the debtor's gross profit margins and the defendant's variable costs, reduced by 60% to reflect these costs as a percentage of SG&A (sales, general and administrative) costs. Rosenfarb multiplied this estimated EBIT by 11.7, and then discounted by 65% to reflect the size difference between the debtor and defendant, to conclude that the diverted business was worth $4.48 million.

In the alternative, Rosenfarb calculated the ratio of defendant's market value ($570.8 million) to annual revenues ($435.9 million) at 130%, multiplied this by the net sales and then applied a 40% discount to reflect the size difference, to reach a value of $4.2 million for the diverted business.

On the whole, however, the court found "unexplained gaps" in Rosenfarb's analysis—such as the 65% discount for the size difference in one approach and the 40% discount for the same differential in a second approach. "I understand why he made these deductions," the Judge explained, "but the percentages he used appear to be 'seat of the pants' estimates rather than grounded in any specific data." Moreover, "the choice of different percentages may have been driven by the desire to achieve consistent valuations" between the two approaches.

Finally, the defendant's CFO had not recalculated Rosenfarb's analysis using the updated financial data, and this further persuaded the court to adopt Aronow's analysis:

> [Aronow] considered all of the Debtor's former customers, and did not limit his analysis to the nine defectors. He took a conservative approach, and thereby lessened the chance of inflating his result. He explained how he calculated the various multiples, ratios and margins more precisely. Finally the substitution of the [updated] operating results ... produced a more precise estimate of the value of diverted business.

Defendant's expert assigns no value to customers—and no value to valuation. As its damages expert, the defendant offered a "crisis and turnaround" manager, a Harvard JD and MBA, whose testimony (according to the court) "was unencumbered by any analysis." It was his opinion that—because customers are generally "at will"—they have little or no value, and neither do their existing relationships. In this case, the defendant acquired nothing but a "hatful of possibilities," the expert said, and also:

> There was no guarantee that they would maintain these customers … [A]nd so to impute some long-term cash flow and then discount it back or apply capitalization factors is what we used to call 'garbage in/garbage out' when we did financial analysis at the Wharton School. [Note: Given the expert's stated Harvard credentials, the Wharton reference is unclear.]

This expert also attacked the use of EBIT multiples as a valuation tool:

> A group—a small group of customers with no long-term contracts, what risk is there in that? Enormous risk. So even to talk about anything long-term and start with multiples which apply to a whole huge enterprise of hundreds of millions of dollars, it's just ridiculous.

The court disagreed: "The customers are the business; without net sales to customers, the business has no value." The expert's demeanor was also "that of an advocate rather than an expert, and his opinion ignored actual practice," including the fact that the debtor had serviced some of its customers for more than 30 years.

More important, the expert's theory ignored the defendant's own business practice, which had involved acquiring approximately 90 reprographics firms in the prior eight years and paying about four times EBIT for each. "In short, the value of a reprographic business is derived from its EBIT, and EBIT is determined by sales to customers."

Stark contrast to *In re Med Diversified*. The courtrooms of the two Judge Bernsteins may be only a few hundred miles apart—but their acceptance and approval of valuation methodologies (and valuation experts) appear to be worlds apart. Let's hope this bankruptcy case bears out as the stronger precedent and that, with time and the work of more good analysts, the complex world of business valuation continues to gain credibility in all courts.

In re Lyall; Monticello Arcade LP v. Lyall

Citation: 191 B.R. 78, 1996 U.S. Dist. LEXIS 854
Date of Decision: January 23, 1996
Country: US
State or Federal: Federal
State/Jurisdiction: Virginia
Court: United States District Court
Type of action: Bankruptcy
Judge: Smith
SIC: 8712 Architectural Services

Should Lease Obligation Be Deducted From Value?

In an action for bankruptcy debtor Raymond Lyall, an architect, testified and produced an analysis valuing his 100% stock ownership in Lyall Design Inc., a professional corporation, at $1,558.41. His valuation method was simple: Liabilities, which included a $12,959.52 unexpired lease obligation, were subtracted from the corporation's total assets.

The issue is whether the lease obligation was a proper deduction in arriving at the bankruptcy court's valuation of the stock. The issue is important in this case because the resulting value did not exceed $5,000, and therefore the bankruptcy court ruled that the stock was protected under Virginia's homestead exemption.

Creditor, Monticello, holder of a nonpriority, unsecured claim for $20,000 in back rent, appealed the exemption. Monticello reasoned that "the lease payments at issue are only due post-petition.... These payments will be made from post-petition accounts and will contribute to post-petition income for Mr. Lyall. Because post-petition income is not included in the bankruptcy estate ... the lease obligation here should not be subtracted from the value of the corporation's assets when placing a value on debtor's stock interest."

The appellate court looked to the law, which states that a trustee in a Chapter 7 bankruptcy must "promptly liquidate the non-exempt assets of the estate." Mr. Lyall offered uncontested testimony that there is no ready market for stock in professional corporations rendering architectural services.

The court considered the cost for discharging the lease obligation, which plaintiff conceded would be a cost of liquidation, and held that it *"must look to the value of the stock in the hands of the trustee rather than in the hands of the debtor."* (emphasis supplied) The appellate court, therefore, affirmed the bankruptcy court's decision to allow the value of the unexpired lease agreement to be subtracted from the corporation's total assets to "arrive at a true valuation of debtor's stock."

In re Magna Cum Latte, Inc.

Citation: 2008 WL 2047937
Date of Decision: May 9, 2008
Country: US
State or Federal: Federal
State/Jurisdiction: Texas
Court: United States Bankruptcy Court
Type of action: Bankruptcy
Experts: Not specified
Judge: Isgur
SIC: 5812 Eating Places (limited-service restaurants)

Lost Profits Turn on Risk-Free vs. Risk-Adjusted Discount Rates

The defendant was a California-based coffeehouse franchise doing business under the Diedrich brand. In 2001, the plaintiff (Magna Cum Latte) entered into sublease and purchase agreements for three Houston coffeehouses that the defendant owned for $1.02 million.

Certain provisions of the sublease agreement quickly became contentious, namely the renewal provisions, which did not specify the conditions under which the defendant could exercise/decline the renewal options, and a "rent formula" provision, which based the plaintiff's rent in part on a percentage of gross sales. Sales never met projections, however, and as the plaintiff's rent declined the defendant's obligations on its master lease continued to increase—in one store by over $1,000 per month. The defendant attempted to renegotiate the plaintiff's sublease, threatening to not exercise the renewal options, despite the plaintiff's assertion that the contract obligated their exercise. Finally, in 2006, the defendant declined to exercise its lease option on one store, and the plaintiff failed to negotiate rent directly with the landlord or find a replacement location. The store closed, and the plaintiff defaulted on its obligations to the defendant, filing for Chapter 11 bankruptcy in early 2007. The plaintiff/debtor sued the defendant for breach of contract, among 14 other claims, seeking damages in excess of $10 million for its "doomed" business. At the original trial, the court found the defendant liable on two claims and held a hearing on damages. The plaintiff sought over $3.6 million—including $2.4 million in lost profits for the one closed store (or, alternatively, $150,000 for its lost value) and another $150,000 for the lost value of a second store.

Forecasts of future performance vary. Plaintiff based its lost profits claims on the remaining lease term as well as the 10-year renewal term for the one closed store. Addressing the latter first, the U.S. Bankruptcy Court (S.D. Texas) found the plaintiff was not entitled to recover lost profits related to the renewal term because it had not met its obligations under the franchise agreements, including payment of past due rents. Even if the plaintiff's default was due to the defendant's failure to renew the lease option, it failed to prove that it could have extended the lease directly with the landlord or relocate.

Both parties presented experts related to the original lease term. Both forecasted future earnings discounted through a yield formula. They varied widely in their inputs and assumptions, however. The plaintiff's expert used a 6% growth rate and a risk-free discount rate over a five-year forecast;

he excluded management fees, amortization, and depreciation deductions. By contrast, the defendant's expert applied a 2.5% growth rate and a "risk-adjusted" discount rate of 27.7% over 4.5 years and included management fees as well as amortization and depreciation deductions. The plaintiff projected over $900,000 in lost profits. The defendant calculated just over $200,000. The court found errors in both and addressed each separately:

- *Base-year revenues.* Plaintiff shut down in November 2006, so no complete operational records were available for that year. Its expert conducted a six-step extrapolation of the first 10 months of 2006, an approach the court described as "contorted," "[made] no sense," and was intended to "artificially inflate" the base year for his forecast. The defendant's expert simply used the actual trailing 12 months for his base year; the court adopted this approach.

- *Expenses.* To offset revenues, the plaintiff's expert used a 30% average (cost of goods sold to generate revenues). This reflected recent expenditures, compared to the 33% that defendant's expert calculated from historic data. Even though more recent data are generally preferable to historic data, the court found it unclear that the plaintiff could have maintained 33% and adopted a 31% ratio.

- *Depreciation and amortization (D&A).* The court found the defendant's inclusion of D&A to be "frivolous," noting that he came "armed to the witness stand" with numerous texts on calculation of business losses, "not one of [which] suggested that depreciation and amortization should be included in the calculation." Because a present value calculation predicts future cash flow, "it is nonsense," the court said, to include D&A.

- *Management fees.* In this business, good management did indeed have value, the court said, and should be deducted from cash flows.

- *Growth rate.* The plaintiff's expert used Starbucks growth rates to predict 6% for the closed store, even though it had never showed such a high rate. Accordingly, the court adopted 2.5%, which was in line with the rate of inflation.

Based, in part, on the foregoing determinations, the court calculated an initial lost profits amount of $570,539. This amount, however, needed to be adjusted to present value. The question became whether a "risk-free" discount rate—as advocated by the plaintiff—or a "risk-adjusted" rate—as advanced by the defendant— should be applied. Under California law, the issue remains unsettled, the Texas court noted, as different courts have applied each type of rate under different circumstances.

In this case, though, the court determined that a risk-adjusted discount rate was the more appropriate. In doing so, the court pointed to the "substantially risky" nature of the forecasts. The court nearly split between the 0% risk-free rate advocated by the plaintiff and the 27.7% rate used by the defendant and settled on a 15% rate. This resulted in an adjusted, present value damages amount of $371,462—to which the court added prejudgment interest of 10%, to increase the total award to $403,825.

Finally, the court denied the plaintiff's claim of "consequential damages" arising from the alleged lost value of two of their stores' purchase prices. "To award an alleged lost value of the [closed] store's purchase price in addition to lost profits would be to grant an impermissible double-recovery," the court held.

In re Mahoney

Citation: 251 B.R. 748, 2000 Bankr. LEXIS 1028
Date of Decision: March 29, 2000
Country: US
State or Federal: State
State/Jurisdiction: New Jersey
Court: Supreme Court
Experts: Peter Gampel, CPA, ASA, CVA (for Mahoney) Rick Gaskins (for Ungaro)
Type of action: Bankruptcy
Judge: Friedman
SIC: 7372 Prepackaged Software (software publishing)
Key words: Bankruptcy, Fair market value (FMV), Fair value, Income approach, Market approach

Bankruptcy Court Determines Fair Market Value Under Pennsylvania Judgment—Court Details Claimant's Expert's Valuation Shortcomings

The issue in this bankruptcy court proceeding is the appropriate valuation of 4,500 shares of stock of Quality Systems Associates Inc. (QSA). Pursuant to a Pennsylvania state court judgment, the debtor, Mahoney, was required to pay the claimant, Steven Ungaro, the fair market value of the shares under the terms of the parties' contract.

The Pennsylvania court did not determine what the fair market value of the stock was. Ungaro filed a claim in the Mahoney bankruptcy proceeding in the amount of $1,035,000, which Mahoney disputes. At trial on the matter, both parties presented expert business valuation reports and testimony.

Debtor's expert used income approach. Mahoney's expert, Peter Gampel, CPA, ASA, CVA, of Arthur Andersen LLP, calculated the value of QSA as an entity using the income approach. In particular, he used the capitalization of income method based on the average of the four most recently completed fiscal years prior to the valuation date. Gampel used the capitalization of income method and not the discounted cash flow method:

> (a) QSA did not prepare budgets or forecasts necessary for the discounted cash flow method; (b) the nature of QSA's business operations and sources of revenue was not expected to change drastically in the future; and (c) QSA's revenue and earnings history served as the best guide, in [Gampel's] opinion, to project the future prospects of QSA.

Debtor's expert rejects market approach. Gampel did not use the market approach to value QSA because the market information that was available was limited from a financial perspective and therefore did not allow for meaningful analysis and comparison to QSA.

Discounts applied to reach fair market value. After determining the fair market value of 100% of QSA, Gampel then calculated 45% to represent Ungaro's pro rata share of the company. To determine the fair market value of Ungaro's interest, he applied a 15% minority discount and a 35% marketability discount. Ungaro did not address whether the size of the discounts was appropriate. In the absence of evidence that the size of the discounts was inappropriate, the court accepted them.

Claimant's expert calculates fair value. Ungaro's expert, Rick Gaskins, of Gaskins Associates P.C., calculated the value of QSA using both the income approach, weighted 35%, and the market approach, weighted 65%. He then calculated Ungaro's 45% pro rata interest and testified that this was the amount of Ungaro's claim. He did not apply any valuation discounts and essentially determined the "fair value" of Ungaro's QSA stock.

The court specifically found that this was incorrect because the Pennsylvania judgment upon which the claim was based unambiguously stated that Ungaro was entitled to receive *fair market value* for his stock.

Court finds flaws in application DCF method. In discussing Gaskins' application of the discounted cash flow method, the court found several flaws in Gaskins' report and testimony:

- He failed to include information regarding additional working capital or capital expenditures that would be required for QSA to expand its business as he projected;
- He projected earnings without management input;
- He failed to account for Mahoney's salary as president and CEO of QSA; and
- He assumed that QSA would terminate a distributorship contract and further assumed an estimated cost savings associated with this termination.

Court finds flaws in application of market approach. The court also found substantial flaws in Gaskins' application of the market approach:

- He upwardly adjusted QSA's gross revenues based upon his assumption that the distributorship agreement would be terminated but did not provide backup for this adjustment;
- He applied a multiplier of 2.00 to 2.18 to his adjusted gross revenues but did not explain his basis for the multiplier;
- He did not consider the accounting method of the comparable companies versus the accounting method of QSA;
- He did not consider the fact that the comparables did not involve strictly cash transactions;
- He did not consider potential synergies that would have affected the sales price in the comparable transactions;

- He did not consider several other factors generally considered relevant in evaluating comparable transactions, such as the legal rights being transferred, the financing terms, or the assets being conveyed; and

- He used comparable companies that had annual revenues in excess of $5 million, whereas QSA's annual revenues never exceeded $650,000.

Management interviews critical. In preparing his valuation, Gampel interviewed current management of QSA and other key employees to assist him in determining appropriate adjustments and the potential impact of future prospects and new product lines.

Gaskins, on the other hand, did not consult with management or key employees regarding his earnings projections for inclusion in his discounted cash flow analysis or other adjustments and assumptions that he made.

This factor in the expert's valuations was an important aspect of the court's acceptance of Gampel's valuation and rejection of Gaskins. Without reference in his valuation report to management input, the court pointed out, "it is impossible to determine whether the assumptions made by Gaskins were reasonable under the circumstances."

The court ultimately determined that the value of Ungaro's claim was $70,000, the fair market value of his QSA stock as opined by Gampel.

Makula v. Sanwa Business Credit Corp.

Citation: 1997 U.S. Dist. LEXIS 11741
Date of Decision: August 7, 1997
Country: US
State or Federal: Federal
State/Jurisdiction: Illinois
Court: United States District Court
Experts: Jerome Lipman (for Makula), Barry Steinberg (for Sanwa)
Type of action: Bankruptcy
Judge: Kocoras
SIC: 8721 Accounting, Auditing, and Bookkeeping Services (other accounting services)
Key words: Bankruptcy, Partnership dissolution

Undervaluing Partnership Interest Comes at a Price

On his Chapter 7 bankruptcy petition, John Makula valued his 67 partnership units in Thomas Havey & Co., an Illinois accounting partnership, at a total of $67,000. The bankruptcy court ruled that Makula had intentionally undervalued his partnership interest and therefore was not entitled to a discharge of indebtedness under the Bankruptcy Code.

Citing Illinois partnership law and the partnership agreement, the appellate court upheld the bankruptcy court's decision to value Makula's interest on a voluntary withdrawal basis rather than on a partnership liquidation basis, resulting in a "conservative" value of $650,000. Expert for Makula was Jerome Lipman, and expert for appellees was Barry Steinberg.

In re McCook Metals v. Lynch

Citation: 2005 Bankr. LEXIS 49
Date of Decision: January 14, 2005
Country: US
State or Federal: Federal
State/Jurisdiction: Illinois
Court: United States Bankruptcy Court
Type of action: Bankruptcy
Experts: Scott Peltz (for trustee), Frederic Lieber (for Lynch)
Judge: Wedoff
Key words: Bankruptcy

Valuation Results in $2.7 Million Disgorgement

The valuation issue in this bankruptcy case focused on the value of a limited liability company. Lynch was found to be a benefiting party of a transfer and was forced to disgorge $2.7 million based on the court's valuation of the company.

McDuffie v. O'Neal

Citation: 324 S.C. 297, 476 S.E.2d 702, 1996 S.C. App. LEXIS 123
Date of Decision: August 12, 1996
Country: US
State or Federal: State
State/Jurisdiction: South Carolina
Court: Court of Appeals
Type of action: Bankruptcy
Experts: Joe M. Gasaway (for McDuffie), Gregory Padgett, CPA (for Blue Flame MTP)
Judge: Stilwell
SIC: 5989 Fuel Dealers, NEC
Key words: Damages, Income approach

Appeals Court Accepts Averaging of Two Experts' Values

Respondent, Steven McDuffie, brought a stockholder oppression action against defendants, Thomas and Patricia O'Neal, Joseph Minshew, and Blue Flame Gas Co. The three main valuation issues in this case are the relative ownership percentages between McDuffie and O'Neal, the amount of money Blue Flame MTP was entitled to receive from the O'Neals for misappropriation of corporate funds, and the price at which McDuffie's shares should be purchased by Thomas O'Neal and/or Blue Flame MTP, a distributor of propane gas.

The original action was heard by a Special Master, who found McDuffie and O'Neal to be equal owners of Blue Flame MTP, who found all of the transactions that McDuffie challenged to be corporate misappropriations, and who required Blue Flame MTP and/or Thomas O'Neal to purchase McDuffie's shares for $467,317. Appellants, Thomas and Patricia O'Neal, dispute all three findings.

After the appellate court upheld the Master's finding of a 50/50 ownership, it turned its attention to the valuation. The Master heard testimony from two expert witnesses: Joe M. Gasaway for McDuffie and Gregory Padgett, CPA, for Blue Flame MTP.

Gasaway conducted an asset valuation of Blue Flame MTP based primarily upon information provided to him by McDuffie, which included estimates of Blue Flame MTP's profit margins, the number of gallons of fuel it owned and its total number of customers, including retail clients. He also looked at lists of vehicles, real estate, equipment, and accounts receivable belonging to the corporation. According to the transcript, "not considering the debts of the corporation or its cash on hand, Gasaway valued Blue Flame MTP at $889,609."

Padgett reviewed financial statements, capital costs, and real estate. Then, utilizing the income approach, he valued Blue Flame MTP at $410,000.

Two ancillary issues were critical to the Master's valuation. First, McDuffie alleged a $270,000 misappropriation of funds. Second, the O'Neals argued that the lack of a covenant not to compete reduced the value of Blue Flame MTP and that reduction of value was not properly considered by the Master.

The Master determined funds in the amount of $270,000 were, indeed, misappropriated. He then averaged Padgett's and Gasaway's values and added half of the misappropriated funds to the amount to be paid to McDuffie.

Regarding the issue of the covenant not to compete, the Master's order included language that, according to the transcript, "clearly prohibited McDuffie from utilizing any customer list, business manual, or other business procedure of the corporation for three years in competition with Blue Flame MTP."

The appellate court upheld the Master's calculations regarding damages and stated, "While we do not necessarily recommend this method (averaging), we find no error in the Master's decision in this case. Faced with conflicting opinions from two apparently qualified experts, both with seemingly reasonable opinions, and not having more reason to accept one than the other, the Master split the difference between the two."

The appellate court adjusted the Master's average by taking into account the corporate debts and cash on hand that Gasaway's valuation did not consider, and it held the final valuation of Blue Flame MTP to be $633,993.80.

Adding $135,000 (half the misappropriated funds), the appellate court affirmed, "but modified it to require the defendant corporation and/or defendant, Thomas O'Neal, to purchase McDuffie's shares for $452,063.87."

In re Med Diversified, Inc. (I)

Citation: 2005 Bankr. LEXIS 2236
Date of Decision: November 14, 2005
Country: US
State/Jurisdiction: New York
Court: United States Bankruptcy Court
Type of action: Bankruptcy
Experts: Scott P. Peltz (for Addus Healthcare, Inc.) Robert Cimasi (for Chartwell Litigation Trust)
Judge: Bernstein
Key words: Bankruptcy, Daubert, Discounted cash flow method (DCF), Guideline company method, Transaction method, Earnings Before Interest, Taxes, Depreciation, Amortization (EBITDA), Enterprise value (MVIC), Illiquidity discount, Black Scholes model

Report Is Inadmissible Where Purported Valuator Is Not Certified, Uses Incorrect Methodology, and Does No Independent Analysis

In a case of first impression in a bankruptcy adversary proceeding, the narrow issue was whether Scott P. Peltz, the proposed business valuation expert witness for Addus Healthcare Inc. (Addus), was qualified and whether his purported expertise satisfied the standards of relevance and reliability under *Daubert v. Merrill Dow Pharmaceuticals, Inc.*, 509 U.S. 579, (1993).

Addus, the defendant in the case, called Peltz to testify on the value of 100% of Addus's shares, as well as on the reasonably equivalent value of an alleged option payment of $7.5 million paid by Med Diversified Inc. (Med D) for a six-and-a-half-month extension to close its purchase of these shares. Med D was insolvent at the time of the payment, and the bankruptcy trustee for Chartwell Litigation Trust (Chartwell), Med D's successor, was attempting to set aside the payment as a constructive fraudulent transfer.

Qualification and reliability of alleged valuator rejected. Chartwell filed a motion in limine to exclude all of Peltz's testimony on the ground that he did not qualify as an expert on valuation of all of the shares of a privately held healthcare services company. This motion gave rise to the court's exercise of its gatekeeper function in excluding expert testimony that is neither relevant nor reliable. Under *Daubert,* the court has a duty to "ensure that the courtroom door remains closed to junk science while admitting reliable expert testimony that will assist the trier of fact."

Peltz testified on voir dire that he had no peer-granted certifications as an expert on business valuations and that his Expert Report was not to be read as a certified business valuation. He also revealed that he had no formal education or training in business valuation. Although Peltz asserted that his support staff were certified business valuators who provided input into the Expert Report, those valuators were not available for cross-examination.

The court indicated it was not prepared to admit an Expert Report submitted by a corporate entity, saying that "the person who signs the report has to testify until the admission of his Report for all evidentiary purposes has been stipulated to." The court also indicated that it would not qualify Peltz as an expert because he had neither sufficient experience in the field nor formal training or certification.

The court rejected Addus's argument that Peltz's substantive experience over 20-plus years as an accountant and as a liquidating agent or bankruptcy trustee in bringing avoidance actions in the bankruptcy court added up to a satisfactory substitute for formal education and training in business valuations and in peer-recognition in this sub-branch of substantive expertise in business valuations, especially in such a unique and highly regulated business of in-home healthcare services.

The court also found that, even if Peltz was found to be otherwise qualified as an expert on business valuation, his testimony would still be inadmissible because he "showed a discernible measure of negligence in purportedly applying the alleged professional standards and techniques found in the published practical treatises, including the standards and techniques published in the writings of Dr. Shannon Pratt and his co-authors, which were repeatedly propounded by both the Defendants and the Plaintiffs."

The court concluded that it could not accept the testimony of an alleged expert in business valuations when he failed to employ the necessary peer-reviewed methods of business valuation, when he based his analysis on inadequate data, and when he thoroughly conflated the discreetly different concepts of gross cash flow and net cash flow from operations. The court also concluded that Peltz's failure to use the DCF method—and to offer a satisfactory explanation as to why he omitted this method—amounted to a material flaw in his methodology sufficient to bar his testimony as an expert witness because his conclusions lacked "good grounds."

Moreover, the court found that the data on which Peltz's conclusions were based were inadequate because he did not do any independent analysis of these companies and did not independently analyze the data from the databases from which he derived his figures—"Mergerstat" and "Factset"; in choosing the comparable companies and transactions upon which his analysis was based, Peltz admittedly never considered the nature or products of the businesses, or the market in which these businesses operated.

***Daubert* holding.** Ultimately, the court ruled that Peltz had not satisfied the *Daubert* standard as to his direct testimony but that he could testify as a rebuttal witness to Chartwell's proposed expert witness in valuation, limited, however, to issues of methodology used by Chartwell's expert witness, Robert Cimasi, in valuing these shares and the "option price" or the extension payment. Accordingly, the court struck Peltz's Expert Report and direct testimony from the record.

Black-Scholes method. As to a substantive issue in the case, the court refused to allow the Black-Scholes Method to be used to value the option involved, saying that the "Black-Scholes Method has simply not been shown to provide a reliable measure of the value of an option to purchase 100% of controlled shares in a privately held company and the parties failed to set forth any credible evidence otherwise."

In re Med Diversified, Inc. (II)

Citation: 2006 Bankr. LEXIS 1677
Date of Decision: August 2, 2006
Country: US
State or Federal: Federal
State/Jurisdiction: New York
Court: United States Bankruptcy Court
Type of action: Bankruptcy
Experts: Robert Cimasi (plaintiffs)
Judge: Bernstein
SIC: 8082 Home Health Care Services

BV on Trial in Bankruptcy? New York Court Excludes Appraisal as 'Junk Science'

Several months ago, this Bankruptcy Court (Eastern District of New York) disqualified the defendant's business valuation expert for failing to meet the federal evidentiary standards of reliability set forth in *Daubert* and progeny.[1]

You'd think the plaintiff would have gained significant leverage in the litigation, but then Judge Stan Bernstein applied the same federal standards to disqualify the report by plaintiff's expert Robert Cimasi, MHA, ASA, CBA, AVA , FCBI, CM&A, CMP (Health Capital Consultants, St. Louis), one of the more recognized authorities in the healthcare valuation field. Notably, in prior proceedings, the court had already qualified Cimasi as an expert in business valuation; this decision came on defendant's pretrial motion alleging that Cimasi's report exhibited such "deliberate, manifest, pervasive, and systematic bias" that it was "fundamentally unreliable" under the federal rules.

But from the beginning, the court's inquiry appears to extend well beyond any bias in one appraisal to business valuation as a whole. "Perhaps this memorandum … may assist other bankruptcy courts in framing their decisions on motions *in limine* under the evolving standards of disqualification of purported non-scientific expert witnesses." These standards include the much-touted "gatekeeper" function, which ensures that the "courtroom door remains closed to junk science"—which may include, in this courtroom at least, the "science" of business valuation.

Benchmarking studies are 'self-fulfilling hearsay.' For example, regarding the benchmarking analysis used in many BV methods, the judge admits his "fundamental skepticism" regarding "whether it is methodologically sound to compare the data from public companies with that of a closely-held business."

That is a huge quantum leap that this court is unwilling to make. The literature cited by Cimasi is severely limited and little of it appears to satisfy the rigorous standard of peer-reviewed publications. The dominant citations are to the writings of two or three consulting firms that hold themselves out as valuation experts either by self-designation or by designation through the very small professional valuation societies they have formed for themselves. This is evidenced by the

1 *Daubert v. Merrill Dow Pharmaceuticals, Inc.*, 509 U.S. 579, 597 (1993); see also, *Kumho Tire Co. Ltd v. Carmichael*, 526 U.S. 137 (1999).

number of acronyms for the six professional designations Cimasi adds after his name, each of which is awarded by one of these professional valuation societies.

Despite otherwise meticulous footnoting, here the court fails to cite the "literature" to which it refers. But most likely, these "dominant citations" include publications by Ibbotson's, Mergerstat, Shannon Pratt, Robert Schweihs, Robert Reilly, Eric Nath, Mark Lee, and others.

In the accompanying sidebar, an excerpt from the trial transcript (also obtained from Mr. Cimasi) provides additional insight into the court's "debunking" of business valuation.

Judge finds 'old math' more persuasive. Up front, the court also admits a "vexing intuitive difficulty" regarding the financial facts. Briefly, the debtor, Med Diversified Inc. (Med D), had agreed in 2002 to purchase all the shares of privately owned Addus Healthcare Inc. for $119 million. Prior to the scheduled closing, the parties negotiated (but did not sign) an amendment to extend the purchase option for six and a half months, for which Med D paid an additional $7.5 million. The parties disputed the amendment's enforceability—but agreed that Med D was insolvent at its execution. This lawsuit arose from Med D's Chapter 11 proceedings, in which the Trustee for Med D's successor (plaintiff) attempted to recover the $7.5 million payment from Addus (defendant) based on the amendment's lack of enforceability, and/or the lack of "reasonably equivalent value."

The Trustee offered Cimasi's report to prove the latter as well as the value of 100% of Addus's shares, which Cimasi concluded was worth $21 million. But, as a preliminary matter, the court points to Addus's 2001 audited financial statements, which reported gross revenues of $234 million—yet, due to adjustment for allegedly nonrecurring expenses, posted EBITDA of *negative* $157,340:

> No matter what industry multiple was used for estimating the value of Addus based on the standard metric of EBITDA ... the Court has serious reservations how, based upon a negative EBITDA number, the company could have any positive value. According to the old math, (0) × (n), with n = EBITDA, is always 0.

The court admits there are ways to avoid estimating "no value" by using another base for computing value, or adjusting EBITDA to remove the nonrecurring adjustments. "But it is not this Court's function to perform an analysis that saves the plaintiff's case in chief (or the defendant's ...) from the unreliable and excluded testimony of the plaintiff's expert on valuation (or the defendant's expert)."

However tempting it may be for a bankruptcy judge to show the parties how the valuation analysis should be done, a bankruptcy judge has to direct the law clerks to tie up the judge to the mast like Ulysses and plug the judge's ears from heeding the Sirens' calls.

Valuation methodologies, data fatally flawed. The court reviews the three valuation approaches in Cimasi's report, finding errors significant enough to undermine not just its credibility, but also its admissibility. More troubling, the court finds fatal flaws with the more common, accepted valuation methodologies and data.

The discounted cash flow (DCF) method bears the brunt of the court's opinion. The judge first focuses on Cimasi's specific assumptions and calculations, finding "no meaningful explanation" for his use of two financial variables (projected reimbursements and projected services)—or the exclusion of other possible variables—to project future revenues. The court also finds no support for normalizing the cost figures of the benchmarking companies (but not those of the subject company) and takes exception to the on one-third/two-thirds weighting scheme Cimasi applied to the company's historic cost of sales and operating expenses.

Next, the judge criticizes Cimasi's calculation of the discount rate and weighted average cost of capital, including the five separate elements that Cimasi employed to calculate the specific risk premium. To the actual cost of debt, Cimasi had added 12% to account for the personal guaranty of the debt by Addus's principal—a factor for which there is "nothing in the literature" to support it, the court says. "In this respect, there is no peer recognized technical knowledge for computing the cost of debt when there is or is not a guarantee by the controlling shareholder."

Similarly, by applying the Gordon growth model, Cimasi had calculated a "conservative" 4% growth rate in the terminal period. But "in light of all the other flaws in applying this method, the Court cannot simply give deference to professional judgment ... in this instance."

Finally, the court rejects Cimasi's 10% control premium for the healthcare company (based on Mergerstat and other data). Although Cimasi attributed the low premium to poor senior management, "there was no showing that he had any expertise in evaluating the quality of management," and no foundation had been laid for such expertise.

Once again, the court could have levied these criticisms against the report's overall credibility—not its *admissibility*. But narrowing its evidentiary "gate," the court also excluded the underlying data:

> [T]o the extent there purports to be any empirical data on the real range of control premiums, Cimasi did not establish that this data and any inferences drawn from the data have reached the level of peer-recognition as an accepted methodology. A passing reference to some limited studies does not establish that this methodology ... has reached the level of a standardized technique or specialized knowledge.... As a gatekeeper, this Court must look to the methodology used ... [and if it is] fatally flawed, as here, the Court must exclude the evidence, regardless of its effect on the ultimate outcome.

Marketability discounts fall prey to the same exclusion. After reviewing 14 separate restricted stock studies, two pre-IPO studies, more Mergerstat data as well as numerous industry and company-specific factors, Cimasi had determined a 30% DLOM. But the court finds the application of marketability discounts for the privately held company "counterintuitive," based on an "impracticably impossible standard."

So the foundational premise for attributing a lack of marketability builds in a very severe diminution in the value of the privately held shares. In this sense, the theory is entirely suspect and inherently unreliable.

The gate clangs shut. In the remaining paragraphs, the court swiftly disposes of Cimasi's guideline company and comparable transactions methods. And, after precluding admission of the entire report, it finishes with this final flourish of the gatekeeper function:

> This ... should serve as a warning to other litigants in future ... cases to make sure that their experts apply the standard methods correctly lest they find their experts' reports denied admission. For if they do not heed this stricture, they may not have any evidence in the record to sustain their burden [sic] of proof.

After finding the "standard methods" fundamentally flawed, however, the court implies that few business valuation experts, their data or methodologies, may find welcome in this courtroom. Bankruptcy bloggers are already buzzing about the opinion (e.g., www.bankruptcylitigationblog.com, Aug. 9, 2006).

Excerpt From Trial Transcript of In re Med Diversified; Cimasi Direct Testimony (8-29-05)

THE COURT: You're assuming that I should rely upon this body of data published by Integra and published by Risk Management Associates, that you didn't look behind that data. You simply accepted their statistical analysis of this data, and started that -- started with that as givens?

THE WITNESS: Yes. We cited those sources of data, 25 as well as citing the data that we received from the -- [...]

THE COURT: I understand about the publicly held companies, and you're saying when you're benchmarking, you're including within that database other reports generated by other companies, and it may be used in the industry, but basically from my standpoint that's hearsay. You haven't looked within that database of health care companies. I don't know how many health care companies comparable to Addus are in the RMA database. I don't know how many companies are in the Integra database. All you're doing is accepting these conclusions, and I don't know whether courts in determining valuation analyses in the health care industry have accepted as probative the analysis prepared by Integra or by RMA.

THE WITNESS: We did investigate, your Honor, in terms of the underlying efficacy and validity of the data sample in the -- in the survey techniques of both of those surveys, and aside from the fact that they are generally accepted surveys and that are widely, almost universally used in the valuation profession and in testimony --

THE COURT: That's just accepted -- that's just internal to your profession. You seem to misunderstand me. I'm trying to get out of your closed universe. I'm trying to get out of the situation in which everything is self-fulfilling. I'm trying to get to how we test empirically the validity of these assumptions, and you can tell me that appraisers use this stuff in connection with preparing valuations for their own clients. I'm trying to determine what kind of validity they should be given in an evidentiary setting in court, and I know about RMA. I said that was for bankers. I understood what you decided -- described as Integra, but what I'm looking for is any court that has concluded that a proper basis for valuation may include these studies.

Source: Robert Cimasi (Health Capital Consultants Inc.)

Where Perceived Bias Infects Entire Valuation, Expert Excluded as Unreliable Under FRE 702(3)

In *In re Med Diversified, Inc.: Chartwell Litigation Trust v. Addus Healthcare, Inc.*, No. 02-88564 (E.D.N.Y. Bankr. Aug. 2, 2006) the Bankruptcy Court for the Eastern District of New York determined the admissibility of a valuation expert's report on a motion in limine. In early 2002, Med Diversified (Med D) agreed to purchase Addus, a private company, for $119.9 million. As the closing date approached, Med D, who was insolvent, and Addus drafted an amended agreement extending the closing date for up to 6.5 months in exchange for $7.5 million. For each month that the deal did not close, Med D would forfeit $1 million; if the deal closed before the 6.5 months expired, any nonforfeited monies would be applied toward the purchase price. The $7.5 million was released to Addus, but the amended contract was never signed by the parties. In November 2002, Med D entered bankruptcy. Med D's fraudulent transfer claim against Addus, seeking return of the $7.5 million, was transferred to Chartwell Litigation Trust under the reorganization plan. Chartwell sued for return of the money as a fraudulent transfer.

Both parties presented expert testimony as to the value of Addus in 2002. Addus's expert was excluded on a motion in limine granted in 2005. Chartwell's expert, who held valuation credentials from a variety of appraisal organizations and specialized in the healthcare industry, was also challenged on a motion in limine. This expert valued Addus using a discounted cash flow, guideline company, and comparable transaction method. Addus argued in its motion that this expert's opinion was unreliable because the methodology and the expert's application thereof were flawed.

The bankruptcy court noted that FRE 702 permits reliable expert testimony where "(1) the testimony is based upon sufficient facts or data, (2) the testimony is the product of reliable principles and methods, and (3) the witness has applied the principles and methods reliably to the facts of the case." *Daubert v. Merrill Dow Pharmaceuticals*, 509 U.S. 579 (1993), required the trial judge to be the gatekeeper. "The trial court acts as a gatekeeper by ensuring that *every step* of the expert's analysis is reliable." (Emphasis in original) The court further noted, "While minor flaws will not automatically bar expert testimony, the court must exclude the evidence 'if the flaw is large enough that the expert lacks 'good grounds' for his or her conclusions.'" The court applied these rules and found the expert "exhibited such a deliberate, manifest, pervasive, and systematic bias in selecting his data points, in adjusting the data points, and in assigning weights to the data points in order to drive his valuation opinion toward its lowest levels ["in order to accomplish his client's implicit bidding"] that his report and testimony have to be excluded as fundamentally unreliable."

The bankruptcy court granted the motion in limine because of the bias it perceived in the expert's selections of judgmental or subjective inputs, whether it existed or not. The court noted many judgments that it perceived as cumulatively indicating infectious bias. While benchmarking, (i) the expert used a universe of 13 public companies, which the judge perceived to be small; (ii) normalized those companies, but not the subject company; (iii) applied weighting schemes such that private company information from two studies was given low weight (the court also footnoted that the specific company information regarding the private company participants was not provided, a lament frequently heard in the Tax Court).

The court also believed that there was bias in the expert's application of the discounted cash flow method: (iv) he failed to provide detailed information on the percentages used to forecast projected revenues. Moreover, (v) the perceived flawed benchmarking, particularly the failure to normalize the subject company, skewed the expert's computation of projected cost of sales. In addition, (vi) he double counted factors in applying a 10% company-specific risk premium in the computation of cost on equity; (vii) increased the cost of debt from the historical costs by 1,200 basis points due to the presence of the owner's personal guarantee of the debt without adequate explanation for such an increase; and (vii) used 4% growth in computing the terminal value under the Gordon growth model without justifying that percentage.

The expert applied both a control premium and a lack of marketability discount in performing his discounted cash flow and public company guideline methods. The court faulted the expert for applying a 10% control premium when the two studies indicated a premium in the low 30% range for healthcare corporations: It found that the expert reduced the discount for lack of management expertise, but the expert was not qualified to opine on management expertise and such was reflected in the low EBITDA multiple. As to the discount for lack of marketability, the expert utilized 30% after considering 14 studies and adjusting for: (1) lack of real prospect of public offering; (2) control value of 100%; (3) financial performance comparable to industry average; and (4) the market for home healthcare companies. The court found the application of a discount for lack of marketability counterintuitive: (1) the hypothetical sale of private stock in a short period of time is "clearly an impracticable impossible standard to meet" and "entirely suspect and inherently unreliable"; (2) a discount was not warranted since Addus had an actual buyer—Med D; (3) the studies looked at sales of minority rather than controlling interests; and (4) the financial health of Addus and the market for Addus had already been considered in the application of the DCF model.

In the expert's application of the public guideline company method, the court found that the expert utilized different periods to calculate each multiple he used: he computed MVIC/revenue using numbers for only one year but computed MVIC/EBITDA using three-year averages. The court found the expert failed to adequately explain the rationale for using different time frames. Moreover, it noted that the initial benchmarking, which it found flawed, impacted this calculation.

Lastly, the court found the expert's application of comparable transactions method similarly flawed. The court faulted the expert for selecting a small group of 11 comparables and excluding transactions whose price/revenue multiple fell outside two standard deviations. Since the comparables' revenues were substantially smaller than the subject company and since the excluded transaction was the most comparable, the court found the transactions were not comparable. It additionally faulted the expert for applying a 10% discount for lack of marketability in his analysis. The discount was to account for the costs of performing the transaction. The court found that the discount was unwarranted because the costs would be reflected in the transaction price.

Considering the faults it perceived in the expert's application of the valuation methodologies, the court concluded that the expert's valuations were unreliable and excluded his opinion under the third prong of FRE 702, requiring "the witness [to] appl[y] the principles and methods reliably to the facts of the case." In reaching this opinion, the court stated, "Perhaps this memorandum of decision may assist other bankruptcy courts in framing their decisions on motions *in limine* under the evolving standards of disqualification of purported non-scientific expert witnesses under the United States Supreme Court's *Kumho* decision with respect to financial matters." The court further stated, "It should serve as a warning to other litigants in future constructive fraudulent transfer cases to make sure that their experts apply the standard methods correctly lest they find their experts' reports denied admission. For if they do not heed this stricture, they may not have any evidence in the record to sustain their burden of proof to avoid the alleged constructive fraudulent transfers."

The judge orally ruled that this expert was admissible but later changed his mind and issued this opinion. Sources have revealed that the opinion was issued after the judge had notice of the parties' settlement of this matter. Moreover, both parties have requested that this decision be withdrawn.

'BV on Trial' in Bankruptcy: Exclusive Insights From the *In Re Med Diversified* Expert

By Robert James Cimasi, MHA, ASA, CBA, AVA, FCBI, CM&AA, CMP[2]

From ghoulies and ghosties
And long-leggedy beasties
And things that go bump in the night, Good Lord, deliver us!
—Old Scottish Prayer

In 1889, to ease overcrowding at the New York City Asylum for the Insane on Ward's Island, 40 men were sent to Central Islip, Long Island, where they built what was then called The Branch Lunatic, a facility for the criminally insane. Today, on that very site, sits the Alfonse D'Amato Federal Courthouse, in which a bankruptcy case was recently tried—so bizarre in its conduct and Byzantine twists—that even the most rationale observer was left to wonder whether the previous inhabitants had somehow returned. In my opinion, this almost surreal proceeding resulted in the business valuation profession being "put on trial."

Puzzling procedural path. Early in the case, in November 2005, the plaintiff (Med Diversified) filed a pretrial motion to exclude the testimony and report of defendant's expert witness, Scott Peltz. Judge Stan Bernstein granted the motion, permitting Mr. Peltz to appear only in rebuttal to my testimony.[3] The defendants had filed a similar motion to exclude my appearance at trial, but the judge denied it, stating at the time:

> I don't see a failure on the grounds of relevancy, reliability and personal qualifications to grant the *motion in limine* to strike or to preclude Mr. Cimasi from testimony ... I think he does have the qualifications as an expert in this industry. I think he testified to that very extensively. I think he does have all kinds of peer-granted recognitions, although I do think it's a rather small, select self-validating society, but he did seem to apply it as evidence of his expertise ... I think the rest of [his testimony] goes to his weight.... So I'm going to deny the motion.

2 Mr. Cimasi is president of Health Capital Consultants (St Louis), a nationally recognized healthcare financial and economic consulting firm.

3 *Chartwell Litigation Trust v. Addus Healthcare, Inc. (In re Med Diversified, Inc.)*, 334 B.R. 89 (Bankr. E.D.N.Y. 2005).

But then, nearly a year later, Judge Bernstein unexpectedly reversed his earlier ruling and granted defendants' motion in limine to exclude my testimony, without any mention of his earlier order or explanation of his reversal.[4] Of course, by that time, plaintiff's established trial strategy didn't permit me to rebut defendants' critique of my report.

If you read only the judge's latest order, you won't get a fair reading of the case. (The August 2006 *Memorandum of Decision and Order* was an interlocutory opinion and is not yet final, pending any appeals). Notably, of the approximately 228,000 words in the trial transcript recorded during my testimony, about 99,000 words—or approximately 43%—were those of Judge Bernstein. The complete record of trial transcripts, reports, and court's orders clearly reveal that Judge Bernstein brought an expressed agenda to this case:

1. To bring *Daubert* and *Kumho Tire*[5] gatekeeping functions to bear directly on business valuation in the bankruptcy courts;

2. To decry established business valuation methodology and authoritative data, which the profession generally accepts as reliable; and

3. Overall, to place the validity and credibility of business valuation, as a profession, on trial.

Don't take our word for it. Below is a sampling of direct excerpts from the hearing transcripts, in Judge Bernstein's own words.

THE COURT: ...I have a discreet understanding of my limitations, but I also have an understanding of what my experience tells me in having listened for the past thirty years to appraisers, and while they may not bear all the credentials and all the publications, I have yet to find an appraiser of value of non-real estate that ever says anything that's cogent and persuasive. Go ahead. I'm always willing to be persuaded.

THE COURT: I'd love to finally found [sic] an appraiser who convinces me that through a rigorous application of a methodology, that person can effectively value a company. Several have tried. None have succeeded, no one as sophisticated as you, but in the universe of companies rather than real estate projects or cash flows, the science isn't there yet, at least as you're presenting it to me because I'm testing it at every single conceivable angle simply because I have a tremendous degree of skepticism....

THE COURT: I don't really care about your certifications, although I do appreciate that this is somehow made up by persons who have some professional standing in connection with some effort by the government to improve the quality and integrity of appraisals. I would much rather hear about your experience as an author and the number of cases in which you've testified in a similar capacity. I want to see what kind of forensic experience you've had. So you don't need to go through all of these. I'm sure they're all noble, but I really want to know what cases you appeared in what books you've written or major articles.

4 *In re Med Diversified, Inc.*, 2006 Bankr. LEXIS 1677 (August 2, 2006).
5 *Daubert v. Merrill Dow Pharmaceuticals, Inc.*, 509 U.S. 579 (1993); *Kumho Tire Co., Ltd. v. Carmichael*, 526 U.S. 137 (1999).

THE COURT: … The only primary sources you look to are the fellow publications of your fellow members of the Appraisal Institute … I don't know what empirical data you're using to tell me it's widely accepted in the profession. I don't know how many—what's the concept of 'widely accepted,' other than citations in each and other's footnotes, and I don't know what the size of the profession, and I don't know what independent scrutiny has been given to these by persons who aren't members of the profession ... and I'm just telling you … that's what I understand the gatekeeper function to be because all I get are people who are self-certifying and self-validating, and it's the same pack that travels around the country and testifies in the cases or serves as consultants, and all they do is quote one another, and it gets to a certain point, am I supposed to take this for real?

THE COURT: I just want everyone to be having an opportunity to look at a standardized text that has some recognition in the field. I'm the only judge in this courthouse who orders books for the library on law and economics, finance, and things of that sort …

… And I make them available to the lawyers and the Bar because I don't think my job is curtailed or limited to reading the statute in light of legislative history. I need other working expertise.

THE COURT: You're assuming that I should rely upon … this body of data published by Integra and published by Risk Management Associates, that you didn't look behind that data. You simply accepted their statistical analysis of this data, and started that—started with that as givens? … That's just accepted—that's just internal to your profession.

You seem to misunderstand me. I'm trying to get out of your closed universe. I'm trying to get out of the situation in which everything is self-fulfilling. I'm trying to get to how we test empirically the validity of these assumptions, and you can tell me that appraisers use this stuff in connection with preparing valuations for their own clients. I'm trying to determine what kind of validity they should be given in an evidentiary setting in court, and I know about RMA. I said that was for bankers. I understood what you decided -- described as Integra, but what I'm looking for is any court that has concluded that a proper basis for valuation may include these studies.

THE COURT: Okay. Thank you, Mr. Cimasi. Thank you for persisting with us. I found it very instructive. I've learned more than I really wanted to know about valuations. I've been reading more of Shannon Pratt than I really wanted to know, but I do appreciate your professionalism in standing up to this inquiry, and it probably convinces you want to go back to the transactional market rather than continue as a forensic witness, or at least before any judge other than me [sic] …

Under the circumstances of the case, and given the totality of his statements, I have taken little solace in Judge Bernstein's last comments. However, I do take from this case a renewed commitment to producing independent, credible reports in accordance with the standards and accepted methods of the business valuation profession, as well as generally acknowledged, valid sources of data, when appropriate. I will also continue making every effort to educate the trier of fact through well-prepared testimony, to encourage fair hearings, unburdened by a prejudged bias against the business valuation profession.

Mercury Companies, Inc. v. FNF Security Acquisition, Inc. (In re Mercury Companies, Inc.)

Citation: 2014 Bank. LEXIS 1230
Date of decision: March 31, 2014
Country: US
State or Federal: Federal
State/Jurisdiction: Colorado
Court: United States Bankruptcy Court
Type of action: Bankruptcy
Judge: Romero
Experts: Neil H. Demchick (plaintiff); Scott P. Peltz (defendant)
SIC: 6361 Title Insurance (title insurers-direct)
Key words: Bankruptcy Code Section 548a1, Discounted cash flow method (DCF), Fraudulent transfer, Reasonably equivalent value, Totality of Circumstances

'Reasonably Equivalent Value' Analysis Is Not a Dollars-and-Cents Issue

What does the Bankruptcy Court look for when it assesses "reasonably equivalent value"? A recent decision describes in technical detail the discounted cash flow analyses the parties' experts performed and the limitations of the calculations. The court also explains what factors other than the contract price and appraisals it considers for its conclusion.

Avoidable sale of subsidiaries? The plaintiff was a title agency organization that began in Colorado but expanded into California, Arizona, and several other states in the 1990s. Its downfall began in 2007 when the California housing market cooled. In April 2008, the plaintiff executed a credit agreement as part of a $45 million loan that was secured by most of its and its subsidiaries' assets, including accounts receivable. On July 2008, the lead creditor swept $40 million from the plaintiff's accounts. Based on this event and other considerations, company management decided to stop doing business in 161 locations and close down many subsidiaries. The company had four Colorado-based subsidiaries—three title companies and a software and computer consulting business—for which management anticipated a payroll of nearly $1.6 million due about a week after the sweep.

Since the title company subsidiaries had a 30% share of Colorado's real estate market, management believed they made an attractive acquisition target. But when it offered to sell them immediately to their largest underwriter the intended buyer rejected the offer. Subsequently, management proposed a quick sale of stock in the subsidiaries to the defendant—a major national title insurance company. On Aug. 5, 2008, the parties executed a purchase agreement, which specified a purchase price of $5 million in cash. The defendant immediately wired $1 million of the amount and took control of the Colorado subsidiaries that same day. A day later, it wired an additional $1.48 million toward the purchase price, leaving just over $2.5 million of the purchase price outstanding. Twenty-three days after the sale, the plaintiff filed for Chapter 11 bankruptcy.

Subsequently, the plaintiff sued in Bankruptcy Court (D. Colo.) to recover the alleged value of the Colorado subsidiaries from the defendant, claiming the sale was a fraudulent transfer under Section

548(a)(1) of the Bankruptcy Code. The transaction was avoidable because the plaintiff received less than reasonable equivalent value for the stock in the four subsidiaries and was insolvent on the date of transfer.

Since both parties agreed on the insolvency issue, the court had to rule on reasonably equivalent value.

It considered expert testimony from both parties. The experts' approaches, the court found, were remarkably similar, but their conclusions "vastly different." The plaintiff's expert determined that, on the date of sale, the stock had a positive value of nearly $15 million, whereas the defendant's expert assigned a negative value of about $5 million.

Immediate versus nonimmediate sale. As to the similarities, both experts agreed the three title subsidiaries required a different valuation from the fourth subsidiary because the latter was in a different line of business. Both experts used a going concern value because the entities were operating businesses at the time of sale. And both opted for an income approach. For the title companies, this meant employing the discounted cash flow (DCF) method: projecting their revenues and expenses in the future and discounting them back to a present value as of the date of sale.

Both experts projected a 0.1% revenue growth in 2009 and 6.4% growth in 2010 based on national forecasts and assumed 3.0% growth for 2011 and all subsequent years. But they disagreed about projections for 2008 following the sale. The plaintiff's expert assumed a sale did not have to be immediate. The Colorado subsidiaries could have stayed in business for 30 to 60 days to get to a sale. In contrast, the defendant's expert built his valuation on the immediacy of the sale and the plaintiff's financial distress at the time of sale.

As to specifics, the plaintiff's expert used data from the title companies' income statements covering the period from January 2004 through July 2008. He determined revenue mostly consisted of title revenue and escrow revenue. He also considered the value of "earned credits." The title companies accrued the credits in exchange for holding large amounts of trust funds—the result of their escrow services—in financial institutions. Since they don't own the funds, state law does not allow the financial institutions to pay interest on the funds. Instead, the financial institutions give earned credits, which the title companies use to buy in-kind merchandise and reduce expenses.

The plaintiff's expert explained that the title companies' fair market value was the net present value of the companies during the projection period, plus their terminal value, minus adjustments for dark office liability and adjustments for working capital, minus a discount for lack of marketability because the plaintiff was a closely held company. To determine cash flow, he looked to financial data from January 2008 through July 2008, adjusted for capital expenses and working capital, and added depreciation back to the resulting amount because it was a noncash expense. For future cash flow, he used projections for 2009 through 2012, deducted potential dark office liability, and adjusted for the weighted average cost of capital (WACC), which he obtained from the *Ibbotson Cost of Capital Yearbook.* He determined a cost of capital of 30.28% of debt and based his projections on the current-year median and the five-year average.

The defendant's expert also used Ibbotson, but a different capital structure resulting in 6.38% of debt; moreover, he used the current-year mean figures. In terms of cost of equity, the plaintiff's expert used 22.8% and the defendant's expert 25.5%. Both experts used the Gordon growth model for terminal value.

The plaintiff's expert computed an unadjusted fair market value of over $28.7 million. He then accounted for dark office liability, the working capital shortfall that existed on the sale date, and the lack of marketability; he also adjusted for the fact that the sale resulted in a transfer of 100% of the stock to the buyer. These adjustments yielded a value of over $14.6 million, to which he added the value of the fourth Colorado subsidiary—nearly $290,000.

In critiquing the defendant expert's valuation, the plaintiff claimed he excluded "shadow revenue," confusing it with the seasonality of the title business, and even after learning about it failed to modify his valuation. Shadow revenue was an accounting tool encouraging title companies to refer business to the plaintiff's non-Colorado subsidiaries. In case of a successful referral, both companies received credit for revenue generated on their income statements and qualified for a commission from the parent company. To prevent "double booking" of revenue, at the end of the year, the shadow revenues were deducted from the title companies' income statements.

The defendant's expert responded that he "made up" for the exclusion. For example, he used management projections existing before the sweep, which tended to be overly optimistic. He agreed that a projected decline in revenues should be in the 30%-to-40% range, rather than the 22% decrease resulting from the projections. He held onto the rate; it and other factors balanced his earlier exclusion of shadow revenue from the projections.

The court called the expert's approach "inappropriate" and said it weakened his conclusion of "negative" value.

The plaintiff also claimed the defendant's expert should not have made a lost business adjustment to account for the effect of the sweep. The court disagreed, finding that fear of lost business was a critical factor in plaintiff management's decision to offer the stock for $5 million and insist on an immediate sale.

Valuations 'excessive' and 'too low.' Neither valuation hit the mark, the court found. It agreed with the plaintiff's expert that a nonimmediate sale would have increased the sales price. But there was no certainty it would have been $10 million higher than the agreed-upon price.

Although it disapproved of the way in which the defendant's expert tried to account for excluding shadow revenue, it approved of his consideration of the immediacy of the sale. But it also found he did not reckon that the defendant was willing to pay $5 million for the four subsidiaries and indeed considered the deal a good one. In sum, one valuation appeared "excessive" and the other "too low."

Ultimately, the court's determination of reasonably equivalent value did not require it to compute a specific dollar value, the court explained. The term "reasonably equivalent value" was not defined in the Bankruptcy Code. But relevant case law provided for a two-step analysis: (1) determine whether the debtor received any value at all; and (2) look to the totality of the circumstances to compare the value of what the debtor received with the value of what it gave. As to the second inquiry, a court could look beyond the contract price and the valuations. And it could factor "indirect" or noneconomic benefits into its determination of the value received, the court added.

In this case, the court found there was no question that the debtor received some value, in the form of the payments from the defendant. As to the circumstances of the sale, the plaintiff's officers held the mistaken belief that they had to sell the subsidiaries immediately. To say the plaintiff lacked the cash to cover the impending payroll was wrong because the plaintiff had access to cash. One day after the sale, the parent company's president stated in court the company had "substantial cash that because of its nature, it did not try to use as working capital." This included $13 million in a nonqualified deferred compensation plan and $4 million in its health and benefits account. According to the court, the more pertinent issue was why experienced business people acted on those mistaken beliefs rather than take steps to obtain accurate information. For one, the company's president panicked. But there also was evidence that he "desired an immediate sale." He contacted the defendant and proposed a discounted $5 million purchase price to enable a quick sale. When the defendant asked for more time to do due diligence, he replied there was no time "for haggling." Management received what it asked for, the court pointed out. It concluded that the sale was conducted for reasonably equivalent value and, therefore, was not avoidable.

Miller Bros. Coal v. Consol of Kentucky, Inc.

Citation: 2009 WL 4904032 (Bkrtcy. E.D. Ky.))
Date of Decision: December 11, 2009
Country: US
State or Federal: Federal
State/Jurisdiction: Kentucky
Court: United States Bankruptcy Court
Type of action: Bankruptcy
Experts: Emily Medine (plaintiffs), Gleason & Associates (defendants)
Judge: Howard

Court Adjusts Discount Rate to Reflect Current Economic Risks

Cases on the appropriate discount rate are relatively rare, so even this brief discussion by a federal bankruptcy court indicates how current economic conditions may impact this critical cost of capital calculation.

Downturn is not an 'act of God.' In the first half of the opinion, the defendant tried to excuse its breach of a coal mining agreement by claiming that the severe economic downturn in 2009 amounted to a force majeure—an exterior event, completely outside its control. However, declining consumer demand, rising inventories, and stalled operations are "normal" market risks, the court ruled, and not the result of a "superior force," or unforeseeable act of God. In agreeing to the fixed-price contract, the defendant assumed "the normal risk ... that the market will change," the court said, and it could not escape responsibility despite a precipitous drop in coal prices and contract opportunities.

The plaintiff claimed it was entitled to lost profits damages in excess of $10.2 million. In particular, the expert applied a discount rate of 10%, based on the plaintiff's actual cost of capital (which had been under 8% prior to its parent's bankruptcy) plus a slight risk premium. She also believed the 10% discount rate was consistent with the effective annuity nature of the income stream under the coal mining agreement, especially given its fixed-price aspect and its costs. "However, the court believes a ten percent rate is too low," it said, and found a 15% rate "more reasonable in light of the normal attendant risks of mining coal." (Essentially, the court appears to have shifted the defendant's arguments regarding an economic "force majeure" from the question of overall liability to the determination of damages—in particular, the risks inherent in the determination of a discount rate.)

The court made additional market-related adjustments to the expert's damages analysis. For instance, she failed to include the plaintiff's forecasts of losses on its surface mining operations, which, during the contract period, conservatively amounted to $2 million. The plaintiff also would have incurred nearly $500,000 in additional fees to a subcontractor. Finally, offsets for development, permitting, gas relocation, reclamation, and other cost reimbursements totaled nearly $3.65 million.

Overall, the expert's analysis was "convincing" and supported the plaintiff's claims for damages calculations in this case, the court held. After its own adjustments for current market conditions and costs, including a more realistic discount rate, it awarded net damages of $3.96 million.

In re The Minnelusa Co.

Citation: 176 B.R. 954
Date of Decision: September 29, 1994
Country: US
State or Federal: Federal
State/Jurisdiction: Florida
Court: United States Bankruptcy Court
Type of action: Bankruptcy
Judge: Paskay

Share Value Can Consider Discounts, Says Court

At issue was the value of shares in a closely held business of a Chapter 11 debtor. These shares were pledged to a group of creditors as collateral for a promissory note provided to the debtor. Each creditor received shares representing a 6% holding. No specific marketability or minority discount was mentioned in the debtor's valuation of the real estate assets and business operation. The creditors valued the real estate assets based upon appraisals; the business operations were accorded net value since the operations had always operated at a loss. A 35% discount was applied to the creditors' valuation to reflect the minority position of each creditor holding stock; an additional 40% discount for lack of marketability was applied, due to the pending Chapter 11, lack of dividends declared in the last few years, and losses sustained. The court accepted the value suggested in the creditors' expert witness report, based in part upon the court's view that it was appropriate to consider discounts for lack of marketability and minority interest.

Monsanto Co. v. Roeder

Citation: 2009 WL 4907014 (Bankr. N. D. Iowa)
Date of Decision: December 14, 2009
Country: US
State or Federal: Federal
State/Jurisdiction: Federal Circuit
Court: United States Bankruptcy Court
Type of action: Bankruptcy
Experts: Timothy G. Taylor (plaintiff)
Judge: Edmonds

Bankrupt Farmer Gets Plowed by Another Patented Seed Case

For several years, the Monsanto Co. has successfully defended its patented, herbicide-resistant "Roundup Ready" seed (mostly soybeans) against infringement by farmers. Federal courts have held that, by law, damages must exceed the "technology fee" that Monsanto charges farmers for each purchased bag of seed. See, e.g., *Monsanto v. McFarling* (Fed. Cir. 2007). In fact, in a later decision, *Monsanto v. Tidball* (E.D. Mo., 2009), the court found that the full cost of a bag of seed is a valid starting point for calculating a reasonable royalty; should damages fall below this point, they create a windfall for infringing farmers.

Stolen seed didn't save the farm. At age 67, Ronald Roeder had been an Iowa farmer for most of his life. For over 20 years, he was also a seed dealer who distributed Roundup Ready seed to other farmers. He knew that the patented seed included a technology fee; he also knew that planting the seed and then harvesting (and saving) resistant seed violated Monsanto's patent.

Nevertheless, in 2003—when Roeder's farm operations were overextended—he stole Roundup Ready seed from his son. For the next three years, he saved and planted resistant seeds, but he also bought Roundup seed in a rough 3-to-1 ratio (saved seed to new). From 2003 to 2006, he used approximately 640 bags of saved seed. The price per bag at the time was $26.00 to $27.00. Roeder couldn't save his farm, however, and he filed for Chapter 11 bankruptcy in 2007. Monsanto filed its claim for a nondischargeable debt for patent infringement. Before trial, the farmer admitted his infringement; the only disputed issues were damages and the maliciousness of his conduct (enhanced damages).

Monsanto retained a professor in "food and resource economics" to testify as its damages expert. Under his first approach, the expert calculated a reasonable royalty using the hypothetical negotiation standard in *Georgia-Pacific Corp. v. U.S. Plywood Corp.* (S.D.N.Y. 1970) and net income/variable costs model. Specifically, he used average Iowa market prices and crop yields for the three years of infringement to estimate the farmer's return per acre. Given Monsanto's superior bargaining power, the expert assumed it would settle for no less than 75% of the farmer's net income, resulting in a hypothetical rate of $135 to $149 per acre. The expert admitted that he did not include leasing expenses for the land because the farmer failed to provide this information.

The expert's second approach relied on capturing the following four benefits/risks resulting from the farmer using saved seed:

1. Cost savings—including cleaning and opportunity costs, as well as the farmer's legitimate purchases of patented seed;

2. Value of higher yields, based on an industry study that patented seed increased soybean yields by five to seven bushels per acre over conventional seed;

3. Monsanto monitoring costs—including field sampling and testing to measure compliance, which amounted to $16 per acre according to company estimates; and

4. Additional benefits, as identified by a nationwide survey of farmers (2004), which priced the extra financial savings of the patented seed (time, convenience, and human and environmental safety) at $37 per acre.

Combining these components, the expert calculated per-acre royalties ranging from $96 to $114 over the three infringing years. Multiplying these by the number of soybean acres per year, he reached a total of $100,113 in damages. The farmer had also produced enough resistant seed to plant "tens of thousands of acres," the expert said—an "exponential effect" that could possibly damage Monsanto's market share.

Court begins with the price of a bag. Citing the *McFarling* decision, the court started with a baseline reasonable royalty rate measured by the dealer's price for a bag of patented seed, including the technology fee. Multiplying this by the number of bags the farmer would have needed to plant his soybean acres during the three years of infringement, the court reached a total of approximately $16,855 in baseline damages.

The court also found that the farmer acted maliciously and with full knowledge that his conduct was wrong and would cause Monsanto financial harm. (As an experienced seed dealer, he was "fully aware of the critical features" of the patented technology; he'd also stolen seed and tried to conceal his repeated infringement through legitimate purchases.) "Enhanced damages are appropriate in this case," the court held, and it multiplied the baseline rate by three to determine roughly $50,565 in damages.

Monsanto claimed this amount essentially required the farmer to pay no more than the price of a bag and "only because he got caught." The court agreed, adopting the expert's benefits/risk model with one adjustment: It eliminated the fourth component ($37 per acre in additional benefits) because the survey of farmers' opinions was "far too subjective" a yardstick to determine damages.

Under this approach, damages equaled $64,353, which the court doubled to reach $128,706. Had there been any evidence the farmer sold or transferred saved seed, the court might have found his conduct more egregious (and trebled the damages), but "there was not." It did charge him with $100,000 of Monsanto's attorneys' fees and costs, bringing the farmer's total nondischargeable debt to $230,408.

Mungo v. Taylor

Citation: 2003 U.S. Dist. LEXIS 3412
Date of Decision: March 7, 2003
Country: US
State or Federal: Federal
State/Jurisdiction: Illinois
Court: United States District Court
Type of action: Bankruptcy
Experts: Lori Henert (for Mungo)
Judge: St. Eve

Acceptance of Lower Valuation Based on Declining Profits Upheld

Defendant Taylor was plaintiff Mungo's attorney in her divorce. The divorce settlement agreement included the marital estates interest in CLP Group Inc. The divorce court had before it two valuations by the same accounting firm, one for $160,000 and a later one for $40,000. The lower valuation was the result of the company's declining profits.

Malpractice adversary proceeding. Mungo later filed bankruptcy and listed Taylor as a disputed creditor. Mungo objected to Taylor's proof of claim for attorney fees and filed an adversary proceeding against her, alleging legal malpractice. The bankruptcy court consolidated the objection to the claim and the adversary proceeding and held a nonjury trial.

To recover damages for a legal malpractice action in Illinois, a plaintiff must prove by a preponderance of the evidence that she would have prevailed in the underlying action. As the underlying action in this case was a divorce, Mungo's measure of damages is the "difference between her recovery under the settlement agreement and what she would have recovered in the divorce action but for Taylor's legal malpractice."

The bankruptcy judge found several breaches of duty by Taylor but held that Mungo had failed to prove any damages resulting from these breaches. Mungo filed a motion asking the court to reconsider this ruling. The judge granted the motion and amended his ruling.

In his amended ruling, the judge determined that the value of the marital estate was $301,075.73 and found that Mungo would have received 60% of the property, or $180,645.43, had the case gone to trial. He determined that Mungo had been awarded $173,305 under the settlement agreement. Accordingly, the judge awarded Mungo the difference of $7,340.43 as damages.

Valuation of stock upheld. Mungo appealed, arguing that the bankruptcy judge erred in his valuation of the marital estate, specifically, the value of the parties stock in CLP Group Inc. She contended that the judge should have valued the stock at $160,000, based upon the original valuation prepared by the accounting firm, instead of $40,000. Mungo argued that the $40,000 valuation was allowed in the divorce action only due to Taylor's negligence. Because the valuation date must be as close as practicable to the date of trial, the district court held that the bankruptcy judge did not err in basing his damages calculation on the subsequent $40,000 valuation.

In re Nanovation Technologies, Inc.

Citation: 2007 Bankr. LEXIS 1862
Date of Decision: May 17, 2007
Country: US
State or Federal: Federal
State/Jurisdiction: Illinois
Court: Court of Appeals
Type of action: Fraud
Experts: Robert Reilly (trustee); KPMG and Sherwin
Judge: Hollis
SIC: 3357 Drawing and Insulating of Nonferrous Wire

Bankruptcy Trustee's Efforts to Go After Valuation Group Backfire

Nanovation Technologies, a private company and provider of fiber optic technologies, was one of many to fall victim to the "irrational exuberance" (Alan Greenspan's phrase) of the American economy in the late 1990s and, in particular, of the telecommunications industry. Shortly after the telecomm bubble burst in 2001, the company filed for Chapter 11 bankruptcy protection, later converted to Chapter 7. The trustee brought this adversarial proceeding against the debtor's financial and valuation advisors, a consulting group formerly within the KPMG umbrella.

Specifically, KPMG prepared two valuations of the debtor, in December 1999 and September 2000, respectively. Their primary use was to determine, for income tax purposes, the value of stock options granted to executives and other insiders (1999, $7.02 per share) and employee stock purchase plans (2000, $9.20 per share). Each study applied similar assumptions in its discounted cash flow (DCF) method and similar comparables and multiples in its market analysis.

The trustee sought to show that, in preparing the 2000 study, however, KPMG had inflated the value of the debtor's stock to permit insiders to repay loans from the company with stock that was in fact worthless. The trustee retained an accredited business appraiser to value the debtor as of the Sept. 30, 2000, valuation date; his valuation concluded that the debtor was worth only *15 cents* per share. Had KPMG not "grossly overvalued" the stock, the trustee claimed, the insiders could not have repaid their loans with company stock and thus owed the bankruptcy estate more than $20 million.

The trustee's 'exuberant' claims. But two critical errors "haunted" the trustee's claims, according to the Bankruptcy Court. While not quite "irrational," the trustee's "exuberant" pursuit of KPMG suffered first and foremost from an internal contradiction. That is, since KPMG used the same assumptions in its 1999 analysis as it did in 2000, if the debtor's stock was worthless at the later date, then the stock should have been worthless months earlier. "Accordingly, the face amount of the notes to purchase 'worthless' stock would have been miniscule at best," the court said, "and not the twenty million dollars or so that the trustee seeks to recover here."

The trustee's failure to ask its expert, an accredited appraiser, to value the debtor at an earlier date—the time it extended the insider loans—"exposes this incongruity," the court added. If the expert had done so, then he would have used the same assumptions as in his September 30 analysis—critical among these a 5% perpetual growth rate in his DCF (compared to KPMG's 15%) and a single pricing fundamental in his market analysis (compared to KPMG's four). The expert would have concluded that the stock was also nearly worthless at the earlier date, and, as a result, the debtor would not have had to extend loans to insiders to purchase "penny" stock.

Similarly, if KPMG had adopted the expert's 5% growth rate (or his other assumptions) at the time the debtor sold stock to insiders, then KPMG's valuation would have been dramatically lower, and the insider loans would have been unnecessary. "The end result is the same," the court emphasized, "*as long as the approach is consistently applied.*"

If there was any inconsistency, it was on the part of the trustee, who "depended on KPMG's valuation methods at the time the loans were extended but assailed the same valuation approach when the loans were repaid. The court is not fooled."

Failure to include actual market transactions. "The second major flaw in the trustee's case was his expert's refusal to take into account *any* real market transactions involving the purchase and sale of [the debtor's] stock." Several independent parties, including Motorola and four investor groups, paid $15.00 per share—or nearly $6.00 more than KPMG's September 30 value. "Not one stock sale came close to fifteen cents." While valid reasons exist to discount such "real world" sales, ignoring them completely was imprudent. "What appraiser considers theoretical textbook valuation methods *exclusively* when the asset is repeatedly bought and sold in the real world?" the court asked, its rhetoric betraying its rising irritation:

> This case consumed eight days of trial time ... [t]housand of pages of exhibits.... The court's own personal notes exceeded 50 pages. After poring through this material, the court is left with the firm conviction that KPMG's September 30 valuation was not only within the bounds of professional care and applicable standards, it was at least as credible as [the trustee's expert's].

After the blistering introduction—and its implicit lessons for lawyers and analysts alike—the court conducts an in-depth analysis of the competing September 30 valuations. This includes detailed discussion of the key assumptions by KPMG, the trustee's expert, and also the trial expert retained by KPMG (who concluded a $12.50 per share value as of Sept. 30, 2000):

1. *Growth rate.* In their DCF analyses, all three experts accepted management growth projections for 2001-2003, including "supernormal" rates. All three used the same discount rate (24%). The only material difference: KPMG and its trial expert used a 15% perpetual growth rate, consistent with management expectations, while the trustee's expert dropped the growth rate from 15% in the terminal year (2006) to 5% thereafter. This was inconsistent with his acceptance of management projections for 2001-2003.

The trustee's expert also testified that, ideally, an analyst would want to reduce growth by perhaps 1% per year from the terminal year to the perpetual growth rate, to make the growth curve "smoother and realistic." By using a 15% growth rate, KPMG's trial expert "essentially replicated a longer discrete period with a more smoothly sloping growth curve," the court found, "the kind that [the trustee's expert] testified would be ideal." KPMG and its expert also checked the 15% growth rate against market comparables, finding it to be reasonable and a 5% growth rate to be far less than what even mature companies in the debtor's industry sector were experiencing. The court found the 15% growth rate to be "reasonable and consistent with generally accepted valuation principles."

2. *Market multiples.* KPMG's September 30 analysis also employed a market approach; it selected nine public companies and four pricing multiples, each with an assigned weight: business enterprise value (BEV) to total assets (15%), BEV to book BEV (15%), BEV to revenue (35%), and BEV to 2001 estimated revenue (35%). The trustee's expert used three of KPMG's four comparables and added one additional company, but he used only one pricing ratio: BEV to last 12 months' revenue.

"The decision to include or not include a pricing fundamental that considers the [debtor's] anticipated future revenues accounts for almost all of the difference in the indicated values [that the trustee's expert] and KPMG reached," the court said. Moreover, "the use of only a single pricing fundamental in a market multiples analysis is not consistent with generally accepted valuation practice." The trustee's expert not only applied a single multiple, but he also applied the lowest possible indicated for that fundamental.

By contrast, KPMG selected a multiple for each price ratio that was higher than the low end of the range indicated by the comparables, but lower than either the mean or the median. It also considered forward-looking pricing multiples that took the debtor's future prospects into account, unlike the trustee's expert, whose single pricing multiple used past revenues only. In 2000, fiber optic investors were "generally looking at the expected future performance of development stage companies rather their past performance," the court found. KPMG's approach was "more consistent with generally accepted practices."

In re Nellson Nutraceutical (I)

Citation: 2006 U.S. Bankr. LEXIS 3186
Date of Decision: November 29, 2006
Country: US
State or Federal: Federal
State/Jurisdiction: Delaware
Court: United States Bankruptcy Court
Type of action: Bankruptcy
Experts: James Harris (taxpayer) (other experts unnamed)
Judge: Sontchi
SIC: 2099 Food Preparations, NEC

Expert Valuation Report Disqualified Under *Daubert* for 'Maverick' DCF Analysis

All four experts in this Chapter 11 bankruptcy case performed a discounted cash flow (DCF) analysis in calculating the enterprise value of the debtors, a privately held affiliation that manufactures nutrition bars and supplements. In conducting the DCF analysis, each expert divided the debtors' future cash flows into two parts: (1) their projected "free cash flows" for 2006-2011, derived from their long-range business plan; and (2) their 2011 terminal value.

To calculate the latter, the three experts representing the secured and unsecured lenders used the debtors' projected EBITDA as the metric of value. But only the debtors' expert used EBITDA minus capital expenditures (Cap Ex) as the metric in determining terminal value.

Procedural positioning—and ominous precedent? At the end of this year, the debtors will owe their secured lenders an aggregate of about $355 million, while their unsecured debt will be $10 million. Thus, for the debtors to be "in the money," their enterprise value must exceed approximately $365 million.

Last September, the bankruptcy court held a specific hearing to determine the debtors' enterprise value. At trial, the secured and unsecured lenders objected to the qualifications of the debtors' expert, James Harris (Seneca Financial Group; Greenwich, Conn.). Notably, at the time the court qualified Harris as an expert but reserved judgment on the admissibility of his testimony pursuant to Rule 702 of the Federal Rules of Evidence (FRE). This opinion came on the lenders' post-trial motion to preclude Harris's expert testimony based on its lack of Rule 702 relevance and reliability, as defined by the well-known Supreme Court decisions in *Daubert* and *Kumho Tire*.

Also notable—but unfortunately not surprising—is the court's citation of the *In re Med Diversified* opinion, a recent bankruptcy case that used *Daubert* criteria to disqualify a healthcare valuation specialist and his report and to discredit the valuation profession generally.

The 'heart' of any valuation methodology. The court began by noting what it called the three "standard" methodologies in business valuation: the DCF analysis, comparable transaction analysis, and comparable company analysis. "At the heart of any valuation methodology is a simple task: the expert determines an appropriate metric of value and applies a multiple to that metric to determine the enterprise value of the company." For the DCF analysis, the metric of value is the company's future cash flows, while the multiple is the applied discount factor, "which is derived from a combination of firm-specific and more general information." Among other tasks, the valuation expert selects the appropriate source material and performs the calculations.

After selecting EBITDA minus Cap Ex as his metric in his DCF analysis, Harris concluded that the net present value of the debtors' free cash flows was $89.7 million and the net present value of their terminal value was $274.7 million, for a total of $364.4 million. After adding cash on hand ($24.5 million) and the present value of amortized goodwill arising from the purchase of a Canadian business ($15.6 million), he ultimately concluded that the debtors' enterprise value was $404.5 million.

Harris also performed comparable transaction and company analyses, concluding enterprise values for the debtors of $435.5 million in the former and a range of values ($340 million to $428.4 million) for the latter, in which he also used an EBITDA minus Cap Ex metric. But for reasons not clear from the court's opinion, Harris declined to consider anything but his DCF analysis, according it a 100% weight.

An 'invented' methodology. In their objections to Harris's testimony, the lenders characterized his use of EBITDA minus Cap Ex in his DCF analysis as "maverick" and "unprecedented" in both the legal and business valuation communities. Indeed, their experts (as well as Harris) had testified that:

> While EBITDA minus Cap Ex is used as a "credit statistic" to measure, among other things, whether a company can adequately service its debt, it has never before been used by any expert before any court in the United States to determine a company's terminal value under a DCF analysis.

Harris had also conceded that he had "never used this methodology in any expert report that he [had] ever submitted to a court." His 85-page training manual did not mention EBITDA minus Cap Ex as an available metric in a DCF analysis; nor was he able to identify any publication, treatise, or article that validated this use.

Further, under FRE 702 and the *Daubert* standard, the court found that the methodology had not been tested, peer reviewed, or generally accepted in the "scientific community" of business valuation, and so its potential error rate was unknown. Although Mr. Harris was a qualified expert and his testimony relevant, it relied heavily on the debtors' projection of capital expenditures, which are generally more volatile and unreliable than projections of EBIT or EBITDA.

"In short," the court concluded, "the evidence clearly indicates that Mr. Harris simply invented the methodology of using EBITDA minus Cap Ex to determine a company's terminal value under a DCF analysis." Because his conclusion of terminal value constituted the bulk of his ultimate conclusions regarding the debtors' enterprise value—and was, in fact, "inseparable" from his ultimate conclusion—the court struck the entirety of his testimony and report from the record.

In re Nellson Nutraceutical (II)

Citation: 2007 Bankr. LEXIS 99
Date of Decision: January 18, 2007
Country: US
State or Federal: Federal
State/Jurisdiction: Delaware
Court: United States Bankruptcy Court
Type of action: Bankruptcy
Experts: Richard Braun, ASA (Official Committee) William Hardie (Informal Committee) Russell Belinsky (secured creditor)
Judge: Sontchi
SIC: 2834 Pharmaceutical Preparations

Experts Left 'in the Dark' by Deliberately Manipulated Management Projections

It's every valuation expert's nightmare: learning after the fact that the long-range financial plans provided by management did not represent their "best and most honest thinking," to use the Bankruptcy Court's more delicate phrasing.

And that wasn't the worst of this Chapter 11 case, concerning a privately held manufacturer of nutrition bars and supplements. To be "in the money" on their investment, the principal equity holders needed to have the debtors' enterprise value declared in excess of $365 million. After screening potential valuation analysts to predetermine their methodologies, the investors and their attorneys sent the selected expert certain values to be attributed to the growth initiatives and then discussed in private as well as email how to "figure out a way" the expert could assist the investors.

Further, the investors hurriedly pushed through a "puffed up" business plan for the debtors, which layered on growth initiatives with inflated revenues and EBITDA projections, ignored price compressions and increased market competition, and eliminated "millions" in capital expenditures (CapEx). The latter turned out to be the "way" the investors could reach the equity hurdle—but, in a decision late last year, the court struck their expert's report for his use of the "maverick" Cap Ex metric in his DCF analysis.

The court does not mince words in condemning these events:

> In sum, [the investors] utilized [their] control over [the debtors] to manipulate both the business planning and valuation process to come up with an artificially inflated enterprise value … to claim some residual value for their existing equity position. There is no other credible interpretation of the evidence before the Court.

The emphasis appears in the original opinion, which next poses the court's dilemma: When each of the three remaining experts in the case (retained by the various creditors) relied on the compromised management projections, "how does the court rely on the expert testimony?" In particular, should it exclude their discounted cash flow analyses, or should it continue an already lengthy and expensive trial to permit revised reports?

Creditors' experts all credible. The court specifically exonerated the experts, who applied "usual and customary" valuation techniques and who "justly relied" on the debtors' information, which was "deliberately inaccurate." Accordingly, the court decided to: (i) accept all three expert opinions; (ii) adjust them for perceived errors and inaccuracies; (iii) weigh them according to credibility; and (iv) adjust the weighted average to account for the debtor's performance since the appraisals. (Note: The appropriate valuation date was the date of the hearing, and expert reports, prepared several months prior, helped "assist" rather than supplant the trier of fact in its determination of enterprise value.)

The court did not completely absolve the debtors' expert, noting he'd sent a draft appraisal to the debtors' board using a traditional DCF analysis that did not reach the desired equity. During a "lively and lengthy" telephone call, board members apparently told the appraiser it would be a "good idea" to use the CapEx methodology. A week later, the board received his new report using the CapEx methodology and approved it immediately.

Valuation highlights. After describing the low points of the proceedings, the court conducted a careful analysis of the three expert reports by Richard Braun, ASA (FTI Consulting Inc.), William Hardie (Houlihan Lokey Howard & Zukin), and Russell Belinsky (Chanin Capital Partners). All three used a traditional DCF analysis as well as a comparable company and comparable transaction analyses—and all three reached the same basic conclusion, that "the [debtors'] enterprise value is *not* sufficient to leave any value for [the investors]."

Their median values were also within 10% of each other, from a low of $314 million to a high of $349 million, with the third at $322 million. But all three testified they would have to reduce their respective valuations significantly, given the extent of the management manipulations (revealed at trial) and the debtors' severely deteriorated financial performances since the reports.

Factoring these points into its stated adjustment/weighting procedure, the court determined the debtors' enterprise value. Highlights of its analysis include:

1. *Separate consideration of 'growth initiatives.'* Only one expert used a separate discount rate in his DCF analysis to account for the debtors' growth plans, thereby assigning a separate value to the increased risk of these income streams as opposed to folding the risk into the discount rate applied to the base business. The debtors argued this double counted the risks of the growth initiatives; the court disagreed, noting the technique was acceptable when certain projects are riskier than the entire business.

2. *No ironclad rule regarding management projections.* While precedent generally favors management projections, courts should examine the track record and motives of management to determine the credibility of their forecasts on a case-by-case basis.

3. *Application of risk premiums.* In determining the appropriate discount rate, one expert used a 2.05% "emergence risk premium" and the other a 6% company-specific risk premium (CSRP) to account for the increased risk in the debtors' earning capacity post-reorganization. By any terminology, the debtor claimed the risk premiums inappropriately considered market

perceptions, but the court found they adequately reflected bankruptcy's potential impact on future earnings. However, it also found the 6% CSRP excessive and adjusted it to 4%.

4. *Selection of terminal multiples.* The debtor said two experts should have derived the terminal multiples for the DCFs from the comparable companies analysis rather than the comparable transactions, which contained "stale" sales over two years old. The court said the experts had correctly derived their multiples from transactions data, as their estimations concerned the debtors' worth to an acquirer. Moreover, there is no "bright line rule" branding transactions older than two years as irrelevant to a comparable transactions analysis: It's the similarity that matters.

5. *Valid criticism of selection of multiples.* Two experts had failed to use the median EBITDA multiple of the selected comparable companies and transactions analysis; instead, they used a lower figure based on "expert judgment and not simple arithmetic," reflecting the critical qualitative differences between the debtors and the guideline companies/transactions. "That may be so," the court said—but then noted that where an expert preferred "judgment" over math, the effect was generally to lower enterprise value, even in face of evidence that it should be higher.

6. *Size risk premium.* Similarly, according to the math, the debtors fit into the 9th decile of Ibbotson data. The resulting equity value straddled the 9th and 10th deciles, and, though two experts had resolved this by using the micro-cap risk premium, one expert had chosen to use the 10th decile data—which was an error, the court said, as it helped "pre-determine" the conclusion of enterprise value.

7. *Nonoperating assets.* One expert properly excluded a large debt from the debtors' cash balance and properly attributed a zero value to certain tax attributes where these were highly uncertain.

Can you recite the Gordon growth formula? The court found all of the experts highly qualified and experienced, even those the debtors challenged for lacking formal valuation training and/or credentials (two were attorneys/investment professionals). Each had made some errors—including one who was unable to recite the formula for the Gordon growth model on cross-examination. But, overall, each expert had established and maintained his credibility.

Notably, the court singled out the accredited appraiser as the most persuasive, not only for his valuation training, but also for his independence, as he'd had no knowledge of the debtors' secured debt prior to the valuation. The court weighted his report 40%, the others 30%, to reach its final conclusion of the debtors' enterprise value at $320 million.

Nelson v. Walnut Investment Partners, LP

Citation: 2011 WL 2711318 (S.D. Ohio)
Date of decision: July 13, 2011
Country: US
State or Federal: Federal
State/Jurisdiction: Ohio
Court: United States District Court
Experts: Robert Ferguson (plaintiff); Jeffrey Risius (defendants)
Judge: Spiegel

Expert's 'Hyperbole' in Article Comes Back to Haunt Him in *Daubert* Hearing

Experienced litigation experts know that their published articles and statements are "fair game" in the courtroom—but this case serves as some reassurance that the context of the publication and common sense should eventually prevail.

Court doesn't need to hold a *Daubert* hearing. In 2000, an investment fund paid $5 million for a 45% minority interest in the debtor, which owned 80 gas and convenience stores. Pursuant to the terms of a repurchase agreement, the debtor was to begin repaying the investors in February 2005, but it made only five payments totaling $2.75 million before filing for bankruptcy in November 2007. The trustee sued the investors to recover payments as a fraudulent conveyance under applicable state and federal bankruptcy law and filed a motion for summary judgment. To support the motion, the plaintiff's expert used the balance sheet test to show that, as of the first repayment, the fair value of the debtor's liabilities exceeded its assets by $2.3 million to $5.4 million. Using a discounted cash flow (DCF) approach, the expert found the excess of liabilities over assets to equal $1.2 million. By either test, therefore, he determined that the debtor was insolvent during the relevant time period.

The defendant/investors filed a *Daubert* motion, seeking to preclude the expert's insolvency analysis. They claimed his methodology was "entirely unreliable" because the expert:

- Did not consult with company management to develop the facts necessary to determine insolvency;
- Did not inspect the physical properties;
- Did not consider the impact of current and future market forces on the debtor's cash flow;
- Did not use reliable data to calculate the small-stock premium;
- Did not use the correct cost-of-debt data;
- Did not use the correct metric in analyzing the debtor's capital structure;
- Based his company-specific risk premium on subjective opinion; and
- Valued accounts receivable and other assets on subjective opinion.

To buttress these claims, the defendants made much of the expert's article, "The 'Dirty Dozen' Mistakes When Using a Valuation Expert," originally published in the *American Journal of Family Law*, Summer 2005. In it, he wrote that it was "malpractice" if an expert conducts a business valuation without talking to the owner or inspecting the physical site. Because the expert failed to speak to the debtor's owners or inspect their properties in this case, the defendants argued his methodology was per se unreliable.

The federal district court read the article in its entirety and found that, in context, the expert's statements were "not so damning." The article was directed primarily toward family law attorneys using valuation experts in divorce. In those cases, the court "could certainly understand the importance of the valuation expert having access to information" that only a management interview and a site inspection could provide.

"Of course, the context here is quite different," the court added. The plaintiff's expert was assessing the debtor as of a past date; a site visit in the present would not necessarily provide relevant information. In lieu of talking to the debtor's owner, who was largely responsible for the debtor's downfall, the expert based his analysis on "extensive" financial documentation. As a result, the court found nothing under *Daubert* that would require the exclusion of the expert's report "merely because he made some hyperbolic statements in an article that was exploring valuation issues in a context entirely different from the present one."

Authorities conflict on using 10b data. The defendants also argued that the expert's use of the 10b size category for deriving his small-stock premium rendered his calculations unreliable. According to their expert, the "data contained in 10b is fraught with problems." The defendant's expert quoted Shannon Pratt and Roger Grabowski for this proposition (presumably from *Cost of Capital: Applications and Examples*, 4th edition, although the court does not cite the specific source). The defendant's expert relied on the same authority to assess the small-stock premium—but he used the 10a size category instead of the 10b. Accordingly, there was authority for both experts' propositions, the plaintiff argued; the choice to use 10b or 10a data was a "matter of professional difference" and not a basis to exclude an expert's opinion.

The court agreed that the question went more to the credibility and weight of the evidence than its reliability. This held equally true for the defendant's claims that the plaintiff's expert did not use the correct cost-of-debt data to calculate the debtor's cash flow and that he did not use the correct metric in analyzing its capital structure. The expert "clearly made judgment calls the defendant disagrees with," the court held, "but that does not mean his methods were unreliable."

Finally, although the expert admitted that his calculation of a company-specific risk premium and his valuation of accounts receivable relied in part on his subjective opinion, he also testified that he arrived at those numbers based on a "thorough review" of the debtor's financial records, including minutes from board meetings, management memoranda, etc. This qualified for sufficient support to take his opinion "out of the realm of speculation," the court ruled, and denied the defendant's *Daubert* motion.

Turning to the plaintiff's motion for summary judgment, the court considered the defendant's primary challenge: that the debtor's audited financials showed it was solvent during the relevant time period. Such statements "can be useful" for assessing a firm's financial viability, the court said, but, in this case, the financials were not "compelling" evidence of solvency because they did not reflect the fair market value of all of the debtor's assets but merely the company's book value. In contrast, the plaintiff's expert included assets such as goodwill in his DCF and balance sheet analyses, demonstrating under both that the debtor was insolvent at the time of the payments.

Since the defendant's expert declined to conduct his own insolvency assessment, this left the plaintiff's expert's conclusions "uncontroverted," the court held. Based on all the evidence, it granted summary judgment entitling the plaintiff to recover the $2.75 million payments, plus interest.

In re Nesser; Boston Restaurants v. Nesser

Citation: 2006 B.R. 372, 1997 Bankr. LEXIS 245
Date of Decision: March 7, 1997
Country: US
State or Federal: Federal
State/Jurisdiction: Pennsylvania
Court: United States Bankruptcy Court
Experts: M. Dagnon, CPA (for Nesser) Mark M. Gleason, CPA (for Boston)
Type of action: Bankruptcy
Judge: Fitzgerald
SIC: 5812 Eating Places (limited-service restaurants)
Key words: Bankruptcy, Fair market value (FMV), Franchise, Marketability

Court Determines Feasibility Requirements Not Met

The charge of the Bankruptcy Court was to determine whether the requirements for confirmation of a Chapter 13 personal bankruptcy reorganization were met or whether the Chapter 7 liquidation case should be reopened. Motions filed included:

- A motion filed on behalf of Fayette Bank attempted to revoke the order of discharge entered in Nesser's (Debtor) prior Chapter 7 case and to reopen the Chapter 7 case; and
- A motion filed on behalf of Nesser to permit him to incur additional debt, allowing him to open a pub that he contended would provide him sufficient income to fund his Chapter 13 plan.

Plan relies on sources of funds. The Chapter 13 plan required funding. Nesser conceded that his current income would not fund the plan but cited as sources of funds the value of his 50% stock interest in Boston Restaurants Inc., a single-restaurant franchise of Boston Beanery, and operation of a pub to be opened if motion to incur additional debt were granted.

With respect to the fair market value of Nesser's Boston Restaurants Inc. stock, the court heard testimony from two experts. Nesser called John M. Dagnon, CPA, with Carbis Walker and Associates. Using figures only from 1995, he projected pretax income of $83,000 per year and used a pretax buildup capitalization rate of 25.16% to derive a value of $331,725.

However, Dagnon failed to consider the terms of the lease agreement, the fact that the lessor owned the liquor license, the value of the restaurant's assets and liabilities, and the fact that an anchor tenant, Hess Department Store, vacated the mall in which the restaurant was located. Dagnon did not visit the location. Accordingly, Dagnon's analysis and conclusions were based on incomplete information.

Discounts reflected in cap rate. Boston Restaurants presented testimony from Mark M. Gleason, a self-employed CPA. Gleason normalized expenses, adjusting for bad debts, advertising, and rent. Gleason developed a capitalization rate of 40% via the buildup method, assuming a no-growth situation based on discussions with Forte. He also included a minority interest discount and discount for lack of marketability in his cap rate.

Furthermore, Gleason reviewed the stock agreement between Nesser and Forte, the other 50% owner. Based on his analysis, Gleason valued Nesser's 50% interest at $10,147.

Court reopens Chapter 7 case. The court found Gleason's testimony to be more credible, resulting from his focus on the valuation of Nesser's 50% noncontrolling interest and the lack of a ready market. The court found the value of Nesser's stock interest to be $10,147 and also found that the feasibility confirmation requirements were not satisfied because success of the plan relied on an unopened pubs income potential. The court concluded by reopening the Chapter 7 case and called for the appointment of a Chapter 7 trustee.

In re Oglesby

Citation: 221 B.R. 515, 1998 Bankr. LEXIS 695
Date of Decision: June 12, 1998
Country: US
State or Federal: Federal
State/Jurisdiction: Colorado
Court: United States Bankruptcy Court
Type of action: Bankruptcy
Judge: Brooks
Key words: Bankruptcy, Interest rate

Bankruptcy Reorganization Uses Market Rates of Interest

The common issue in these two cases is setting appropriate interest rates to establish present value in "cram-down" situations. In "cram-down" situations, the bankruptcy court, in effect, forces the creditor to accept a new loan for the property rather than allowing the creditor to repossess the secured property.

Debtors propose 9% rate. Louis and Pamela Oglesby filed a Voluntary Petition under Chapter 13 of the bankruptcy code on Nov. 24, 1997. Michael and Nicole Jones filed a Voluntary Petition for bankruptcy on Dec. 2, 1997. In both cases, the debtors' Chapter 13 Plan proposed to provide a 9% interest rate on the balances due the creditors on automobiles in the debtors' possession.

Both creditors maintain that a 9% rate is inadequate to provide them with an amount equal to the present value of their claims as required by 11 U.S.C. 1325(a)(5). Both creditors argued the appropriate capitalization rate should be based on the rate of interest they currently charge for similar loans in the region. According to the creditors, the appropriate rate should be 20.19% in one case and 21% in the other.

Court says market rates apply. The court determined that any analysis of this issue necessarily begins with the 10th Circuit opinion *In re Hardzog*, 901F.2d 858 (10th Cir. 1990). The 10th Circuit held that, "in the absence of special circumstances, such as the market rate being higher than the contract rate, bankruptcy courts should use the current market rate of interest used for similar loans in the region."

The debtors argue that the "current market rate of interest" should be some variation on the "prime lending rate" or "prevailing market rate" as reflected, for example, in *The Wall Street Journal*. The creditors in these cases argued that the correct interpretation of "current market rate of interest," as used in *Hardzog*, means the rate charged by the particular or objecting creditor for similar loans in the region in the recent past.

Citing *Hardzog*, the court determined that "similar" loans means a loan that the creditor regularly extends to other borrowers who are not in bankruptcy but who are otherwise similarly situated to the debtor. Thus, the court ordered that the appropriate rate for the claim of Community Credit Co. in the Oglesby case shall be 20.1%, and the appropriate rate in the case of Jones should be 21%.

Decision consistent with prior cases. This conclusion is consistent with previous rulings in many other cases, such as *Rankin v. DeSarno*, *General Motors Acceptance Corp. v. Alphonso Jones*, and *Green Tree Financial Servicing Corporation v. Ruben R. Smithwick, Jr.*, all discussed in Chapter 19, "Cost of Capital in the Courts," in *Cost of Capital—Estimation and Applications* by Shannon Pratt.

Joseph D. Olsen, Trustee of Huntley Ready Mix, Inc. v. Gary A. Floit

Citation: No. 00-1107 (7th Cir. 2000)
Date of decision: July 14, 2000
Country: US
State or Federal: Federal
State/Jurisdiction: 7th Circuit
Court: United States Court of Appeals
Type of action: Bankruptcy
Judge: Easterbrok
SIC: 3272 Concrete Products, Except Block and Brick (concrete products, except dry mix concrete and pipe)

Value of Noncompete Agreement Considered in Bankruptcy Case

The U.S. Court of Appeals for the 7th Circuit considered whether Floit breached his fiduciary duty to Huntley Ready Mix (Huntley) when he sold the corporation. Floit was the sole owner of Huntley, a company with aging equipment and an outdated plant. In 1993, Floit sold Huntley to Harvard Ready Mix for $151,000 plus a three-year employment contract and a five-year noncompete agreement, payable at $50,000 per year. The $151,000 was used to repay the Huntley's debt, which was personally guaranteed by Floit. Fifteen months later, Huntley entered bankruptcy. Since the 12-month time limit for recovery under 11 U.S.C. sec. 548(a)(1)(B)(i) expired, the trustee sought to recover the amount paid for the noncompete agreement under state corporate law, on the theory that Floit breached his fiduciary duty as a director of Huntley by obtaining too little for the company.

Both parties presented expert testimony on the value of the company and the noncompete agreement before the bankruptcy court. The trustee's expert valued the business as a going concern using a discounted cash flow method. In his valuation, this expert assumed that Floit would remain with the company. He concluded that the company had a value between $380,000 and $410,000. Floit's expert valued the business, inclusive of Floit's services, at $440,000. However, he opined that the majority of the value was due to Floit's services, and that Huntley's assets were worth $151,000 or less.

To bolster this opinion, Floit presented evidence of the value of the noncompete agreement. This evidence included the amount allocated to the noncompete in the 1996 sale of Harvard. In that sale, the remaining two years of the noncompete agreement were valued at $200,000. The trustee also presented evidence of the value of a noncompete agreement in the cement industry. He determined that "a covenant not to compete in the cement business should be valued at between 0.7 and 1.5 times the promisor's annual earnings." Thus, he concluded that the noncompete agreement was worth $93,000, based on Floit's $63,000 annual salary from Huntley. However, this expert also indicated that one company had executed a noncompete agreement for 16% of the company's annual sales. Using this method, the noncompete agreement was worth $240,000. Based on this evidence, the bankruptcy court concluded that Floit had not breached his fiduciary duty and negotiated a price that was fair to the company. The trustee appealed.

The 7th Circuit affirmed the bankruptcy court's decision. It began by noting that "[v]aluation of closely held businesses is something of a black art," which relies on the assumptions the valuators make. It further indicated that the opposing experts relied on opposite assumptions: The trustee's expert assumed that Huntley's future operations would be similar to its past operations, while Floit's expert assumed that the cost to renovate Huntley "decrepit" plant could not be justified.

It then considered the discretionary income generated by Huntley and available to Floit. The appellate court found that Huntley's average annual discretionary income was $115,000 with a high of $166,000 in 1992. It then noted that this was precisely the amount Harvard was willing to pay Floit ($65,000 in salary plus $50,00 for the noncompete agreement). It stated, "Viewed this way, the numbers imply that Huntley didn't have much if any value beyond its physical assets; its net cash flow was needed to retain Floit's services."

It then considered the experts' opinions. While the Trustee argued that its expert had more experience and better credentials than Floit's expert, the 7th Circuit found various problems with the opinion of the Trustee's expert, stating:

> The trustee's expert did not do all that would be expected of a specialist in valuing closely held firms. Why leap to a discounted cash flow analysis when other methods are available? Most trade associations maintain records of sale prices for firms in the business. What multiple of free cash flow did other small cement ready-mix producers sell for?

The appellate court went on to note that Floit and Huntley had not executed a noncompete agreement, and, therefore, Floit owned his human capital and could leave at will. Thus, the court reasoned, "It would have been especially interesting to know the answer to this question for sales following the departure (or death) of the founding entrepreneur." The court noted further, "A solid demonstration that Huntley was worth more than $150,000 even if Floit was planning to leave would have gone a long way toward establishing that the bankruptcy judge made a clear error." The appellate court then affirmed the trial court's decision in favor of Floit because "the trustee's position depends on allocating the value of Floit's human capital to Huntley, and we do not think that the bankruptcy judge committed clear error in ruling otherwise."

In re Oneida Ltd.

Citation: 2006 Bankr. LEXIS 1985
Date of Decision: August 30, 2006
Country: US
State or Federal: Federal
State/Jurisdiction: New York
Court: United States Bankruptcy Court
Type of action: Bankruptcy
Experts: Credit Suisse (Debtors), Alvarez & Marsal (Lenders) Imperial Capital, LLC (Equity Committee) Mesirow Financial Consulting, LLC (rebuttal)
Judge: Gropper
SIC: 3914 Silverware, Plated Ware, and Stainless Steel Ware (cutlery and flatware, nonprecious and precious plated)

Discovered Emails Plus a Contingent Fee Discredit Appraiser's DCF Analysis

"Oneida is on the move," according to an online statement of its president (at www.oneida.com). Indeed, after seeking Chapter 11 bankruptcy protection in March 2006—and filing its reorganization plan on the same day—the international flatware company received confirmation of its plan in less than six months and is already moving forward with plans of "global expansion."

The company also avoided a potential roadblock: An ad hoc committee of equity security holders had intervened in the bankruptcy case, arguing that Oneida was solvent. They objected to the plan—which the company had negotiated with its secured lenders prior to filing and which would convert a large portion of secured debt into 100% of the outstanding common stock of the reorganized company.

Although the standard was high, the court approved the special Equity Committee, not because it found any bad faith, but because it wanted to dispel "any implication" that the lenders had taken control of the company to "neutralize" the unsecured creditors and take the value of the remaining equity.

Approval turns on four valuation reports. The Bankruptcy Court received four expert valuations of the Debtors (Oneida and its related companies and subsidiaries), all from investment bankers:

- *Debtors.* Credit Suisse concluded a total enterprise value of $190 million to $230 million, with a midpoint value of $210 million.
- *Secured lenders.* Alvarez & Marsal, the lender's financial advisors, concluded a total enterprise value ranging from $190 million to $225 million, with a $207 million midpoint.
- *Equity Committee.* Imperial Capital LLC (Beverly Hills) presented a total enterprise value of $260 million to $330 million, with a $295 million midpoint value.
- *Creditor's committee.* Mesirow Financial Consulting LLC (Chicago) critiqued the three reports, adjusting each total enterprise value for alleged errors in math and methodologies.

The first three valuations relied on a discounted cash flow (DCF) analysis, agreeing that it was the most "probative." The experts also started with the company's "aggressive" but optimistic financials, applying a weighted average cost of capital (WACC) to arrive at a discount rate; they agreed that WACC depended on an appropriate projection of debt and equity costs as well as the split between the two. All of the experts used substantially the same cost of equity (19.9% to 20.5%), acknowledging that the cost of debt would be much lower.

Equity Committee goes much lower. Where the experts diverged was on the cost and apportionment of debt: While the other experts used the interest rate that would be charged on the debtors' actual exit financing (12% to 13%), only the Equity Committee's expert used the cost of debt for comparable companies, arriving at a 7.9% rate. He cited "several valuation texts" in support, and, while the court agreed that the (unnamed) authority existed, it found the expert's selection of comparables "problematic at best."

> For example, [he] used debt issued by Lifetime Brands, Inc. at a 4% interest rate, despite ... that this was convertible debt, which has both an equity and a debt component that have different pricing points. [He] merely took "the face value of the coupon." The most nearly comparable company, Libbey, Inc., had a recent debt financing with a cost of debt at around 14%. Use of Lifetime convertible debt skewed the results of the ... analysis.

In addition, the court found "little support" for the expert's use of a 60/40 debt to equity split in the WACC, compared to the 40/60 split that the debtors' and lenders' experts had used and the 70/30 split the rebuttal expert recommended. "It is pure speculation ... that these debtors will be able to borrow so much at such low rates in the near-term future," the court said, as was the expert's assumption that they'd secure a "B" bond rating. The Equity Committee argued that using the cost of debt and the debt-to-equity ratings of comparable companies removes "the stigma of bankruptcy" as well as the nonrecurring nature of restructuring—but it apparently failed to present any supporting evidence. "There is no reason to believe that the cost of the Credit Suisse exit facility is an unfair indicator of the cost of debt of the Reorganized Debtor," the court found, "for a reasonable time going forward."

Finally, the Equity Committee's expert made two other "dubious" adjustments to the debtors' already aggressive projections: He assumed that they could stretch out the payment terms on their overseas debt; and he speculated that the cost of nickel would decrease over time. In light of all the evidence, the court found the DCF analysis by the lenders and the debtors to be more reliable.

Never-before used normalizations. For the comparable company and "precedent transaction" analyses, all three experts used, for the most part, the same companies and transactions as comparables and agreed on the same basic methodology. However, only the Equity Committee expert normalized the debtor's revenues and EBITDA by reaching backward and forward five years. His reasoning: The company had underperformed in past years and also projected substantial growth into the future.

On cross-examination, however, he admitted that he had "never before used a normalization analysis in a published valuation report." Moreover, he had relied on a 1920 U.S. Treasury publication regarding the intangible value of goodwill lost by breweries during Prohibition. And though the

Equity Committee presented additional authority for the appropriateness of replacing current with "normalized" earnings for a restructuring company, its expert had reached back to years when the debtors generated revenue from business segments that had since closed, adding nearly $8 million to EBITDA and $34 million in revenue, which the court also found unreliable.

Conflicting testimony, emails, and interest. In presenting its case for appointment, the Equity Committee had used the same expert to opine on the debtors' solvency—and, at the time, approximately two months after the bankruptcy filing, the expert had used the actual cost of the debtors' exit facility in his analysis (despite later testifying that valuation texts discredited this approach).

Worse, in an email to an associate around the time of the final valuation, the expert had admitted: "We are using the cost of debt of the comps vs. [Credit Suisse] and Alvarez using the cost of borrowing. What is our rationale? Do we have academic support for this? I testified previously that the cost should approximate the cost of the entire facility."

But the final blow was the expert's acceptance of a contingency fee—after he had "emphatically" told the Bankruptcy Court at the appointment/approval hearing that he "absolutely would not" enter into such an arrangement with the Equity Committee.

"Nevertheless, he entered into exactly such an arrangement," having accepted in addition to a monthly advisory fee, a "success fee" of 1% of any equity recovery. "This contingent fee and the circumstances surrounding it," the court concluded, "seriously undermine [the expert's] credibility."

Paloian v. LaSalle Bank

Citation: 2010 WL 3363596 (C.A.7 (Ill.))
Date of Decision: Aug. 27, 2010
Country: US
State or Federal: Federal
State/Jurisdiction: Federal Circuit
Court: United States Court of Appeals
Type of action: Bankruptcy
Experts: None
Judge: Easterbrook
SIC: 8062 General Medical and Surgical Hospitals

DCF, Including Tax Affecting and Discounts, May Not Apply to Insolvency Opinions

The saga of the financially destitute (and fraud-ridden) Doctor's Hospital in Chicago takes yet another spin. In an opinion by Judge Frank Easterbrook, a former University of Chicago law professor who is "widely respected for his creative applications of economic theory to legal issues,"[6] the U.S. Court of Appeals for the 7th Circuit adjudged two "first impression" issues for the federal

6 BVR's *Comprehensive Guide to Lost Profits Damages, for Experts and Attorneys*, 2010 edition, Chapter 15B ("Discounting Damages: *Case Law*"), by Professor Robert M. Lloyd (University of Tennessee); available at BVResources.com.

circuits. One concerned the use of a discounted cash flow (DCF) analysis in forming insolvency opinions, and the other considered whether to permit fraudulent conveyance claims against banks that merely hold securitized assets.

Court records are encyclopedic. Doctors Hospital of Hyde Park first filed for Chapter 11 relief in 2000. Several years and multiple adversary proceedings later, the bankruptcy court concluded the hospital was insolvent no later than August 1997. (See *In re Doctors Hospital of Hyde Park, Inc.*, 2007 Bankr. App. LEXIS 605.) Based on this finding, the court avoided two loans to the hospital and its owner-controlled affiliates: a $25 million line of credit, in which the lender took a security interest in the hospital's current and future accounts receivable, and a $50 million loan, collateralized in part by an interest in the hospital's rent payments. Shortly after funding, this second loan was securitized (along with billions of dollars of commercial credit) and transferred to a trust overseen by LaSalle National Bank. (The first named party in these proceedings, Gus Paloian, is trustee for the debtor.)

The parties appealed, and, in *LaSalle Nat'l Bank. v. Paloian*, 2009 WL 721510 (N.D. Ill.), the federal district court upheld the insolvency findings based in large part on three valuations by the trustee's experts. In particular, the court confirmed the bankruptcy judge's adoption of a "fair market balance sheet" test (essentially a DCF analysis) that viewed the hospital as a going concern by capitalizing its normalized cash flows. The court also found that the trustee's experts had appropriately reduced the hospital's earnings by its fraudulent Medicaid and Medicare overpayments. (The hospital was under federal investigation in 1997, at the time of the loans, but the government didn't charge it—for $18.5 million—until 1999-2000). Even the bank's experts believed "some" reduction in cash flow was warranted based on known future liability for the hospital's fraud, and thus the DCF value was not driven by improper hindsight bias, the district court ruled.

The court also approved a combined 40% tax-affecting discount applied by the trustee's experts, based on their opinions (substantiated by valuation literature) that it was "standard" practice to do so when valuing a controlling interest in an S corporation. Although it criticized the bankruptcy court for its broad finding that the "object of an insolvency analysis is to determine the value of [the hospital] to a theoretical buyer," the district court nevertheless found the dispositive factor in tax affecting the hospital, an S corporation, was the 100% ownership interest at stake. It also confirmed the 10% company-specific risk premium applied in the experts' DCF as "reasonable" and even "conservative" under the circumstances that plagued the hospital prior to bankruptcy.

The appeal to the 7th Circuit presented more than 20 issues; the appellate briefs approached 300 pages, and the bankruptcy and district court opinions were "thick enough to outweigh a dictionary," Judge Easterbrook noted. Fortunately, the parties resolved most of the issues, he said, making it "unnecessary to traipse through them again." That left three primary questions for his consideration.

Lender claims it is not an 'initial transferee.' In its appeal to the 7th Circuit, LaSalle Bank argued that, as trustee for the securitized pool of assets, it was "merely a conduit" for the loan proceeds and was not an initial transferee of the funds for purposes of Sec. 505(a)(1) of the Bankruptcy Code (concerning preferential transfers). The Bankruptcy Code does not define "initial transferee," Judge Easterbrook noted, and no appellate decision has yet considered whether a trustee of a securitized investment qualifies as one. The leading case in the 7th Circuit adopts an approach that tracks the bankruptcy trustee's ability to recoup money from the "real" recipients of the alleged preferences, Judge Easterbrook explained.

Applying that approach to this case, if the bank were to be found liable for an avoided transfer, it would reach into the trust assets and not its own to pay the assessment. "This means that the money really comes from the trust's investors—the persons 'for whose benefit the transfer was made,'" Judge Easterbrook said, quoting the 7th Circuit precedent. Rather than require the trustee to sue thousands of investors who may have received interest payments that were, even in slight measure, enhanced by funds from the hospital's coffers, "a single suit suffices." If the hospital had made a preferential transfer to Exxon, the trustee would sue the corporation, not its millions of stockholders. "Similarly with a preferential transfer to a hedge fund," the judge observed, in finding the bank an initial transferee.

Having dispatched the first issue (which may have broad implications for a securities pool trustee with a depleted or nonexistent corpus, forced to rely on its own funds or sue investors for reimbursement), the court turned to the valuation issue. Until it filed bankruptcy in 2000, the hospital had stayed current in payments to creditors and had consistently posted positive EBITDA. "Yet the bankruptcy judge concluded that it had been insolvent for almost three years," Judge Easterbrook observed. "How was that possible?" Even subtracting $18.5 million, the amount that federal audits later charged the hospital for fraudulent overpayments, was not enough to turn the hospital's "bottom line red," he added:

> What did the trick was lopping off the portion of the Hospital's assets that represented the present value of future income. The rationale for this adjustment was that the Hospital was a Subchapter S corporation that did not pay taxes, and a taxable buyer would reduce the purchase price in recognition … that its profits must be shared with state and federal treasuries.
> In this appeal, the bank didn't resurrect its hindsight arguments so much as claim that the bankruptcy court erred by applying the actual value of federal overpayments ($18.5 million) in 2000 rather than their expected value as of 1997. The trustee claimed the bank forfeited this argument on appeal, because it had neglected to raise it at trial. But Judge Easterbrook saw "an even more glaring error," obviating the need to consider "the right way" to value contingent liabilities. "Contingent liabilities must be matched against contingent assets," he said.

In fact, the missing matching asset was the wealth of the doctor who bought the hospital back in 1992 (and who was also held accountable for its fraud). As it happened, the doctor paid the entire $18.5 million of the hospital's federal liability in or around 2000. The trustee claimed this was not foreseeable, resurrecting the hindsight argument, but the judge disagreed. The doctor's substantial personal wealth was not "pie in the sky." If the doctor had executed a note in the hospital's favor, a court would not ignore it as an asset but would simply discount the note to reflect the probability that it might not be paid. Yet, in this case, the bankruptcy court essentially valued the contingent assets at zero cents on the dollar but valued contingent liabilities at 100 cents on the dollar.

"The treatment must be symmetrical," Judge Easterbrook reasoned. "So too with hindsight: If a court uses hindsight to value the liability at $18.5 million, it must … [also] value [the doctor's contribution] at $18.5 million, for a net zero effect on the Hospital's balance sheet."

"The 40% reduction was likewise a mistake," the judge held. The discount is based in part on the illiquidity of the hospital's shares and its status as a nontaxable S corporation compared to that of a potential buyer. "Neither of these had anything to do with a corporation's solvency," the judge declared. "They concern the market value of its securities, not the state of its balance sheet," he added (citing *Gross v. Comm'r*, 272 F.3d 333 (6th Cir. 2001)).

"Take tax effects," the Judge continued. An S corporation does not pay taxes; some potential buyers do. "But how much a buyer will pay for a revenue stream does not tell us whether a firm is insolvent, except indirectly: If a buyer will pay a positive price for the firm's stock, then it is very likely to be solvent." However, even bankrupt firms will sell for a small price, the Judge noted, reflecting a buyer's belief in the firm's turnaround potential. Moreover, income tax questions arise only when a firm is profitable, i.e., has reportable net income. "So whether an outsider would have paid $50 million or $40 million (a 40% discount) for all stock in the Hospital, *either* price implies that the Hospital's assets are worth more than its liabilities," Judge Easterbrook emphasized. Finally, most prospective buyers for a hospital would be nonprofit (and nontaxable) organizations, which would not reduce their bids to account for taxes.

The judge had much the same to say about discounts. When shares of a closely held company (or other restricted asset) are appraised for purposes of estate and gift tax assessments, for example, the ultimate value is typically discounted from fair market value. But when the judge asked counsel for both parties to cite one decision, from any court, that applied either a liquidity discount or a tax-effect discount to the asset side of a corporation's balance sheet for the purpose of determining solvency, neither side could find one. "Our own research did not turn one up," the judge said. Accordingly, he found the hospital solvent as of 1997 and reversed the bankruptcy court's avoidance of the loan transfers as fraudulent conveyances.

Trustee still has a chance. At the same time, the judge remanded the case for the bankruptcy court to determine whether the hospital was insolvent at any time after 1997, up to and through its filing in 2000. If so, the trustee may still be able to recapture any loan transfers made during that time. To assist this finding, the judge considered the last issue on appeal, whether—by constructing the loans to go through the hospital's affiliate as "bankruptcy-remote vehicles"—the lenders had succeeded in preserving the securitized assets from the reach of the preferential transfer provisions.

"To make the idea work, the separate entity must be, well, separate," Judge Easterbrook said. In this case, there was "scarcely any evidence in the record" that the hospital's wholly owned affiliate had any independent corporate identity, except the name that the lawyers for the hospital (and its nefarious doctor-owner) gave it. If the lenders weren't aware that the affiliates were a corporate shell, they could have "easily" found out. Perhaps on remand, the bank could offer some evidence that a bona fide sale took place and the hospital's affiliate was "more than a name without a business entity to go with it," Judge Easterbrook held, but, as a first matter, the bankruptcy court should determine whether the hospital was insolvent at any time prior to filing. "Unless it was, nothing else matters," the judge said, and sent the case back for reconsideration.

In re Parnes

Citation: 200 B.R. 710, 1996 Bankr. LEXIS 1159
Date of Decision: July 5, 1996
Country: US
State or Federal: Federal
State/Jurisdiction: Georgia
Court: United States Bankruptcy Court
Type of action: Bankruptcy
Experts: Earl Douglas (for Parnes)
Judge: Bihary
SIC: 8021 Offices and Clinics of Dentists
Key words: Bankruptcy

Ex-Wife, Creditors Allege Husband Knew Dental Practices Had Substantial Value When He Filed Bankruptcy

In bankruptcy proceedings, debtor listed "unknown" as the value of his dental practices. Ex-wife and MBNA America, a credit card company, object and argue that debtor knew the practices had substantial value when he filed bankruptcy because he previously valued the practices both in divorce proceedings and on financial statements submitted to lenders. Debtor responds by stating he previously valued the practices as if he and his partner, his father, were willingly selling the practices as a whole with covenants not to compete. Court accepted debtor's reasoning (supported by expert testimony by Earl Douglas) that valuing his half interest in the practices on a forced sale basis without a covenant not to compete would seriously impact value. Judgment in favor of debtor.

In re Pegasus Agency, Inc.

Date of Decision: December 5, 1996
Country: US
State or Federal: Federal
State/Jurisdiction: 2nd Circuit
Court: United States Court of Appeals
Type of action: Bankruptcy

Proper Due Diligence Required for Reorganization Plan Confirmation

The U.S. Court of Appeals for the 2nd Circuit considered the reasonable prospect of the success of a Chapter 11 reorganization plan. The debtor, Pegasus Agency Inc., is a New York City corporation engaged in the business of holding real estate, and its plan called for the subdivision of its one asset, a six-acre beachfront property, into residential lots and constructing 3,000-square-foot homes on those lots. The district court vacated the bankruptcy court's lift of the automatic stay and remanded for valuation and possible bifurcation of Pegasus's debt. This appeal followed.

The appellate court reviewed the plan in accordance with *Timbers of Inwood Forest Assocs.*, 484 U.S. 365, 375-376 (1988), to determine whether the property was necessary to the reorganization and for the "reasonable possibility of a successful reorganization within a reasonable time." The appellate court found that the plan was based on improper assumptions and "shot in the dark" calculations because it assumed that site improvement costs and the sale price of the homes would remain the same whether the property was divided into eight or 18 lots. Furthermore, the only hard documentation submitted to the court was an appraisal report that estimated the return from a sale of the property as eight unimproved lots. The appellate court agreed with the bankruptcy court's assessment that "there is no evidence that [anyone] performed the kind of research, analysis and projections, generally referred to as due diligence, required to make any reliable assessment of the financial feasibility of any plan to develop the property." *In re Pegasus*, 186 B.R. 597. The court reversed the district court decision to reinstate the automatic stay because the plan did not offer the reasonable possibility of success.

Peltz v. Hatten

Citation: 279 B.R. 710, 2002 U.S. Dist. LEXIS 10282
Date of Decision: June 5, 2002
Country: US
State or Federal: Federal
State/Jurisdiction: Delaware
Court: United States District Court
Type of action: Bankruptcy
Experts: Patrick Landry (for debtor)
Colin Blaydon, Sharon Armbrust, Robert Ott (for trustee) Keith Mallinson (for Hatten)
Judge: McKelvie
SIC: 4813 Telephone Communications, Except Radiotelephone
(resellers)
Key words: Bankruptcy, Discount rate, Discounted cash flow method (DCF), Fraudulent transfer, Growth rate, Income approach, Market approach

Bankruptcy Court Indicates Strong Preference for Market Approach, Price Per Subscriber Multiple

This trial court matter involves an adversarial proceeding in bankruptcy in which the liquidating trustee asserts that USN Communications Inc.'s (the debtor) purchase of Connecticut Telephone and Connecticut Mobilecom (CT Tel) stock from the Hatten sellers for $68 million was a fraudulent transfer. The primary issue was whether the debtor received "reasonably equivalent value" for the $68 million it transferred to the Hatten sellers. In other words, was the CT Tel stock worth $68 million at the time of the transfer?

Valuation evidence. The trustee offered the expert testimony of Colin Blaydon, Sharon Armbrust, and Robert Ott in support of his claim that CT Tel was worth significantly less than $68 million.

Blaydon, the trustee's primary witness, testified that CT Tel was worth $43.4 million based upon a three-year discounted cash flow analysis using a 15.9% discount rate. Blaydon used two market approach methods to corroborate his DCF valuation—price to sales and price to subscriber—as well as a cost approach. In his market approach, he included comparable transactions that consisted of asset purchases rather than sales of whole companies.

Armbrust, the trustee's first rebuttal witness, testified that CT Tel was worth $39 million to $40 million. Her valuation was based on a 10-year DCF analysis using a 16.71% discount rate. She testified that her growth rate and discount rate indicated a less optimistic view of the growth of the cellular industry than the parties had considered in their negotiations. Armbrust also used market approach methods to corroborate her valuation, using one whole company transaction and three asset purchases, and determined that a valuation as high as $47.7 million was possible.

Ott, the trustee's second rebuttal witness, testified that CT Tel was worth $38 million. Ott criticized the valuations by the parties to the transaction and by the Hatten seller's expert because they used only the market approach and because within that approach they used only the price per subscriber index. Ott used the EBITDA multiple method and a multiple of revenues method in his valuation, resulting in a much lower valuation conclusion. Ott also completed his own DCF analysis.

The Hatten sellers presented the expert testimony of Keith Mallinson, who opined that the $68 million price paid for CT Tel was fair. He based his valuation on the market approach, using four comparable transactions of whole companies, and comparing the price per subscriber of each transaction to the CT Tel transaction. He also testified that CT Tel's superior financial condition made the company "a very high quality cellular reseller" and that numerous synergies made the company particularly valuable to the debtor. Both of these factors indicated that the price per subscriber would be higher for CT Tel than for the comparable transactions.

Mallinson rejected an asset-based approach because it was not appropriate for a going concern such as CT Tel that was in a great position for growth and expansion. He also criticized the discounted cash flow valuations of the liquidating trustee's experts.

He noted that, while DCF is a widely used technique that can be a good tool when it's used objectively and with impartiality, he had two concerns over its use by the liquidating trustee. First, he stated that a DCF analysis is not necessarily determinative of what a fair price would be for a firm because fair market value is often dictated by marketplace factors apart from pure stand-alone valuation. He noted that CT Tel—a proven solid player at the top end of the resale market and with bundling and expansion—was becoming an increasingly scarce entity that could command a high price on the market. Second, he noted that DCF analyses can yield wildly different valuations depending on the modeler's perspective and assumptions. He disagreed that Blaydon's application of the DCF analysis in an adversarial setting fairly valued CT Tel.

Trial court findings. The trial court noted that "reasonably equivalent value" must be determined objectively from the perspective of the parties to the transaction and that significant deference would be given to marketplace values.

The court accepted the testimony of Mallinson (and implicitly the valuations of the parties) as the most reasonable because it was based on comparable sales close in time to the sale of CT Tel. The court also noted that the price per subscriber was the accepted measure of value in the industry and so was most reasonable for Mallinson and the parties to use.

The court also criticized the DCF valuations performed by Blaydon. First, Blaydon's DCF study was based upon three-year projections that CT Tel had prepared in April 1997 in connection with its recapitalization at that time. These projections, however, were outdated by late fall 1997 and early 1998 and do not accurately value CT Tel on a DCF basis as of Feb. 20, 1998. By that time, CT Tel was well ahead of the new store pace assumed in the April 1997 projections and was planning the addition of many more new stores, mostly out of market, to fuel its growth. Also, the April 1997 projections contained no forecast for local or Internet services, as the systems for such services were not yet proven or in place. Last, in April 1997, CT Tel could not and did not undertake to estimate the growth that could be expected from the fully bundled product that CT Tel began to promote in January 1998. Second, Blaydon chose the prior five-year average of 8.5% for the telecommunications industry for his growth rate. This rate, however, has no necessary relationship to the then-forecasted growth for the cellular resale industry in general or the near-term anticipated growth rate of CT Tel in particular. The effect of Blaydon's choice of growth rate was to reduce the valuation of CT Tel, since high near-term growth contributes significantly to value. Third, Blaydon's choice of a 15.9% discount rate was higher than the discount rate of 15% that was used by both USN and the underwriters at the time of the transaction. Blaydon then added a subjective firm risk factor of 1.5%, yet cited no evidence that an objective assessor of value would feel compelled to so enhance the discount rate for an established company such as CT Tel with sound business fundamentals and a 10-year operating history. The effect of increasing the discount rate is to reduce the present valuation of CT Tel. Last, Blaydon also excluded any incremental or synergistic value in his model, even though CT Tel had such value to any acquirer in the marketplace and USN affirmatively considered such values in the CT Tel acquisition.

The trial court held that $68 million was reasonably equivalent value for the CT Tel stock and that the trustee failed to prove his fraudulent transfer claim.

Pension Benefits Guaranty Corp. v. CF&I Fabricators (In re: CF&I Fabricators)

Citation: 150 F.3d 1293, 1998 U.S. App. LEXIS 17697
Date of decision: August 3, 1998
Country: US
State or Federal: Federal
State/Jurisdiction: 10th Circuit
Court: United States Court of Appeals
Type of action: Bankruptcy
Judge: Porfilio
SIC: 3325 Steel Foundries, NEC
Key words: Bankruptcy, ERISA, Prudent-investor discount, Unfunded Benefit Liabilities

Prudent Investor Method Used to Value Unfunded Pension Benefits Claim

Pension Benefit Guaranty Corp. v. CF&I Fabricators of Utah, Inc. (*In re: CF&I Fabricators of Utah, Inc.*) required the U.S. Court of Appeals for the 10th Circuit to determine the proper valuation method to calculate the present value of the unfunded benefit liabilities a Chapter 11 debtor owed. The appellant, Pension Benefit Guarantee Corp. (PBGC), was a private governmental corporation that was charged statutorily with protecting and preserving private pension plans. CF&I, the debtor, established a pension plan subject to the termination provisions of Title IV of ERISA prior to declaring Chapter 11 bankruptcy. Whereas initiating such a plan is voluntary, once the employer introduces it, it must meet minimum funding requirements set forth by the Internal Revenue Code and ERISA. It must do so until the employer itself terminates the plan or PBGC does so. After petitioning for bankruptcy, CF&I continued operations as a debtor-in-possession. It did not contribute to the pension plan but also did not voluntarily terminate it. When the estate's assets dwindled, PBGC stepped in to terminate the plan and, as its statutory trustee, filed a claim for unfunded benefit liabilities accruing due to the lack of assets in the plan. The parties differed over how to value the claim. Under PBGC's approach, it would be worth nearly $223 million; under CF&I's approach, it valued approximately $124.4 million.

The Bankruptcy Court held that PBGC's unfunded benefits claim must be reduced to present value and should be valued in accordance with PBGC's regulatory system (ERISA) and not following the standards of the Bankruptcy Code.

The district court reversed this part of the Bankruptcy Court's holding. It found an "inexorable conflict between ERISA and the Bankruptcy Code and decided the latter trumped the former. It said: "[T]he actuarian present value of guaranteed benefits in a reorganization context [must be] determined according to bankruptcy law." On remand, the Bankruptcy Court used the "prudential investor" valuation method and allowed PBGC a general unsecured claim in the amount of $124.4 million as the present value of CF&I's unfunded benefit plan future liabilities.

PBGC subsequently appealed to the 10th Circuit contesting the valuation. The appeals court affirmed the district court's approach. It noted that, to the extent the "liabilities are for beneficiaries' payments that extend into the future, the amount of the liability must be reduced to present value so the debt can be dealt with under the reorganization plan." The ERISA provisions on which

PBCG built its calculation conflicted with the Bankruptcy Code; Congress, the appeals court said, established "precise contours of how claims that are administered in Chapter 11 are to be decided, and has pronounced as a cardinal rule that all claims within the same class must be treated alike." To allow one discount rate for PBGC claims but not any other unsecured creditor would violate that rule. "Congress has made clear when ERISA conflicts with another provision of federal law, ERISA must be subordinated," the Court of Appeals added. Consequently, it concluded that the district court did not err in using the prudent-investor discount in computing the present value of PBGC's claim.

Pereira v. Dow Chem. Co. (In re Trace Int'l Holdings, Inc.)

Citation: 2003 Bankr. LEXIS 1619
Date of Decision: December 10, 2003
Country: US
State/Jurisdiction: New York
Court: United States Bankruptcy Court
Type of action: Bankruptcy
Experts: Thomas M. Blake (for trustee)
Judge: Bernstein
SIC: 6719 Offices of Holding Companies, NEC
Key words: Bankruptcy, Solvency opinion, Dividends

Inconsistent Legal Theory and Valuation Methods Cost Trustee Fraudulent Transfer

The issue in this bankruptcy adversary proceeding is whether certain payments made by the debtor shortly before the filing of the petition were fraudulent transfers recoverable by the trustee for the benefit of all the creditors.

Dow Chemical Co. bought preferred stock from Trace International Holdings Inc. in 1992. Trace was obligated by contract to pay dividends when lawfully able to do so and, if it redeemed the stock, to pay accrued dividends at that time. Trace paid dividends to Dow totaling $3,575,150 between 1995 and the petition date in 1999. The trustee sought to recover those payments as fraudulent transfers, claiming that the payments were made by Trace when it was insolvent.

Valuation evidence. The trustee's expert, Thomas Blake, relied on two methods to show insolvency. Under the fair market balance sheet method, he characterized the dividend obligation as a cash obligation and treated it like Trace's other liabilities. He concluded that Trace was insolvent at "various points in time" from 1995 through 1998.

Using the cash flow and capital adequacy method, Blake treated Trace's dividend obligation as a component of cash outflow, just like Trace's corporate and interest expenses. He concluded that Trace was insolvent at all times from 1995 through 1998.

District court findings. With only minor modifications, the district court accepted Blake's insolvency analysis and concluded that Trace was "either insolvent or in the zone or vicinity of insolvency" for the entire period of 1995 through 1999, except for the fourth quarter of 1996. Thus, all dividend payments Trace made to Dow during that period were illegal.

Bankruptcy court holdings. The court began by stating that the payment of an "antecedent debt" satisfies the requirement of fair consideration and reasonably equivalent value and payment of an existing liability is not a fraudulent transfer. Although the court said it could be debated whether Trace paid a debt rather than a dividend to Dow, the trustee was stopped from arguing that it was not a debt, since its expert treated it like all Trace's other liabilities.

Having successfully characterized the dividend obligation as an expense, and hence, a liability, for valuation purposes, he is stuck with that characterization. He cannot argue in this forum that the payment of the dividend obligation did not satisfy an "antecedent debt."

Accordingly, the court held that the payments to Dow were not fraudulent transfers and could not be recovered by the trustee.

In re PieceGoods Shops Co.

Citation: 188 B.R. 778
Date of Decision: October 10, 1995
Country: US
Federal or State: Federal
State/Jurisdiction: Maryland
Court: United States Bankruptcy Court
Type of action: Bankruptcy
Judge: Wolfe

Is Marketability Discount Offset by Possible Sale of Debtor?

At issue was the reasonableness of the equity value determined and whether it met the "best interests" test. That test requires each holder of a claim or interest in an impaired class to accept the debtor's plan or, alternatively, to receive or retain under the plan property having a present value at least equal to what the holder would receive or retain if the debtor were liquidated under Chapter 7 on the effective date of the plan.

The debtor's experts, Richard Holmes and Steven Matt, ASA, both of Arthur Andersen, determined the equity value of the company in question by using a market multiple approach. Both indicated that a control premium of at least 20% would be likely in the event the company were sold. Although Holmes believed that some lack of marketability discount was appropriate, he felt that such a discount was offset because his experience suggested that a secondary market would be created for trading in the new common stock created. He also felt a marketability discount would be offset by a possible sale of the debtor after the effective date. Accordingly, no marketability discount was applied. Although an objecting creditor, through expert witness W. Allen Rogers, presented expert witness testimony on valuation, the court did not find the argument persuasive. The court accepted Holmes' and Matt's equity determination.

In re Premier Entertainment Biloxi LLC

Citation: 2010 WL 3504105 (Bkrtcy. S.D. Miss)
Date of Decision: Sept. 3, 2010
Country: US
State or Federal: Federal
State/Jurisdiction: Federal Circuit
Court: United States Bankruptcy Court
Type of action: Bankruptcy
Experts: Saul Solomon (debtors)
Judge: Olack
SIC: 7011 Hotels and Motels (casino hotels)

Bankruptcy Court Prefers Adjusted Balance Sheet Test, Including FMV of Brand License

In 2002, the debtors began constructing the Hard Rock Hotel and Casino Biloxi, a full-service gaming resort located along 8.5 acres of Mississippi coastline. To underwrite construction, the debtors entered into an indenture agreement by which they pledged over $160 million in first lien mortgage notes secured by the resort's assets and supervised by U.S. Bank as trustee. To protect the noteholders against prepayment, the indenture agreement precluded the debtors from redeeming the notes unless they paid a liquidated damages premium.

To prepare for the resort's grand opening, the debtors procured over $181 million of insurance in August 2005. Just two weeks later, Hurricane Katrina hit, completely destroying the casino and severely damaging the hotel. The debtors eventually recovered the $181 million of insurance proceeds but delivered them to the indenture trustee on behalf of the noteholders. The parties disputed their respective rights to the proceeds, and the debtors ultimately filed for Chapter 11 bankruptcy relief (in 2006) in part because they could not get access to the funds to finish construction.

Confirmation plan contemplates prepayment. Almost immediately after filing their petition (and based on a plan developed during their negotiations with the noteholders for the funds), the debtors proposed to pay the notes at par value plus interest, thereby extinguishing the noteholders' liens and releasing the insurance proceeds. The noteholders opposed the plan because it did not provide for a $10.75 million prepayment penalty pursuant to the indenture agreement. The debtors disputed their right to any liquidated damages but nevertheless agreed to place $10.75 million in escrow.

The court approved the plan in August 2007, releasing the insurance proceeds and permitting the debtors to finish reconstruction. The parties still disputed the liquidated damages claims, with the noteholders arguing their entitlement to the prepayment premium under various provisions of the Bankruptcy Code, including Sec. 505(b), which permits oversecured creditors to recoup any reasonable charges provided by the underlying security agreement, and Sec. 502(b), which allows unsecured creditors to recoup damages from a solvent debtor.

After a lengthy discussion, the court rejected the former argument but upheld the application of Sec. 502(b). In particular, bankruptcy courts will generally enforce a debtor's valid contractual obligations, including liquidated damages provisions, if the debtor was solvent. The debtors insisted they were "equitably" insolvent as of the date of their bankruptcy petition because, without access to the insurance proceeds, they had only $200,000 in cash and over $230 million in outstanding liabilities. More importantly, they were in danger of losing their Hard Rock license and any opportunity to successfully rebuild the resort.

By contrast, the noteholders claimed the debtors were solvent at all times, because, simply put, "their debts never exceeded their assets, notwithstanding any perceived cash flow problems." The debtors had access to more than $40 million in financing from a secondary source, which had already invested over $150 million in rebuilding the resort. After hearing a "wealth of testimony and evidence" from both parties regarding the debtor's financial status, the court ultimately decided the issue came down to which solvency test applied: the debtors' "equitable insolvency" test, derived largely from statutory case law concerning fraudulent transfers, or the adjusted balance sheet test proposed by the noteholders.

Between a rock and a hard place. To show the latter, the noteholders presented a valuation and solvency expert, a CPA/ABV and CVA who had testified numerous times in federal courts. He reviewed the debtors' bankruptcy schedules, which showed nearly $253 million in assets and only $230 million in liabilities. He also examined the financial statements the debtors submitted to secure their secondary financing. Using an asset approach and a cost-based balance sheet prepared according to GAAP, the expert made two notable adjustments to the debtors' asset values to equate them with the Bankruptcy Code's requirement of "fair valuation," which he construed as "fair market value premised on the debtors' going concern status."

First, he changed the value of the Hard Rock license from its book value of just over $472,000, the amount shown in the bankruptcy schedules, to just over $11.7 million, the same amount the debtors assigned to the license in their funding applications and SEC filings. Second, he included the $17.5 million value of construction in progress, which the debtors also reported to their lenders but which they omitted from their cost-basis balance sheet. After making these adjustments, the expert concluded that the debtors' assets exceeded their liabilities by roughly $50 million on the date of the petition. Even on a cost-basis approach, assets exceeded liabilities by over $28 million.

The debtors still maintained they were "in between a rock ... and a hard place" on the date of bankruptcy, having only $200,000 in usable cash and owing hundreds of millions, including $160 million to the noteholders. Several trade vendors had filed lawsuits and liens, and three or more could have filed an involuntary bankruptcy petition. The debtors challenged the adjustments made by the noteholders' expert but did not present an expert of their own and generally held to the "equitable insolvency test."

But that test applied only in limited factual circumstances, the court ruled, and did not apply here. Instead, it found the adjusted balance sheet was "the traditional bankruptcy test of insolvency." The adjustments by the noteholders' expert were appropriate—in particular, his use of the market value of the Hard Rock license, as corroborated by its assigned value in the debtors' public filings and loan documentation. Accordingly, the court found the debtors solvent at all relevant times and awarded the noteholders their unsecured claims for liquidated damages.

In re Prince

Citation: 85 F.3d 314, 1996 U.S. App. LEXIS 13151
Date of Decision: May 31, 1996
Country: US
State or Federal: Federal
State/Jurisdiction: 7th Circuit
Court: United States Court of Appeals
Type of action: Bankruptcy
Judge: Kanne
SIC: 8021 Offices and Clinics of Dentists
Key words: Bankruptcy, Personal goodwill

Personal Goodwill Deemed Corporate Asset in Chapter 11 Bankruptcy Reorganization

Dr. Prince operated his orthodontics practice as a wholly owned professional corporation. He and his wife filed a voluntary petition for bankruptcy reorganization under Chapter 11 on Aug. 17, 1981. The sole issue in this case is whether Dr. Prince's personal goodwill should be included in the calculation of the value of the professional corporation's stock for the purpose of the Chapter 11 reorganization.

The bankruptcy court determined that Dr. Prince's goodwill fell within the personal earnings exception of 11 U.S.C. § 541(a)(6), which excludes the debtor's post-commencement earnings from the bankruptcy estate in a liquidation. The bankruptcy court valued the stock, on the basis of its net physical assets, at $7,500.

District court says no exemption. On appeal, the U.S. District Court (N.D. IL) held that Dr. Prince's goodwill did not fall within the personal earnings exemption and remanded the case, instructing the bankruptcy court to include the worth of Dr. Prince's goodwill in the stock's value.

Practice sold after reorganization. About four months after the bankruptcy reorganization confirmation, Dr. Prince negotiated a sale of his practice. The sale included the stock, a covenant not to compete, and eight months of transitional services, for a total price of $450,000 for the package. However, about four months into the transitional period, the buyer and seller had a falling out, and the actual sale was never consummated.

The district court directed the bankruptcy court to consider the sale agreement an accurate proxy for the worth of the stock and to value the stock by starting with the package purchase price and subtracting the salary and expenses paid to the purchasing doctor and the value of Dr. Prince's services during the transition period. On this basis, the bankruptcy court recalculated the value of Dr. Prince's stock to be $292,290.

Company had no noncompete covenant. The Princes maintain that the stock's value was no more than the $7,500 physical asset value because the corporation did not possess a covenant not to compete.

The court of appeals said, however, "at the time of the confirmation, when Dr. Prince owned the stock himself, there was no need for a covenant not to compete in order to protect Dr. Prince's substantial goodwill, which constituted the lion's share of the stock's value ... the covenant not to compete and Dr. Prince's best efforts did not represent the transfer of extra value ... over and above the value of the stock.... Rather, they were used (as they are in virtually every sale of a medical or dental practice) merely to insure that after the sale the practice would be as valuable in (the buyer's) hands as it had been in Dr. Prince's."

Court defines goodwill. The court of appeals defined goodwill as "an intangible asset that resembles the ability of a company to generate earnings over and above the operating value of the company's other tangible and intangible assets."

The court of appeals concluded, "The value of Dr. Prince's goodwill represents future cash flows not from earnings for future services actually performed by Dr. Prince, but from return on an intangible capital asset that could be sold and transferred with the sale of the practice. The value of Dr. Prince's goodwill is therefore not excluded from the estate by virtue of 541(a)(6), and according to the plan of reorganization it must be paid by the Princes to the creditors fund."

Pryor v. Tiffen (In re TC Liquidations LLC)

Citation: 2011 Bankr. LEXIS 4950
Date of decision: Dec. 6, 2011
Country: US
State or Federal: Federal
State/Jurisdiction: New York
Court: United States Bankruptcy Court
Experts: Michael Goodman (trustee); David Berliner and G. William Kennedy (debtor)
Judge: Eisenberg

Certain Intangibles Only Have Value in Ongoing Business

The Tiffen Manufacturing Corp., a maker of photographic supplies, enjoyed a meteoric rise to success beginning in 1998, when it acquired three companies with distributorship agreements to big-box stores (Walmart, Target, etc.) and also licensed the Kodak brand.

To finance these acquisitions, the company received a $20 million infusion from equity investors in exchange for a 28% interest in a subsidiary. It also received a $7 million bank loan, guaranteed by its three controlling stockholders—all members of the Tiffen family—who served in various executive capacities, their responsibilities (and salaries) increasing as the business expanded. The shareholders also received dividends sufficient to cover their tax obligations in connection with the company, a Subchapter S corporation, as well as their personal obligations under the bank financing.

A catastrophic decline. By 2001, the company began defaulting on its bank obligations. Delayed product shipments from China caused large losses, as did Kodak's decision to pull its license in 2003, after which the company filed for Chapter 11 bankruptcy. On that day, Feb. 28, 2003, the bankruptcy court found that the company was "clearly" insolvent, with $28 million in liabilities but only $18 million in assets. In August 2003, the court approved a sale of substantially all of the debtor's assets to an affiliate (Tiffen Acquisition LLC) for $8.25 million and converted the proceedings from Chapter 11 to Chapter 7, appointing a trustee to oversee the winding down of the remaining assets and claims.

In these proceedings, the trustee attempted to recover the dividends as well as certain salary increases (collectively, the "transfers") issued from 2001 to 2003 that the company had distributed to its controlling shareholders to cover their tax liabilities as well as their loan obligations. To prevail under its fraudulent conveyance claims, the trustee needed to show that: (1) the debtor did not receive "fair consideration" for the transfers; and (2) it was either insolvent or rendered insolvent by the transfers.

As a preliminary matter, the court found that the salary increases, instituted at or around the time of the company's expansion, were warranted based on the shareholders' increasing business responsibilities. Similarly, the court found that the debtor received fair consideration for the dividends distributed to cover the shareholders' obligations under the bank loan.

The tax dividends were another matter, however. The debtor received no consideration for the distributions made to the shareholders to cover their personal tax liabilities related to the business, the court held. Given this finding (the first step in proving fraudulent conveyance), the court turned to whether and when the debtor was insolvent or rendered insolvent by the distributions.

Intangibles worth over $23 million? To prove that the company was solvent at the time of the dividend distributions, the defendants (the individual shareholders) produced an insolvency expert, whose analysis included valuing the company's goodwill during the appropriate time period (2001-2002) at roughly $11.6 million to $12.5 million. The defendants also retained an intangible asset appraisal by a business valuation expert, who valued the company's patents, unpatented know-how, trademarks, customer relationships, and licensing agreements at just over $23.4 million.

The trustee claimed the intangible asset valuation was speculative because it relied on the debtor's 2003-2006 sales projections as well as discussions with management and a 2003 budget. No projections could ever be reliable, the trustee said, because they were based on "conjecture" and "represent only a potential economic future." Further, the defendants' intangible experts had failed to explain how the 2003 budget was created or why he'd used it in his valuation, particularly when its projections might have been obsolete within a year.

The court agreed with the trustee, finding the defendants' intangible valuation expert lacked credibility. "There is no evidence that any specific intangible had any value independent of its value in an ongoing business," it held, particularly unpatented know-how and customer relations. Further, the debtor's value was tied into its contracts with Kodak and other licensing agreements. When the business began to fail in 2003 and stopped making royalty payments, it risked the loss of these licenses, "which would likely further devalue the business's intangibles," the court observed. Indeed, when Kodak pulled its license, the company went bankrupt.

A review of 1998-2000 financial statements also revealed that the company's accountants valued intangibles from roughly $3 million to $11.5 million. A draft of the 2001 financial statement listed intangibles at no more than $12 million. This was the "peak" of the debtor's business, the court said; once it stopped paying its bills, the value of any "intangible properties became a guess."

At the same time, the debtor's financial statements calculated a valuation of the company's intangibles that was consistent with the goodwill value by the defendants' primary expert. If the court deducted the intangible asset valuation but left the goodwill valuation intact, then the evidence showed that the debtor was insolvent from the end of February 2002 through February 2003.

Trustee's expert shows only 'year-end' insolvency. The trustee tried to show that the debtor was insolvent at least one year earlier, or as of January 2001. In support, its solvency expert reviewed the relevant tax returns, financial statements, and accounts receivables for the years 1999 through 2003. Relying primarily on the tax returns, he formulated a 1998-2002 balance sheet for the debtor and then adjusted the receivables and goodwill downward and accelerated debt payments. In particular, he reclassified the equity investors' and other stock interests as liabilities because they shared characteristics of debt, he said, and because financial accounting standards (FAS 150) required the reclassification of equity if "the equity holder receives interest payments and if the equity interest is mandatorily redeemable for cash."

However, at trial, the expert also conceded that neither of these characteristics applied to the equity interests in this case and that FAS 150 was not in effect at the time of the debtor's bankruptcy filing. Moreover, all his balance sheet analysis showed was that the debtor was insolvent at year's end (December 31) in each of the years 2000-2003; he did not show insolvency on the actual dates that the distributions were made. Under a "retrojection" analysis, the court could have imputed insolvency from one year's end to another but only if the trustee (or its expert) established that no books or records were available to ascertain solvency between those dates.

In this case, those records were clearly available to the trustee as well as its expert, the court said. At the same time, it was clear that the debtor's 2001 and 2002 loans as well as its obligations to equity investors would have shifted its liabilities along a "downward trend," as the trustee's expert suggested. However, his failure to use the available financial evidence to support a retrojection analysis led the court to dismiss the expert's insolvency conclusions prior to February 2002. Accordingly, under all the evidence presented, the court found only those dividends that the debtor distributed between February 2002 and March 2003 could be avoided as fraudulent conveyances and dismissed the trustee's remaining claims.

In re PWS Holding Corp.

Citation: 228 F.3d 224, 2000 U.S. App LEXIS 23393
Date of Decision: September 18, 2000
Country: US
State or Federal: Federal
State/Jurisdiction: 3rd Circuit
Court: United States Court of Appeals
Experts: Harrison J. Goldin (court appointed)
Type of action: Bankruptcy
Judge: Becker
SIC: 5411 Grocery Stores (grocery stores and supermarkets selling substantial amounts of nonfood items)
Key words: Bankruptcy, Going concern, Net asset value, Reorganization

Business Enterprise Valuation Showing Solvency Precludes Fraudulent Transfer Claims

The issue in this Chapter 11 reorganization plan appeal involved the court-appointed examiner's assessment of Bruno's Inc.'s leveraged recapitalization. Harrison J. Goldin, the court-appointed examiner, performed a detailed financial analysis of the recapitalization to determine Bruno's solvency and its ability to use capital resources to meet future needs, including debt payments and liability satisfactions.

Business enterprise valuation shows solvency. Goldin tested the company's solvency by using two approaches. An asset-by-asset valuation compared the sum of each asset's value to total liabilities.

The business enterprise valuation valued the business as a going concern and included intangibles such as relationships with customers and suppliers and the name, profile, and reputation of the business. Goldin applied the business enterprise valuation because participants in the recapitaliza tion acquired Bruno's as a going concern.

Of three formulations applied under this valuation method, all but one determined that Bruno's was solvent at the time of recapitalization. Goldin compared the discounted cash flow to long-term debt and found that Bruno's value exceeded its long-term debt by $270 million to $690 million. The asset-to-liabilities analysis, which compared total adjusted enterprise value from a discounted cash flow analysis to total liabilities, showed solvency by $215 million to $635 million. The only test that indicated insolvency considered a sales multiple for comparable enterprises operating in the southeastern United States only.

Solvency Determination Using Going Concern Premise Affirmed

In *In re: PWS Holding Corporation*, 228 F.3d 224 (3rd Cir. 2000), the U.S. Court of Appeals for the 3rd Circuit considered whether a solvency test should be completed on an asset-by-asset or a going concern basis. PWS Holding Corp. and affiliates (hereinafter, debtors) operated a 200-store grocery chain in the southeastern United States, based in Alabama. 88.3% of the chain was sold in a leveraged recapitalization in 1995 for approximately $880 million. The business operated successfully for two years after the recapitalization. In early 1997, the debtors refinanced their acquisition debt. However, by late 1997, the business began to fail, and, in early 1998, the debtors filed for Chapter 11 bankruptcy protection. In 1999, the creditors' committee decided to release the debtors from any claims arising from the leveraged recapitalization (e.g., constructive fraudulent transfers) as part of the reorganization plan. Huff, the largest creditor on the committee, held $290 million in subordinated notes issued by the debtors. Huff petitioned the bankruptcy court to appoint an examiner to review the committee's decision.

The examiner was appointed to analyze the viability of a constructive fraudulent transfer claim. "A constructive fraudulent transfer occurs when a debtor transfers assets to another without consideration, and the debtor was, or became, insolvent at the time of the transfer." Thus, the examiner set out to perform a solvency opinion. He noted that solvency might be determined either piecemeal (asset by asset) or by valuing the business as a going concern. After an extensive review of the case law and the generally accepted accounting principles (GAAP), the examiner determined that it was appropriate to value the business as a going concern. Thus, the examiner appointed an expert to perform the financial analyses.

The financial expert valued the business using three methods: the comparable acquisitions method, the comparable public company method, and the discounted cash flow method. Almost all the analyses indicated that the debtors' assets exceeded their long-term debts after the leveraged recapitalization, and, thus, the debtors were solvent. In addition to the expert's report, the examiner considered the actual transaction. The transaction also indicated that the company was solvent after the transaction by approximately $90 million. While the examiner did not believe the court would consider an asset-by-asset analysis, he performed one. The piecemeal analysis indicated that the company was insolvent after the leveraged recapitalization by approximately $89 million. After considering all the evidence, the examiner concluded that the debtors were solvent after the transaction.

The examiner then considered whether the transaction left the debtors undercapitalized after the transaction. He considered the parties' projections. "The analysis looked at historical data, such as cash flow, net sales, gross profit margins, and net profits and losses, and whether the parties considered difficulties that might arise, such as interest rates fluctuations and market downturns, to gauge the reasonableness of the projections in light of working capital needs in the industry and actual cash available to service needs." The examiner noted that the actual performance of the company was probative and that the company successfully operated, meeting its current obligations, for two years after the transaction. Thus, he concluded that the debtors were properly capitalized after the transaction.

Considering both the solvency opinion and the capitalization analyses, the examiner concluded that it was unlikely that the bankruptcy estate would be successful in a fraudulent transfer action. Based on the examiner's determination, the committee released the debtors from liability resulting from the transaction in the bankruptcy reorganization plan. Huff appealed.

On appeal, Huff argued that the examiner erred when he used the going concern valuation rather than an asset-based valuation and, thus, in the determination that the debtors were solvent after the transaction. The 3rd Circuit affirmed the examiner's use of a going concern valuation. It found that the law did not mandate a valuation using an asset-based approach. Huff did not dispute any of the examiner's other findings regarding the debtors' solvency. Furthermore, the 3rd Circuit found that Huff's own advisors listed the debtors as a "buy" after the transaction and that Huff invested in the debtors in 1995, 1996, and 1997. Thus, the 3rd Circuit affirmed the finding that the debtors were solvent after the transaction.

In re Residential Capital, LLC

Citation: 2013 Bankr. LEXIS 4844
Date of decision: Nov. 15, 2013
Country: US
State or Federal: Federal
State/Jurisdiction: New York
Court: United States Bankruptcy Court
Type of action: Bankruptcy
Experts: Marc D. Puntus (debtors); Michael Fazio, Jeffrey M. Levine, John A. Taylor, and P. Eric Siegert (Houlihan Lokey Capital, Inc.) (defendants)
Judge: Glenn
SIC: 6162 Mortgage Bankers and Loan Correspondents (mortgage bankers and originators)
Key words: Adequate Protection Claim, Diminution in Value, Collateral, Junior Secured Noteholders, Fair market value (FMV), Petition Date, Effective Date, Royalty Base

Creditors' Valuation Spoils Diminution in Value Claim

A recent ruling in the multifaceted Chapter 11 bankruptcy litigation of Residential Capital (ResCap), a large residential mortgage loan company, and its affiliated debtors contains a noteworthy analysis of the alleged diminution in value of the collateral of junior secured noteholders (JSNs). This valuation issue arose in the context of the JSNs' adequate protection claim—one of the many claims they presented in their opposition to the debtors' proposed reorganization plan.

Background. ResCap was a leading originator of residential mortgage loans and, together with nondebtor affiliates, the fifth largest servicer of residential mortgage loans in the country. In May 2012, ResCap and its affiliated debtors petitioned for Chapter 11 bankruptcy. The defendants in this case were entities holding or managing entities that hold junior secured notes. In connection with the bankruptcy, ResCap proposed a reorganization plan. A few days later, the U.S. trustee appointed the Official Committee of Unsecured Creditors, which began investigating what it alleged were security interests the defendants improperly claimed. Subsequently, the defendants filed a series of counterclaims related to the junior secured notes ResCap had issued in 2008 and the collateral securing those notes.

To keep their business operating as debtors in possession, the debtors sought to obtain post-petition financing and authorization to use the cash collateral encumbered by existing debt facilities. In essence, the funding would allow them to continue to issue loans and offer loan modifications to thousands of borrowers; service mortgages and make advances associated with such servicing obligations; comply with the Federal Reserve and FDIC consent order; comply with agreements they had made with government-sponsored entities (GSEs) as to the care they needed to apply in servicing their loans; and retain hundreds of employees to protect against an increase in delinquencies, which could diminish the value and jeopardize the sale of the debtors' mortgage servicing rights (MSRs) and other assets. The debtors and the JSNs negotiated a cash collateral order that established the JSNs' right to adequate protection for the use of their collateral. As of the petition date, the JSNs' secured claims against ResCap and certain affiliated debtors had a face value of $2.2 billion, including $2.1 billion in unpaid principal and $101 million in unpaid prepetition interest.

In the "Phase I" trial in front of the Bankruptcy Court (S.D.N.Y.), the JSNs argued, among other things, that they had a right to recover an adequate protection claim of $515 million based on the diminution in aggregate value of their prepetition collateral as used during the case pursuant to a number of consensual orders.

Both sides agreed that the amount of the adequate protection claim was the difference in the value of collateral between the effective date and the petition date. Moreover, they agreed that $1.88 billion was a baseline value at the effective date. They disagreed over the value of the collateral on the petition date and retained valuation experts to support their arguments.

They also disagreed over how to value the collateral: The JSNs claimed case law required use of the fair market value of the collateral in the hands of the debtors. In contrast, the debtors contended the foreclosure value of the collateral in the hands of the secured creditor was the appropriate measure.

JSNs offer 'global summary' of various valuations. The JSNs had the burden of proving the diminution in value. They presented opinions from four experts who valued different assets. To determine the fair market value of each asset that was part of the collateral, where applicable, the experts considered the prices the debtors' various assets commanded in a post-petition auction process, adjusting for cash flows and loan balances back to the petition date. They also performed a "bottoms-up" fair market valuation as of the petition date. One of the experts presented a single "global summary" of the opinions arriving at a net fair market value of $2.79 billion. He calculated this value by summing: (1) the valuations of the debtors' cash, various assets, unsold servicing advances, loans, equity interests, hedge contracts, and certain other contracts; (2) the valuation of the debtors' sold servicing advances; and (3) his own valuation of the various intangible assets based on his analysis of the other valuations. This approach yielded a value of $4.450 billion, from which he subtracted various liabilities to conclude that the collateral was worth $2.79 billion on the petition date.

Debtors' expert devises methodology. The debtors' expert served for two years as their lead investment banker and in this capacity was involved in their decision to market their assets and in arranging a prepetition marketing process and post-petition sale process. He used two initial bids that did not materialize (stalking horse agreements) to determine a $1.74 billion benchmark value. This benchmark, he said, did not represent his opinion of the value of the collateral for purposes of adequate protection because the purchase prices the stalking horse deals proposed were contingent on the continued operation of the debtors' business in Chapter 11. To estimate the value of the JSNs' collateral as of the petition date in the hands of the creditors' agents upon foreclosure, he made downward adjustments to his benchmark valuation based on two alternative scenarios: "Alternative A" assumed the collateral would be monetized by the collateral agents over a three-to-four-month period ($1.47 billion), while "Alternative B" assumed a five-to-six-month period ($1.59 billion). Other factors required further reductions, he believed, and lowered the "Alternative A" valuation to $1.05 billion and the "Alternative B" valuation to $1.13 billion.

Valuations leave court 'unimpressed.' The court found neither side's valuation was convincing. At the outset of its analysis, it agreed with the defendants that, for the purpose of a finding on whether the secured creditor was adequately protected, "the going concern/fair market value" in the hands of the debtors was the correct measure. The parties in this case did not on the petition date contemplate that the creditors might conduct a foreclosure sale, said the court. Rather, the JSNs agreed to the cash collateral order to enable the sale of assets as a going concern.

But this ruling in favor the defendants did not mean they were able to prove a diminution in the value of their collateral, the Bankruptcy Court continued. Their valuation was defective for various reasons:

(1) The valuation incorrectly assumed the debtors could have sold the JSN collateral on the petition date free and clear of certain obstacles. However, at trial, one of the experts admitted that the sale of mortgage servicing rights would have required consent from the residential mortgage-backed securities (RMBS) trustees and the GSEs. At the same time, that expert's valuation did not account for costs related to obtaining consent. These costs, said the court, were considerable. They included payments of hundreds of millions of dollars to the GSEs to "cure alleged liabilities" prior to obtaining their consent to a sale. Moreover, the debtors agreed to settle billions of dollars of potential RMBS liability to obtain the RMBS trustees' consent to a sale.

(2) Even assuming the debtors could have sold their assets on the petition date, the defendant experts' valuation was not credible. Instead of considering sales other distressed companies "on the brink of bankruptcy" made, they only considered a solvent company that was able to obtain fair market value for its assets. In this case, however, most of the assets could not simply be handed to a buyer who could instantly benefit from full value "as if the assets were commodity products." According to the court, the experts "ignored the reality" of the dire situation in which the debtors were just prior to the bankruptcy. "ResCap was an insolvent company, over-burdened with debt, owning assets that had to be 'fixed' before they could be sold, and facing a real possibility of being shut down."

The Bankruptcy Court added it was "equally unimpressed" with the valuation the debtors' expert had proposed. He performed subjective valuations of risks related to the collateral. At trial, he admitted that he had never seen a valuation analysis relying on a similar methodology before. "Nor is it likely that [the expert's] valuation methodology could be used in other contexts," noted the court. But, even if his methodology was unreliable, "the numbers he reached may well be closer to the actual value of the JSN collateral on the petition date," the Bankruptcy Court stated.

The court was "mindful" of the JSN money the debtors had spent during the case, but, it said, this spending did not mean they incurred a diminution in the aggregate value of their collateral. There was no right to an adequate protection claim on a dollar-for-dollar basis for cash collateral used during the case. Considering the value of the collateral on the petition date was significantly impaired because of existing defaults that prevented the debtors from disposing of most of the collateral, the court did not believe the value then was higher than the value on the effective date. By way of settlements and consents, the debtors were able to sell most of their assets on very favorable terms. "The JSNs and all estate creditors will benefit from this accomplishment," the court concluded. For all these reasons, it denied the request for adequate protection.

Editor's Note. The court noted that a "Phase II" trial and a contested confirmation hearing likely would get underway at the end of 2013 based on the JSNs' strategy to "contest everything and concede nothing," resulting in "protracted proceedings that have burdened the estate and reduced funds available to satisfy creditor claims."

In re Resorts International

Citation: 181 F.3d 505, 1999 U.S. App. LEXIS 14651
Date of Decision: June 30, 1999
Country: US
State or Federal: Federal
State/Jurisdiction: 3rd Circuit
Court: United States Court of Appeals
Type of action: Bankruptcy
Judge: Nygaard
SIC: 7011 Hotels and Motels (hotels, except casino hotels, and motels)

Stockholder's Merger Price Recovery Reversed on Appeal

The District Court reversed a Bankruptcy Court order that awarded Resorts International full restitution for a loss resulting from a stock transaction. The case discussed Resorts' mistakes allowing the stockholder to recover merger prices for his shares as a "settlement transaction."

Samson v. Western Capital Partners LLC (In re Blixseth)

Citation: 2013 Bankr. LEXIS 1001
Date of decision: March 28, 2013
Country: US
State or Federal: Federal
State/Jurisdiction: Montana
Court: United States Bankruptcy Court
Experts: Joseph N. Karas (trustee); Kristina A. Cook (defendant)
Judge: Kirscher

Court Credits Expert's Cash Flow Analysis in Solvency Determination

"The Trustee … continues the fiction that [the debtor], one of the *Forbes' 400* wealthiest Americans in 2007, was insolvent during that very same year" is how the lender tried to defend against the plaintiff trustee's suit for a determination of insolvency. The Bankruptcy Court (D. Mont.) found insolvency was the reality.

In June 2007, the debtor and her estranged husband were in the midst of a "long, costly, and acrimonious" California divorce. The divorce court appointed the husband as manager of the community property; he, in turn, curtailed the debtor's access to all family businesses and cash flow. During that time, the debtor also entered into legal disputes related to her $18 million investment in two technology companies. In July 2007, she described her financial condition as "trying to pay $100 worth of stuff with 10 cents." She was approximately $2 million in arrears to creditors, she stated in an affidavit, even after using all her money from the sale of real estate.

Also, at that time, the husband ended his financial involvement with the businesses of the debtor's son. Searching for funds to develop various projects, the son approached the defendant for money. The latter considered this "the opportunity to do a large loan, anywhere between $5 million and $15 million for a billionaire and her son." Regardless of the family's cachet, it adhered to its standard practice and required personal guarantees from the debtor and her son. Recognizing that the son's assets were all "illiquid," the lender admitted the inducement to make the loan was the debtor's guarantee. When the defendant was unable to obtain the debtor's financial statements for due diligence, it accepted a written statement from her attorney regarding her financial and legal condition. Based on a preliminary review of the assets, the letter stated, it appeared the assets of the couple's estate were community property, totaling "in excess of $1 billion." It further noted that, under California law, the wife was expected to receive assets in excess of $500 million.

The two-year loan to the debtor's son closed on June 15, 2007, for a total amount of over $13 million. The debtor's personal guarantee included an after-acquired property clause. Between May 30, 2007, and Sept. 9, 2008, directly or indirectly, she made payments of over $4.5 million to the defendant. The debtor's divorce only became final in October 2008; along the way, the couple had reached two "minisettlements" and a 42-page final agreement that awarded her several businesses that declared Chapter 11 bankruptcy in November 2008.

In January 2009, the defendant obtained a default judgment against the debtor and her son for nearly $13.3 million, after the son had failed to make payments on the loan. In March 2009, the debtor filed for voluntary Chapter 11 bankruptcy, showing a secured debt of nearly $103 million and an unsecured debt of nearly $57 million.

After conversion to Chapter 7 bankruptcy, the trustee in charge of administering the bankruptcy estate filed an adversary proceeding against the defendant, claiming in essence that the guarantee was avoidable because it was a fraudulent transfer. On the signing date, June 15, 2007, the debtor was insolvent. The defendant claimed the debtor received reasonably equivalent value and was solvent. Both sides presented expert testimony.

'The very definition of insolvency.' To avoid the guarantee, under federal bankruptcy law, the trustee needed to show: (1) that the debtor was insolvent at the time she incurred the obligation or rendered insolvent by it; and (2) that she received less than reasonably equivalent value.

1. *Solvency.* Both sides' experts—both CPAs—agreed that the debtor would be insolvent if she failed one of three tests: the cash flow test, balance sheet test, or adequate capital test. The trustee's expert stated the debtor was insolvent under all three, whereas the defendant's expert found her solvent under all of them.

The disparate conclusions stemmed in part from a disagreement over whether to include community property in the solvency analysis. The trustee's expert considered only the debtor's personal liabilities and the personal assets over which she had control on June 15. While he recognized that "control" of an asset was not a factor under the general balance sheet test, he nevertheless contended it was a critical element for any solvency analysis because all tests "come back to what an asset can generate in terms of cash on a forward looking basis." He considered cash flow, and specifically future cash flows, "the most important determinant as to your ability to repay debts and meet scheduled obligations."

For his analysis, he relied on information the trustee provided, reviewing about 1,000 pages of documents. Four or five of them, he said, had particular relevance, including the debtor's bankruptcy schedules. These showed that in March 2009 she had zero operating cash flow, and, based on her own reports, her liabilities then exceeded her assets by roughly $60 million. Accountants routinely perform a "subsequent event review," that is, "looking at events through the date of the report" when completing audits, he stated. He carefully reviewed a 2009 expert report from the bankruptcy proceedings related to one of the major assets the debtor obtained at divorce. It showed that by 2007 this business was highly leveraged, with insufficient capital to fund its financial plans and projections. He further reviewed affidavits and declarations the debtor had signed in the course of divorce and analyzed her general ledger activity to corroborate her statements. All this information confirmed her claim that in June 2007 her expenses amounted to $2 million and that she was borrowing to pay her daily expenses, he said. He had, the expert continued, looked hard to find assets that would generate cash from day-to-day activities. "The only form of cash generation that could occur would be through the sale of that asset, and that would essentially reduce her committed obligations."

He dismissed the letter the debtor's attorney issued prior to the loan. It conveyed expectations that had no basis in reality; the values for the community property were those the husband had assigned, and they were "pie in the sky."

The trustee's expert concluded that, on June 15, 2005, her debt was roughly $21.5 million; this amount increased to $160 million by March 2009. Her assets on the signing day were only about $16.4 million. Her ability to borrow throughout did not substitute for operating cash flows, he said. He also found that her entering into the marital settlement agreement "exacerbated" her cash flow troubles. "She was taking on assets that required cash, and she didn't have any other source to generate [it] ... other than borrowing." The debtor was "the very definition of insolvency," the expert concluded.

Lack of 'professional skepticism.' The defendant's expert rebutted the opposing testimony and made her own solvency determination. She agreed with the trustee's expert's valuation of non-contingent assets and liabilities. But she assumed, "as a matter of law," that on the signing date the debtor owned half of the marital assets. Therefore, she added assets that the debtor owned pursuant to the first minisettlement and subsequently further adjusted the debtor's balance sheet to include what she called the debtor's "vested 50 percent interest in the community property." She based the second analysis on a June schedule of assets the husband had submitted to the divorce court (the opinion here states two conflicting dates, June 2007 and June 2008).

From a balance-sheet perspective, the debtor had assets in the amount of $377 million in June 2007; their value was roughly $173 million more than her liabilities. At the same time, the debtor had about $47 million in personal assets, excluding community property, and approximately $8.5 million in liabilities, the defendant's expert concluded.

The cash flow test, she stated, centered on a debtor's intent: Did she intend to incur or believe that she would incur debts beyond her ability to repay? The debtor's statements that she planned to repay debt as it matured were "pretty good proof" that she was solvent under this test, the expert concluded.

The defendant's expert also found the debtor was solvent under the adequate capital test, which considers "whether or not the transaction left the debtor with insufficient capital to continue normal business operations." Avenues to obtain capital included operations, borrowing, or equity financing, the expert stated. In June 2007, the debtor was able to borrow money to fund her day-to-day operations.

The trustee's expert failed to use "professional skepticism" in his analysis of documents that came into existence after June 2007, the defendant's expert noted. These did not record "historical circumstances" but were "filed with the court for the purposes of eliciting a result." Moreover, she faulted him for considering the full amount of the debtor's guarantee as liability. He did not account for the value of the primary security, that is, "the probability that the other guarantor, [the son], would not satisfy the remainder of the loan."

The trustee's expert gave his own rebuttal. The competing expert failed to perform a proper analysis under any of the tests. Without questioning, she accepted the values the husband had assigned to assets in determining one-half of the community property and then subtracted certain liabilities.

The court credited the testimony of the trustee's expert for numerous reasons:

- His choice to exclude community property that was under the control of the debtor's husband aligned with case law that stated "[a]sset valuation … should be reduced by the value of the assets not readily susceptible to liquidation and the payment of debt."

- In her solvency analysis, the defendant's expert failed to consider whether any of the community assets generated income. She ignored the fact that "the marital asset which supposedly had the most value" was in financial straits and lacked the ability to generate any cash flow.

- While the defendant's expert criticized the trustee's expert for being insufficiently skeptical, she was the one who "applied no professional skepticism to values assigned to marital assets by [the husband]." By contrast, the trustee's expert "tested the veracity of the documents and declarations he examined."

- As to his ignoring that there were other primary borrowers (the companies the son set up for purposes of the loan) and two primary guarantors, the court pointed out that, before the promissory note matured, the defendant "was looking to Debtor for payment on the obligation," as court documents against the son and debtor showed.

- The trustee's expert "persuasively testified" that a solvency analysis should begin with an entity's operating or future cash flows to determine "the supportable level of debt." He did not fail to give proper weight to the preloan letter, considering its reliance on values the husband provided. In 2007, none of the assets the debtor ultimately received had positive cash flows.

- Regardless of whether one considered only the assets over which the debtor had control or one-half of the community assets, the debtor was insolvent on the day of signing the guarantee.

2. *Reasonably equivalent value.* The defendant tried to argue that the debtor did not need to receive reasonably equivalent value for the full amount of the $13 million loan because there were other assets that secured the loan. The court dismissed this claim, noting the defendant itself admitted that it considered the son's assets "illiquid and high-risk" and relied "almost exclusively" on the divorce settlement to ensure repayment.

The court also disposed of the claim that the debtor received "value" upon signing. "The sole value of the guarantee to Debtor was a mother's satisfaction in helping her child," the court said. There was no other value, "particularly from the standpoint of [her] creditors."

Regardless of how *Forbes* magazine portrayed her, at the relevant time, the debtor did not have sufficient assets to support her lifestyle or carry on any business. In the defendant's opinion, she was "too big to fail"; however, that opinion was based on "unreliable and untested information," the court concluded.

As a remedy, it set aside the guarantee and ordered the defendant to return property it had received from the debtor and her son and still held as well as pay the trustee $4 million for property it had received but no longer held.

Scott v. Universal Fidelity Group

Citation: 42 F. Supp. 2d 837, 1999 U.S. Dist. LEXIS 3260
Date of Decision: March 19, 1999
Country: US
State or Federal: Federal
State/Jurisdiction: Illinois
Court: United States Bankruptcy Court
Type of action: Bankruptcy
Judge: Keys
SIC: 7322 Adjustment and Collection Services
Key words: Fair market value (FMV), Net worth

Net Worth

Scott sought to compel discovery of defendant's financial picture. Discussion of the meaning of "net worth" within the Fair Debt Collection Practices Act ensued. The court found the proper definition to coincide with "fair market value."

In re South Canaan Cellular Investments

Citation: 2011 WL 52558 (E. D. Pa.)
Date of decision: Jan. 6, 2011
Country: US
State or Federal: Federal
State/Jurisdiction: Federal Circuit
Court: United States Bankruptcy Court
Experts: Mark Sherman (neutral); William Redpath (debtors)
Judge: Fox

Should Neutral Appraiser Be Kept 'Blind' to Parties' Competing Valuations?

To fund their plan of reorganization, the debtors agreed to sell their limited partnership interests in a wireless communications provider by May 2011. If the debtors were unable to find an acceptable buyer, then the plan permitted the limited partners (LPs) to compel the debtors, as general partners, to purchase their interests.

To determine the price of the put, the partnership agreement required both parties to determine and then disclose their respective value of the subject LPs' interests. If these valuations differed by more than 10%, then, under the agreement, the parties would jointly appoint an appraiser to determine the fair market value of the LPs' interests using a going concern premise of value. If the parties couldn't agree on an appraiser, then each would appoint its own appraiser, and, within 20 days, these two would appoint a neutral third, who would make the ultimate determination of value. After this third appraiser reached an opinion of value, it would be compared to those that the debtors and LPs had initially exchanged. "The valuation proposed by the limited partner that is closest to the value opined by [the neutral third appraiser] then becomes the agreed upon value of the limited partnership," the bankruptcy court explained, and the purchase price would be calculated.

Parties couldn't agree on anything. The debtors were unable to find a suitable buyer for the limited partnership and invoked the put provisions. The parties exchanged their valuations of the LPs' interests—which differed by more than 10%. After each party chose an expert appraiser, it took another two months (and threatened court intervention) to select a neutral third.

Even then, debtors requested an appraisal "protocol," essentially asking the court to permit both parties to provide the appraiser with whatever information they believed to be relevant—except that neither party could disclose its prior, competing valuation. Further, all communications with the independent appraiser would be in writing, with copies served to the other side, and the appraiser could not interview the LPs' key managers without all parties being present.

The court held a hearing on the proposal, at which the debtors' appraiser acknowledged the professional standards by the various business valuation organizations (including the AICPA and ASA). All of these standards admonished valuation analysts to be objective, independent, and impartial. They also required the analyst or appraiser to use "professional judgment," the court noted, and to "obtain all relevant financial and non-financial information." After this testimony, the debtors withdrew all but one request: that the court still preclude the independent appraiser from about the valuations exchanged by the parties.

In support, the debtors said that because the appraisal provisions required the appraiser to make his fair market determination of value *before* selecting the party's number that was closest to that value, the agreement contemplated "an appraiser who is blind to the numbers put on the table by the parties." Further, because the LPs and their affiliates presented an opportunity for "significant appraisal and transactional work in the future, given the numbers of wireless and wireline companies in which they have invested," the appraiser had incentives for producing "as low a number as possible," to benefit the LPs and "strengthen" this future opportunity. "Any disclosure that would allow the appraiser to know which party 'wins' if he moves his valuation one way or another by a few tens of thousands of dollars seriously risks tainting the independence of the appraisal process," the debtors concluded.

The LPs requested that the appraiser be permitted to see the parties' prior valuations because they were carefully based on a "complex balancing of a number of factors," including various appraisals and value estimates based on several methodologies and the uncertainties regarding the numbers that each side might propose. Each side also knew the risks of the "baseball-like arbitration provisions" of the agreed-on appraisal process and would have hedged against the risk of an unfavorable result due to the "uncertainties" of the appraiser retention process. Finally, the entire process contained no provisions for a court-ordered "protocol," the LPs argued, but was silent on the type of information the appraiser could obtain, thus recognizing his freedom to "exercise his business judgment to obtain and use any information he believes relevant to his engagement."

Neither party called the independent appraiser to testify regarding the information he might request to make his value determination. Nevertheless, the court assumed that, after the protracted selection process of a candidate from their own list, even the debtors believed that the third appraiser would be "competent, independent, objective, and fair in completing his valuation engagement." To the extent the debtors were concerned the appraiser could be influenced by knowing the LPs' prior valuation positions, that concern would have been present during the parties' negotiation of their agreement. "Had the partners intended to restrict their valuation provisions from being revealed, it would have been simple to include such a restraint in the agreement," the court ruled, and denied the debtors' motion to keep the independent appraiser "in the dark."

In re Spansion

Citation: 426 B.R. 114
Date of decision: April 1, 2010
Country: US
State or Federal: Federal
State/Jurisdiction: Delaware
Court: United States Bankruptcy Court
Type of action: Bankruptcy
Experts: Henry Owsley (debtors); Michael Genereux (senior noteholders); and Richard Morgner (Convert Committee)

Management Projections, DCF Discount Rate, and More Are Key to Bankruptcy Valuation

This decision demonstrates "what has and is now occurring in many of the larger Chapter 11 cases," according to the federal bankruptcy court (Delaware). Trading of claims can begin even before the filing, creating various constituencies of creditors—most often institutional investors such as hedge funds and secondary traders—who purchase debt at various levels and then seek to advance their claims by proposing competing plans. Valuation issues become paramount in the proceedings, in particular, whether a proposed plan undervalues the debtors at the expense of dissenting creditors, which can now include these seasoned, strategic debt investors.

Third-largest maker of flash memory. In 2008, they held 14% of the flash memory market, outpaced only by rival manufacturers Toshiba and Samsung. At the time, half of the debtors' flash memory sales came from the wireless market. They entered bankruptcy in part to refocus on the more profitable embedded applications, such as those used in gaming, automotive, and industrial electronics.

After lengthy negotiations, an ad hoc committee of converted noteholders (the "Convert Committee") offered $112 million in equity financing, based on a 12% discount derived from a total enterprise valuation for the debtors of $1.5 billion. The debtors rejected the offer and a month later proposed a plan supported by senior noteholders. Not surprisingly, the Convert Committee objected, claiming the proposal understated total enterprise value (TEV) and its equity incentive provisions allocated too much value to management-employees.

In deciding whether the debtors' proposed plan was fair and equitable, the court heard from three valuation experts. The debtors' expert concluded that the company's TEV ranged from $700 million to $850 million. The expert for the senior noteholders said TEV ranged higher, from $799 million to $944 million. The Convert Committee's expert advocated the highest range, $1.054 billion to $1.419 billion. The court also heard from additional objectors to the plan, who argued that the debtors' value could best be determined from the active market for buying and trading its bankruptcy claims. However, this evidence did not rise to the required level of accuracy. "There is no record on the number of such trades, over what period of time such trades occurred, [and] how open the market is to participants," the court said. As a result, its value determination would turn on a cautious scrutiny of the three "hired experts," with particular attention to their underlying assumptions and data.

Management projections: worst case or base case? During bankruptcy, the debtors prepared a "base" forecast consisting of management's best estimates for an "aggressive but achievable" performance as of May 2009. Two months later, they prepared a "contingency" forecast that adjusted the base projections to account for potential risks and downsides through 2012.

In conducting their valuations, experts for the debtors and the secured noteholders relied on both projections but weighted the base case more heavily (75% and 85%, respectively) than the contingency case (25% and 15%). Some of the contingency risks had mitigated by the time of confirmation hearing, the experts said, while others remained present. The Convert Committee's expert excluded the contingency forecasts entirely because they failed to recognize the mitigated risks as well as certain growth opportunities; he also believed the base forecasts resulted from a "bottoms-up, two-month, rigorous business planning process." However, the court found it proper to include both forecasts, weighting the base case more heavily than the contingency case, and credited the noteholders' expert with the proper apportionment.

All three experts favored the discounted cash flow (DCF) approach, but each accused his opponents of emphasizing certain inputs and assumptions to manipulate ultimate values. In particular:

1. *Discount rate*. The debtors' expert calculated a weighted average cost of capital (WACC) at 15%, compared to the secured noteholders' 14.7% and the Convert Committee's 13.8%. The first two experts criticized the third's beta analysis, claiming he used an "overly broad peer group" to achieve the lower rate. The experts also noted that prior valuations of the bankrupt debtors used rates ranging from 14% to 16%.

2. *Terminal value.* The debtors' and secured noteholders' expert agreed on a perpetuity growth rate of -2.5% to +2.5%, with a midpoint of zero. The zero growth rate relied on industry forecasts that the debtors' market share would grow even while individual sectors declined. Despite this evidence, the debtors' expert used a terminal growth rate of zero to 3%, with a midpoint of 1.5%.

3. *"Out-years" projections.* Under its restructuring plan, the debtors' management planned to outsource 100% of production over five to 10 years. Accordingly, the Convert Committee's expert gradually reduced the debtors' free cash flows from 2012 to 2019 (the "out years"). By contrast, the secured noteholders' expert assumed the debtors would outsource 100% by 2013 and used this as the "out year." At the same time, he prepared a sensitivity analysis that used the gradual out-years projections with the zero growth rate and 14.7% WACC to produce a higher TEV.

Market approach focuses on appropriate multiples and M&A transactions. In addition to their DCFs, the three experts employed a comparable companies analysis, based on EBITDA multiples. Only the Convert Committee's expert also used a revenue multiple, which significantly increased his value conclusion from a range of $871 million to $1.14 billion (EBITDA multiple) to a range of $1.3 billion to $1.9 billion (revenue multiple). "This variance is too great to ignore," the court said, and credited the comparable companies analysis by the debtors' and senior noteholders' expert.

Finally, all three experts applied a comparable transactions (M&A) approach, but only the debtors' and senior noteholders' experts focused on two recent deals related to the company's primary competitor, which they believed were "very relevant." (To ignore these deals would be "foolish and reckless," one expert said, "like me valuing Pepsi and ignoring Coke.") Only the Convert Committee's expert looked at five M&A transactions involving "memory companies," from which he calculated an implied revenue multiple range (1.2x to 1.7x) much broader than those calculated by his opponents' focus on the two key deals (0.60x to 0.72x). However, when applied to the debtors' 2010 revenues, this higher range of multiples resulted in an enterprise value "so far above the ranges calculated by [the same expert's] other methodologies that its soundness and therefore its usefulness is doubtful," the court held.

Overall, after weighing each expert's evidence and criticisms of the others' reports, the court concluded that the valuation by the senior noteholders' expert was appropriately weighted and rested on "the most sound" assumptions for determining the debtors' current value in its industry. It was also more transparent than the report by the debtors' expert, and "more in line with common valuation practices" than the Convert Committee's expert. At the same time, the court believed the DCF analysis by the senior noteholders' expert should be adjusted to account for a more gradual decline in EBITDA over a longer period of "out years" (as performed by his sensitivity check.)

Based on these observations, the court found the debtors' TEV ranged from $872 million to $944 million. After adding various assets available for distribution—such as auction rate securities, net operating losses, and litigation recoveries—the court found a net distributable value range of $1.25 billion to $1.3 billion. Given this valuation, the debtors' proposed plan treated all unsecured creditors fairly, the court ruled. At the same time, it found the debtors' proposed equity incentive plan favored management with a disproportionate allocation of equity value. Certain third-party releases also violated bankruptcy law, and the court declined to confirm the plan in its present form.

Note: Within two weeks of this decision, the Convert Committee raised more than $419 million to fund its rival plan and requested the court to delay proceedings to consider the proposal. The debtors rushed to amend their plan, cutting more than $14 million from its equity incentives, and obtained court confirmation on April 15, 2010. See www.reuters.com/article/2010/04/16/spansion-idUSN1613444520100416.

In re Spielfogel

Citation: 211 B.R. 133, 1997 Bankr. LEXIS 1237
Date of Decision: July 28, 1997
Country: US
State or Federal: Federal
State/Jurisdiction: New York
Court: United States Bankruptcy Court
Type of action: Bankruptcy
Judge: Eisenberg
SIC: 2679 Converted Paper and Paperboard Products, NEC (except corrugated paper, wall paper, gift wrap paper, paper supplies for business machines, and other paper office supplies)
Key words: Bankruptcy, Employment agreement, Minority interest

Company Withholds Data From Minority Owner; Court Rejects Control Stockholder's Valuation

The issue is whether to approve a compromise and settlement that is opposed by the debtor, Sidney Spielfogel. The question is the adequacy of the settlement offer of $700,000 for debtor's 21.585% interest in Bambu, a highly profitable cigarette rolling paper importer and distributor, and the debtor's related employment agreement ($450,000 for the stock and $250,000 for the employment agreement).

Unusual bankruptcy case. According to the court, "this bankruptcy case is unusual (reflected in a lengthy and complicated decision on the settlement proposal) because it involves an individual Chapter 11 debtor, the installation of an operating trustee in an individual reorganization case, and an estate which may arguably not be insolvent."

In support of the settlement, valuation reports were submitted by Goldstein Golub Kessler & Co., P.C., CPAs, engaged by Bambu and the Michael Spielfogel defendants and by Parity & Co., P.A, CPAs, engaged by the trustee.

Controlling stockholders refuse access. The debtor did not submit an expert valuation because Bambu and the Michael Spielfogel defendants (controlling stockholders at the time of the action), claiming confidentiality, would not provide the raw numbers necessary for Sidney to have such a valuation report prepared.

Court rejects settlement. The court rejected the settlement, stating "the valuations submitted in connection with this motion are unreliable for purposes of valuing either Bambu or the Debtor's shares in the context of a Dissolution Action under the Business Corporation Law."

In rejecting the settlement, the decision made several points:

- "The court must consider the individual Debtor's residual rights in the estate.... The Court has searched the Trustee's papers in vain for a mention of any consideration given to the Debtor's interests in negotiating the proposed settlement."
- "This valuation is based on unreliable data compiled from raw numbers and information supplied to the experts solely by Bambu and the Michael Spielfogel Defendants, without any consultation with the Debtor ... who effectively ran Bambu until his ouster and is intimately acquainted with all of the events which affected Bambu's profitability during the years immediately preceding the Valuation Date."
- The valuations were skewed downward by not being adjusted for nonrecurring events and by relying on low 1990 figures and ignoring much higher 1995 figures.

With respect to the Employment Agreement, the court stated, "without more factual information indicating an adverse finding of the issues raised, $250,000 appears to be well below the lowest reasonable value of this asset."

In re Structurlite Plastics Corporation: SPC Corporation v. Robert E. Griffith

Citation: 244 B.R. 27 (B.A.P. 6th Cir. 1998)
Date of Decision: August 25, 1998
Country: US
State or Federal: Federal
State/Jurisdiction: 6th Circuit
Court: United States Court of Appeals
Type of action: Bankruptcy

Previous Valuations Assist in Showing Debtor's Post-LBO Solvency

The U.S. Court of Appeals for the 6th Circuit considered whether an expert's affidavit overcame the presumption that the price paid for a company was equal to the value of that company's assets. Structurlite was sold for $4 million in a leveraged buyout transaction. Sometime after the transaction, Structurlite filed for bankruptcy protection. The unsecured creditors' committee argued that the LBO left Structurlite insolvent and moved for summary judgment regarding its insolvency. For bankruptcy purposes, insolvency is defined as "when the present fair saleable value of his assets is less than the amount that will be required to pay his probable liability on his existing debts as they become absolute and matured." However, the bankruptcy court raised the presumption that the negotiated sale price is equal to the present fair saleable value of the debtor's assets at the time of the LBO. The former shareholders disputed that presumption. They offered the affidavit of a CPA who testified that Structurlite had a value of $1.7 million after the LBO.

The CPA valued the business as a going concern. He relied heavily upon a valuation of the debtor, dated two days before the LBO. However, he also considered valuations of the debtor's assets performed for insurance purposes and the debtor's audited financial statements. (This CPA did not prepare the financials). He further considered the liabilities incurred by the debtor in completing the LBO. He found that the present fair value of Structurlite's assets exceeded its liabilities at the time of the LBO.

The bankruptcy court based its insolvency determination on the presumption that the present fair saleable value of the debtor's assets was equal to the purchase price. Its opinion failed to mention the former shareholders' expert. The appellate reversed the bankruptcy court's insolvency determination. It noted "although purchase price may be highly probative of a company's value immediately after a leveraged buyout, it is not the only evidence." It concluded that the introduction of the affidavit regarding Structurlite's solvency created a genuine issue of material fact, inappropriate for summary judgment.

Superior Offshore International, Inc. v. Schaefer

Citation: 2012 U.S. Dist. LEXIS 174841
Date of decision: Dec. 11, 2012
Country: US
State or Federal: State
State/Jurisdiction: Texas
Court: United States District Court
Experts: Norman Dufour (plaintiff); Christopher M. James, Alan D. Bell (defendants)
Judge: Atlas

Expert May Use Public Information for Company Valuation

Before filing for Chapter 11 bankruptcy, the plaintiff provided subsea construction and diving services to the oil and gas industry. The defendants were members of the board of directors prior to its initial public offering (IPO) in April 2007. In connection with the bankruptcy, a special committee representing the plaintiff sued, alleging breaches of the duty of care and duty of loyalty and good faith, as well as self-dealing; for example, the defendants approved a $28 million special dividend to the board's chairman and awarded him the full benefit of an increased IPO that left the company undercapitalized and unable to continue its operations. Also, two defendants failed to disclose and pursue more lucrative offers for the *Achiever*, a vessel the company tried to sell.

Both sides retained experts. In its pretrial *Daubert* motion in federal court (S.D. Tex.), the plaintiff sought to exclude the testimony of the defendants' two experts regarding the company's capitalization at the time of the IPO. They used public information, including the prices at which the company's stock traded on the exchange following the IPO and the views of security analysts who worked for the underwriters that had performed due diligence on the plaintiff one year before the IPO. (The opinion does not indicate the experts' valuations.)

One of the defendants' experts also critiqued the factors and valuation methodology the plaintiff's expert used in appraising the *Achiever.* While he had valued the vessel at $100 million in 2007 in a business appraisal, he increased the amount to $135 million after the plaintiff had retained him.

***Daubert* safeguards are less critical.** Regarding the company's capitalization, the plaintiff claimed the experts used unreliable information; as to the vessel appraisal, it argued the expert lacked experience in appraising marine vessels. The court dispensed with both objections quickly.

Although reliance on publicly available information is not always the preferred methodology, the court said, "It could be an acceptable procedure when the company's stock is trading in an efficient market." This seemed to be the case here because one source of information was the securities analysts who worked for the underwriters and thus had more access to internal information than other analysts.

As to the plaintiff's second objection, the defendants' expert did not plan to testify about vessel appraisal generally but specifically to address the plaintiff's expert's method and unexplained change in the vessel's value.

In denying the motion, the court noted that the case would be tried to the court, not a jury. In *Daubert,* the Supreme Court's main concern was guarding against jury confusion and exposure to unreliable testimony. Here the court was easily capable of determining whether the experts' testimony was helpful and how much weight to give it.

In the Matter of TCI 2 Holdings, LLC

Citation: 2010 WL 1540115 (Bkrtcy. D.N.J.)
Date of Decision: April 12, 2010
Country: US
State or Federal: Federal
State/Jurisdiction: Federal Circuit
Court: United States Bankruptcy Court
Type of action: Bankruptcy
Experts: William Hardy and Andrew Yearley (debtors); Neil Augustine (competing plan proponents)
Judge: Wizmur

Competing Valuations of Trump Casinos Determine Fate, Feasibility of Restructuring

In a massive bankruptcy case that pitted Donald Trump against Carl Icahn, valuation evidence once again proved pivotal in persuading the court which billionaire's proposed plan of reorganization was the most fair and feasible.

Trump casinos owed billions. Faced with declining gaming revenues during a recession and a failure to make a December 2008 interest payment to its bondholders, TCI 2 Holdings LLC—which owns and operates three Trump hotels and casinos in Atlantic City, N.J. (Trump Entertainment)—filed for Chapter 11 relief. At the time, the debtors owed nearly $490 million on a first line of secured debt and over $1.25 billion to its bondholders, along with $40 million in general unsecured claims.

Within months, two competing reorganization plans emerged. The debtors, supported by Donald Trump and the bondholders, offered to reduce Trump Entertainment's total debt by $1.4 billion and give the celebrity billionaire a 10% stake in the casinos he once ran. The bondholders also offered to invest $225 million in the new venture. After buying 51% of the first lien lenders' claims (from Beal Bank), Carl Icahn proposed to completely deleverage the debtors by converting the entire amount of the first lien debt into equity (Beal/Icahn plan). The second lien bondholders and the general unsecured creditors would not receive a distribution.

In a lengthy opinion that ended the 14-month battle between the billionaires, the federal bankruptcy court considered whether the proposed plans satisfied the "cram-down" requirements of Sec. 1129 of the Bankruptcy Code, in particular its provisions regarding financial feasibility and fairness. Both parties enlisted well-qualified valuation and restructuring experts to prove the viability of their respective plans—but only the debtors' expert had "significant experience with gaming companies," the court noted. By contrast, the Beal/Icahn expert had little gaming experience and no prior exposure to the Northeast casino market. The court first examined the debtors' plan, focusing on whether its projected EBITDA (2010 through 2013) demonstrated capacity to service the proposed new loans.

1. *Capex reduction.* Historically, the debtors targeted a 20% return on investment in capital. To meet projected earnings, however, the debtors all but deferred capital expenditures (capex) in 2010, reducing new projects and maintenance from $54 million to $10 million. The recession, the decline in discretionary consumer spending, and "dramatic" cuts in capex by competitors supported the reductions.

The Beal/Icahn expert challenged the debtors for failing to adjust future earnings for declining capex. Instead, by assuming the debtors' historic 20% ROI in a stable economy, he said the proposed capex reductions resulted in an across-the-board, annual reduction of the debtors' budgeted EBITDA of $10.5 million. However, the expert did not differentiate between project and maintenance capex (or know which the debtor would defer); he also failed to factor in the economic and industry effects. Undeniably, a long-term reduction in capex "may impact … EBITDA," the court held. However, the debtors' proposed deferral of some projects would not have a material impact.

2. *Pennsylvania gaming.* In meeting with the debtors, the Beal/Icahn expert overhead a manager mention that new legislation in Pennsylvania (January 2010) authorizing gaming and casinos might impact earnings by $7 million to $10 million. At the expert's behest, management provided a chart indicating that the potential impact might range from $5 million to $20 million but specifically noted that the numbers did not reflect management projections. Nevertheless, the expert chose the midpoint of the range to reduce the debtors' projected EBITDA by $10.2 million per year. The court found these deductions speculative and discredited them due to the delay in implementing the legislation and the expert's admitted lack of experience in gaming ventures in Pennsylvania.

3. *Historic performance.* The Beal/Icahn expert correctly pointed out that in nine of the past 10 years, the debtors had missed their projected EBITDA. In their proposed plan, however, the debtors' projections were well below EBITDA numbers achieved in 2005 to 2007. Despite industrywide setbacks, the debtors had also maintained their market share and their management since 2006.

4. *Debt service ability.* Assuming the debtors meet their EBITDA projections and secure a 12% interest rate, their plan showed sufficient capacity to service the new loans. Sensitivity analyses by the debtors' expert showed that, even if they missed EBITDA projections the first three years, the debtors would be able to service their debt and operations. Moreover, this "worst case" scenario did not account for a host of likely management responses, including an asset sale (the Trump Marina) to eliminate negative cash flows and costs. By contrast, the Beal/Icahn expert predicted the debtors would run out of cash before the new loans matured in 2015. However, he used a 15% market interest rate and applied his reduced EBITDA figures, "which were largely discredited," the court said. Accordingly, the expert's predictions "cannot be sustained."

5. *Market interest rate.* Both experts selected gaming comparables to determine the applicable market interest rate for the new loans. The debtors' expert focused on 11 gaming companies with 15 debt issuances and a corporate credit rating between a B and a CCC; they owned a similar number of properties (one to four) and operated in one or two markets, including New Jersey. Their paid interest rates ranged from 5.42% to 17.47%, with an average yield of 11.8%; thus he proposed a market rate of 10% to 12%.

The Beal/Icahn expert proposed a market interest rate ranging from 14% to 16.5%, based on six comparables, primarily regional operators in Nevada with B ratings or below (and including a highly leveraged, distressed casino). He also looked at exit financings from companies with similar risk profiles, assuming an implied credit rating of CCC for the debtors; however, five of his comps were not gaming companies, and he admitted that exit financing does not always reflect market rates. Moreover, his implied credit rating used only three out of nine S&P metrics while ignoring other more salient ones. The expert's "cherry-picking process ... slanted his conclusions," the court held, and adopted the 12% rate proposed under the debtors' plan.

6. *Debt capacity.* Using a "total leverage approach and an interest coverage approach," the debtors' expert estimated their post-reorganization debt capacity from $305 million to $390 million. Thus, the debtors' proposed new funding of $334 million was well within this range. But the Beal/Icahn expert said the $334 million new loan would leave the debtors "dramatically overleveraged." He projected their debt capacity from $158 million to $212 million—only once again, he used a high interest rate and a high debt base, plus highly rated market comparables. The expert's choice of "high-performing" comparables with relatively low debt ratios to arrive at a relatively low debt capacity number for the debtors "was suspect," the court held.

7. *Value of lenders' security.* The debtors' expert used a discounted cash flow analysis along with a market multiple and comparable transactions approach to calculate a total enterprise valuation (TEV) of the debtors of $459 million (i.e., the value of the lenders' collateral). This TEV included $24 million for the Trump Marina (based on a qualified expert appraisal that discounted the asset

for myriad market uncertainties) but excluded pending litigation on the value of the Trump brand. The Beal/Icahn expert criticized the debtors for the discounts and exclusions, which would have boosted TEV to $482.5 million (a value required by the Beal/Icahn plan to fulfill financial feasibility). Given the speculative value of the litigation and the rights to the Trump brand, however, plus the debtors' expert's "combined and extensive experience in the gaming industry," the court found their TEV more credible.

Overall, the debtors' plan met the requirements of Sec. 1129 and was confirmable, subject to certain modifications, including modifying the new loan to reflect a 12% interest rate, the court ruled. It turned to the Beal/Icahn plan next.

Debtors receive their own rebukes. The debtors contended that the Beal/Icahn plan was "illusory" because it lacked liquidity financing and a feasible business plan. They pointed to the "poor performance record" that Icahn investors had in other endeavors and pointed out that, in this one, they lacked rights to the Trump brand.

Although the Beal/Icahn plan failed to propose a specific strategy for operating the debtors' casinos, the court found the "intense investment" by Icahn and his managers in this "protracted litigation" demonstrated their commitment to proceed with their plan. The Icahn parties also claimed they could rebrand the casinos at an estimated cost of $15 million, which would be "easily absorbed" by the reorganized debtors' available cash, the court found. "While there might be a temporary disruption to the debtors' operations, there can be no question that the casinos could operate successfully without the Trump brand, particularly on a platform of a debt-free enterprise."

The debtors also objected to the Beal/Icahn plan, which was premised on a higher TEV, for returning a greater than 100% recovery on the first lien holders claims. But "the objectors cannot persuasively contend" that the debtors' TEV is lower for purposes of their plan and something higher under the Beal/Icahn plan, the court held. Although it was true that the Beal/Icahn partners would receive 100% of the equity under their proposal (and other creditors would receive nothing), they also held all of the risk. Overall, and subject to certain modifications, the court also found the Beal/Icahn plan to be confirmable.

To break a tie between two competing, confirmable plans, Sec. 1129 highlights the preferences of creditors. Although both plans provided a full recovery to the first lien lenders, the Beal/Icahn plan provided no return to any other stakeholder in the case. By contrast, the debtors' plan returned a modest outlay to general unsecured creditors and, more importantly, gave the majority (61%) of bondholders the opportunity to participate in any future success of the reorganized companies. An "overwhelming" number of creditors voted for the debtors' proposed plan versus the Beal/Icahn plan, the court observed. Support by the largest creditor constituency, coupled with financial feasibility and the potential for creditors to share in any upside potential, compelled the court to confirm the debtors' plan under Sec. 1129.

In re Terrestar Networks, Inc.

Citation: 2011 WL 3654543 (Bkrtcy. S.D.N.Y.)
Date of decision: Aug. 19, 2011
Country: US
State or Federal: Federal
State/Jurisdiction: New York
Court: United States Bankruptcy Court
Judge: Lane

Security Interest Exists in Economic Value of FCC License

The debtors in this Chapter 11 proceeding provide mobile satellite services pursuant to various FCC licenses. Aware that federal law prohibits using the licenses themselves as collateral, in 2008 the debtors granted their secured noteholders an interest in all economic proceeds from the "sale, transfer, or other disposition" of the FCC licenses as well as any related "goodwill or other intangible rights."

After the debtors filed for bankruptcy in 2010, the Sprint Nextel Corp. (Sprint) sued for $104 million in costs to clear the satellite bandwidth that the debtors previously owned. To satisfy its admittedly unsecured claim, Sprint sought to void or at least gain seniority over the secured noteholders' interest. It filed various motions in federal bankruptcy court, seeking a judicial determination of its claims by essentially arguing that the noteholders' lien in the economic value of the licenses was invalid under the same law that precludes granting a collateral interest in FCC licenses.

An opportunity for bankruptcy valuation analysts? The bankruptcy court agreed that long-standing federal precedent precluded a lien from existing on the FCC license itself. Beginning in 1992, however, federal courts disagreed whether to distinguish a debtor's "private" right to receive the economic value generated by its FCC license from the FCC's "public" right to assign the licenses and regulate their transfer. To clear up the controversy, the FCC issued guidance in 1994 that declared:

> If a security interest holder were to foreclose on the collateral license, by operation of law, the license could transfer hands without the prior approval of the Commission. In contrast, giving a security interest in the proceeds of the sale of a license does not raise the same concerns.

Since this ruling, "it appears to be settled law that a creditor may perfect a lien in the private economic value of an FCC license to the extent that such lien does not violate the FCC's public right to regulate license transfers," the bankruptcy court observed. Applying federal precedent to the current case, the court concluded that the noteholders had a valid secured interest in the "economic value" associated with the debtors' license, "even if they cannot hold a lien on the FCC license itself."

In denying Sprint's motions, the court also found that: (1) Sec. 552 of the Bankruptcy Code did not prevent the noteholders' prepetition liens from attaching to the post-petition sale proceeds of the licenses; and (2) the court—and not the FCC—was the ultimate arbiter of the validity and priority of claims related to the economic value of FCC licenses. Given this clear ruling, the opportunity exists for analysts to appraise the economic value of FCC licenses not only in the bankruptcy setting, but in general valuation and transfer contexts as well.

In re Texans CUSO Insurance Group

Citation: 2010 WL 743291 (Bankr. N.D. Tex.)
Date of Decision: March 2, 2010
Country: US
State or Federal: Federal
State/Jurisdiction: Federal Circuit
Court: United States Bankruptcy Court
Type of action: Contract
Experts: Brian Mroski
Judge: Houser
SIC: 6411 Insurance Agents, Brokers, and Service (insurance agents and brokers)

Textbook Case of Proving Lost Future Profits Based on Past Finances of the Business

In 2007, the owner sold several insurance businesses to a Texas insurance company for $19 million plus an earnout payment of up to $21 million over three years. The parties agreed that the owner would come on board as president to manage his former operations and accrue the additional earnout payments. But less than four months into the transition he was fired. After a bitter and extended arbitration, the company was ordered to reinstate him with all back pay and benefits.

The company failed to comply, however, and this time the former owner sued for breach of the arbitration award and the parties' underlying repurchase and employment agreements. Just two months before trial, the company filed for Chapter 11 bankruptcy, and the owner filed a proof of claim amounting to $22.3 million.

Company never intended to permit earnout. After reviewing the record, the federal bankruptcy court agreed with the arbitrator. The facts clearly demonstrated that the company fired the owner without cause, never intending to reinstate him as president. The parties' employment agreement stipulated the amount of back pay and benefits, which an expert for the owner (now plaintiff) determined to be $348,000.

The plaintiff's expert also presented a detailed description of consequential damages based on how the company would have performed if it had kept the plaintiff in charge. Interestingly, the expert did not prepare a report on damages but relied on his testimony and demonstrative exhibits. The company objected to the expert's proposed testimony under Rule 702 of the Federal Rules of Evidence and the *Daubert* standard. But since the court did not have a written report, it postponed its *Daubert* findings to permit the expert to present his calculations.

The parties' original sale agreement provided a complicated formula to determine the earnout amount based on annual revenues and earnings over the three-year contractual period—2007-2009. Accordingly, the expert began with the company's historical financial performance in 2004, 2005, and 2006, compared it to available industry data for 2004-2008 and the first quarter of 2009, and concluded that the company performed favorably against industry averages.

Next, the expert forecast the company's net revenues during the earnout period by using the average net growth rates for comparably sized insurance agents and brokers (those with $10 million to $25 million in annual revenues) as reported in a Best Practices Study—an annual publication of the insurance industry. To forecast the effect on net revenues from the plaintiff's wrongful termination in 2007, the expert multiplied the actual 2006 net revenues from his former operations by the 2007 "organic net revenue" from the Best Practices comparables. (Organic net revenue excluded any increase in revenues derived purely from acquisitions, the expert explained.) He added the result to the company's 2006 net revenues and then made similar calculations for years 2007 and 2008. To forecast the company's expenses during the same earnout period, the expert first calculated the actual variable costs for each of the years 2004-2006 as a percentage of actual net revenues. He then took the average of that percentage for the three years and applied it to his forecast net revenues for 2007-2009 to calculate variable costs for each of those years. For fixed costs, the expert used the company's actual reported fixed costs for 2007, 2008, and 2009.

Finally, the plaintiff's expert used his net revenue and expense figures to forecast the company's EBITDA for the same years, modifying them by specific adjustments mandated by the earnout formula in the parties' contract. After applying the formula, he concluded that total earnout payments would have amounted to $20.1 million.

Experts need to know industry studies. In considering the *Daubert* challenge, the court was troubled by evidence that during his deposition—which took place three days before the damages hearing—the expert admitted that he was not familiar with the content and methodology of the Best Practices Study. By the day of trial, however, the expert had "cured this deficiency," the court stated. He was able to testify in detail about the survey's method in selecting listed companies, and, more importantly, he was able to demonstrate the "analytical link" between the data and his conclusions. Lastly, during the various reporting periods, the survey cited 10 to 12 companies (out of 35) located in the same region (Texas) as the company.

Based on this testimony, the court concluded that the expert appropriately relied on the Best Practices survey. Further, even though he had no prior experience in the insurance industry, the expert's qualifications as a CPA and CFE (certified fraud examiner), with experience in calculating and reviewing financial damages models in litigation, were sufficient to establish his expertise in this case.

The company claimed that the expert failed to consider independent causes of damages other than the breach—but the court rejected this challenge as well. In particular, the expert took into account "broad economic factors that affected the industry as a whole, including the impact of

Hurricane Katrina and the deterioration of financial markets in 2009" in denying the *Daubert* motion, the court said.

For these same reasons, and based on the expert's testimony, the court concluded that the plaintiff had proven lost profits to a reasonable certainty, and it awarded earnout damages of just over $21.1 million.

In re TOUSA, Inc.

Citation: 2009 WL 3519403 (Bankr. S.D. Fla.)
Date of Decision: October 30, 2009
Country: US
State or Federal: Federal
State/Jurisdiction: Florida
Court: United States Bankruptcy Court
Type of action: Bankruptcy
Experts: Kevin Clancy, Charles Hewlett, Amy Benbrook, William Derrough (unsecured creditors); Michael Canon, Michael Samuels, Rene Stulz, William Lenhart, Andrew Metrick (secured lenders)
Judge: Olson

Teams of Experts Help Court and Creditors Value Huge, Bankrupt Homebuilder

The TOUSA homebuilding company—once the largest in the country—became one of the first multibillion dollar casualties of the collapse of the housing and credit markets. Its bankruptcy provides a sobering look at what went wrong with the economy on so many levels and how top-tier valuation analysts are critical to the ensuing litigation. Most of the numerous experts involved in this high-stakes trial proved credible to the Bankruptcy Court, if not key to its ultimate decision concerning solvency. But one expert evoked a sharp rebuke for "dissembling" and for offering an opinion-for-hire—nothing any valuation professional would want to hear from the bench or have published in the permanent reports.

Caught between boom and burst. After rapidly expanding nationally during the housing boom, Florida-based TOUSA made a last, disastrous acquisition in 2005 funded with over $675 million in secured financing. When the bubble burst in 2007, TOUSA defaulted on the debt, and the bank (Citigroup) insisted that the company borrow—and cause its subsidiaries to borrow—$500 million in restructured debt secured by liens on substantially all of the subsidiaries' assets.

At a board meeting in June 2007, the company's restructuring advisor (Lehman Brothers) presented the $500 million deal as the "best alternative" for shareholders. At the same time, it declined to provide a fairness opinion. Two days later, the CEO emailed a strategic memo to the majority owners, warning that the company was "dangerously overleveraged" and in "desperate need" of equity. Even if the deleveraging plan was successful, he said, the company could not service its debts and was at an "increasing risk of crashing and burning." The CEO did not send the memo to management or the bank, but even Citicorp "harbored significant doubts about TOUSA's solvency," according to court records. The bank nevertheless pressed forward, "motivated by the prospect of substantial fees." More troubling, the CEO's incentive bonus ($4.5 million) was contingent on completing the refinancing, as was $2.9 million of Lehman Brothers' fees.

The deal closed in July 2007. Within months, the consolidated company was saddled with a debt-to-total capitalization ratio of 71.3%—much higher than the ratios of comparable homebuilders, according to trial experts. TOUSA's bonds were trading at a severe discount (48 cents on the dollar), and, by year's end, the company had lost over 98% of its market value. In January 2008, it filed for an orderly dissolution under Chapter 11. In this adversarial proceeding, a committee of unsecured creditors sought to avoid the subsidiary transfers as fraudulent conveyances under applicable state law and provisions of the Bankruptcy Code (Sections 544, 548, and 550).

Expert testimony makes the case. To buttress these dismal (and rather damning) facts, the plaintiffs/creditors sought to prove the subsidiaries were insolvent as of the July refinancing. They presented two valuation and restructuring experts, who in turn relied on a real property appraiser to assess the homebuilder's inventory and a construction expert for the cost inputs. Not to be outdone, the defendant/lenders retained two valuation experts, two real estate experts, and an economist; they also offered an insolvency opinion obtained in the course of the debtors' July 2007 refinancing.

In its 186-page opinion, the court discusses the valuation issues in great detail, focusing on: (1) prefinancing insolvency; (2) post-financing insolvency; (3) validity of the solvency opinion; and (4) proof of reasonably equivalent value. It examined every aspect of expert testimony, including the appraisers' assumptions, methodologies, and possible motives.

1. *Prefinancing insolvency.* To show the debtors' insolvency prior to refinancing, the plaintiffs' valuation expert created adjusted balance sheets for the parent company and two conveying subsidiaries. He started with the debtors' operational data, making adjustments to reflect each entity's ownership of the other, their pro rata share of debt, and the fair market value of their inventory (as provided by real estate and cost appraisals). He eliminated intercompany debt, treating these items as equity investments. The final balances showed the parent company's liabilities exceeded assets by $360 million and the conveying subsidiaries were overleveraged by $180 million.

The defendants challenged the expert's reliance on the third-party asset/inventory appraisals. In particular, the real estate/restructuring expert applied a detailed DCF analysis for over 298 community-held properties, including raw land, by subtracting developmental and carrying costs from the prospective net sale prices. He then "rolled up" the community assets into the company divisions and from there into the full legal entities. When cost-to-complete exceeded forecast revenues (approximately 18% of the communities), the expert assigned a zero value. Doing such ignored the "option value," the defendants claimed, or what a prospective purchaser might pay to hold the property for development, especially since a single parcel sold post-refinancing for a significant sum.

The court found this "cherry-picking" of the data unpersuasive. The plaintiffs' expert's approach was consistent with company procedure, which required writing down any property to zero if developing costs exceeded expected returns—a frequent occurrence in the current housing market when the sale of a single property was an anomaly. The defendants' experts also failed to study total sales, including abandoned properties or those sold at millions *less* than the appraised value assigned by the plaintiffs' expert.

The court also found "serious problems" with the defendants' experts' approach:

- *Housing assumptions.* The defendants' experts forecast average sale prices (ASPs) for TOUSA's residential properties to remain flat for three to six years before returning to predownturn absorption rates, regardless of location or condition. "Historical experience [shows] that different metropolitan areas recover from housing downturns at different rates depending on ... the local economy, supply and demand, and the degree of correction needed in that particular ... market," the court observed. By contrast, the plaintiffs' expert accounted for these differences by using Moody's and other price forecasts "very specific and very sensitive to the geographic market."

- *ASP assumptions.* Further, it was incredible *not* to project any decrease in ASPs, especially given the downturn and industry use of incentives. One of the defendants' experts argued that ASPs have "nothing to do with market value," but that was at odds with all the evidence, the court noted, and his failure to use declining ASPs appeared to be "result-driven" with a goal "to avoid lowering future sale prices."

- *Economist's assumptions.* The defendant's economist said that the plaintiffs' expert was unduly pessimistic because the national economy didn't truly begin to deteriorate until August 2007; and then, it was in ways that TOUSA couldn't have foreseen. But just because "the national housing market went to hell in a handcart" after the refinancing, this did not mean that TOUSA's markets "were not already there" as of July 2007, the court said, warranting a pessimistic outlook.

- *Cost assumptions.* All of the defendants' experts assumed that housing costs would decline, and one "made no effort" to calculate community-based completion costs, relying instead on industry ratios and rules of thumb, e.g., the "60/40" rule that 40% of the value of the finished lot is attributable to the raw land. By contrast, the detailed, site-specific analysis by the plaintiffs' expert was "plainly superior," consistent with historical data regarding material costs (which continue to rise during downturns, albeit at a slower pace) and properly factored in all marketing, maintaining, and closing costs.

- *Discount rates.* The plaintiffs' real estate expert also developed community-specific discount rates, calculating an average of 20%. His range was well within industry and market participant averages. By contrast, the defendants' experts applied "unreasonably low" discount rates (10.63% and 11.5%) inconsistent with industry surveys, the court said. They also failed to account for differences in demographics or asset size, complexity, and quality.

Based on the evidence, the court found the plaintiffs' valuation expert to be more credible and reliable, based in part on his use of third-party appraisals and inputs, and concluded that the company and its subsidiaries were clearly insolvent prior to the refinancing.

2. *Post-transaction solvency.* The plaintiffs' lead valuation expert also provided post-financing balance sheets for the parent company and conveying subsidiaries, this time allocating the $500 million in secured debt proportionately among the entities along with their share of any acquired assets. Post-transaction, TOUSA's liabilities exceeded its assets by $43 million, while the subsidiaries were overleveraged by roughly $619 million. Because the expert used essentially the same methodologies, the court found his post-transaction balance sheets to be credible and reliable, clearly showing that the subsidiaries were "rendered even more deeply insolvent by the transaction."

Leaving nothing to doubt, the plaintiffs presented a second valuation/restructuring expert, who calculated TOUSA's total enterprise value (TEV) by three methods:

- Observable market (-189.4 million);
- Comparable companies (-$357 million to -$114 million); and
- A DCF analysis (-$585 million).

The defendants objected to all three methods as follows:

- *Observable trading price.* The public market is not reliable when securities aren't trading efficiently, one of defendants' experts claimed. He offered no evidence that TOUSA's shares were not trading efficiently, however; nor did he show that its bonds were priced low for any reason other than the market's perception that TOUSA's value was depressed. Another of defendants' experts wanted to apply a control premium to the market price, but the court rejected this "implausible notion," finding no evidence that any purchaser would pay such a premium. Finally, the company's total market cap of $175 million did not contradict its insolvency. "The stock of even notoriously bankrupt companies trades at a positive price," the court said, because certain investors gamble that it may someday rise again.

- *Guideline public companies.* The plaintiffs' expert selected five comparables using book value of inventory because: (1) inventory is a homebuilders largest, most valuable asset; (2) industry investors and analysts typically use this metric; and (3) each of the comparables had similar ratios between their TEVs and booked inventory of approximately 55% to 65%. The defendants' experts claimed an income-based multiple (based on EBITDA) would have been better, as would using all assets instead of a single line item. The court disagreed, finding that an EBITDA metric would be inappropriate because its ratio to TEV varied too widely among the comparables, suggesting that market participants distrusted this variable as well.

- *Discounted cash flow.* The plaintiffs' expert began with TOUSA-generated cash flow projections adjusted according to the ASPs generated by the real estate expert. He then calculated a terminal value by applying an inventory multiple of 60% (midrange in his comparables analysis). The expert also provided a sensitivity chart to illustrate how his conclusions would change with changes in his assumptions. According to that chart, TOUSA would have a positive net equity only under a "vastly more optimistic set of assumptions," the court said. The defendants' experts criticized his failure to lower projected costs and his use of an inventory multiple, but, given the court's prior acceptance of these assumptions, neither undermined his DCF values.

The defendants' two valuation experts tried to present their own TEVs. However, the first relied on faulty cost assumptions (as in the prefinancing scenario) to calculate his balance sheet analysis. Had he used the assumptions that the debtors' expert relied on, the court observed "he too would have found that the consolidated TOUSA enterprise was insolvent both before and after the transaction."

Moreover, this first expert included a $228 million line item for "goodwill and other intangible assets" that did not belong. Nearly a quarter ($63 million) was attributable to the book value of TOUSA's goodwill—which the plaintiffs' expert appropriately wrote off to prevent overstating value. A going concern value is likely to include most of the intangible asset value as goodwill, the court explained. "To add the entire value of TOUSA's booked goodwill on top of that ... creates the risk, if not the certainty, of double-counting."

Even the defendants' expert admitted that the remainder of intangibles—$162 million for trademarks and $5 million for workforce-in-place—might have already been included in booked goodwill. Further, a number of his assumptions, including royalty rates and future growth rates, "lacked empirical and theoretical footing," the court said. "If one were to simply remove the $161 million of trademark value from [the expert's] balance sheet ... it would show the consolidated TOUSA enterprise to be *insolvent* by approximately $16 million just before the transaction."

Will this expert ever testify again? The defendants' second expert presented far more problems, specifically on questions of accountability. First, his report claimed that "no court had ever found his methodology to be unreliable." He also testified under oath that no court had ever rejected his ultimate opinion on solvency.

But these assertions were "simply not true," the court said. Evidence revealed that at least two courts rejected his methods and/or ultimate opinion. With his attorney's help, the expert tried to backpedal based on semantics (it depends on the definition of "ultimate") but then found his "dissembling ... extraordinarily troublesome." Worse, the expert "swore" in a deposition that he'd reviewed the CEO's strategic memo but then testified at trial that he'd never seen the document. "Such a fundamental contradiction about a crucial document ... served only to erode [his] overall credibility further," the court said, concluding the expert's testimony "on this and many other points was simply unbelievable and that, for the right price, [he] would opine as desired on anything." The court summarily dismissed his substantive opinion as unreliable.

By contrast, the court found that each of the analyses provided by the plaintiffs' experts was reliable and credible in isolation. Together, and considered in light of all the evidence, "the analyses derive even greater force." Unlike the defendants' experts' analyses—which were "frequently at odds with one another and with the non-expert evidence"—the plaintiffs' experts provided consistent, credible support for the court's finding that TOUSA and the conveying subsidiaries were "grossly insolvent" as a result of the July 2007 transaction.

An overpriced solvency opinion. In a last effort to prove solvency, the defendants presented the solvency opinion that the company obtained from a corporate turnaround/restructuring firm in the course of refinancing. Notably, the firm evaluated the entire consolidated company rather than its entities. Its creation and content also raised some red flags:

- The firm had not provided a solvency opinion for a homebuilder in at least two years prior to the market downturn. Despite the firm's lack of experience, however, TOUSA did not consider any other provider.
- The fee was contingent on the outcome: If the firm found the company solvent, it would earn $2 million; if it did not, it would receive only its time and costs.
- The firm reached its opinion in "remarkable speed." In less than two weeks, it was circulating a draft saying the company was solvent.
- Its opinion relied heavily on management projections rather than a "rolled-up" approach. The firm also failed to discuss the projections with management or review their accuracy—despite their forecasting increasing ASPs.
- TOUSA also failed to review or revise its projections, even though the market was declining "dramatically" and its own business had collapsed.
- The solvency firm did not adequately "stress test" the models.
- It used an inappropriate EBITDA multiple in valuing the company.

"Because [the firm] blindly relied upon TOUSA's unsupportable financial projections, [its] opinion that TOUSA was solvent as of July 31, 2007 is not credible," the court concluded. Even minor adjustments to the projections would have changed the firm's ultimate opinion. "It remains quite unclear … what value TOUSA received in exchange for the $2 million [fee]."

Experts analyze reasonably equivalent value. The plaintiffs' lead valuation expert also proved instrumental in the court's findings that the conveying subsidiaries failed to receive reasonably equivalent value for assuming the $500 million in restructured debt. In particular, he found that the subsidiaries jointly and severally took on $403 million in new obligations, secured by their assets; in his balance sheet approach, he allocated the debt among three of the entities. The court once again found his apportionment methodology sound and his solvency analysis credible.

Moreover, the subsidiaries received no value in terms of debt relief. TOUSA paid the loan proceeds to settle litigation spawned by its last "disastrous" acquisition, which was directed against the company and one of its partners, *"but not against the conveying subsidiaries,"* the court emphasized. The defendants' experts tried to counter this evidence, but one focused on value to the entire TOUSA group (this was the expert the court had already found not credible by virtue of his dissembling). The second expert also attempted to quantify the benefits for the consolidated company—but even he declined to affirm that the refinancing was necessary for TOUSA to obtain these same benefits.

A last expert for the lenders contended that the liens on the subsidiaries' assets were worth only $161 million, based on the estimated probability that there would be a default on the debt they secured. "I reject that valuation because it conflicts with the legal principles that govern the determination of the value of liens," the court said. The expert didn't account for the critical role the liens played in allowing TOUSA to obtain the new financing and failed to value the subsidiaries' sacrifice of future borrowing ability. Finally, at trial this expert used a chart derived from S&P data to illustrate the historical default rate of similar debts. On cross-examination, he realized the data showed historical *corporate* (not debt) default rates. "Because [he] used the wrong chart and conflated defaults.... I cannot accept his calculations," the court said.

Final orders. In light of the extensive expert testimony and additional findings of fact and conclusions of law, the court ultimately found the conveying subsidiaries were insolvent on the date of the transfer, had unreasonably small capital, and would incur debts beyond their ability to pay within the meaning of applicable state law and provisions of the Bankruptcy Code. Accordingly, it disallowed the lenders' claims against the debtors' estate and ordered them to disgorge any and all amounts received in connection with the July 2007 refinancing, plus prejudgment interest.

Trans World Airlines v. Trans World Airlines Official Committee of Unsecured Creditors

Citation: 134 F.3d 188
Date of Decision: January 20, 1998
Country: US
State or Federal: Federal
State/Jurisdiction: 3rd Circuit
Court: United States Court of Appeals
Type of action: Bankruptcy
Judge: Mansmann, Nygaard, Garth
Experts: Global Aviation Associates (for Travellers) Avmark Inc. (for TWA)
SIC: 4512 Air Transportation, Scheduled (passenger)
Key words: Fair market value (FMV)

Fair Valuation Clarified for Bankruptcy Purposes

The U.S. Court of Appeals for the 3rd Circuit determined Trans World Airlines Inc.'s (TWA) solvency in its action to recover Travellers' $13.7 million judgment as a preferential transfer. TWA claimed that on the date of transfer it was insolvent as defined by the bankruptcy code, 11 U.S.C. 101 (32) (a): "The sum of such entity's debts is greater than all of such entity's property, at *fair valuation*." (emphasis added) The only issue before the 3rd Circuit was the "fair valuation" of TWA on the date of transfer. Both parties presented expert testimony.

Travellers valued TWA's assets at their fair market value. TWA's assets included operating assets, cash, cash equivalents, accounts receivable, and other investments. Travellers assumed TWA would not be under *any* time constraint to liquidate its assets, thereby achieving the highest price for the assets. Travellers then valued TWA's liabilities. Travellers concluded that TWA's publicly held debt should be valued at fair market value. It claimed that this standard of value was within the bankruptcy code's definition of "fair valuation," which applied to liabilities as well as assets. Thus, Travellers devalued TWA public debt from face value to fair market value. Travellers concluded that TWA was solvent by just under $2 billion on the date of transfer.

TWA valued its assets under the assumption that a sale would occur within 12 to 18 months. It also determined that its publicly traded debt should be valued at face value. Further, TWA included the contingent costs of ceasing operations in its liabilities. Those costs included contractual and union payments, medical/dental benefits, wind down expenses, among others. TWA valued itself at $2.5 billion in the red.

The 3rd Circuit began its review by stating "[b]ecause liquidation … was not clearly imminent on the date of … transfer, we concern ourselves with how to achieve a fair valuation of TWA's assets on a 'going concern' basis." The court also noted that "we begin … by recognizing that … a fair valuation of assets contemplates a conversion of assets into cash within a reasonable period of time." The 3rd Circuit determined that Travellers' asset valuation was without merit because it assumed no time constraint on the sale of TWA assets. Thus, it accepted TWA valuation because it contemplated a conversion to cash in under one and a half years.

The court also considered the proper valuation of TWA's liabilities. The court determined that TWA's publicly traded debt should be valued at face value, not fair market value. It stated: Because we treat TWA as a going concern, we cannot consider the market's devaluation of TWA's debt resulting from the possibility as of the date of transfer that TWA would cease operations and be unable to satisfy its promises.… [Face value] represents the net present value of TWA's obligations, while [Fair Market Value] represents the net present value of TWA's obligations but discounted by the likelihood that TWA will be unable to pay its debts in full. Along the same line, the court determined that TWA could not consider in its calculations any liabilities contingent upon its dissolution. The court further noted that "it is the antithesis of a 'going concern' valuation to include such costs."

The court concluded that TWA should be valued as a going concern for the purposes of a fair valuation under the bankruptcy code. The court allowed a reasonable time constraint to be considered when valuing TWA's assets and disallowed any liabilities contingent upon or in anticipation of TWA's dissolution. The court concluded that TWA was insolvent on the date of transfer by $1.1 billion and, thus, could recover the judgment monies.

In re Tribune Co.

Citation: 2011 Bankr. LEXIS 4128 (D. Del.)
Date of decision: Oct. 31, 2011
Country: US
State or Federal: Federal
State/Jurisdiction: Delaware
Court: United States Bankruptcy Court
Experts: John Chachas, Suneel Mandava, and Daniel Fischel (debtors); Rajinder Singh and Ralph Tuliano (noteholders)
Judge: Carey

Tribune Bankruptcy Court Prefers Current Data to Fill Valuation 'Chasm'

The financial woes of the Tribune Co. may have peaked in 2007, when noted real estate baron Sam Zell closed a two-step, heavily leveraged buyout (LBO) of the publishing and media conglomerate, owner of the *Los Angeles Times* and the *Chicago Tribune*, with minority interests in private entities such as TV's The Food Network.

In "Step One" of the LBO, a Zell-controlled trust sold the company to an employee stock ownership plan (ESOP), leveraged with $8.2 billion of senior secured financing. "Step Two" consisted of a merger that added another $3.7 billion in debt, cancelled all issued and outstanding shares of Tribune stock, and left the ESOP as sole owner of the new entity. Within a year of the going-private transaction, however, the company's pre-LBO and LBO indebtedness totaled over $12.7 billion, and, in December 2008, the Tribune and its related entities filed for Chapter 11 bankruptcy relief.

LBO-related claims critical to reorganization. From the outset of the bankruptcy, the resolution of certain LBO-related claims became central to the formulation of any reorganization plan. These consisted primarily of the debtors' claims to avoid the LBO as a fraudulent conveyance, that is, that either or both steps of the transaction took place when the debtors were insolvent or left them insolvent. By April 2010, the debtors had proposed a plan of reorganization, but, given the complexity of the LBO claims, the bankruptcy court deferred its hearing on the plan and appointed an independent examiner, Kenneth Klee, to investigate the validity and potential value of the LBO claims.

The examiner subsequently developed a comprehensive financial analysis, including issues concerning the debtors' solvency, its available capital at the time of the two-part transaction, and the flow of funds among the various entities. Of particular interest to business appraisers, the examiner also evaluated a solvency opinion conducted by the Valuation Research Corp. (VRC) in April 2007, which concluded that the debtors could meet their obligations under the heavily leveraged buyout. In his July 2010 summary to the court, the examiner found three major flaws in the process surrounding the procurement of the VRC opinion:

- Evidence indicated that Tribune "did not act forthrightly in procuring the solvency opinion issued by VRC at Step Two," the examiner said. Instead, "the procurement of the solvency opinion was marred by dishonesty and lack of candor about the role played by [the Tribune's investment bankers] in connection with VRC's solvency opinion and on the question of Tribune's solvency generally."

- Additional evidence indicated that Tribune's senior financial management "failed to apprise the Tribune Board and Special Committee of relevant information underlying management's October 2007 projections on which VRC relied in giving its Step Two solvency opinion."
- "One important component of those projections went beyond the optimism that sometimes characterizes management projections," the examiner found. Although no direct evidence indicated that Tribune's management had been deceitful in preparing this aspect of the forecasts, "this component of the projections bears the earmarks of a conscious effort to counterbalance the decline in Tribune's 2007 financial performance … to furnish a source of additional value to support a solvency conclusion."

Despite these findings, the examiner ultimately concluded that Step One of the LBO, while highly leveraged, was "not likely" to be found by a court to be a fraudulent conveyance. However, a court would be "somewhat likely" to find that Step Two was an intentional fraudulent transfer, Klee reported. As a result, the debtors abandoned their original proposal while other parties considered a competing plan.

In October 2010, the debtors submitted a joint proposal with certain senior lenders and unsecured creditors (the debtors' plan), and certain holders of pre-IBO debt jointly filed a competing proposal (the noteholders' plan). Once again, the treatment of LBO claims proved the pivotal difference. The debtors' plan would settle all the LBO claims involving the more senior lenders, who'd invested more than $10 billion in connection with the 2007 buyout. The noteholders argued that this proposed settlement was unreasonable because it undervalued the LBO claims—which could potentially provide "substantial" recoveries, they said.

For that reason, the noteholders' plan preserved all LBO causes of actions for "vigorous" prosecution after confirmation. The debtors criticized this course of action, calling it a "gamble" by institutional investors who bought their claims "deep into bankruptcy" that would "hazard the fortunes" of other creditors, including former Tribune employees. Moreover, at a December 2010 vote, the vast majority (over 90%) of LBO and non-LBO creditors supported the debtors' plan, while a slim minority—primarily institutional investors—supported the noteholders' plan.

Valuation also at the core of confirmation. From March 2011 through June 2011, the bankruptcy court held confirmation hearings and oral argument on the competing plans. On October 31, it issued a 126-page opinion that began with a valuation determination, the consequence of which "permeates more than one aspect of the confirmation disputes between respective plan proponents," the court noted, such as the fairness of the debtors' proposed settlement of the LBO claims.

In support of their proposed plan, the debtors presented three valuation/insolvency experts. Together, they argued that the debtors' "total distributable value" ranged between $6.3 billion and $7.1 billion, with a midpoint of $6.75 billion. In comparison, the noteholders' two valuation experts maintained that the debtors were worth between $7.9 billion and $8.7 billion, with a midpoint of approximately $8.3 billion. "This leaves a staggering valuation chasm—measured by the distance between the competing valuation midpoints—of $1.589 billion," the court observed. To bridge this expanse, it examined the basis for the competing valuations in greater depth.

To reach their conclusion, the debtors' experts relied on an analysis by the company's financial advisors, Lazard Freres, prepared as of October 2010 (the deadline for filing competing plans). This 2010 analysis relied on then-current projections by the debtors' management as well as a current comparable companies analysis. In January 2011, however, Lazard updated its analysis to conclude a $269 million increase in the debtors' total value. As a result, the noteholders' experts said the debtors' valuation relied on "stale" and unreliable data.

In response, the debtors' experts acknowledged that Lazard properly "refreshed" its 2010 report in 2011. Nevertheless, they argued that Lazard's 2011 midpoint value ($7.019 billion) fell in the high end of their 2010 valuation range. Moreover, the increase between the 2010 and 2011 Lazard analyses was not derived from the Tribune's "core" publishing and broadcasting business—which actually decreased during the same time period—but was due to the Tribune's minority interests in TV's The Food Network and other private entities. Importantly, the 2011 analysis did not discount these holdings for a lack of marketability, the debtors' experts said, and gave no weight to a DCF analysis and so was an unreliable basis for increasing the debtors' total distributable value.

Accordingly, the midpoint value of $6.75 billion, based on the October 2010 analysis, was still the most reasonable estimate of the company's value, one of the debtors' experts maintained, because:

> The midpoint best takes into consideration the chance or risk or opportunity of the valuation either improving between now and then or going down between now and then. One only has to look at the stock market every day for the last two weeks to realize markets are highly volatile, and they will change.... It will continue to change every day between now and June 30. So $6.75 [billion] as the approximate midpoint best reflects that risk.

In addition, another of the debtors' experts—with particular experience in the publishing and media industries—emphasized that the increased value of the Tribune's noncontrolled interests did not warrant an increase in the company's overall value. Further, he believed that the value of these interests supported a 10% to 30% marketability discount and that even a 10% discount would negate the $269 million overall increase from 2010 to 2011.

Noteholders prepare rebuttal valuation. In addition to critiquing the debtors' experts for not relying on the updated 2011 Lazard analysis, one of the noteholders' experts prepared a rebuttal report. Among other inputs, he used: (i) updated Tribune financial data through February 2011; (ii) updated comparable company and market data through February 2011; and (iii) an adjusted weighting for values of the publishing and broadcasting segments, according 10% for the DCF approach and 90% for a comparable companies analysis. This resulted in a $7.9 billion-to-$8.7 billion range of value for the company, with a midpoint at $8.3 billion.

The debtors criticized this rebuttal report, noting that, by the time of the confirmation hearing, the company had lost any of the asserted increase in value. Thus, "changes based on updated market data are hard to gauge," the debtors said, especially given current volatilities. Further, using actual (better than expected) 2010 financial results for the company's publishing segments, which had experienced "secular declines year after year," rather than "less enthusiastic forward-looking forecasts" improperly raised the company's purported value.

The debtors also argued that his weighting of approaches reflected the noteholders' experts' lack of knowledge and experience in the publishing industry. A comparable companies analysis assumes the industry will "revitalize itself," the debtors experts said, "while the DCF analysis assumes the industry will continue to struggle with the secular challenges it is facing and will not be able to turn the business around." A 10% DCF weighting was also akin to "giving no consideration to management's projections." Instead, the debtors' experts applied a 30% weighting to the DCF and a 70% weighting to the comparable companies methods, thereby balancing the latter's more "optimistic view of the future" with management's continued projections of steep declines in the publishing industry.

Finally, the debtors claimed that by "cherry-picking" certain companies and transactions for his comparable companies analysis, the noteholders' rebuttal expert improperly revised the value of the company's noncontrolled interests upward. Due to his inexperience in the industry, his judgment in selecting comparables should be given "considerably less weight" than that of their experts, the debtors said—particularly the one expert who held over 20 years' valuation experience in the publishing sector.

Hired experts approach advocacy? Predictably, "hired experts often approach their valuation task from an advocate's point of view," the court observed. In this case, it agreed with the debtors' experts that the 2010 Lazard report was reasonable and credible "when completed." Overall, however, the court found that the data had become stale as of the confirmation hearing in April 2011. "A valuation should be based on the most up to date information available," it held.

At the same time, it found that the debtors' experts accorded more reasonable weightings to the respective DCF and comparable companies approaches, particularly given their "experience and knowledge of the applicable industries." Throughout this case, all the parties had agreed that the publishing industry was "in a serious decline," the court said. Although the company's 2010 results were better than expected, the evidence demonstrated that the updated market data was "a moving target. Further, the noteholders' rebuttal expert failed to adequately explain how his "cherry-picked" revisions would impact his report as a whole, the court said, in finding that his conclusions were not "reliable, reasonable, or complete."

Accordingly, the court relied on "the most recent complete valuation report presented at the confirmation hearing" (the 2011 Lazard analysis) to conclude that the debtors' total distributable value is the midpoint of the 2011 report, or $7.019 billion.

Based on this valuation, the court spent the remainder of its opinion determining whether either the debtors' or the noteholders' plan was confirmable under Section 1129 of the Bankruptcy Code. Although it found many aspects of both plans fair, reasonable, and financially feasible, the court ultimately rejected *both* plans because neither had been accepted "by at least one impaired class" of creditors as required by § 1129(a)(10). This ruling has particular import for jointly filed plans in Chapter 11 cases, as the court applied the § 1129(a)(10) requirement for each of the debtors included in the proposed plan instead of applying it on a per-plan basis.

After more than a thousand days in bankruptcy, the court also said it was "determined" that the debtors must "promptly find an exit door." Moreover, "if a viable exit strategy does not present itself with alacrity," the court warned that it might, on its own motion, appoint a bankruptcy trustee to oversee the proceedings.

In re Tronox Inc.

Citation: 2013 Bankr. LEXIS 5232
Date of decision: Dec. 12, 2013
Country: US
State or Federal: Federal
State/Jurisdiction: New York
Court: United States Bankruptcy Court
Type of action: Bankruptcy
Experts: Prof. Grant Newton (plaintiffs, solvency analysis), Prof. Daniel Fischel (defendants, solvency analysis); Prof. Jack Williams (plaintiffs, REV analysis), Jeffrey Balcombe (defendants, REV and damages analyses); Dr. Neil Ram (plaintiffs, environmental liability)
Judge: Gropper
SIC: 1311 Crude Petroleum and Natural Gas

Expert's Market-Based, 'Self-Contained' Solvency Analysis Crumbles

Valuation experts of various stripes took center stage in a recent fraudulent conveyance suit regarding a parent company's decision to spin off its chemical manufacturing business from its highly profitable oil and gas exploration and production business. The transaction left the former with billions of legacy environmental and tort liabilities and ultimately led to bankruptcy. The litigation trust sued to recover from the defendants the value of the transferred oil and gas assets. The court's 82-page decision explored claims as to reasonably equivalent value, business enterprise value, and environmental and tort liabilities.

Liberating assets from liabilities. The plaintiffs and defendants started as a many-tentacled enterprise that included an oil and gas exploration business as well as a uranium mining business and various chemical plants. By November 2005, only two businesses remained: the oil and gas exploration and production (E&P) business and the chemical—titanium dioxide—business. The E&P business was dominant, with operating profits of about $1.8 billion for that year; in comparison, the chemical business brought in about $106 million. The conglomerate's enormous environmental and tort liabilities represented a major problem: Since 2000, it had incurred more than $1 billion in environmental response costs and was spending more than $160 million a year on remediation. This made it an "unattractive" acquisition candidate. In 2002, the eventual buyer of the E&P business rejected a merger, reasoning that future environmental liability would be "$BILLIONS" and could last for "at least 30 more years." (After the spinoff, it paid more than $18 billion for the nearly liability-free E&P business.)

As early as 2002, the parent company's top management hired Lehman Brothers to pursue a corporate reorganization. Essentially, it meant transferring the E&P business—the oil and gas assets—to a new holding company (one of the defendants in the suit) and transferring the ownership interests in the E&P subsidiaries to a new company; the old company was refashioned into the stand-alone titanium dioxide company.

In preparation for an IPO/spinoff of the chemical company, management prepared projections but, at the direction of its CFO, abandoned its customary methodology. Until February 2005, it had forecast titanium dioxide pricing using a mean treadline based on decades of historical pricing data, but the March 2005 forecast that was the source of the IPO numbers showed dramatic increases. Specifically, projected results increased by $99 million in 2008 (to a total of $228 million) and $128 million in 2009 (to a total of $325 million).

In November 2005, the split culminated in a master separation agreement in which the parent company dictated the terms. The chemical business would assume every legacy liability of every discontinued business the original company had owned in the prior 75 years. The E&P business would only assume liability based on "currently conducted" E&P operations. The net cash proceeds from the spinoff were $537.1 million, after expenses, but the chemical business was made to pay everything but $40 million in cash to the E&P entities. Last, but not least, it was to assume $442 million in pension obligations and $186 million in unfunded "other post-employment benefits."

At one point in 2005, Lehman Brothers prepared for a possible sale of the chemical business, but most potential purchasers balked at taking on the large legacy liabilities. Only one of the four finalists, Apollo, made a "final offer," which envisioned a purchase price of $1.3 billion, $300 million in indemnities from the new entity for the environmental liabilities the buyer would assume, and an additional $200 million indemnity for breaches of representation and warranties. The contract contained numerous open items and terms the new E&P company previously had rejected. The sale did not go through. As part of doing due diligence, Apollo also hired an environmental consultant to value the legacy liabilities; the latter calculated them to be $556.1 million on an undiscounted basis.

A one-product business, the chemical company floundered almost immediately after the spinoff. From November 2005 through the third quarter of 2008, it lost $199.7 million. As it was struggling with poor cash flow, it had to fund legacy liabilities. It only was able to fund $90 million per year, net of reimbursements, but even that reduced amount was 56% of its 2006 EBITDA and 95% of its 2007 EBITDA. A financial analyst involved in the negotiations leading up to the spinoff summed up the situation in a picture that showed a flower (the chemical business) and a weed (the legacy liabilities) strangling the flower.

In January 2009, it petitioned for bankruptcy. The litigation trust sued in Bankruptcy Court (S.D.N.Y.) on behalf of a number of plaintiffs, including the three debtor entities that made up the estate of the chemical company and public and private entities that had claims against the debtors for environmental cleanup costs and tort liabilities. The defendants were the parent company and the entities making up the E&P business. The plaintiffs' principal claim for relief was that the transaction that removed substantially all of the parent company's assets from the legacy liabilities was an actual or constructive fraudulent conveyance. It left the debtor insolvent. The defendants characterized the transaction as an attempt "to unlock the value inherent in each of [the businesses]."

Actual fraud beyond dispute. Whether the transfers were actually fraudulent was a question of whether they "hinder[ed] and delay[ed] creditors," the court explained. In this case, it was beyond dispute that [the defendants] acted to free substantially all its assets—"certainly its most valuable assets"—from decades of historic liabilities, said the court. By the defendants' own admission, the assets represented 86.4% of the old entity's assets and accounted for 83.2% of its revenue and 112.6% of its net income as of December 2001. As a result, the legacy creditors would be left with a minimal asset base on which to recover in the future; accordingly, they were "hindered or delayed" as a direct consequence of the transaction, the court concluded.

REV expert undergirds constructive fraud claim. Whether the transfers were constructively fraudulent was a question of whether the chemical business received "reasonably equivalent value" for distributing the E&P assets and other property as part of the spinoff, said the court. Both sides used REV experts.

The plaintiffs retained a reputed bankruptcy analyst to show there was no REV. He determined that the debtor companies conveyed property worth approximately $17 billion (including the E&P assets) and received in return $2.6 billion, a $14.5 billion reduction in value. To calculate the market value for the conveyed E&P assets, he compared the company's oil and gas business to seven independent, comparable E&P companies and determined it was worth approximately $12 billion as of November 2005. He then added a 30% control premium, concluding that the value of the transferred oil and gas assets was approximately $15.8 billion as of that date. His valuation aligned with valuation estimates from Lehman Brothers and Salomon Smith Barney and the actual price the future buyer paid only a few months after the spinoff, he said.

The defendants did not question the calculations, but their REV (and backup damages) expert, who, the court pointed out, testified for the first time in a fraudulent conveyance suit, objected that the REV and solvency analyses should be on a strict entity-by-entity basis. This would mean that two of the debtor companies did not receive REV, but one did receive REV with the transfer of interests in an Australian titanium dioxide plant. The court dismissed that argument, finding that "the 'market' dealt with [the entities] on a consolidated basis." They appeared as one entity for purposes of the spinoff, and every one of them was liable on the debt issued as either a borrower or guarantor. It adopted the conclusions of the plaintiffs' REV expert.

Solvency experts with 'sterling credentials.' The critical next question was whether the transfers left the chemical company insolvent. The answer lies in a "balance sheet test," which requires a determination of whether the debts in the aggregate are greater than assets in the aggregate, said the court. In this case, the parties called insolvency experts with "sterling credentials," it added. In commenting on the experts' qualifications, it explained that the defendants' expert was well known for his view that "market prices typically are more reliable evidence of a company's value than ex post analyses prepared by experts in the context of litigation." For his solvency opinion, he said he did not rely on any of the defendants' other experts but strove for a "completely self-contained analysis."

To determine the chemical company's business enterprise value (BEV) as of November 2005, both experts used a three-prong approach: a discounted cash flow (DCF) analysis, a comparable company analysis, and a comparable transaction analysis. The plaintiffs' expert computed a BEV of $1.03 billion, whereas the defendants' expert said it was $1.7 billion.

1. *DCF analysis.* The major difference in the experts' DCF analyses related to the use of cash flow projections. The plaintiffs' expert believed the company's internal projections required a downward adjustment. As he saw it, they were "sell-side" projections based on overly optimistic assumptions and key numbers "were imposed at the direction of [the parent company's] chief financial officer." For this reason, the expert used the February 2005 projections.

In contrast, the defendants' expert adopted the management projections without independent analysis or view to the chemical business's historical performance. He said his BEV aligned with the BEV that would result from using the projections of future cash flow of third parties "who were either potential bidders or banks that served as advisors and/or lenders" to such bidders.

The court strongly rejected the defendant expert's approach. The use of "sell-side" projections was "particularly insupportable," it said, because titanium dioxide prices began to erode in April 2005, as the defendants' industry expert admitted. They also far exceeded the chemical business's "peak" and "very strong" years of 2000 and 2005. And they were "particularly unreasonable" given uncontroverted evidence that the company's titanium dioxide business peaked in early 2005 and "was on the downturn" by November 2005. Further, use of the third-party projections would result in a BEV of only $1.5 million—almost $200 million lower than the defendants' expert had calculated. Moreover, it was clear that nearly all of the third-party projections used the company's inflated IPO forecasts or outdated data as their starting point, the court added.

For all of these reasons, the plaintiffs' expert was correct to use the earlier projections.

The court found little disagreement as to other inputs. The plaintiffs' expert determined 11% was an appropriate weighted average cost of capital, while the defendants' expert used one that was slightly lower (not specified). The plaintiffs' expert calculated the terminal values based on the Gordon growth model and applied a constant growth rate in perpetuity of 2.5%. The defendants' expert agreed that this was an accepted method but proposed a slightly higher 2.87% rate, which, he said, was based on a market approach.

The plaintiffs' expert concluded the DCF-derived BEV was $1.01 billion; the defendants' expert arrived at $1.7 billion. The court credited the value the plaintiffs' expert proposed.

2. *Comparable company analysis.* The plaintiffs' expert chose 10 commodity chemical companies, calculated EBIT and EBITDA for each, and added a reasonable control premium of 5%. His selection

resulted in a LTM EBITDA multiple of 6.2. Based on this method, he arrived at an IPO value of between $770 million and $1.23 billion, with a midpoint value of $1.0 billion.

The defendants' expert selected 15 companies based on whether potential buyers or industry analysts considered the company comparable to the subject company. He admitted he had not performed an independent analysis of the comparables. He calculated a substantially higher LTM EBITDA multiple of 7.63 and concluded the subject company's BEV was between $1.48 billion and $1.6 billion.

The court found the defendant expert's comparables were not sufficiently similar to the subject company. They included DuPont, which was much larger and more diversified; some other diversified companies; and some specialty companies that "typically trade at a higher multiple than commodity chemical companies like [the subject company]." Consequently, his LTM EBITDA was too high, and his BEV was not persuasive.

3. *Comparable transactions.* The plaintiffs' expert identified seven comparable transactions, calculated EBITDA and EBIT for each, and applied the median to the subject company's adjusted LTM September 2005 operating results. Based on this approach, the company's BEV was between $960 million and $1.24 billion, with a midpoint of $1.1 billion.

The defendants' expert used three data sources (Capital IQ, FactSet, and Thomson SDC) to select comparable companies and included a transaction if it involved chemicals, took place during the three years prior to the IPO, and had a value greater than $50 million. The resulting LTM EBITDA multiple was 8.0, which again was significantly higher than the 6.6x the competing expert determined. Applying it to the management projections, he arrived at a BEV of $1.7 billion.

The court noted that the defendant expert's selection process included transactions involving an Indian fertilizer company, a Swiss company that manufactured waterproofing materials and parts for car manufacturers, and a company making foam-related products for diapers and adult incontinence products. Applying the multiple to the "overstated" internal projections added another flaw to the analysis.

Averaging his three BEVs, the plaintiffs' expert arrived at a BEV of $1.03 billion. Adding the value of nonoperating assets, he calculated a total of $1.22 billion. In contrast, the defendants' expert determined the total asset value was $1.81 billion. The court found the latter value "not persuasive."

Only one in-depth liabilities valuation. The second component in the solvency analysis was the amount of debt that the chemical business faced at the time of the IPO. There was little argument over many of the liabilities, including the company's financial debt, tax liabilities, liabilities for discontinued operations, and unfunded retiree liability. Instead, the parties' disagreement concentrated on the amount of environmental and tort liabilities, "which, again, is what this case is all about," said the court. Expert testimony figured prominently in this part of the trial, as well.

The plaintiffs' expert had decades of experience in environmental engineering, site remediation, and cost accounting. He concluded that the present value of the future response costs of environmental remediation at over 2,740 sites related to the parent company's activities was between $1.5 billion and $1.7 billion as of November 2005.

The defendants recruited two experts, but, as the court noted, the latter made it clear that the resulting 8,000-page report was not a comprehensive analysis, just a rebuttal. The final expert report estimated costs to be approximately $376 million.

"It is significant that [the plaintiffs' expert's] analysis is the only comprehensive valuation in the vast record of this case of [the chemical business's] environmental liabilities," the court said at the outset of its analysis. The defendants' failure to come forward with a comprehensive analysis at any point represented a "major failure of proof."

In keeping with his principle to rely on contemporaneous market information, the defendants' solvency expert "built his solvency analysis around" the findings in Apollo's 2005 environmental study. However, the court found this analysis unreliable because it only considered "known environmental sites," where a third party actually had filed a claim and even the solvency expert admitted on cross-examination that it did not measure the enterprise's "total environmental footprint."

The 2005 "Standard Guide for Disclosure of Environmental Liabilities" described four cost-estimating approaches: expected value, most likely value, range of values, and known minimum values. The plaintiffs' expert used a "most likely value" approach because, he said, he concluded that "the sites were either sufficiently well-developed to conclude that one remedy was likely or information was insufficient to assign reliable probabilities to remedial outcomes."

The defendants contended that the "expected value" approach was a probabilistic approach and the preferred methodology for estimating future environmental costs. The plaintiffs' expert's approach "fail[ed] to address future uncertainty, particularly the question of whether any environmental response action would be required at a site."

The court found the plaintiffs' expert had used his judgment and reasonably decided to adopt another acceptable methodology. Also, it explained, the object of a solvency analysis was "to assign a 'fair valuation' to all debts, with the term 'debt' defined as a liability on a claim, and 'claim' defined in the 'broadest possible sense' to include contingent, unmatured and unliquidated claims." The resulting solvency analysis often accompanied a bankruptcy filing, "where all debts are accelerated and debtors are obligated to send notice of the requirement of filing a proof of claim to every known potential environmental creditor." Ultimately, the court used the plaintiffs' expert's lower figure, valuing the environmental liabilities at $1.5 billion.

The value of the chemical company's other liabilities, it said, was not disputed and totaled approximately $803 million. Accordingly, the fair value of its liabilities was nearly $2.1 billion. These findings meant that the chemical business was insolvent as of the IPO/spinoff date "in that its liabilities at a fair valuation exceeded the value of its assets, even if we use Defendants' highest and most aggressive value for the assets," the Bankruptcy Court concluded.

Still awaiting final conclusion. Resolution of the fraudulent conveyance claim did not spell the end of litigation. The Bankruptcy Court recognized the defendants' right under the Bankruptcy Code to pursue claims against the debtors for, among other things, their failure to adhere to the terms of the spinoff generally and the MSA in particular. The defendants argue that damages the debtors owed would offset the damages the debtors were allowed to recover.

Editor's note: The court's discussion of what methodology to use in assessing environmental liabilities brings to mind a session at the November 2013 AICPA that explored the issue of how to deal with uncertainty in a conceptually correct way but did so in a different context: projecting and discounting future lost profits. According to the presenters, only the "expected value" was statistically valid, whereas the "most likely value" might "work by accident" but failed to account for the range of possible outcomes and ignored the possibilities of extreme outcomes.

In re UDC Homes, Inc.

Citation: 203 B.R. 218, 1996 Bankr. LEXIS 1583
Date of Decision: December 6, 1996
Country: US
State or Federal: Federal
State/Jurisdiction: Delaware
Court: United States Bankruptcy Court
Experts: Donaldson, Lufkin and Jeanrette
Houlihan, Lokey, Howard and Zukin
Type of action: Bankruptcy
Judge: Balick
SIC: 1521 General Contractors--Single Family Houses (except remodeling contractors)

Bankruptcy Expert Fees: UDC Homes

The court ruled that reimbursement of expenses in Chapter 11 cases can be based upon a restructuring fee concept, such as compensation on the basis of a percentage of certain financial benchmarks relating to the resulting transaction. Donaldson, Lufkin and Jeanrette used a percentage of the transaction value and the transaction's accredited security value as a representation for their fees. The court decided that these methods were both reasonable and consistent with the industry average over the last five years.

Houlihan, Lokey, Howard and Zukin was denied portions of its fees because the compensation request was not found to be reasonable by the court and was shown to benefit the completion of the restructuring of the company. Instead of using a monthly fee, the court utilized hourly rates as a proxy for HLHZ.

United Airlines, Inc. v. Regional Airports Improvement Corp.

Citation: 2009 WL 1181852 (C. A. 7 (Ill))
Date of Decision: May 5, 2009
Country: US
State or Federal: Federal
State/Jurisdiction: 7th Circuit
Court: United States Court of Appeals
Type of action: Bankruptcy
Judge: Easterbrook
SIC: 4512 Air Transportation, Scheduled (passenger)

Bankruptcy Court Cannot Just 'Split the Difference' in Divergent Discount Rates

In a case that grew out of the United Airlines Chapter 11 reorganization, the bankruptcy court considered how much the airline owed lenders that financed the improvements to its gates at Los Angeles International Airport (LAX). The original 2004 loan amount was $60 million. According to its reorganization plan, United would have to pay the full, present value of the assets that served as security, i.e., the improved, leased space at the airport. Any excess would be unsecured debt, which the airline could write down.

"Valuation would be straightforward if there were a market for improved space at airports," the U.S. Court of Appeals for the 7th Circuit noted, in reviewing the bankruptcy court's and the intervening district court's decisions. Absent a liquid market, the fair market value of the property turned on the amounts that would be agreed upon by a hypothetical willing buyer and willing seller. Accordingly, the bankruptcy court applied a discounted cash flow (DCF) analysis and considered divergent opinions from three experts: one for the airline, another for the lender, and another for the trustee.

The experts disputed two critical elements of DCF. The bankruptcy court first considered an appropriate, annual rental rate for the 345,167 square feet of leased space. The United expert used $17 per square foot, the historic market rate that LAX charged to airlines. The lenders disagreed, arguing that this was the rate that the airport offered prior to the 1984 Olympics for *unimproved* space. It also reflected a discount, to persuade carriers to improve the terminal; and it locked in any rental increases to the airport's costs rather than to supply and demand. Since that time, the demand for air travel and gates had risen, the lenders said. As secured creditors, they were entitled to a higher price, even if the airline authority had "disabled" itself from increasing current rental rates to market levels.

For instance, the trustee's expert looked at rental rates charged by a consortium of airlines that operated out of the airport's second terminal (LAX2). In 2004, the year of the loan, the consortium leased gates to other carriers at $63 per square foot.

The bankruptcy court found this number inflated. "It was inappropriate to use the net revenues as a measure of market rent," it said. Moreover, it did not indicate the internal rate of return that a hypothetical investor in LAX2 would require. The court also found significant gaps in any projection of hypothetical revenues and expenses, making an estimation of market rental rates too speculative. Accordingly, it adopted the airline's $17 figure.

On review, the district court agreed, adding its own criticism that the trustee's expert did not account for comparable scaling. United operated only seven out of the 20 gates in its terminal; its ratio of costs to revenue would not be the same as that to operate an entire terminal such as LAX2. "Would a bidder on the ... [United] facilities ... pay the same amount as a bidder who acquired [all] 20 gates?" the district court asked. "The answer is obviously no."

The 7th Circuit found fault with both decisions. Neither lower court explained how a ratio of costs to revenue or an operator's internal rate of return was relevant to the market price. "An operator (airline or trustee) would not charge less than avoidable cost; it could do better by giving the space back to the airport authority." How much more it could get depended not on some ratio, but on demand for the space and the price its competitors charged. Because the supply of gates at LAX was fixed (inelastic), the owners could command an economic rent in excess of costs. Even if it was proportionately less costly to operate seven gates compared to the LAX2 consortium's 20, this did not warrant ignoring the $63 per square foot that some carriers willingly paid, which was the only estimate in the record of the price for improved airport space.

"Nor can the $63 figure be thrown out the window" in favor of $17 for vacant space, just because the LAX2 consortium provides additional services to its lessees, the 7th Circuit said. "The bankruptcy court did not attempt to determine how much of the $63 is attributable to these services, and it was most unlikely that they accounted for more than half the price." Ultimately, it did not matter whether the bankruptcy trustee could have leased United's improved gates at $63 a foot or only $40. "Any potential rental price higher than $30 would make the collateral worth at least [the] $60 million [loan amount]," the court ruled, even with the discount rate that the bankruptcy court selected. That is where the court turned its attention next.

The difference 2% makes. In its DFC analysis, the lender's expert chose an 8% discount rate, citing the rate that LAX currently paid on unsecured general revenue bonds. By contrast, United's expert selected 12% as the rate that investors would demand, given the industry's volatility. "The bankruptcy judge added the two estimates and divided by two," the 7th Circuit explained. "An arbitrator might choose such a method, and perhaps a jury would do so behind closed doors, but a judge should choose the *right* discount rate rather than split the difference between the parties," it said, with emphasis.

Instead of looking at the general industry risk, it would have been more credible to look at the risks of *this* airport, the court added. "Real prices are much more informative than lawyers' talk." Although it would have been best to know the rate that actual investors and borrowers negotiated on secured loans to LAX during the valuation period, "it is unnecessary to track down that detail" in this case. LAX was currently operating at capacity; airlines were "clamoring for gates" at the terminal, despite the "fluctuating fortunes" of the industry. The airport was building a new, 10-gate terminal, the first since the early 1980s. These facts implied that space at *this* airport was "not particularly risky," the court said. If the airport could raise money at 8% without giving security, then secured debt investors would not demand more, and that "is all we need to know" to conclude that the discount rate could not exceed 8%.

The 10% discount rate selected by the bankruptcy court made an enormous difference in its conclusion. Using the $17 per square foot rental rate, it projected industry-rate increases over the term of the loan (2021) and then discounted the result ($146 million) at 10% per annum to reach a present value for the security of roughly $35 million. Subtracting this from the $60 million loan amount left $25 million unsecured and available for a write-off. By comparison, using an 8% discount rate, the same $146 million would have a present value of $46 million, the 7th Circuit said. "Thus simply changing the discount rate from 10% to 8% would mean that an extra $11 million of the loan is secured, even holding the rental rate at $17 per square foot." Increasing the rent to $23 would make the lenders fully secured, the court held, in reversing the lower courts' judgments. "Because improved space in [LAX2] fetches almost three times the price needed to make these loans … secured, the lenders are entitled to a full recovery."

U.S. Bank N.A. v. Verizon Communications Inc.

Citation: 2013 U.S. Dist. LEXIS 8521
Date of decision: Jan. 22, 2013
Country: US
State or Federal: Federal
State/Jurisdiction: Texas
Court: United States District Court
Experts: Carlyn Taylor (plaintiff); Mark Hopkins (defendants)
Judge: Fish

Expert's 'Unsupportable' Inputs Undermine DCF Analysis and Credibility

A 10-day bench trial in federal court (N.D. Tex.) focused on a single factual issue: What was the enterprise value of a directories business on the day Verizon spun it off?

Prior to Nov. 17, 2006, the entity was a wholly owned subsidiary of Verizon. Subsequently, it operated for two years as an independent company that was traded on the New York Stock Exchange, before filing for Chapter 11 bankruptcy in early 2009. The plaintiff was the litigation trustee, which, in the context of reorganization, pursued a variety of claims against Verizon and related entities.

Business in for 'secular change.' The plaintiff's chief arguments were that the transaction was a fraudulent conveyance and the defendants had misrepresented the company's value to the market. Verizon's key executives recognized that its directories business was undergoing a "secular" change. Publicly they portrayed the subject as having the potential for significant growth, while secretly they considered it a "dying harvest business" that they needed to sell off.

Under the divestiture, the subject incurred $9.1 billion in debt in exchange for Verizon's domestic print and electronic directories. To structure the transaction as a tax-free event, the parties entered into a tax sharing agreement (TSA) that allocated liability should the IRS later determine that the event did not qualify as such.

At the time of the spinoff, there was significant investor interest in directories companies because of their high and stable cash flow. Verizon's directories business historically produced more than $3.4 billion in annual revenue and its EBITDA margins were about 50%. But while stand-alone directories companies traded at as much as 10 times EBITDA, Verizon's was trading at only 5 to 5.5 times EBITDA.

Also, Verizon's and the subject's SEC filings indicated declining revenues from 2001 through 2006, and industry analysts projected future revenue declines in the incumbent print business. The management forecasts that Verizon provided only to private-side investors showed a flat EBITDA from 2006 through 2010; free cash flow forecasts for the subject showed declines from $459 million in 2006 to $437 million in 2010.

Three private-side investors undertook their own valuations. Morgan Stanley concluded that, on the day of the spinoff, the subject would have a total enterprise value of $12.5 billion and an equity value of about $3.4 billion. Citibank determined an enterprise value of $11.7 billion to $14.4 billion, and Goldman Sachs calculated a value of $12.5 billion, with an equity value of approximately $3.4 billion. In November 2005, the Verizon board received a "strategic update" that indicated a valuation range of $10.5 billion to $15 billion resulting from a discounted cash flow (DCF) analysis, based on "plan of records" forecasts for the previous five years, 2005-2009.

In contrast, an internal Verizon document from summer 2005 suggested a value of only $6.5 billion. This was the result of a "downside case" DCF analysis evaluating a worst-case scenario for the print business alone, a company executive explained. He subsequently "refined" the analysis, using a lower discount rate and correcting earlier analytical flaws. The final valuation, he said, "was what it was when the transaction was completed," that is, $12.8 billion.

Not all calculations count the same. At trial, the plaintiff presented a valuation expert and the defendants a rebuttal as well as a tax expert. The plaintiff's expert was a CPA, who was also a certified insolvency and restructuring accountant, a credentialed business valuator, and held licenses from the Financial Industry Regulatory Authority (FINRA). To determine the value on the spinoff date, she made three separate calculations using: (1) the "market multiple method"; (2) the "comparable transaction method"; and (3) the DCF method.

Under the market multiple approach, she used the same five directories companies and multiples that the investment bank Houlihan Lokey had used when it performed a valuation analysis for a solvency opinion for the subject in fall 2006. She determined the value ranged from $11.7 billion to $13.2 billion but only weighted the outcome at 15%. Verizon's directories business performed worse than the comparables, she said. Also, the selected companies were not truly comparable: Only one was, like the spinoff, an incumbent print company doing business in the U.S. However, that company received significant tax benefits related to the purchase of another directories company—benefits not available to the subject.

Under the comparable transaction method, she again drew on data—in this instance, 17 company transactions—Houlihan Lokey had used for its solvency opinion. Ultimately, she arrived at a value range of $13.4 billion to $15.8 billion, but again she only assigned 15% weight to the result, reasoning that the 17 transactions did not involve sufficiently comparable companies and the TSA prevented the subject from accessing the transactions market. This restriction, she found, conflicted with the premise of the comparable transaction method—that the subject is able to access the market.

For the DCF valuation, she made three different calculations based on three different projections of the subject company's free cash flow for the projection period. For one projection, she adjusted a "base case" projection that Verizon had prepared in 2006; for a second, she used a stress-test projection Houlihan Lokey had made before presenting its solvency opinion; and, for a third projection, she used a mathematical extrapolation of the trend of the actual historical performance of Verizon's directory business from 2003 to 2006. She derived her terminal growth rate from the Gordon growth model, assuming an annual rate of EBITDA decline in perpetuity.

She determined a discount rate of 9.75% using the standard weighted average cost of capital (WACC) formula, which she applied to the three sets of projected cash flow in the projection period and the terminal value. Moreover, she applied a 2% company-specific risk premium in calculating the company's cost of equity. As a result, the overall discount rate was 1% higher than it would have been without the premium. The adjustment was appropriate, given certain disadvantages that were specific to the subject, she explained, including its operating in lower-growth, highly competitive urban markets, lagging behind competitors in terms of performance, having inexperienced management, and facing restrictions in the strategic and financial options it could pursue because of the TSA.

She concluded that the value ranged from $5.4 billion to $6.3 billion and that the midpoint—$5.85 billion—most accurately reflected the enterprise value under the DCF. She stated that she "looked deeply" at any potential flaws in her analysis, given that the result deviated sharply from the other valuations, but ultimately decided to weight the result at 70%.

The weighted calculations produced a value range of $7.5 billion to $8.8 billion. The midpoint—$8.15 billion—was the enterprise value on the day of the transaction, she concluded; this meant the company was insolvent after, including its spinoff debt.

Finally, although she agreed that a valuation professional normally would consider the price at which the company stock traded as "a prime indicator" of its value, she thought in this case it was "completely unreliable" and chose to disregard it. Because of Verizon's misrepresentations and omissions, investors were prone to inflate the subject's equity value by at least $4 billion. She also asserted that Verizon had not disclosed the significant differences in EBITDA margins from the incumbent print and electronic businesses; concealed the steady annual declines in revenue in specific Northeastern urban markets; and failed to disclose consistent missed management projections, as well as a consulting group's pessimistic forecast about the future of the directories business.

Accusations of 'double counting.' The defendants' rebuttal expert focused most of his critique on his counterpart's DCF analysis. Under accepted valuation principles, it was "incorrect" to use a purely historical average for a projection, as she did in her third projection, he noted. It also was inappropriate to use the Houlihan Lokey stress-test projection because that originally was for a sensitivity analysis, not for the purpose of valuation. And she made inappropriate adjustments to Verizon's base case projection. For example, Verizon's incumbent print revenue projection was already more conservative than industry reports suggested; similarly, there was no reason to downward adjust projections of independent market growth because the company historically had seen strong growth in this revenue segment and its projections were again more conservative than industry expectations.

As for the terminal value, to assume an annual rate of EBITDA decline in perpetuity was "commercially unreasonable and inappropriate in a DCF valuation." Most analysts would assume that management would take drastic steps to assure such steep declines did not occur, he said. In fact, the subject had planned for an annual $200 million dividend from which it could withdraw if projected revenues were not on target.

Her discount rate was too high. For one, it assumed a capital structure of 44% debt, 56% equity, which he said was common in European companies but inappropriate for a U.S. business. The one comparable most similar to the subject had a capital structure that was weighted much more heavily toward the debt side, which most analysts would "mimic" in their calculation. He also objected to the 2% company-specific risk premium. Those risk premiums generally were disfavored because they allowed analysts to improperly inject subjective hindsight; moreover, their use in this case led to "double counting," since the plaintiff's expert already had assumed "drastically" lower cash flows than contemporaneous analysts.

As the defendants' expert saw it, merely correcting for the errors in her discount rate and terminal value calculations would have led to a DCF value that was $4.3 billion higher. The result would have been a range of $9.7 billion to $10.6 billion even before weighting it and adding it to the weighted results of the market-based valuations.

He asserted that the plaintiff's expert's DCF analysis produced "a significant outlier" in relation to the calculations she achieved under the other methods and noted that Shannon Pratt's authoritative treatise prescribed ways of how to handle this type of irregularity. An expert might disregard the outlier, assign more weight to the consistent valuations, or more closely examine the model that produced the irregular result to determine what went wrong.

The defendants' tax expert stated that TSAs were typical in spinoff transactions; they provided an incentive for the spun-off company to use diligence before entering into post-spin transactions that might undermine the tax-free status of the earlier event. The agreement here did not impose onerous burdens on the subject to repay or refinance its debts following the transaction.

Reliance on market evidence. The court found the defendants' valuation expert convincing. "For nearly every step of the DCF analysis, [the plaintiff's expert] selected inputs that forced [the company's] value lower," it said, producing a valuation "that is low in the extreme and that implied an incredibly low trading multiple for [the subject]."

It further agreed that numerous instances of double counting "infected" the DCF analysis and the expert's overall conclusions. She not only applied an unjustified company-specific risk premium, but also weighted the market multiple method at 15%, ostensibly because the companies Houlihan Lokey had selected were not sufficiently comparable. But the bank, in its earlier analysis, had already applied a multiple discount to account for any dissimilarity.

It was beyond dispute that the plaintiff's expert's valuation under the DCF method "produced an extreme outlier even within her own analysis," the court stated. But rather than disregard or assign low weight to this valuation, she did the opposite: assign low weight to the consistent valuations. Consequently, the court dismissed the valuation.

All credible evidence indicated that the subject company was solvent on the spinoff date, it noted. Also, there was no misrepresentation. Verizon's and the subject's public filings contained comprehensive risk disclosures informing the market of a general decline in the use of print directories.

Relying on market evidence, the court found that the value "implied by trading on the NYSE was no less than $12.8 billion." But choosing to "remain agnostic" about the precise final figure, it held that the value on the spinoff date was "at least $12 billion."

In re Mary Beth Usery (Ewing B. Gourley v. Mary Beth Usery)

Citation: 123 F.3d 1089 (8th Cir. 1997)
Date of Decision: August 22, 1997
Country: US
State or Federal: Federal
State/Jurisdiction: 8th Circuit
Court: United States Court of Appeals
Type of action: Bankruptcy

The Same Capitalization Rate Must Be Used When Determining Actual Value and Value as Represented for Damages From a Fraudulent Business Sale

The U.S. Court of Appeals for the 8th Circuit considered a nondischargeable damage award stemming from a prepetition fraudulent sale of businesses. In contemplation of divorce, the Userys sold two nursing homes, an apartment complex, and a laundry to the Gourleys in 1989 for $8 million note. Ms. Usery received the note in the divorce. The Gourleys later discovered that the businesses' cash flow was less and the accounts receivable were greater than the Userys represented, and some of the long-term debt assumed in connection with the sale was not business related. The Gourleys invested large amounts of personal funds to continue to operate the businesses and ceased paying on the note due to cash flow problems stemming from the misrepresentation. Ms. Usery subsequently filed for bankruptcy thereafter because the note was her primary source of income. The Gourleys filed an adversarial proceeding claiming the sale was fraudulent and the note was void and unenforceable. The bankruptcy court determined that the sale was fraudulent and awarded the Gourleys $5.4 million in damages, the amount of damages in excess of the note. A district court affirmed the bankruptcy court and this appeal followed.

The 8th Circuit affirmed the bankruptcy court's determination that the sale was fraudulent but reversed and remanded the computation of damages. The circuit court stated that the correct measure of general damages was either rescission of the sale or "benefit of the bargain" (the difference between the actual value and the value as represented at the time of the transaction). The Gourleys presented expert business valuation testimony regarding the value of the nursing homes. Their expert valued the nursing homes at $5.175 million using the capitalization of cash flows methodology. The bankruptcy court accepted this value and subtracted it from the purchase price to arrive at general damages. The circuit court concluded that the general damages award could not stand because it failed to consider that an apartment complex and a laundry were also included in the sale price. The court also concluded that the general damage award could not stand for a more "fundamental" reason: The bankruptcy court confused the actual purchase price with the value of the business but for the Userys' misrepresentations. This court found that "the Gourleys undoubtedly paid more for the nursing homes than they were worth, but the record and testimony of the Gourleys' own expert suggest they did so for two reasons: the Urserys' misrepresentations and the Gourleys' bad judgment." It further noted, "Principles of causation and damages are equally relevant in this situation. Any harm resulting from expectations that are overly optimistic even in light of defendant's fraudulent statements is not a 'natural and probable consequence' of the defendants fraud." *Herberer v. Shell Oil Co.*, 744 S. W .2d 441, 444 (Mo. 1988).

The court went on to note that benefit of the bargain focuses on actual value at the time of the transaction, which is not necessarily the contract price. Here the purchase price and actual value were based on different assumptions. "A fact finder cannot compare figures derived from different capitalization rates (and therefore different risk assumptions) to determine damages attributable to fraud, because part of the difference will be due to the change in risk perception and not due to the fraud at all."

The court further considered the bankruptcy court's determination of special damages, the majority of which was consequential damages relating to amounts the Gourleys invested to make the homes as profitable as the Urserys represented. The court found that this argument amounted to attempting to recover fewer than two different theories for the cash flow misrepresentation. It ordered the bankruptcy court, on remand, to limit the Gourleys to a single recovery for cash flow misrepresentation.

In re Valley-Vulcan Mold Co. (I)

Citation: I1999 Bankr. LEXIS 991
Date of decision: August 19, 1999
Country: US
State or Federal: Federal
State/Jurisdiction: 6th Circuit
Court: United States Bankruptcy Court
Type of action: Bankruptcy
Experts: Jeffrey R. Greene (for Valley-Vulcan Mold Co.)
SIC: 3312 Steel Works, Blast Furnaces (Including Coke Ovens), and Rolling Mills (except coke ovens not integrated with steel mills and hot-rolling purchased steel)
Key words: Expert testimony

Solvency Opinions Admissible in Bankruptcy Court

The U.S. Court of Appeals for the 6th Circuit considered whether the bankruptcy court improperly considered expert valuation testimony when determining whether the committee could recover $9 million as a fraudulent conveyance. "In 1986 and 1987, changes within the steel industry, most notably the increasing use of the 'continuous casting' process which does not use ingot molds in steel production, prompted many ingot mold manufacturers to pursue partnerships and mergers in order to remain competitive." In this environment, Vulcan, a subsidiary of Ampco, sought an alliance. It received an offer to purchase from Underwood for $10.4 million plus debt assumption. Vulcan rejected this offer in favor of a partnership with Valley, another ingot mold manufacturer. Valley was a subsidiary of Microdot and in Chapter 11.

Both Valley and Vulcan agreed to transfer all their assets and liabilities relating to their ingot mold business to the new entity, Valley-Vulcan. Both parties would become equal partners in the new entity. Since Vulcan was substantially more valuable than Valley, Valley-Vulcan was required to pay a $9 million equalization payment to Vulcan. The payment was drawn from Valley-Vulcan's line of credit. The $9 million was transferred to Ampco in satisfaction of intracompany debt and as dividend on Vulcan's liquidation.

The new entity, Valley-Vulcan, initially did well. However, problems with its hot metal supply and labor eventually forced the company into bankruptcy. The unsecured creditors committee sought to recover the $9 million equalization payment from Ampco as a fraudulent conveyance. Before the bankruptcy court, Ampco presented expert valuation evidence that showed that the value of Vulcan's assets justified the equalization payment of $9 million. Its expert, a "national director of a valuation services group with a leading financial firm," valued Vulcan's assets as a going concern between $16.2 million and $27.9 million, excluding liabilities, on the date of Valley-Vulcan's formation. This expert also relied on Underwood's offer to purchase Vulcan, showing that the offer was $1.83 million greater than the equalization payment. The creditors' committee argued that this expert's valuation was incorrect because he did not determine the assets' "fair salable value." However, the committee did not present any expert testimony. The bankruptcy court agreed with Ampco's position and denied recovery of the $9 million payment. The creditors committee appealed.

On appeal, the committee argued, among other things, that the bankruptcy court erred by admitting the testimony of Ampco's valuation expert. They claim that: (1) the expert was not qualified to give "solvency opinions"; and (2) "this area of analysis is not widely accepted in the appropriate professional venues." The 6th Circuit considered the claims in light of *Daubert v. Merrell Dow Pharmaceuticals, Inc.*, 509 U.S. 579, 589, 113 S. Ct. 2786, 2794-95, 125 L. Ed.2d 469 (1993), and *Kumho Tire Co., Ltd. v. Carmichael*, 119 S. Ct. 1167, 1175, 143 L. Ed.2d 238 (1999). The appellate court affirmed the bankruptcy court's decision to admit the expert's testimony. It found that the "bankruptcy court overruled the Committee's objection to the appropriateness of solvency opinions as a field of inquiry, noting that the opinion of a person experienced in evaluating the solvency of a business would assist the court in the determination of facts at issue in the proceeding." Further, the 6th Circuit stated, "In light of [the expert's] experience in determining the solvency of companies in complex financial circumstances and the nature of the factual issues regarding the effect of the transfers challenged by the Committee, [the expert's] testimony easily satisfies the flexible standard for admissibility enunciated in *Daubert* and *Kumho*."

In re Valley-Vulcan Mold Co. (II)

Citation: 2001 U.S. App. LEXIS 3212
Date of Decision: February 26, 2001
Country: US
State or Federal: Federal
State/Jurisdiction: 6th Circuit
Court: United States Court of Appeals
Type of action: Bankruptcy
Experts: Jeffrey Greene
Judge: Siler
Key words: Daubert, Expert testimony

Expert Testimony Using DCF Method to Determine Solvency Admissible

The relevant issue in this bankruptcy litigation matter was whether the bankruptcy court erred in permitting the expert testimony of Jeffrey Greene. Greene testified as to the solvency of Valley-Vulcan and to the value of one of the entities that formed Valley-Vulcan at the time of its formation. The Official Unsecured Creditors Committee claimed that the testimony should not have been allowed on the grounds that solvency expertise was not a widely accepted field in "appropriate professional venues."

DCF is well-recognized methodology. Citing *Daubert* and *Kumho,* and the broad flexibility permitted the trial court under FRE 702, the 6th Circuit held that the bankruptcy judge did not abuse his discretion by admitting Greene's testimony.

Interestingly, the court did not address the Committee's contention that solvency expertise was not a widely accepted field. It simply stated that Greene's qualifications as an expert were "well established" and that his valuations were based on a discounted cash flow valuation, a "well-recognized methodology for determining a business's going-concern value."

Expert qualified. The court concluded the matter by saying that, "[b]ased on the bankruptcy court's articulated desire for assistance and Greene's qualifications," the bankruptcy court's determination that Greene qualified as an expert witness satisfied Federal Rule of Evidence 702.

In re Stephen L. Vecchitto (I)

Citation: 235 B.R. 231, 1999 Bankr. LEXIS 388
Date of Decision: March 30, 1999
Country: US
State or Federal: Federal
State/Jurisdiction: Connecticut
Court: United States Bankruptcy Court
Type of action: Bankruptcy
Experts: Alec R. Bobrow (for plaintiff) Walter C. King (for defendants)
Judge: Krechevsky
SIC: 8721 Accounting, Auditing, and Bookkeeping Services (other accounting services)
Key words: Bankruptcy, Valuation methods

Can Debtor Transfer Valueless Stock?

A Chapter 7 bankruptcy debtor was sued by the trustee to avoid the transfer of certain shares of stock that debtor declared valueless. Discussion of noncompete clause, a stockholder's agreement, and valuation methods by experts.

In re Stephen L. Vecchitto (II)

Citation: No. 00-5010 (unpublished)
Date of Decision: October 11, 2000
Country: US
State or Federal: Federal
State/Jurisdiction: 2nd Circuit
Court: United States Court of Appeals
Type of action: Bankruptcy

Stock in an Accounting Firm Valued at Zero

The United States Court of Appeals for the 2nd Circuit considered the valuation of stock in an accounting firm. The debtor's estate contained 220 shares in the accounting firm. The stock was subject to a buy-sell agreement, which spelled out the valuation of the stock in the event the debtor resigned, retired, or was terminated. After filing for Chapter 7 bankruptcy protection, the estate valued the shares at zero and sought to exclude the stock from the bankruptcy. The trustee claimed the stock should be valued under the firm's shareholders' agreement.

Before the bankruptcy court, the debtor's expert valued the stock using the net asset and income valuation methods. The expert concluded the stock had no value. The trustee argued that, according to the shareholders' agreement, the stock had a value of $397,825. The bankruptcy court found "that the Shareholder Agreement was an executory contract for purposes of the Bankruptcy Code." Because the trustee did not assume the agreement, it was not binding. Therefore, the bankruptcy court valued the stock at zero. On appeal, the district court affirmed the bankruptcy court. The trustee then appealed to the 2nd Circuit. The 2nd Circuit affirmed, finding that, "because the trustee did not assume the agreement, its terms were no longer in effect and its valuation methodology was inapplicable."

The 2nd Circuit also examined the trustee's argument that the stock had market value even though its principals were not subject to a no compete agreement in favor of the firm. The trustee argued that *In re Prince,* 85 F.3 314 (7th Cir.), *cert. denied,* 519 U.S. 1040 (1996), "held that goodwill is not to be excluded as a matter of law simply due to the absence of a covenant not-to compete." The 2nd Circuit noted that *Prince* provides that exclusion of goodwill be determined "case by case." It found that the bankruptcy court did not automatically exclude any goodwill value but had appropriately determined a lack of goodwill based on testimony regarding the firm's risk of losing its client base. Therefore, it denied the trustee's claims and affirmed the bankruptcy court's findings.

VFB LLC v. Campbell Soup Co.

Citation: 2007 U.S. App. LEXIS 7407
Date of Decision: March 30, 2007
Country: US
State or Federal: Federal
State/Jurisdiction: 3rd Circuit
Court: Court of Appeals
Type of action: Bankruptcy
Experts: Henry Owsley (plaintiff), Timothy Leurhman (defendant)
Judge: Cudahy
SIC: 2099 Food Preparations, NEC (except bouillon, marshmallow creme, spices, peanut butter, perishable prepared foods, tortillas, tea and tea extracts, dry dip mix, prepared dips, dry salad dressing mix, seasoning mix, dried potatoes, pasta)

Expert Valuations a 'Sideshow' Compared to Capital Pricing Markets

The plaintiff faced an enormous hurdle in its appeal of the Delaware U.S. District Court's decision in this case. Essentially, it had to convince the 3rd Circuit Court to set aside findings that the public securities market provided the "most disinterested" if not "ideal data point" regarding the price of a company's publicly traded common stock at the time of the target transaction.

This is not an absolutely insurmountable challenge, although it does require the right facts. Compare, for example, the decision of the United States Bankruptcy Court, also in Delaware, in *In re Winstar Communications, Inc.* There, the valuation expert was able to show that despite a "large and active" market for the public company's shares, the typical investor had no idea of its true financial condition, and management's 10-year earnings projections were unreasonable if not unreliable. He was helped by a telecomm market that was "simply too unstable" at the time to provide an adequate indicator of value.

The plaintiff in *VFB LLC* had no such luck with the facts.

Campbell's spins off specialty foods. Briefly, back in 1998, Campbell's incorporated a wholly owned subsidiary (VFI) and then sold off several of its food companies (Vlasic pickles, Swanson frozen dinners) in exchange for borrowed cash, then issued VFI's stock to its own shareholders.

The $500 million spin was "particularly hard" on VFI—more so than the public knew at the time. District managers had tried several techniques such as bulk discounts and product loading to increase short-term sales, but none changed the company's longer-term prospects. Within three months of the spin, VFI's earnings had dropped by half. To avoid default, VFI secured new lending, the price of its shares steadied, and the company outperformed the S&P midcap food index for more than a year. As required by its refinancing, VFI also reissued $200 million in unsecured debt to its institutional investors, despite disclosing discouraging financial data for FY 1999, including declining sales, limited advertising, "and other worrisome news."

The problems were public. The company's decline continued, and, over the next two years, VFI sold off the former specialty food assets for $115 million less than the $500 million received from Campbell's. By then, VFI was bankrupt, and its successor-in-interest, VFB, claimed the entire amount as a fraudulent conveyance.

To do so, VFB needed to prove that VFI was insolvent (worth less than $500 million) at the 1998 sale. In its trial to the District Court, VFB argued that, because of the company's promotional sales tactics, Campbell's SEC disclosures—particularly those related to its FY 1997 and 1998 earnings—were inflated, sufficient to mislead not only the public securities markets, but also the banks that underwrote the spin.

But, in looking at the market price, the U.S. District Court of Delaware found that, on March 30, 1998, VFI's stock traded at over $25 per share, giving it a $1.1 billion capitalization rate, an amount "greatly in excess" of the $500 million transaction. After the spin, the court also noted that the company's inflated sales figures had quickly corrected themselves, as the market rapidly "learned the truth" about VFI's earning prospects. And yet, despite its "very public problems," the company's market capitalization did not drop below $1.1 billion until 1999. Even if the market was suffering from "irrational exuberance," as VFB claimed, the court found no basis for setting aside a value "that was fairly established in open and informed trading."

Market price more reliable than experts. In its appeal to the 3rd Circuit, VFB tried to resurrect its arguments, attacking the District Court's reliance on market capitalization. Indeed:

> Some portions of VFB's brief seem to argue that courts should never measure the value of a business by its market capitalization because the market price of a corporation's stock "is based on expectations (projections) of future income," which may turn out to be inaccurate.

"That contention is clearly wrong," the 3rd Circuit said. "Equity markets allow participants to voluntarily take on or transfer among themselves the risk that their projections will be inaccurate; fraudulent conveyance law cannot rationally be invoked to undermine that function."

VFB also tried to reargue that Campbell's manipulations had inflated VFI's market capitalization, misleading investors at the time of the spin. But the District Court had specifically considered the company's capitalization six months later, after the market had absorbed the "truth" of VFI's situation; VFB failed to show that the market was somehow still affected by Campbell's spin tactics several months after the fact.

Its final argument claimed the District Court erred by "dismissing" its expert valuation reports in favor of market prices. The 3rd Circuit agreed that the expert valuations were more or less a "sideshow" at trial, but "we do not think that the District Court erred in choosing to rely on the objective evidence from the public equity and debt markets."

To the extent that the experts purport to measure actual post-spin performance, as by, for example, a discounted cash flow analysis, they are measuring the wrong thing. To the extent they purport to reconstruct a reasonable valuation of the company in light of uncertain future performance, they are using inapt tools. Absent some reason to distrust it, the market price is a more reliable measure of the stock's value than the subjective estimates of one or two expert witnesses.

These are strong words, which may reappear in the *Winstar* litigation, currently under appeal—to the U.S. District Court of Delaware.

In re Village at Camp Bowie I, L.P.

Citation: 2011 Bankr. LEXIS 3033
Date of decision: Aug. 4, 2011
Country: US
State or Federal: Federal
State/Jurisdiction: New York
Court: United States Bankruptcy Court
Experts: Allyn Bryant Needham (debtor); Paul French (lender)
Judge: Lynn

Court Adopts Expert's Interest Rate, Based in Part on B/P Calculator

The debtor owned a mixed-use development in one of the busier sections of Fort Worth, Texas. After several extensions of its underlying financing, however, the debtor defaulted and declared Chapter 11 bankruptcy. At the time, it owed more than $31.2 million on the property to its secured lender.

Investment group buys debt at a discount. At the lender's auction, Western Real Estate Equities purchased the debt at a discount. Western was not in the lending business; rather, it wanted to own and operate the property and had no interest in negotiating a reorganization plan with the debtor.

Thus, when the debtor proposed a plan that would infuse $1.5 million of new equity into the property and pay off its debt in five years, at an interest rate of 5.83%, Western objected, stating that this proposed rate failed to return the present value of its claim. At a hearing on the feasibility of the debtor's proposed plan pursuant to Sec. 1129(b)(2)(A) of the Bankruptcy Code, both parties offered competing real estate and interest rate experts.

In particular, the debtor offered a real estate appraisal of the property at $38.4 million, but Western's real estate expert said it was worth closer to $28.4 million. Without any discussion of its findings, the bankruptcy court valued the property at $34 million, or approximately halfway between the experts' amounts.

With respect to the sufficiency of the proposed interest rate, the court first looked to the U.S. Supreme Court's decision in *Till v. SCS Credit Corporation*, 541 U.S. 465 (2007), a Chapter 13 bankruptcy case that nevertheless applies to the feasibility requirements under Sec. 1129. In *Till*, the court approved a formula approach to calculate a proper "cram-down" interest rate, although it suggested that, in some cases, a market approach might be appropriate.

In this case, both of the parties' interest rate experts agreed that no efficient market existed for Western's loan. Accordingly, both experts adopted a formula approach, beginning with the "risk-free" rate. The debtor's expert, like the *Till* court, used the prime rate as his base, but Western's expert applied the rate for five-year Treasury notes of 1.71%. Finding that the *Till* case did not require using the prime rate as a starting point, the bankruptcy court adopted the approach by Western's expert, also finding it "more thoughtful and better documented" than that of the debtor's expert.

After starting with a 1.71% risk-free rate, Western's expert adjusted it to account for certain risk factors as applied to three separate tranches of debt: (1) a senior secured position equal to 65% of collateral (property) value; (2) a junior or mezzanine position equal to 20% of collateral value; and (3) an "equity band" equal to the remaining 15% of collateral value. These three levels reflected the current realities of commercial lending practices, the expert believed.

Based on these same risk factors and realities, the expert first computed a baseline interest rate for senior debt of between 4.76% and 5.01%, and a range of 13.02% to 14.88% for junior lenders. The lower and upper ranges reflected the expert's reliance on the two competing real estate appraisals, but, since, using the higher appraisal, Western's debt equaled 84% of the property's value, he calculated only a single interest rate of 18.63% for equity investors.

The expert next determined what each of the senior, junior, and equity tranches represented as a percentage of the debt (Western's claim). Based on these proportions, he calculated a combined interest rate ranging from 7% (based on the higher real estate appraisal) and 9.25% (based on the lower appraisal). Lastly, he adjusted these rates for the reduced risk at the junior debt and equity, including the existence of only one lender, and the benefits of bankruptcy, such as court supervision and feasibility determinations. Ultimately, Western's expert calculated final interest rates between 6.25% and 7.75%.

Court approves methodology, with adjustments. "The court has not detailed here the data from which [Western's expert] derived his numbers," the court observed in a footnote to its feasibility opinion. "Suffice it to say that his research was extensive and well-planned, [and] ... his opinions are defensible under the most rigorous *Daubert* analysis." (Editor's note: Among other tools and techniques, he used the *Butler Pinkerton Calculator—Total Risk Calculator* (BPC).)

At the same time, the court noted the expert worked with "several flawed assumptions"—first and foremost, the parties' divergent real estate appraisals. Since the court found the property was worth $34 million, or the rough midpoint of these values, it decided to use the averages of the expert's interest rate ranges for each of the three debt tranches, or 4.89% for the senior level, 13.95% for the junior level, and 18.63% for the equity level. The court also added the proposed capital infusion of $1.5 million to the value of the property and then added the cost of Western's attorney fees (per a prior court order) to the amount of Western's claims.

Having "pegged the debt to Western and the value of the debtor," the court allocated the three interest rates proportionally to Western's claim, determining an overall interest rate of 7.422%, before final adjustments for the benefits of bankruptcy and having a single lender. Western's expert calculated the former between 0.5% and 0.8%, but the court rejected these as too high, finding that the benefits of bankruptcy in this case were "minimal."

Similarly, the court rejected the expert's 0.85% upward adjustment of the interest rate to reflect a profit for the lender. Although the *Till* applied the prime rate, which has a built-in assumption of lender profit, this court found that *Till* "simply adopted prime rate as a useful starting point," and the case did not promise any profit margin to the cram-down lender. Instead, all that the Bankruptcy Code required was the present value of the secured claim, including an interest rate that "arguably leaves the lender where it would have been absent cram down under the applicable plan."

Accordingly, the court adjusted its 7.44% rate downward by 0.85% and 1.17%, to arrive at a cram-down interest rate of 6.27% to 6.59%. Since this range was higher than the debtor's proposed rate of 5.83%, the court rejected the proposed plan unless and until it provided an interest rate of "at least 6.4%" and directed the parties to meet and confer regarding an amended plan.

Villaje del Rio, Ltd. v. Colina del Rio, L.P.

Citation: 2009 WL 1606431 (W.D. Tex.)
Date of Decision: June 8, 2009
Country: US
State or Federal: Federal
State/Jurisdiction: Texas
Court: United States District Court
Type of action: Bankruptcy
Experts: Paul Hornsby and Martyn Glenn (plaintiff)
Judge: Rodriguez
SIC: 1522 General Contractors—Residential Buildings Other Than Single-Family

Cutting Costs on Expert Testimony and Appraisals Doesn't Always Pay Off

A large office and residential/retail project failed to get off the ground in San Antonio, leaving the development company bankrupt and owing more than $26 million on the construction financing. To recover some of the funds, the developer claimed that the bank "forced" his company to overpay the general contractor by more than $2.8 million. The overpayments constituted fraudulent conveyances, the developer claimed, because the project was insolvent at the time and incurred the obligations without receiving "reasonably equivalent value" in exchange. (The developer had also personally loaned the project $1.5 million and was seeking enough to recover this unsecured debt.)

Attempts to pull in three 'experts.' The developer designated two experts to provide damages and valuation testimony, based on appraisals prepared in connection with the project's financing. In what appears to be another effort to cut costs, the developer also designated himself to testify as an expert concerning the property's value and damages.

The defendant bank objected to all three witnesses, arguing that none met the standards for reliable testimony under Rule 702 of the Federal Rules of Evidence. In particular, the owner was not qualified by experience, training, or skill to testify as an insolvency or valuation expert. The valuation experts were disqualified because they prepared their appraisals in 2001 and 2002, during the project's underwriting phases, but the alleged overpayments took place in 2004. The court considered each witness in turn.

1. *Owner's testimony as expert.* Although the owner may have possessed sufficient personal knowledge to testify as a lay witness regarding the solvency of this particular project, the court observed, he was not qualified to testify as an expert on the financial solvency of construction projects in general. "[L]ay testimony results from a process of reasoning familiar in everyday life, while expert testimony results from a process of reasoning which can be mastered only by specialists in the field." Even an owner who is "intimately familiar" with a business may not qualify as an expert to testify regarding the company's value or lost profits, the court held.

2. *Appraisal experts.* Because they prepared their valuation reports two years prior to the project's alleged insolvency, the appraisal experts did not consider the relevant facts, data, or issues to support a finding of insolvency. A fraudulent conveyance doesn't require "exact" proof of a debtor's

assets and liabilities at the time of the transfer, the court held. In this case, however, "even if the reports and appraisal somehow purport to value the construction project at various stages of completion ... the data [the experts] relied on could be, at best, mere projections and not actual data." As a result, their methodologies and testimony were neither reliable nor helpful, and the court struck these two expert witnesses—leaving the plaintiff with none.

Vision-Park Properties v. Seaside Engineering

Citation: 2014 U.S. Dist. LEXIS 41923
Date of decision: March 27, 2014
Country: US
State or Federal: Federal
State/Jurisdiction: Florida
Court: United States District Court
Type of action: Bankruptcy
Experts: John Reuben Bice (appellants); Robert McCullar (debtor)
Judge: Walker
SIC: 8713 Surveying Services (except geophysical surveying)
Key words: Going concern premise, Build-up Discount Rate, Emergence Risk Premium, Income approach, Plan Confirmation, Liquidation method

Debtor's Challenges Justify Bankruptcy Court's Emergence Risk Premium

In appealing the Bankruptcy Court's plan confirmation, the appellants took particular issue with the court's rejection of their expert's valuation of the debtor company. In their opinion, the court overrated certain risk factors surrounding the debtor and as a result determined an improperly low value. Ultimately, the discussion boiled down to the applicable discount rate.

The debtor was a small, closely held engineering and surveying company that specialized in hydrographic surveying and navigational mapping—a niche business. Based on their unique mapping and people skills, the company's five principal shareholders established a special rapport with the U.S. Army Corps of Engineers. Eventually, 90% of the company's revenues came from projects for the Corps. Because the government contracts were qualification contracts, not awards based on the lowest bid, the principals' experience was critical to securing the contracts and to the company's survival.

The company historically maintained three months' worth of operating capital on hand, but its financial situation devolved as a result of the economic downturn in late 2000, a change in its way of doing business, and the principal shareholders' unsuccessful real estate ventures. The ventures received funding from the appellants in the case, and the shareholders guaranteed the debt. Once the company and the individual shareholders filed for bankruptcy, the appellants acquired an equity interest in the company.

The debtor succeeded in obtaining approval from the Bankruptcy Court of its reorganization plan, which envisioned keeping its structure as a small business—and not allowing the appellants to acquire a majority interest in it—and continuing to employ all of its 23 workers. The Bankruptcy Court's approval turned on its valuation of the debtor.

'Way understated' discount rate. The Bankruptcy Court considered valuation testimony from the appellants' expert and a rebuttal opinion from the debtor's expert.

The appellants' expert valued the company under the going concern standard, using an income approach. He considered "the earning capacity of the business" and used "a discount rate that is reflective of the risk associated with the business [which] determines what the value of a future stream of income would be utilizing such a discount rate." He arrived at a "build-up" discount rate of 18.44%, allocating only 1.5% of it to the company-specific risk. He did not believe the departure of any one of the five principal employees would seriously affect the company's ability to preserve its contracts with the Corps. He concluded that the debtor was worth $960,000.

When testifying on direct, the debtor's expert advanced a liquidation analysis, which showed a negative $628,000 value. The appellants objected, and the Bankruptcy Court rejected that analysis as inappropriate. Consequently, the debtor's expert critiqued the appellant expert's opinion, particularly the latter's selected discount rate. That element, he said, was perhaps the most subjective factor of the analysis and critical because "just a few tweaks in the discount rate that is used can make a huge difference in the valuation that you end up with." By way of example, he explained that increasing the 18.44% rate used by the rival expert by just seven points would reduce the value of the company from $960,000 to $575,460.

He called the 18.44% rate "way understated" and said the company-specific risk in this case was "major." In his view, the appellants' expert "failed to separate the value of the business from the value of the professional owners of the business." The opposing expert did not adequately appreciate the debtor's difficulty of replacing key personnel given the principals' unique technical skills. The rebuttal expert believed the company would "not have the resources to withstand any sort of interruption of its services and to go through the process of finding key personnel."

Also, he said his review of the debtor's financial statements revealed an $80,000 liability for back wages and taxes to its employees that the appellants' expert had not considered. He projected a loss of approximately a quarter million for the most recent year, whereas the appellants' expert only recorded a loss of $57,000. According to the rebuttal expert, a financial analysis should account for a loss of that magnitude for the most recent year when the company historically had operating profits.

He noted that one of the authorities the rivaling expert used to support his analysis had proposed an 80% discount rate for a company in financial distress. Were he asked to state an applicable rate for this case, he would say it should be in the range from 40% to 75%.

Bankruptcy Court homes in on 'willing buyer.' The Bankruptcy Court noted that there were "two different experts talking about what each of them viewed as a discount rate" and acknowledged the impact of the discount rate on the valuation number. The court found it "extraordinary" that the value the appellants' expert had computed was only $40,000 less than the value the principals had placed on the company several years earlier, in 2008, 2009, and 2010. Yet, in 2011, the record showed a loss of almost $240,000. This factor indicated that the expert failed to give adequate consideration to the fact that the company was in bankruptcy—which "not only affected their value, it affected their credit rating, borrowing power and potential for obtaining new business," said the court.

It also emphasized that there were considerable other risk factors that a willing buyer would weigh in assessing the company. These related to the key role the principal shareholders played in dealing with the Corps and the company's deriving 90% of its revenues from contracts with the Corps. In the court's view, "if you don't have the employees and you don't have the contracts, what have you got left?"

Ultimately, the Bankruptcy Court arrived at a value of $200,000, without identifying the discount rate it applied or specifying the adjustments it made to the appellant expert's valuation. Based on its valuation, the court approved the debtor's reorganization plan.

No undue focus on risk factors. The appellants appealed the decision at the district court (N.D. Fl.), spotlighting the valuation issue. They alleged a host of errors resulting in the Bankruptcy Court's undervaluation of the company and its erroneous approval of the plan.

First, the appellants contended that the Bankruptcy Court's focus on the risk of losing certain key employees meant it valued something other than the entity that was featured in the plan, which contemplated retention of all employees.

The district court disagreed. The Bankruptcy Court simply took note of the unique circumstances in the case: The value of the company depended on "the human capital of a small number of employees with a unique skill set and a relationship with the U.S. Army Corps of Engineers." In this case, the district court added, the company's value did not lie in tangible assets. To consider the risks arising from the nature of the company did not mean the Bankruptcy Court "valued something other than the plan proposed."

Second, the appellants claimed the Bankruptcy Court was wrong to reject the only competent going-concern value—their expert's $960,000 valuation—in front of the court. They suggested that, since the court did not articulate its adjustments, it "effectively pulled a number out of thin air or merely split the difference between the two experts' valuation figures."

This argument also got no traction with the district court. "The Bankruptcy Court was free to accept the testimony of any witness, including an expert witness, in whole or in part." Here, it rejected the liquidation analysis that the debtor's expert proposed. At the same time, it relied on evidence discrediting the valuation that the appellants' expert advanced and particularly his discount rate. The district court found the rebuttal expert's testimony about the drastic effects of a change in discount rate on the overall valuation was particularly relevant. Using a discount rate in the suggested range of 40% to 75% "would produce results as reached by the Bankruptcy Court or a lesser value." Therefore, the Bankruptcy Court's valuation had support in the record.

Three, the appellants objected that the Bankruptcy Court's focus on a prospective buyer's concern over the alleged risks of a company coming out of bankruptcy reflected a market analysis and its attendant undervaluation of the company.

The district court found this claim unconvincing as well. The Bankruptcy Court's observation about the appellant expert's failure to consider the effects of bankruptcy did not mean it valued the company "strictly on a market analysis," rather it was analogous to the court's applying an emergence risk premium to reflect the challenges the company faced as it emerged from bankruptcy.

For all these reasons, the district court upheld the Bankruptcy Court's valuation and its confirmation of the reorganization plan.

Whyte v. C/R Energy Coinvestment II, L.P. (In re SemCrud)

Citation: 2013 Bankr. LEXIS 2351
Date of decision: June 10, 2013
Country: US
State or Federal: Federal
State/Jurisdiction: Delaware
Court: United States Bankruptcy Court
Type of action: Bankruptcy
Experts: M. Freddie Reiss (debtor); Michael Lederman (defendants)
Judge: Shannon
SIC: 1389 Oil and Gas Field Services, NEC (except construction of field gathering lines, site preparation and related construction activities performed on a contract or fee basis)
Key words: Bankruptcy, Chapter 11, Solvency, Asset approach, Income approach, Market approach

Bankruptcy Court Wary of Asset Approach in Solvency Analysis

Five months before it filed for Chapter 11, the debtor made partnership distributions to the defendant equity interest owners for over $29 million, which the plaintiff trustee sought to avoid and recover. The Bankruptcy Court considered expert testimony on the issue of solvency at the time of the distributions.

The debtor primarily serviced the energy industry, moving oil and gas products via trucks and pipelines and storing them; its revenues for 2007 were about $13.2 billion. But it also had a marketing business that was trading in derivatives on the New York Mercantile Exchange (NYMEX) and the over-the-counter markets. Ultimately, these activities caused a liquidity crisis and the debtor's Chapter 11 bankruptcy filing in July 2008.

The defendants were equity owners in the debtor and as such received equity distributions, including over $29 million in February 2008. In challenging the distributions, the litigation trustee claimed that the debtor's CEO had engaged in speculative derivatives trading in violation of the company's loan agreements. Also, the debtor allegedly had moved millions of dollars into a company the CEO owned to enable him to do his own commodities trading.

Agreement on valuation basics. In trial in Bankruptcy Court (D. Del.), the trustee argued the transfer was avoidable because the debtor received no value for the distributions considering they were equity distributions. The defendants tried to claim that the debtor's status as a limited partnership allowed for taxes to pass through to the individual partners, which meant there was a value. The court dismissed that claim, pointing out that the Bankruptcy Code and case law taught that equity distributions did not confer "value" on the transferor.

To succeed on its fraudulent transfer claim, the trustee next had to show the debtor was insolvent on the distribution date. For the solvency analysis, both sides presented expert testimony to determine the debtor's fair value.

The experts agreed—and so did the court—that the debtor should be valued on a going-concern basis because liquidation in bankruptcy was not "clearly imminent" on the distribution date. Rather, the business was fully functioning, with plans to continue operations. The experts, and the court, further agreed that there were three standard approaches to valuing the company—the income approach, the market approach, and the asset-based approach—and that the income approach was the preferred method for valuing a company on a going-concern basis.

Trustee's expert advocates asset approach. But when it came to choosing the appropriate method for *this* case, the experts disagreed. Accordingly, their conclusions as to solvency diverged considerably.

Specifically, the trustee's expert claimed the asset approach was the only reliable approach here. It alone accounted for the speculative trading activities. He used Jan. 31, 2008, as the valuation date and analyzed the company's consolidated financial statements for 2007 and the unaudited financials for January 2008. He made several key adjustments to the balance sheet line items. For one, he reduced the receivables for the CEO's company from $263.4 million to zero, reasoning it was "very unlikely" that the debtor would be able to collect on the money owed. The records showed a lack of documentation for that company's receivables and "lackluster" collection efforts on the debtor's part. An informed buyer would have assigned little or no value to the receivables, he argued. He explained that "debt issuance costs" were the "upfront costs a company pays when issuing debt and it is capitalized as an asset on the company's balance sheet and amortized over the life of the debt issued." He decided to reduce the debt issuance balance from $28 million to zero, he said, because "there is no value of this 'asset' to a third party." The asset only reflected the costs the company previously had incurred, he continued. He reduced "the investment in affiliates" item by $13.5 million because of the sale of one entity.

He made no adjustment for "goodwill," stating that the balance sheet already took it into consideration. The same logic, he said, applied to "customer relations," which was "an intangible asset created through the acquisition of a business." Even though it was appropriate to make downward adjustments for items related to the CEO's speculative trading and concomitant significant unrealized losses, he found it unnecessary to do so for his report.

He also described certain limitations the income approach and market approach showed in this case. The income approach was inappropriate here, he found, because of "the lack of reliable, detailed financial projections and corresponding assumptions with which to create a discounted cash flow

(DCF) valuation." He acknowledged that a Goldman Sachs valuation from June 2008 used both the income and market approaches (see below) and, specifically, the DCF. But, he said, that analysis relied on financial projections whose assumptions Goldman Sachs did not provide; therefore, he was unable to assess their reasonableness. He also believed the Goldman valuation rested on the "incorrect premise" that the debtor was not involved in speculative trading.

He concluded that the market approach was inapplicable because the company's "risk profile was materially different" from other companies in the same industry. Accordingly, he could use no comparable companies to obtain a transaction multiple. He noted that Goldman, under the market approach, resorted to an "adjusted EBITDA" figure as a multiple metric. As he saw it, that metric was inappropriate because of significant unrealized derivative losses and the incorrect assumption that the debtor's trading activities had physical inventory behind them.

He concluded that only the asset approach applied, and it showed the debtors were insolvent by at least $429 million as of Jan. 31, 2008.

Defendants' expert opts for income approach. The defendants' expert relied primarily on Goldman's June 2008 valuation, which, he reasoned, was close to the distribution date. Further, Goldman valued the debtor on a going concern basis, using the income and market approaches. It prepared the valuation in the context of an actual 144A securities offering, which, again, ensured reliability, the expert believed. Moreover, Goldman had substantial access to the debtor's due diligence documents, including projections, and to management. The valuation, he said, was easily adjustable for "any negative economic impact that [the debtor's] trading activities may have had on the Company's value and its solvency cushion."

Goldman's valuation indicated a range of value from $4.3 billion to $6.1 billion. The defendants' expert adjusted those values to account for market multiples from February to June, adding $384 million to $543 million in value. He also increased the value by $206 million to account for "construction-in-progress," which he said would have value to a buyer. Goldman's valuation was for a securities offering rather than a mergers and acquisitions transaction. He decreased the value by $14 million to account for the sale of the affiliate entity. Next, he subtracted "net long-term debt" from the adjusted value to arrive at "net equity," which, he concluded, ranged from $3 billion to $5 billion. After subtracting other balance sheet liabilities totaling $2.2 billion, as well as $143 million related to "net trade book deficiency" from the net equity, he determined there was a "solvency cushion" ranging from $670 million to $2.7 billion.

The defendants also presented a trading expert to calculate the net trade book deficiency so as to measure the negative economic impact the debtor's trading activities had. He maintained that $143 million was a "conservative risk premium" the debtor had to pay.

For his part, the defendants' valuation expert criticized several aspects of the competing expert's asset approach. For one, he disagreed with the latter's decision not to adjust "goodwill" for fair value by distinguishing between book value based on accounting principles and value. He also objected to eliminating the $263.4 million receivables, relying on statements from the trading expert that they were not a credit risk as of March 2008. The company had paid $102.4 million in January and February. Lastly, he pointed out that the item "minority interest" that appeared as a liability on the balance sheet in the amount of $320.3 million represented the value of the equity ownership of minority shareholders and was not in fact a liability. He concluded that, if he adjusted the asset approach accordingly, he was able to show the debtor was solvent even then, from anywhere between $183 million to $250 million.

Court rejects receivables valuation. The court said it was "not convinced by the trustee's arguments against adopting the income approach in this case." They were based on the expert's unsupported contention that there was a lack of reliable financial projections and accompanying assumptions. Even though neither expert had access to the debtor's financial forecasts and assumptions, or to management, there was the Goldman valuation, which relied on them and which the court found reliable. It was contemporaneous and not generated "in anticipation of litigation." Because Goldman prepared the valuation in connection with a 144A securities offering, it did significant due diligence; preparations included sessions with debtor management throughout 2008 and access to a data room that stored documents going forward from 2005 when the debtor's credit agreement originally was drafted. It was appropriate for the defendants' expert to apply the income approach and use the Goldman valuation as a starting point.

As to the criticism that Goldman did not know about the speculative trading and, therefore, could not produce an accurate valuation, the court said the defendants' expert adequately quantified and adjusted for the activity's effects by relying on the analysis of the trade expert and applying a $143 million risk premium.

The asset approach was problematic, said the court. Even if one acknowledged the "insider nature of these transactions," it was impossible to conclude the receivables from the CEO's company were uncollectible. There were the $102.4 million payments at the beginning of 2008. Considering that the trustee's expert determined that insolvency amounted to $429 million, decreasing the value by $263.4 million—that is, the full amount of the receivables—amounted to a significant portion of the calculation and was not necessarily accurate. For all these reasons, the Bankruptcy Court held the trustee had failed to prove the debtor's insolvency at the date of distribution.

In re Wallace G. Wilkinson, Jr., debtor: Charles J. Lisle, Trustee v. John Wiley & Sons, Inc.

Citation: No. 05-5744 (6th Cir.)
Date of Decision: August 17, 2006
Country: US
State or Federal: Federal
State/Jurisdiction: 6th Circuit
Court: Court of Appeals
Type of action: Bankruptcy

Reasonably Equivalent Value Tested on Date of Transfer

The U.S. Court of Appeals for the 6th Circuit considered whether a debtor's payment could be recovered as a fraudulent transfer. Wilkinson was the majority shareholder in Wallace Bookstore Inc. (WBI), a chain of college textbook stores. In 2000, WBI was indebted to John Wiley & Sons (Wiley) for $2.4 million and Wiley refused to ship more books without receiving payment. Wilkinson and WBI were deeply indebted. Wilkinson had assets of $41 million and liabilities of $349 million. In January 2001, he paid $1 million to Wiley and WBI received a reduction in debt of $1 million. In February 2001, Wilkinson's creditors filed an involuntary petition for bankruptcy, which was converted to a voluntary petition in March. WBI followed suit and declared Chapter 11 bankruptcy.

The trustee for the Wilkinson bankruptcy estate sought to avoid the $1 million transfer to Wiley as a fraudulent transfer. The trustee alleged that Wilkinson did not receive reasonably equivalent value for his transfer and presented expert testimony supporting that position. The expert determined that Wilkinson's unsecured creditors received, at most, $118,300 as a result of the Wiley payment. This was determined by multiplying the amount of the payment by the best-case scenario for what the creditors could receive on their claims (11.83%). The bankruptcy court rejected this argument. It found that Wilkinson received an indirect benefit in the reduction of WBI debt for his payment on a dollar-for-dollar basis and his net worth did not change as a result of the payment. The trustee appealed.

On appeal, the trustee argued that Wilkinson did not receive reasonably equivalent value for the $1 million payment and the bankruptcy estate should recover that payment. The appellate court disagreed. It found that the trustee is only permitted to recover the transfer where the debtor is insolvent or has become insolvent as a result of the transfer and where the debtor did not receive reasonably equivalent value. It noted that the appropriate valuation date for determining reasonably equivalent value is the date of the transaction. It further noted that what constitutes value is determined on a case-by-case basis and fair market value is but one factor to consider. Moreover, "courts have held that a reduction in debt is sufficient to establish equivalent value."

The appellate court found that Wilkinson received an indirect dollar-for-dollar reduction in WBI's debt for his $1 million payment. In making this determination, it rejected the trustee's expert's analysis. It found that the expert's opinion "does not eliminate reliance on events subsequent to the payment to Wiley.... Value is to be tested on the date of transfer, not with reference to when distributions are made to creditors." Therefore, since the debtor received an equivalent debt reduction for his payment that indirectly benefited him and since his net worth did not change after the transfer (he remained insolvent before and after the transfer to the extent of $308 million), the transaction was not a fraudulent transfer within the meaning of Bankruptcy Code sec. 548(a).

Waller v. Pidgeon

Citation: 2008 WL 2338217
Date of Decision: June 5, 2008
Country: US
State or Federal: Federal
State/Jurisdiction: Texas
Court: United States District Court
Type of action: Bankruptcy
Experts: unspecified
Judge: Fitzwater
SIC: 6282 Investment Advice (portfolio managers)

Insolvency of Hedge Funds Turns on Book Value Versus 'Fair Valuation' of Debts

Must debts be valued at book value, or can they be treated similarly to assets, and adjusted to a "fair valuation" for purposes of determining insolvency? These are the questions the U.S. District Court (N.D. Texas) considered in this opinion, which may well impact both state and federal solvency cases.

Closely related entity holds debt. The plaintiff in this case was the receiver (a person appointed to take possession of an insolvent company's accounts and property by order of the court) for four closely related entities: two hedge funds and the two partner organizations that served as investment advisors to the funds. The defendant had invested $4 million in one of the funds (Dobbins Partners) over the course of four years. Over the same time period, he received significant redemption payments, totaling nearly $5 million. A final payment of $650,000 was made to the defendant on Dec. 27, 2002.

The entities declared bankruptcy on Dec. 31, 2002, and the plaintiff subsequently sued to recover the $650,000 payment as a fraudulent transfer. Under the Texas fraudulent transfer statute, the fund would be entitled to recover the payment if the fund was insolvent on the date of the transfer or became insolvent as a result. The plaintiff believed that, due to a fraudulent overstatement of the fund's value, Dobbins Partners was insolvent as early as Sept. 30, 2002.

The parties actually stipulated to most of the facts at trial: The fair value of the assets of the fund was approximately $4.95 million as of Dec. 31, 2002, and the book value of its liabilities was roughly $8.9 million. However, more than $6.8 million of that liability amount was owed to the other Dobbins hedge fund. The plaintiff argued that, because the book value of the fund's liabilities exceeded the fair value of its assets, the fund was insolvent, and the $650,000 transfer to the defendant must be recovered. The defendant, in contrast, believed that "the court should adjust liabilities to a fair valuation by deducting related-party transactions" between the two funds. In essence, the defendant argued to reduce Dobbins Partners' $6.8 million in debts owed to $2.08 million. With this adjustment, the fund's assets would have exceeded its debts, and the transfer would stand.

Analyzing the parties' arguments under the Texas statute, the court narrowed its discussion to the "simple" issue of whether it was required to value a debtor's liabilities at book value, as the plaintiff contended.

Does the law 'compel' book value of debts? To support his position, the plaintiff pointed to the language of the statute itself, and its definition of "insolvency," as well as the "similarly worded" text of the Bankruptcy Code. He also argued that applying the fair valuation standard to debt was "inconsistent with the broad definition of 'debt,' as interpreted by several courts."

While the majority of the court's opinion focuses strictly on legal issues involving statutory construction and interpretation, the court rejected the plaintiff's arguments. Neither the legislative intent behind enactment of the statute nor subsequent judicial interpretations supported a finding that "compel[led] the conclusion that debts can *only* be valued at book value" and could never be adjusted.

> Although the [Texas statute] definitions of insolvency at issue here would *permit* debts be valued at book value, they do not *command* that they be valued at book value. (emphasis in original)

Accordingly, the court dismissed the plaintiff's claims. The court declined to make any findings specific to the valuation of the fund's liabilities, but it was clearly concerned with the close relationship between the funds, with one holding the debt for the other. It remains to be seen whether courts interpreting the U.S. Bankruptcy Code will similarly find a "fair valuation" of debts to be permitted.

In re Washington Mutual, Inc.

Citation: 2011 WL 4090757 (Bkrtcy.D.Del.)
Date of decision: Sept 13, 2011
Country: US
State or Federal: Federal
State/Jurisdiction: Federal Circuit
Court: United States Bankruptcy Court
Experts: Steven Zelin (debtors); Peter Maxwell (plan objectors)
Judge: Walrath

WaMu Bankruptcy Court Credits the More 'Complete' Valuation

When Washington Mutual Bank—once the nation's largest savings and loan association—was seized by federal regulators in September 2008, it became the largest bank failure in the nation's history. That same day, the feds sold substantially all of WaMu's assets to JPMorgan Chase Bank, amounting to nearly $147 billion. One day after being placed in receivership, WaMu's parent company, Washington Mutual Inc., and its investment affiliate filed for bankruptcy.

Three years later, and still no plan. At stake were at least $4 billion in cash and billions more in potential tax refunds from carrying forward net operating losses (NOLs). By March 2010, the debtors had proposed a plan of reorganization. Although the bankruptcy court found the plan fair and reasonable, it declined to confirm it due to several deficiencies, primarily involving litigation related to WaMu's seizure and insider trading claims against the hedge fund investors who helped negotiate the reorganization.

To address the court's concerns, the debtors reproposed a plan in July 2011. In essence, the plan would cancel all stock in the debtors, leaving the common and preferred shareholders with nothing, and issue stock in the reorganized entity, giving the most senior creditors and equity investors one share of stock for each dollar of claimed debt. The assets of the reorganized entity would consist primarily of the debtors' former subsidiary, a mortgage reinsurance company, and the tax attributes of the NOLs.

Not surprisingly, most of the major stakeholders, including JPMorgan Chase and the FDIC, supported the plan, but the equity committee and others reasserted their claims that it was neither fair nor reasonable. They also argued that, in its proposal to distribute stock in the reorganized debtor, the plan was substantially undervaluing the stock, thus giving the creditor/recipients more than the amount of their claims (in violation of §1129 of the Bankruptcy Code). Further, the plan objectors argued that this "excess value" should be distributed to other stakeholders—notably, the preferred and common shareholders.

The plan objectors presented a valuation expert to support their positions, and the debtors filed a *Daubert* objection, claiming the expert did not use accepted methodologies and relied on hypothetical scenarios—namely that the reorganized debtor would raise substantial amounts of debt and equity and/or acquire new businesses to maximize the value of the NOLs. In response, the plan objectors pointed out that even the debtors' valuation expert considered the possible "corporate opportunities" that the reorganized entity would have, and any flaws in such assumptions went to the weight and not the credibility of the expert's opinion.

In this context, the court did not discuss the parties' "dueling" expert valuations in much detail. Instead, it summarily concluded that *Daubert* did not bar the plan objectors' expert from testifying. Although the expert "did not follow normal methodologies for valuing a business," the court said, neither was he preparing a complete valuation but offering only a critique at trial. To that extent, his testimony was relevant and useful to the court, which, as trier of fact, was competent to evaluate the expert's credibility and his reliance on hypothetical scenarios.

Debtors tend to undervalue, objectors to overvalue. Turning to the more substantive objections to the proposed plan, the court considered the respective values that the parties' experts assigned to the two main assets of the reorganized debtor:

1. *Reinsurance subsidiary.* The debtors' subsidiary was a captive reinsurance company that wrote policies on the mortgage loans issued by WaMu and its affiliates. As of the bankruptcy, the subsidiary had been in a "run-off" mode, not issuing new policies but simply collecting premiums and paying claims on existing ones. The company had no independent management, no independent sales force, and no employees.

Interestingly, the valuation experts weren't far apart: The debtors' expert said the company was worth between $115 million and $140 million, while the plan objectors' expert posited a narrower range, from $129 million to $135 million. In his capacity as rebuttal witness, the latter also highlighted some internal consistencies and flaws in the analysis by the debtors' expert. For instance, the debtors' expert drew a weighted average cost of capital (WACC) from a December 2010 report, even though that number had fallen by 5% to 10% since then, which would have increased the value. Moreover, his selected WACC of 13% to 15% was higher than historical returns for comparable businesses (8% to 12.5%) and also their current returns (6% to 10%). Finally, the debtors' expert gave little weight to comparable transactions, which would have yielded a value well above his concluded range of $145 million to $205 million. Instead, he assigned most of the weight to his discounted cash flow analysis.

The court gave credit to the debtors' expert for valuing the company using accepted methodologies. At the same time, it recognized the inclinations of all debtors to "undervalue themselves" and the plan objectors' equal but opposite tendency to inflate values. In this vein, the court agreed that there were flaws in the analysis by the debtors' expert, as pointed out by the plan objectors. Based on these considerations, it determined that the value of the reinsurance company, assuming it acquired no new business, was at the high end of the range posed by the debtors' expert, or $140 million.

2. *Net operating losses.* The face value of the reinsurance company's NOLs amounted to nearly $17.7 billion. Much of this could be lost, however, due to the company's change in ownership under the debtors' proposed plan and the application of IRC §382, which disallows a new entity from claiming loss-carry forwards attributable to a predecessor, and/or IRC §269, which disallows deductions from a corporate transaction if the main purpose was tax avoidance.

The debtors' expert attempted to determine the net present value of the subsidiary's NOLs under two alternative scenarios: as a static, "run-off" business and a potential future business with ongoing operations. Under the first, he testified that IRC §382 would limit the value of the NOLs to the run-off business to $7 million, which was worth $10 million to $20 million on a present value basis. The plan objectors did not really dispute this value, except to note that it did not take into account possible future revenues that could be generated by the income. Accordingly, the court adopted the highest value posited by the debtors' expert, or $20 million.

The debtors' expert valued the NOLs used by the future business between $10 million and $25 million. The plan objectors' criticized his approach for using a liquidation rather than going concern value, which would recognize the ability of the subsidiary or even the reorganized debtor to apply the NOLs through the acquisition of new businesses. Their expert also critiqued his use of a 25% to 35% WACC for future acquisitions but then adjusted this downward by 33% to account for the risks associated with the same. The plan objectors' expert characterized this as "double discounting" resulting in an effective WACC of 38% to 52%, when he believed a more appropriate rate ranged from 15.8% to 20%

Moreover, the plan objectors' expert testified that the reorganized debtor could have a net present value of $275 million, based on assuming a mix of capital and debt infusions totaling approximately $500 million. The reinsurance market is a "prime area for new investment given the recent turmoil in the real estate market," he added. The new entity could even reach a value of $240 million to $420 million, if it raised "billions of dollars in additional equity," he said.

The plan supporters once again accused the expert of failing to use typical methodologies to perform a "conventional" valuation of the reorganized debtor. It also pointed out these technical flaws in his analysis:

- His comparables for the debt-to-equity ratios were not reinsurance companies;
- His cost of debt was based on double-B-rated securities though none of the reinsurance comparables had that high a rating;
- His rate of return was based on going-concern reinsurance companies rather than startups or run-offs;
- He gave 40% weight to precedent transactions, despite his "normal" practice, because he mistakenly believed the debtors' expert had also; and
- He did not account for any tax risk, ignoring the possibility that the IRS could disallow all the NOLs.

Finally, the plan supporters said that any assumption the reinsurance company would continue as a going concern was speculative because it was not based on the proposed reorganization plan—or indeed, any existing business plan or strategy by the future shareholders. In response, the debtors' expert admitted that, to achieve his going concern value, the reorganized debtor would have to "get new management, hire employees, develop a business plan, get customers and vendors, and acquire hard assets." Further, he could not give an opinion whether the reorganized entity could raise the equity or debt projection in his model, which amounted to "just one of a number of possible future scenarios." Finally, he conceded that his calculations of debt and equity did not account for all the costs and risks of converting a liquidating company into a going concern, including the time to incorporate new operations and acquisitions.

'Serious flaws' in the analysis. "The court agrees with the plan supporters that these are all serious flaws in [the expert's] analysis," the court said. It outright rejected any conclusion by the plan objectors' expert that the reorganized debtor could be worth anything over $275 million, much less have "billions" of additional value, because the expert's assumptions in this regard were "purely speculative and unrealistic."

At the same time, the court agreed with the critique by the plan objectors' expert of the valuation done by the debtors' expert, which gave "too little value to the possible future earning capacity of the reorganized debtor" due to "imaginary" tax restrictions. Any value of the NOLs must account for the tax risks, the court stated, but, after a review of the applicable IRS regulations and case law, it concluded the risk wasn't as great as the debtors' expert assumed. In this case, the creditors would acquire the reorganized debtors' stock not to shelter their own income or merge it with a company of their own but "simply in repayment of debt owed them," the court said.

"Based on the two expert opinions, one of which is too conservative and the other of which is too aggressive," the court concluded that the present value of the NOLs to the reorganized debtor was $50 million. This assumed that the new entity should be able to raise additional capital and debt over the next 20 years equal to twice the value of its current assets by investing these assets either in regenerating its reinsurance business or acquiring new businesses.

Based on all of the evidence presented, the court found the reorganized debtor and its NOLs would have a value of $210 million. Given this value and an extensive review of the facts already on record, the court also found that the debtors' proposed reorganization plan was fair and feasible and in the best interest of creditors.

However, the court was still troubled by the outstanding legal claims against the debtors and its findings (after another extensive review of facts and case law) that the equity committee and others had stated an actionable claim of insider trading against several hedge fund investors who helped negotiate the settlement process. Concerned that the case could "devolve into a litigation morass," the court declined to confirm the plan for a second time and ordered the parties to mediate the issues in an attempt to resolve the litigation along with any other outstanding issues.

In re Westpointe (I)

Citation: 234 B.R. 431, 1999 U.S. Dist. LEXIS 7831
Date of Decision: May 26, 1999
Country: US
State or Federal: Federal
State/Jurisdiction: Missouri
Court: United States District Court
Type of action: Bankruptcy
Judge: Limbaugh
SIC: 6513 Operators of Apartment Buildings

What Valuation Methods Are Appropriate for a Going Concern in Bankruptcy?

In this Chapter 11 bankruptcy proceeding, the valuation method relied upon by the Bankruptcy Court in valuing the "going concern" of the properties is in dispute. The court thoroughly discussed the appraisal methods it finds appropriate in this situation.

In re Westpointe (II)

Citation: 241 F.3d 1005, 2001 U.S. App. LEXIS 3854
Date of Decision: March 14, 2001
Country: US
State/Jurisdiction: 8th Circuit
Court: United States Court of Appeals
Type of action: Bankruptcy
Experts: James K. Tellatin, MAI Bryson Randolph (for debtors)
Judge: Hansen
SIC: 6513 Operators of Apartment Buildings
Key words: Bankruptcy, Fair market value (FMV), Going concern, Real Estate Limited Partnerships (RELP)

8th Circuit Upholds Use of Preconfirmation Value

The bankruptcy court adopted a reorganization plan over the debtors' objection. The debtors appealed to the U.S. District Court, which upheld the bankruptcy court, finding that the debtors' equity interests were without value. Debtors appealed to the 8th Circuit.

Facts. Five real estate limited partnerships filed for Chapter 11 bankruptcy after defaulting on their HUD mortgages. Each partnership consisted of two general partners, Pentad Properties Inc. and Kevin Kelly—each with a 50% share—and one limited partner, St. Louis Associates Ltd. (SLA), a limited partnership. Kelly was also a general partner of SLA.

The properties were previously owned by William E. Franke, who bought them in 1983 for $38,000,000 and sold them in 1984 to SLA for $57,300,000. The purchase was financed, in part, by a promissory note by SLA in favor of Franke in the amount of $57,300,000, secured by a second mortgage on the properties. SLA entered into a contract with Gannon Management Corp., owned by Franke, to manage the properties.

Debtors and Gannon/Franke filed different reorganization plans. HUD accepted the Gannon/Franke plan and the bankruptcy court confirmed the plan. Debtors appealed the confirmation, arguing that the plan was not "fair and equitable." The U.S. District Court remanded the case to the bankruptcy court for a valuation hearing.

Valuation evidence in bankruptcy court. The parties stipulated to a preconfirmation fair market value of the properties at $38,600,000, but they disagreed as to the properties' "reorganization value." The bankruptcy court excluded testimony of the debtors' valuation expert witness, Randolph, who was to testify about future cash flows of the properties *as reorganized* under the Gannon/Franke plan. The court stated the hearing was limited to a determination of the estate's value *prior* to confirmation of the plan.

The court reviewed the appraisal of the properties, conducted by Tellatin, Andreas & Short Inc., which resulted in the stipulated fair market value. The appraiser used three methods: (1) the cost approach; (2) the direct sales comparison approach; and (3) the income capitalization approach, which measured the present net worth of anticipated future net operating income. Under this approach, the value of the properties was between $37,180,000 and $40,850,000. The bankruptcy court found that the value stipulated by the parties was supported by the record and that this amount represented the value of the properties prior to confirmation.

District court findings. Debtors appealed the bankruptcy court's findings to the U.S. District Court for the Eastern District of Mississippi. Their main argument was that the bankruptcy court erred in considering the preconfirmation value of the properties and not the "reorganization value." They argued that the appraisal did not take into account the favorable financing conditions under the Gannon/Franke plan, so that the value of the properties to a third-party purchaser would be considerably less than under the plan. Gannon/Franke argued that the debtors were insolvent and that the bankruptcy court properly considered future cash flow in its "going concern" valuation.

The district court held that there was nothing in the record to suggest that the income capitalization approach relied on by the bankruptcy court was not an appropriate valuation method. It adequately took into account anticipated future profits, and, thus, there was no reversible error in the bankruptcy court's rejection of debtors' expert.

The court affirmed the bankruptcy court, finding that the estate was insolvent and, therefore, the debtors' equity interests in the estate were without value and were properly extinguished. The debtors appealed to the 8th Circuit, arguing that the estate's assets actually exceeded its liabilities and that they were entitled to the excess value of the estate.

Holding on appeal and rationale. The court of appeals began by noting that a primary consideration for determining whether a plan that extinguishes equity interests is fair and equitable is whether the debtor is solvent. Thus, the main issue on appeal was the debtors' solvency.

The debtors argued that the bankruptcy court used an erroneous valuation method, which underestimated the value of the estate's assets. The bankruptcy court relied primarily upon the Tellatin appraisal. This appraisal was compiled by "a recognized expert according to accepted professional standards," the court noted. In its appraisal, Tellatin applied the income capitalization method in determining the value of the estate. This method "incorporated anticipated future profits and the anticipated reversion value of the apartments into the final present going concern value of the estate."

But the debtors insisted that the court should have taken into consideration special financing terms of the reorganization. The appellate court disagreed. The appellate court stated that the special financing terms were not a market condition available to the debtors and that the market financing assumption behind the appraisal was adequate for purposes of determining solvency.

Further, the debtors argued that the bankruptcy court was wrong in failing to qualify their expert witness in valuation. Upon review of the bankruptcy court's record, the appellate court found that the bankruptcy court did not abuse its discretion in refusing to qualify Randolph as an expert witness or in its finding that Randolph's testimony was irrelevant.

The court of appeals upheld the district court's judgment that accepted the proposed reorganization plan.

In re White

Citation: 2010 WL 786292 (Bkrptcy. S.D. Tex.)
Date of Decision: March 4, 2010
Country: US
State or Federal: Federal
State/Jurisdiction: Federal Circuit
Court: United States Bankruptcy Court
Type of action: Bankruptcy
Judge: Isgur
SIC: 7353 Heavy Construction Equipment Rental and Leasing (rental of construction equipment [except cranes] with operator)

'Devastating' Cross-Exam in Shareholder Buy-Out Case Leads to Discredited Expert

In a shareholder oppression case that should be a red flag to the IRS, the federal bankruptcy court first found that $4.9 million in executive bonuses paid by a profitable construction equipment company over a span of two years (2006 and 2007) were in fact disguised dividends. "Uncontroverted" testimony at trial established that the company paid shareholder-employee bonuses to avoid double taxation, first as corporate profits and then as individual income to the recipients.

Further, with the exception of the CEO and the oppressed shareholder, the company paid the bonuses in proportion to each employee-shareholder's ownership interest, based on the company's performance. If the company had paid its combined tax burden on the disguised dividends, which the court estimated at 40%, then the $4.9 million dividend pool would decline to $2,940,000. The oppressed shareholder owned an 8% interest; thus his share of the disguised dividends amounted to $235,200.

Shareholder wants a forced buyout, too. In reviewing the shareholder's request for a statutory buyout under Texas law, the bankruptcy court concluded that it had three options to value his 8% interest:

1. The shareholder's expert valuation;
2. Book value; or
3. The buy-sell provision in the company's shareholders' agreement.

The shareholder's expert used a capitalization of income approach and the company's annual EBITDA of $9 million. Based on a number of factors—including then-current market conditions and a prior sale using a 5.17 multiplier—he applied a 6.0 multiple and arrived at a gross value of $54 million. After subtracting $22 million in liabilities and applying discounts for lack of control and marketability, the expert valued the minority shareholder's interest at $1.23 million. (The court opinion does not detail the combined discounts, but, by extrapolating from the expert's conclusion, they total roughly 30%.)

Cross-examination by the company's attorney dealt a "devastating" blow to the expert, according to the court. First, his March valuation report forecast annual revenues of $120 million, when actual revenues were only $77 million. More importantly, the company's fiscal year ended in June. "Therefore, the expert's forecast was only for a three month period of time," the court said, "yet his forecast erred by $43 million."

The expert suffered a second blow when he said that he'd never been excluded from a case—yet evidence revealed that at least one prior court had rejected his testimony. And finally, when the expert testified on his choice of earnings multiples, "he gave completely different testimony in court from that given in his deposition," the court said. "[He] testified as to facts and conclusions that were convenient at the time," and the court refused to credit any of his testimony or conclusions in this case.

The company offered a valuation expert only to critique the shareholder's expert, leaving the court with little guidance regarding the validity of applying book value to the particulars of the case. Moreover, no witness testified how to apply the minority's 8% interest to book value. "Would there be a discount?" the court asked, and "if so, how much?" Due to lack of answers or evidence, it declined to apply book value.

Buy-sell value by default. The shareholders' agreement established a simple formula for determining the buyout price for a departing owner's shares: the difference between total fixed assets and total long-term liabilities. The parties disputed whether liabilities should be calculated before or after depreciation; in a footnote, the court decided that the final value should be net of depreciation.

The buy-sell agreement did not provide any discounts for lack of marketability or control, and the company was allowed to purchase the interest over 25 months, interest-free.

The court acknowledged "substantial pitfalls" in the formula. For example, if the company converted 100% of its assets to cash and paid off all of its debts, a departing shareholder would receive nothing. At the same time, the agreement was negotiated at arm's length and without coercion. The formula excluded both short-term assets and short-term debt and allowed for the extended payment period. Both elements could implicitly recognize or build in a discount, the court observed.

In any event, the court saw "little reason to substitute [its] own judgment as to the fair terms of a buy-out." In applying the formula to the company's most recent balance sheet, it found total fixed assets of about $53 million, minus $15.3 million in depreciation, leaving net fixed assets of $38.6 million. Long-term liabilities were about $29.4 million, resulting in a total value for the company of $9.2 million. The minority shareholder's interest was worth just over $739,000. The company would pay the shareholder that amount, plus the disguised dividend award. Or, in the alternative and pursuant to an equitable remedy available in Texas, it could pay the shareholder dividends according to a court-issued injunction, outlined in the remainder of the opinion. "In these difficult economic times," the court said, it was "loathe to mandate a particular dividend policy for the company." Its sole purpose in issuing the injunction, in addition to complying with applicable law, was "to protect [the shareholder's] future expectations that have thus far been frustrated by [the company's] conduct," and it gave the company one month to elect its option.

In re Susan E. Wick

Citation: No. 01-1312MN
Date of Decision: January 9, 2002
Country: US
State or Federal: Federal
State/Jurisdiction: 8th Circuit
Court: United States Court of Appeals
Type of action: Bankruptcy

Stock Options Valued for Inclusion in a Bankruptcy Estate

The U.S. Court of Appeals for the 8th Circuit considered whether a debtor could exclude stock options from her bankruptcy estate. Wick, the debtor, sold her company in March 1997. Pursuant to the sale, she received a right to 24.5% of the company's stock if she remained employed with the company for one year following the sale. In July 1997, Wick filed for bankruptcy protection under Chapter 7. She listed the stock options as an asset of the estate having an unknown value. She also exempted the asset under 11 U.S.C. § 522(d)(5), which was limited to $3,925 in her case. The trustee permitted the options' exemption, and the bankruptcy estate's debts were discharged in November 1997. The trustee followed up on the options in July 1998 and was told that Wick had attempted to exercise the options but had been denied. However, she continued to work for the option granter and did eventually exercise the options in September 1998. In October 1998, Wick brought suit against the company for a court-ordered buyout of her interest and her bankruptcy case was closed. Prior to fixing the fair value of Wick's 24.5% interest, the trustee asserted a claim to a share of the proceeds from the sale of the stock. The court fixed the value of Wick's stock at $97,200, the amount she received in the buyout. Thereafter the trustee reopened the bankruptcy case to determine the bankruptcy estate's interest in the stock proceeds.

The bankruptcy court permitted the reopening of the case. It determined that the bankruptcy estate was entitled to share in the proceeds of the stock. However, it concluded that the bankruptcy estate was limited to share in one-third of the stock proceeds, since Wick had worked for four months toward the vesting of the options when she filed for bankruptcy. Since Wick had to work for eight months following the bankruptcy filing to generate value for the options, the bankruptcy court found that two-thirds of the options were generated by her post-petition services and thus were her individual property. Wick presented expert testimony, which valued the options on the date of filing at $4,863, making the bankruptcy estate's one-third interest worth less than the allowable 522(d)(5) exemption. The bankruptcy court rejected that valuation and calculated the amount due to the bankruptcy estate.

It determined one-third of the stock proceeds and deducted the amount of Wick's 522(d)(5) ($3,925). Wick appealed.

On appeal to the district court, Wick successfully argued that the bankruptcy court erred. The district court valued the options based on Wick's expert's testimony. It further found that the trustee failed to challenge the value of the options for the purposes of the exemption within the 30-day period. Thus, it reversed and permitted Wick to retain the entire amount of the stock proceeds. The trustee appealed.

The 8th Circuit reversed the district court and reinstated the decision of the bankruptcy court. It found that Wick's listing of the options' value as unknown was "presumably designed to reflect the fact that contingent, unvested options are not easy to value." It further noted that her exemption was limited to $3,925. It then stated, "We reject Ms. Wick's contention that listing 'unknown' as the current market value of the exemptions is sufficient as a matter of law to make an asset fully exempt." Thus, the appellate court agreed with the bankruptcy court that the options were partially exempted, limited by the amount of available exemption. It further agreed with the bankruptcy court that under 11 U.S.C. § 541(a)(6), "the estate's interest is limited to the pro rata portion of the proceeds that are related to the debtor's pre-petition services." The bankruptcy court limited the services provided prior to the date of filing. The appellate court then affirmed the bankruptcy court's determination of the amount of the options' proceeds includible in the bankruptcy estate. In reaching this decision, the appellate court rejected the debtor's position that the trustee had abandoned the asset by failing to challenge the valuation of the asset within the 30-day period. It stated, "We do not think that the Bankruptcy Code and Rules oblige a trustee to object every time a debtor partially exempts an asset in order to preserve the estate's interest."

In re Winstar Communication, Inc.

Citation: Case No. 01-1430, United States Bankruptcy Court
Date of Decision: December 21, 2005
Country: US
State or Federal: Federal
State/Jurisdiction: Delaware
Court: United States Bankruptcy Court
Type of action: Bankruptcy
Experts: Peter Scherf (Trustee, on behalf of Winstar Communications) Kevin Collins (Lucent Technologies, Inc.)
Judge: Rosenthal
SIC: 4813 Telephone Communications, Except Radiotelephone (except resellers)
Key words: Bankruptcy, Preference, Insolvency, Fair market value (FMV), Balance sheet test

Analyst Convinces Court to Reject Stock Value as 'Fair'

In the most recent case to come out of its litigation-plagued bankruptcy proceedings (and its ill-fated alliance with Lucent Technologies), former telecom company Winstar Communications Inc. needed to show that it had gone belly-up nearly five months before filing its petition.

Specifically, to prove that Winstar had made an unlawful preference in favor of Lucent—to the tune of nearly $200 million—the Chapter 7 Trustee had to convince the court that the company was "insolvent" on the date of the preference, which took place on Dec. 7, 2000. Winstar, a publicly traded company, didn't solicit bankruptcy protection until April 18, 2001.

The federal Bankruptcy Code defines "insolvency" using a balance sheet test: If the "fair value" of all the assets is less than its stated liabilities on the date in question, then the debtor is insolvent. The emphasis is on fair valuation, however, and, while GAAP is relevant, the court noted, "It is not determinative."

Stephen Scherf, a principal with Parente Rudolph LLC (Philadelphia) presented valuation evidence on behalf of the trustee; his counterpart at Houlihan Lokey Howard & Zukin (New York City) and head of its corporate valuation practice, Kevin Collins, testified on behalf of Lucent.

To arrive at the fair value of the company's assets, Scherf used three standard approaches: market, income, and asset. Collins used the first two but not the last. Under the market approach, Collins testified that there was a "large and active" market for Winstar, which was trading at $12.50 on the relevant date, down from a high of over $60.00 but far from a patently distressed value. Adjusting the market value upward to account for a buyer purchasing a complete and controlling interest, Collins concluded that Winstar was solvent on Dec. 7, 2000.

Scherf rejected the stock market valuation of Winstar. First, he testified that the typical investor had no idea of Winstar's true financial picture, which only Lucent knew was much "bleaker" than the debtor's publicized financials would show. Moreover, as even Collins acknowledged, the telecom market was "simply too unstable to be an adequate indicator of value." A year before the average stock price of an emerging broadband group had appreciated 63%, but a year later the same group of stocks had declined an average of 87%.

The court found these facts persuasive—even more so because Collins had cited them in his report for Lucent, then Scherf was able to use them to Winstar's advantage. "My biggest obstacle was to see if we could get the court to reject publicly traded value" and override the assumption of efficient markets, Scherf admitted, "but I found the facts that enabled me to do that."

In another coup—and in using the discounted cash flow method under the income approach, Scherf was able to convince the court to ignore Winstar's own 10-year earnings projections. The projections were speculative at best, he said, and included growth rates "significantly in excess" of reasonable projections for the industry. As an example, Scherf noted one projection that predicted a growth rate in perpetuity of 28%.

"There's a good word of caution for all analysts," he added, "that you can't always take a client's documentation at face value." Digging below surface assumptions and stock values to find the facts on fair value also found a winning case for Winstar—but a final word of caution: This decision just came out at the District Court level. According to Scherf, Lucent has filed a notice of appeal, so stay tuned for further developments.

Retrojection Used to Determine Fair Valuation of Assets in Bankruptcy Case

In *In re Winstar Communications, Inc.*, No. 01-1430 (JBR) (Del. Bankr. Dec. 21, 2005), the Delaware Bankruptcy Court found the discounted future cash flow method inappropriate when determining the fair value of the debtor's assets for solvency purposes in this preferential treatment action. Winstar was a publicly held company engaged in the build out of broadband communications networks. It entered into a credit facility agreement with Lucent, another public company. Winstar and Lucent also had other contractual dealings.

In November 2000, Winstar obtained an additional $200 million in bank financing. Despite the fact that Winstar's obligation to Lucent was not due until 2005, Lucent demanded that Winstar pay it the proceeds from the new financing. Winstar paid $188 million, the net proceeds of the loan, to Lucent. When Winstar sought Chapter 11 bankruptcy protection in early 2001, the trustee sought to avoid the payment to Lucent as a preferential transfer.

The bankruptcy court noted that one element of establishing a preferential transfer was that the company be insolvent at the time of the transfer. Both parties presented the bankruptcy court with valuation experts who testified as to the solvency of Winstar on the date of the transfer. Solvency is measured by a fair valuation of assets, which is often interpreted to be fair market value, less face value of the liabilities.

Winstar's expert, a credentialed business appraiser, concluded that it was insolvent. He used the market approach but rejected it because the market overvalued Winstar since the financial picture of Winstar was "much bleaker than the debtor's publicized financials would indicate."

He also considered the asset approach. Because Winstar did not have audited financials for December 2000 but had them for December 2002, the expert utilized retrojection. "That rule [retrojection] provides that when a debtor was insolvent on the first known date and insolvent on the last relevant date, and the trustee demonstrates 'the absence of any substantial or radical changes in the assets or liabilities of the bankrupt between the retrojection date,' …, the debtor is deemed to have been insolvent at all intermediate times." The expert identified four events subsequent to the filing date that required adjustment. These included an impairment charge for the fourth quarter of 2000, a 2001 sale of the assets of Winstar without an assumption of liabilities, the valuation prepared in connection with the allocation of that purchase price, and the administrative insolvency of the debtor's estate. He concluded that Winstar was insolvent on the date of the transfer.

Lastly, Winstar's expert considered the valuation of its assets under a capitalization of earnings method. Since Winstar consistently lost money during its life, this method resulted in a finding of insolvency.

Lucent's expert, an investment banker, used the same methods but arrived at a different conclusion. He concluded that the market appropriately valued Winstar on the date of the transfer, and therefore it was solvent. In reaching this conclusion, he also considered the purchase of similar companies during the relevant period.

He also utilized the asset approach and retrojection. Since the book value of Winstar was positive on the date of transfer based on in-house financials for December 1, 2000, and Dec. 31, 2000, he concluded that Winstar was solvent.

Lastly, he valued the business using a discounted future cash flow method. The company had profit projections for a 10-year period ending in 2009, which the expert took at face value. Based on his analysis, he concluded that Winstar was solvent.

The bankruptcy court adopted Winstar's expert's solvency opinion. It agreed that the market approach was inapplicable because the market price was overvalued since it was uninformed of the true state of Winstar's financial picture. It adopted the application of the doctrine of retrojection to determine the asset value and concluded that Winstar was insolvent under that approach in light of the subsequent events noted by Winstar's expert. Lastly it adopted the capitalization of earnings method and the results determined by Winstar's expert. It rejected the application of the discounted cash flow method under the facts of this case because the management projections were unreliable in light of the fact that the business never turned a profit. Thus, the court determined that Winstar was insolvent and the trustee could recover the $188 million payment as a preferential transfer.

In re Yellowstone Mountain Club, LLC

Citation: 2010 WL 3222534 (Bkrtcy. D. Mont.)
Date of Decision: Aug. 16, 2010
Country: US
State or Federal: Federal
State/Jurisdiction: Federal Circuit
Court: United States Bankruptcy Court
Type of action: Bankruptcy
Experts: Robert Reilly and Joanne Sheridan (owner); David Abshier, Kent Mordy, and John Hekman (debtors)
Judge: Kirscher
SIC: 7997 Membership Sports and Recreation Clubs (recreation clubs with facilities)

Experienced BV Expert Manipulated by Resort Owner and Attorneys?

In the aftermath of the recent economic crisis, valuation experts may have to apply an extra layer of caution when reviewing management projections related to certain lending practices and/or troubled assets—or risk getting caught in the middle of what this court called a case of "naked greed."

Credit Suisse specifically targets high-end developers. In 2004, a team at Credit Suisse First Boston crafted a new syndicated loan product for the owners of high-end, master-planned resorts. The new product had several unique aspects: For example, it relied on an appraisal methodology (the "total net value method") based on future gross revenues without any discount to present value. This did not meet federal requirements (under FIRREA) to include a fair market value appraisal of the underlying assets, which meant that Credit Suisse could only offer the loan through its newly formed Cayman Islands branch. Finally (and what the court later called "the most shocking aspect" of this loan product), the owners could take a substantial portion of the proceeds as an immediate distribution, for purposes unrelated to the property development—in essence, permitting them to realize anticipated future revenue streams directly on funding.

In 2005, the Credit Suisse team targeted Timothy Blixseth, founder of the Yellowstone Mountain Club—a private ski and golf resort for the very rich (such as early member Bill Gates). Blixseth eventually negotiated a $375 million facility—including a 2% transaction fee (decided by a coin toss) and $209 million distribution. Blixseth didn't want to split the distribution with his fellow shareholders, however, and so convinced Credit Suisse to characterize the $209 million distribution as a loan to a wholly owned affiliate, permitting Blixseth to personally access the funds while saddling the Yellowstone entity with the debt. Blixseth didn't book the "loan" to the affiliate until months after the deal closed, backdating the promissory notes.

The bank didn't care how Blixseth dealt with his shareholders or capitalized on his asset; according to the court, the Credit Suisse team cared only for the "fat fees" it made by syndicating such "unnecessary" loans to wealthy developers. Moreover, the bank's financial due diligence "was almost non-existent," the court said. It relied almost entirely on "exuberant" financial projections provided by Blixseth without requesting audited or historic financials. It also commissioned a national firm to conduct the "total net value appraisal," based on the same gross revenues forecasts, to find the Yellowstone Club was worth over $1.16 billion in 2005. (Just a year before, the same appraisal firm had valued Yellowstone on an "as-is, market basis" at $375 million.)

After the deal closed, the Yellowstone Club had a "consistent and often desperate need for cash" to pay its creditors, including Credit Suisse. Blixseth never demanded payment on the "loan" to his affiliate, however, and used the $209 million largely to pad his personal expenses. In November 2008, the club filed for Chapter 11 relief. Among a multitude of claims, the bankruptcy court considered whether the debtors could avoid the $375 million Credit Suisse loan as a fraudulent transfer.

Credible BV experts caught in the middle. The debtors presented several experts to prove their claims, including a CPA and certified insolvency expert, who concluded that the $209 million transfer was not a loan under generally accepted accounting principles but rather a distribution and return of capital, which left the debtors overleveraged and undercapitalized.

To rebut these claims, Blixseth presented two experts. The first, a well-known business valuation expert, explained the three tests for solvency: (1) the balance sheet test (does the value of the entity's assets exceed its liabilities?); (2) the cash flow test (can the entity pay its debts as they become due?); and (3) the capital adequacy test (does the entity have sufficient capital to continue as a going concern?). If it fails any one of these tests, an entity is considered insolvent, the expert said.

Under all three tests, the expert concluded that Blixseth and his affiliate were solvent at the time of the Credit Suisse transaction. The expert based his opinion on financial information provided to him by Blixseth and his attorney, which he later learned overstated cash reserves by over $240 million and should have been booked as a note receivable. The attorney also characterized the financial data as "WAG" ("wild-a__ guess") and kept sending revised "WAG" statements up to the date of the expert's report.

Finally, Blixseth and his attorney told this expert to apply only two solvency tests, the cash flow and capital adequacy, when assessing the Yellowstone Club because they were assigning the balance sheet test to a second expert. That way, neither expert could give an ultimate solvency opinion regarding Yellowstone. It also forced the first expert to rely on the second expert's balance sheet test of Yellowstone in his solvency analysis of Blixseth and the affiliate. To make matters more questionable, the second expert was told to rely on the 2005 "total net value appraisal," which relied on gross values without an as-is, fair market value appraisal of the commercial assets.

The court clearly discredited these tactics. As an initial matter, it found the Credit Suisse transfer was a distribution rather than a loan, thus rendering both expert opinions "moot," because both presumed the affiliate had a substantial receivable on its books. Even if the loan was legitimate, however, the court declined to rely on the experts' opinions, "because Blixseth's counsel masterfully divided the work between [them] so as to cast Blixseth in a light that simply does not shine in this Court."

Further, although the second expert "ostensibly" discounted the total net value appraisal to present value, its cash flow projections were based on Blixseth's "over-inflated" forecasts, which "had no basis in historical reality and appeared to be nothing more than unsupported puffery," the court said, in dismissing the second expert's balance sheet test.

That left the opinions of the first expert, who was "extremely qualified and compelling," the court observed, but who nevertheless failed to perform a complete solvency analysis of the Yellowstone Club. His analysis of Blixseth and his affiliate also incorporated the second expert's flawed balance sheet conclusions, and, though he claimed to test the reliability of the projections, he compared the projected gross revenues to actual gross revenues rather than comparing projected cash flow to actual cash flow (as the debtors' expert did). He defended his choice by saying there was too much "noise" in the cash flow data, meaning nonrecurring income and expenses, but later conceded that a normalization adjustment would have "easily" accounted for the few items. "It is also noteworthy that [the expert] chose to ignore, or was instructed to ignore, the actual historical financial performance" of the debtors prior to the Credit Suisse transaction, the court found. The reason: The debtors' historical data could not support its future projections and "demonstrated conclusively" that it could not take on the Credit Suisse debt.

Finally, this expert also acknowledged relying on financial information provided by counsel and Blixseth without independently verifying its accuracy or completeness. On cross-examination, the expert said he agreed with the adage "garbage in, garbage out." After considering the information underlying this expert's opinions, "this Court finds … that the garbage in/garbage out maxim is applicable." Although "generally credible," the first expert "was so restricted by Blixseth and his counsel" that his opinion in this case "was simply inapplicable," the court held.

BV standards discredit the debtors' expert? In an attempt to impeach the debtors' expert, Blixseth's first expert also summarized the requirements of the AICPA's *Statement on Standards for Valuation Services* (SSVS-1). In particular, CPAs can give a solvency opinion without complying with SSVS-1 but not if they give a valuation opinion. "If an independent valuation opinion is contained within a solvency opinion, CPAs must comply with the AICPA standards, including SSVS-1," the expert explained.

He contended that the debtors' expert insolvency opinion amounted to an independent valuation and that he violated the "known or knowable rule" under SSVS-1. However, Blixseth's expert also conceded that SSVS-1 does not apply to the typical solvency analysis in the bankruptcy context and that violation of SSVS-1 or the known and knowable rule does not render a solvency opinion invalid. Further, by relying on historical financial data, including cash flows rather than gross revenues, the debtors' expert opinion was far more credible, confirming that there was insufficient cash flow to pay the Credit Suisse debt.

Overall, the debtors' experts also demonstrated that the "total net value" appraisal proved devastating to the Yellowstone Club. Several experts had never seen this type of appraisal and questioned why any lender would prefer it to a FIRREA-compliant, market value appraisal—unless, as the court observed in this case, "Credit Suisse, with Blixseth's tacit approval, wanted to bulk up the alleged value of the Yellowstone Club … to inflate the size of the loan." Had the bank requested a fair market value appraisal, it likely would have loaned substantially less than $375 million, the court found. Instead:

> The only plausible explanation for Credit Suisse's actions is that it was simply driven by the fees it was extracting from the loans it was selling, and letting the chips fall where they may. Unfortunately for Credit Suisse, those chips fell in this Court with respect to the Yellowstone Club loan. The naked greed in this case combined with Credit Suisse's complete disregard for the Debtors or any other person or entity who was subordinated to Credit Suisse's first lien position, shocks the conscience of this Court. While Credit Suisse's new loan product resulted in enormous fees to Credit Suisse in 2005, it resulted in financial ruin for several residential resort communities. Credit Suisse lined its pockets on the backs of the unsecured creditors.

To compensate for Credit Suisse's overreaching and "predatory" lending practices, the court subordinated the bank's first lien position to that of a general unsecured creditor. The court also found that Blixseth's removal of over $200 million in funds was the sole reason the debtors went bankrupt and avoided the Credit Suisse transaction as a fraudulent transfer.

In re Young Broadcasting, Inc.

Citation: 2010 WL 1544401 (Bkrtcy. S.D.N.Y.)
Date of Decision: April 19, 2010
Country: US
State or Federal: Federal
State/Jurisdiction: Federal Circuit
Court: United States Bankruptcy Court
Type of action: Bankruptcy
Experts: Timothy Kuhn (creditor's committee)
Judge: Gonalez

'Levered' DCF for Bankrupt Business Fits the Facts but Falls to *Daubert* Standard

Daubert challenges to financial experts are practically becoming de rigeur. In just this month's issue, we've digested nearly half a dozen new cases attacking the relevance and reliability of the valuation evidence (and/or the valuator's qualifications). Admittedly, most *Daubert* motions are like depositions: Another opportunity for a party to "try" the evidence, either to encourage settlement or glean an opponent's litigation strategy prior to a full hearing on the merits. In some of the more complex bankruptcy and securities litigation cases, however, *Daubert* challenges have become an effective means to separate the "true" and tested methodologies (and experts) from the simply untried.

Expert attempts to value the effect of deleveraging. In this Chapter 11 proceeding, the debtors—a consolidation of related broadcasting companies—owed nearly $338 million on secured loans and $484.3 million on senior subordinated notes. In their deleveraging plan, the debtors proposed creating a new company in which the secured lenders and senior noteholders would take sufficient equity to satisfy all their outstanding claims, but the pool of unsecured creditors would be entitled to no more than a pro rata share of $1 million.

The committee of unsecured creditors proposed an alternative plan, which would reinstate all of the secured lenders' debt (due in November 2012) and provide the senior noteholders with certain pro rata equity participation. To support its plan, the Committee presented a valuation expert to testify regarding the company's ability to sell or refinance at the maturity of the secured loans and the current, overall value of the company. The lenders objected under Rule 702 of the Federal Rules of Evidence and the *Daubert* standard, claiming that the expert was not sufficiently qualified and both parts of his valuation evidence were unreliable.

The Committee's expert was neither a credentialed valuation expert nor an economist; he did not have an M.B.A. or a published article on the restructuring of media companies. He was, however, the director of a consulting firm, with experience advising media and entertainment clients in M&A, financing, asset sales, and restructuring. "Academic training is not necessary if an expert's practical experience is sufficient to qualify him," the bankruptcy court observed. In fact, an expert's working background is likely "more relevant" than education or published articles, the court added. In this case, the expert's "knowledge of issues relevant to media financing deals" and his significant experience on the borrower's side qualified him to testify.

Similarly, his evidence regarding the debtors' future sale or refinancing was based on extensive research. The expert analyzed industry data—including prior transactions and current public comparables—from which he determined a range of "broadcast cash flow" and selected an exit multiple. He also considered the leverage ratios of recent broadcast company sales. Although the expert assumed that the general economy would improve, his assumption did not create such a wide "analytical gap between the data and the opinion" as to render his conclusions unreliable, the court held. "Since exclusion is the exception rather than the rule," it admitted the expert's opinion on the company's refinancing and sale options, noting that any weakness in his analysis would go to its weight at trial, after "vigorous cross-examination."

A DCF in name only. The expert's valuation of the company was a different matter. Although he performed a comparable company and transactions analysis, he relied primarily on a "levered DCF" (discounted cash flow) analysis consisting of the following :

1. Zero projected distributable cash flow, resulting from the Committee's assumption that all cash would go toward paying off the secured debt by November 2012;
2. A determination of the approximate value of equity in 2012 and assumed sale of the Company at that value;
3. A "terminal value" determined by subtracting net debt and outstanding preferred stock from the projected sale value; and
4. The application of a discount rate, derived from the cost of equity, to conclude a present value for the company.

The lenders claimed that this approach was misleading because it omitted all the necessary steps of a traditional DCF, and the court agreed. "Although [the expert] uses DCF terminologies, there are practically no substantive similarities between the generally accepted DCF method and the Levered DCF method," the court said.

In particular, the expert made "multiple novel assumptions," such as an assumed sale of the company and a discount rate that failed to account for both the cost of debt *and* the cost of equity. He also altered another key component of the DCF method: By simply assuming a sale of the company in 2012, the expert failed to apply the appropriate "metrics to multiples" and calculate a terminal value, the court said. Further, his levered DCF failed to meet any of the *Daubert* factors: It had not been tested, peer-reviewed, published, or relied on by any other experts in the field. Its error rate was unknown, and there was "no evidence that this method was ever employed, discussed, and certainly not generally accepted in any academic or professional community," the court held.

The Committee defended its expert, stating that the levered DCF more closely fit this case because it accounted for the substantially below-market value of the reinstated debt under the Committee's plan. The court was still not convinced; the facts of the case did not give the Committee's expert "free rein to employ a brand new valuation method that … had never been used by any other valuation expert in court."

Indeed, the expert's application of the facts to an untested method did not match the "intellectual rigor that characterizes [the] practice of an expert in the field of media valuation," the court held, and it disqualified all of the expert's conclusions derived from his levered DCF analysis under *Daubert*, finding it was neither an acceptable variant of the DCF or a reliable stand-alone method.

www.ingramcontent.com/pod-product-compliance
Ingram Content Group UK Ltd.
Pitfield, Milton Keynes, MK11 3LW, UK
UKHW050951290926
15470UKWH00005B/1767

9 781621 500421